BURT FRANKLIN: BIBLIOGRAPHY & REFERENCE SERIES 334
Essays in Literature & Criticism 65

HANDBOOK TO TENNYSON'S WORKS.

A HANDBOOK

TO THE WORKS OF

ALFRED LORD TENNYSON.

BY

MORTON LUCE.

BURT FRANKLIN
NEW YORK

Published by BURT FRANKLIN
235 East 44th St., New York, N.Y.
Originally Published: 1908
Reprinted: 1970
Printed in the U.S.A.

Library of Congress Card Catalog No.: 77-122841
Burt Franklin: Bibliography and Reference Series 334
Essays in Literature and Criticism 65

PREFACE.

THE Preface to the First Edition of " New Studies in Tennyson " read as follows :

"This little book is intended to precede, possibly by several years, a much larger work which has long been in course of preparation, and which will contain complete commentaries on ' In Memoriam,' ' Maud,' ' The Princess,' and ' The Idylls of the King,' together with critical and explanatory notes on all the other writings of the late Laureate."

Although this " Handbook to Tennyson," which retains a few extracts from the preliminary " New Studies," may serve in future years as a companion volume to the larger undertaking mentioned above, it has nevertheless been designed as a Complete Introduction to the Works of Tennyson for the present use of the general reader, as well as for the requirements of schools and colleges.

The whole of the poems have been brought under review ; and they are considered as nearly as possible in the order of the Table of Contents prefixed to the one volume edition of Tennyson's works.[1] The number in

---

[1] "The Complete Works of Alfred Lord Tennyson." With a Portrait, Crown 8vo. 7s. 6d. Macmillan and Co., London.

brackets gives the page of that volume on which the poem will be found.

In preparing the present work of wider scope the author has kept within view some principles expressed in the Introduction to " New Studies in Tennyson " :

" It has been the main object of the writer to stimulate the higher emotion and to cultivate the finer imagination of the student, rather than to check the growth of these artistic faculties by an accumulation of unsympathetic facts. . . . Some help the student and the general reader must have, and the commentator has merely to see to it that the information he offers is of the right kind. The author, many years ago, met with a series of magazine articles entitled ' How to look at a Picture ; ' with their aid he was able to discover and appreciate in any good painting a thousand beauties hitherto concealed from his most careful gaze. Possibly, then, the following Chapters may help some student or casual reader to look at and listen to a poem."

To the above it may here be added that in this more comprehensive volume evidence has often been brought forward in support of criticism ; and space has sometimes been given to details for the purpose of ascertaining the truth.

The author's best thanks are due to Mr. W. J. Lias, of the Downs School, Clifton, late Scholar of Jesus College, Cambridge, for his kindness in revising the proof sheets.

UPPER BELGRAVE ROAD,
  CLIFTON,
    September, 1895

CONTENTS.

HANDBOOK TO TENNYSON'S WORKS.

CHAPTER I.

TENNYSON'S LIFE, TIMES, AND CHARACTERISTICS.

PART I.—LIFE OF TENNYSON.

"THE hero and the bard is gone." By this first line of an ode[1] that celebrates Byron as a hero, but has little to say about his poetry, we are reminded that there have been poets whose mere lives were poems, and whose poetry was the House of Life built to music. As we might expect, such poets are rarer in our less eventful days, when, if the leaders of thought gain something from uninterrupted study, they yet, according to Milton, also lose something:

> "The wisest, unexperienced, will be ever
> Timorous and loath."
> *Paradise Regained*, iii. 240-1.

What Milton means by "unexperienced" may be gathered from the context; and many years before, in

---

[1] "On the Death of Lord Byron," in "Poems by Two Brothers." (Signed A. T. in the ed. of 1893.)

plainer prose, he had set forth the doctrine that a poet's education, if nothing more than " studious and contemplative," is very incomplete. It must have a living share, he says, in events that stir human experience widely and to the depths.

Of course we can never separate a poet's work from his life, however sequestered and contemplative that life may have been; but if only this, for example—if Tennyson had been more frequently compelled to breast the blows of circumstance, he might have become a more powerful poet and a greater dramatist.

On the other hand, we lost Chatterton altogether. Sometimes the stars above us seem to govern our conditions, and poor Chatterton failed to grapple with his evil star. Possibly, therefore, we may rest well content with Lord Tennyson's long life of ease and seclusion ; content also to read his biography not so much in the pages of history as in his own poetical work, where it is clearly written, interesting and instructive.

There is yet one other consideration. The words "more frequently," above, were used advisedly. Circumstance did deal Tennyson one blow, and that a terrible one, and while he was still young ; and the shock of it was diffused through all his life. But though this private sorrow gave some power and some passion to his poetry, and brought him closer to the hearts of his countrymen, it left him without that wide knowledge of men and things which fell to the lot of Shakespeare and Milton ; perhaps it even tended to keep him apart from some of the mighty activities of a rapidly growing nation and a world-advancing era.

We have mentioned incidentally that Lord Tennyson's life may be read in his works ; we may now add that his poems are undoubtedly his best biography. Nevertheless it is useful to recall the glimpses which recording friends have given to us of the great poet as he moved through life, at that stately distance, to a resting-place where the meanest of his fellows may now stand near his dust.

Alfred Tennyson was born on August 6th, 1809, the year which gave birth to two other great men, Darwin and Mr. Gladstone. His father, Dr. G. Clayton Tennyson, was rector of Somersby, a small parish in Lincolnshire.

Alfred was one of twelve children, and the fourth of eight brothers, most of whom have written poetry ; two of his elder brothers, Frederick and Charles (afterwards Charles Tennyson Turner) being poets of some note. His father died in 1831, but his mother, who will be mentioned again in these pages, lived to see her son famous. Tennyson's childhood was uneventful, but such as allowed him to be nursed by Nature, to observe her ways, and to love her ; and it encouraged the growth of fine emotion, though at the same time it helped to render the poet retiring and sensitive. From the time that Alfred and his brother Charles left Louth Grammar School in 1820 (Alfred was then eleven and Charles thirteen) until they were both entered at Trinity College, Cambridge, in 1828, they were educated at home—or rather, they were often left to educate themselves ; a piece of good fortune that falls to few in these days when, as the schoolmaster in Mr. Davidson's play confesses,

> " I, for food,
> Have made myself a grindstone, edging souls
> Meant most for flying."

The early flights of these affectionate poet brothers were frequent and free and far ; their wits were not sharpened with the knife that had cut their wings. Thus it came to pass that they were led to all the Castalies, and fed with the milk of every Muse ; and thus it further came to pass that after six years of this almost perfect poetical apprenticehood, they published at Louth (1826-7) the now famous " Poems by Two Brothers."

For this collection of boyish verses the venturesome
publisher gave them £17 in cash, together with three
pounds' worth of books. The "Poems" found very few
purchasers and fewer readers. But for the copyright of
the same book £230 was subsequently paid; the original
manuscript was sold in December, 1892, for no less than
£430; and at about the same time booksellers were ask-
ing £24 for a copy of the precious volume.

From one point of view these particulars are somewhat
melancholy; for they may be regarded as a mournful
illustration of a reflection in "In Memoriam," lxxv. 4.
They are yet more melancholy on this account; the book,
as we shall see hereafter, contained no pieces of great
promise, nothing that could compare, for example, with
the early work of Chatterton.

The date printed on the title-page of this notable
volume is 1827. Lord Tennyson refers it to the year
before.

We now lose sight of Charles Tennyson who, as stated
above, entered Trinity College with Alfred in October,
1828. At the same time, being then in his eighteenth
year, Arthur Henry Hallam went up to Cambridge, and
he and Tennyson soon formed a lasting friendship. Both
were competitors for the Chancellor's prize poem of
1829, the subject being "Timbuctoo;" and the prize fell
to Tennyson. But Hallam's attempt was remarkable,
especially for a man so young (nearly two years younger
than his friend). Like Tennyson he broke through the
traditional verse of this college exercise, and his work—
again considering his age—gave promise of the future
scarcely less trustworthy than Tennyson's. Hallam was a
wonderful and a good man; two fragments of testimony
shall be allotted to him here. Tennyson spoke of him
as being "as near perfection as man might be," and
Monckton Milnes wrote: "We are deprived, not only of
a beloved friend, of a delightful companion, but of a most

wise and influential counsellor . . . and of the example of one who was as much before us in everything else as he is now in the way of life."[1]

In 1830, while he was yet at Cambridge, Tennyson published in London, "Poems, Chiefly Lyrical," a book that aroused criticism, mostly favourable. During the summer of the same year he journeyed in company with Hallam to the Pyrenees. After the death of his father in 1831, Tennyson did not return to Cambridge; but Hallam remained at the University till 1832, when he took his degree. In spite of this, the two friends continued to see a good deal of each other, and there is in "In Memoriam"[2] a description of one of the visits paid by Hallam to the Somersby rectory. In the year 1832, Tennyson published his second volume,[3] entitled "Poems," which showed a considerable advance upon the first. Hallam, who had been studying law in London, travelled to the Continent with his father in 1833; his health had for some time been delicate, and while abroad he was seized with a sudden and fatal illness, and died at Vienna on September 15th. On January 3rd, 1834, his remains were interred at Clevedon.

The loss of his friend, together with some adverse criticism of the 1833 volume, kept the poet almost silent for nearly ten years. But all this time he was preparing his wings for a surer flight, the volume of 1842; and during these years some part of "In Memoriam" was written. His life at this period may be left to the words of Margaret Fuller in a letter of August 1842: "Much has he thought, much suffered." Though the poet was not actually compelled to get his living by treading some rougher road than the flowery walk of letters, his means were scanty. We hear of him living "in poverty with his friends and golden dreams."

---

[1] See also "In Memoriam," cix-cxiv.
[2] lxxxix.   [3] Dated 1833.

These friends included the foremost men and women of letters. Many of them he met in London, where the Cock Tavern was a favourite haunt, as he seems [1] to tell us in "Will Waterproof's Lyrical Monologue." His place of abode was often changed. In 1837 the Tennyson family left Somersby,[2] and after living at High Beech, Tunbridge Wells, and Boxley, they removed to Cheltenham, where they remained till 1850. In that memorable year Tennyson published his "In Memoriam," was appointed Poet Laureate in succession to Wordsworth, married Emily Sellwood, and with her took up his residence at Twickenham. Here Hallam Tennyson was born, August 11th, 1852. In 1853 the poet removed to his famous retreat, Farringford, at Freshwater, where Lionel Tennyson was born, March 16th, 1854. This was his home until 1867, when he purchased the estate of Aldworth in Sussex. There he resided for the remainder of his life, though for many years he continued to spend the winter and spring at Farringford. He died on October 6th, 1892.

Such is the outline of a life that appears somewhat commonplace; yet is it truly wonderful, most wonderful in what may best be called its completeness. Certainly, as we have seen, it wants the earnestness, the austerity, the strenuous effort which Milton associates with the life of the ideal poet; yet in some respects it is so ideally perfect as to be almost bewildering. The poet lisped in numbers; he won the prize poem at his university; he published poems while yet in his teens; he published when more than fourscore years old. Though he was not always inclined to kiss the rod, no writer profited more by the discipline of adverse criticism, and from the outset he was accorded approbation of sufficient authority to save

---

[1] To a fastidious taste it is healthier and sweeter to avoid the wine and tobacco of modern biography or novel.

[2] "In Memoriam," c. ci. cii.

him from despair, if not from self-distrust. His life was one long service of song, yet was there in it a period of years (1833-1842) with just enough in them of mystery, suffering, romance, and dealings with the world to thaw the ice of regularity. He was a most learned man, and with that a wise man. He was happy in his family, his friends, his friendship, his fortunes. He received a pension from the State and he was made Poet Laureate. Oxford bestowed on him its proudest token of esteem, the honorary degree of D.C.L. He had the privilege of refusing a baronetcy; he had the privilege of becoming a lord. An honoured son succeeds him in the peerage. Though heir of all the ages, he produced work that was strikingly original. He excelled in lyrical, mono-dramatic, and narrative poetry; he wrote a long and beautiful poem on a subject of almost national interest, and one that so many poets before him had attempted or thought of attempting;[1] then he produced several important dramas. Poetry seemed to wait upon his dying bed;[2] he was buried in the Poet's Corner of Westminster Abbey. In life he secured what most great men have missed in life—a meed of praise; only in one thing might it be said that he fell short of fruition, for death alone could tell him how much he was loved.

PART II.—TENNYSON'S POSITION IN THE HISTORY OF ENGLISH POETRY.

" Man is man, and master of his fate,"[3] is among Tennyson's earlier doctrines. In later years it assumes the form " Man can half control his doom."[4]

[1] " Idylls of the King."
[2] " His proud head pillowed on Shakespeare's breast."—SWINBURNE.
[3] " Marriage of Geraint."
[4] " Locksley Hall Sixty Years After," couplet 139.

Even the poet, most independent of men, will be moulded—in part—by circumstances. He cannot altogether stand aside from his age. And in order to know him thoroughly, we should first learn something about the times to which he was born.

If we look back through the centuries of life and letters, we shall hardly fail to notice how often the literary period connects itself with some important phase of national life; and we also find that a great poet almost universally represents a great historic age.

Speaking roughly, and with especial reference to English poetry, the times of Tennyson were preceded by three important periods.

The first period has Chaucer for "morning star,"[1] Shakespeare for noonday sun, and, to repeat Tennyson's figure, Milton for evening star. If we assign dates to it, they are 1350—1675, though given in such round but convenient numbers they overlap. A central date would be 1600, and a central historical epoch the reign of Elizabeth. This, the first period, and especially the first part of it, has the characteristics of youth; it has freshness, beauty, strength, and joy. It includes much of the making of our composite English race, its victory in the struggle for existence among races; new freedom, a new world, new learning, and along with that, the religious, political, social, and literary influence of the Bible. No wonder that such an age should give birth to our two great poets, Shakespeare and Milton.

The next is a period of reaction, dating roughly from 1650 to 1750, leading names being Dryden, Pope, and Johnson, and a central epoch the reign of Queen Anne. Its characteristics are well marked; its poets appeal to the intellect rather than to the emotions; they neatly dress the body of poetry, but they put into it the soul of prose; the book of humanity and the book of nature are

---

1 "Dream of Fair Women," stanza 1.

alike closed to them; they deal with the limited and often petty life of "society" and "the town;" their fancy seldom attains to imagination, nor their wit to humour; and they mostly affect a satire whose pungency is bitterness rather than saltness. Their poetry affords pleasure to some people, but it is pleasure of a low and scarcely an artistic order, such pleasure as we derive from watching a clever chemical experiment, or a game of chess, or the sleight of hand of a juggler, or from listening to the mouthing of a mob orator in Hyde Park. Even in the one great poem of this school, Pope's "Eloisa to Abelard," our emotional attention is too often distracted by mere tricks of conscious rhetoric.

Nothing could be more natural than a new rise in poetry after such a decline—or rather, a new birth after such a death. It was due to many causes; such as, in history, the Declaration of Independence and the fall of the Bastille.

Its literary origins are numerous; among them are the romantic movement in Germany and the writings of Voltaire and Rousseau, preceded by others in England. There is a general return from artifice to art, from the town to nature, from society to mankind, from intellect to emotion, from philosophy to romance, from politics to the people, and, with one or two exceptions, from satire to love. Cowper appears as the morning star of this new day, and Keats is its evening star. But while Cowper is nearer to the age he heralds than Chaucer was to the Elizabethan epoch, and represents many of its elements, Keats in spirit stands farther apart than did Milton. Scott, like Keats, seldom looks beneath the surface of the life of his own day; he lives rather in a past of romance, and Keats in a past both romantic and classical. Burns, standing for Scotland, reflects in his poetry many of the new emotions of the new era.

Of the others who are more closely identified with the

stir of the time, Wordsworth was the wisest, Byron the strongest, and Shelley the sweetest singer. Another to be named with these, one who bequeathed to Tennyson so much that is precious in poetry, was Coleridge—musical, mysterious, beautiful, capricious.

Among notable features of the new poetry is a certain looking forward, sometimes eager, sometimes wistful, sometimes sublime. It is a feature of Tennyson's poetry. Byron, Shelley, and Wordsworth might well turn their faces towards the other distance and the hues of promise ; the French Revolution behind them was an exhausted volcano with a desert of ashes around. It had introduced no new principles ; at best it had merely directed attention to principles already existing ; but even that use of it was made barren by excesses and by the subsequent disgust of right-minded men. It would have been better for the world, perhaps, if these new principles had arisen not as a destructive volcano in France, but as a well-spring of water in England ; indeed, just as Tennyson was becoming an author, those waters, after being pent up for half a century, gushed forth from English ground, cool, pure, and refreshing.

Like the French Revolution, Byron was furious to pull down, careless to build up. Yet even his misanthropic eye looked onward to a time "When the heart and the mind And the voice of mankind Shall arise in communion." These are almost the words of Tennyson in "Locksley Hall."[1] To the French Revolution Shelley was

> " As the last cloud of an expiring storm,
> Whose thunder is its knell."
>
> *Adonais.*

He had striven to redeem the present, though he found greater hope in the future ; and these offices of love and trust were part of Tennyson's inheritance from Shelley.

[1] Couplets 64 and 65.

The bequest of Keats,[1] who knew not of these things, was a luxurious dallying with external beauty. But the poet from whom Tennyson received the laurel wreath gave him also the goodliest gifts of song. It was Wordsworth's privilege to learn the lesson of revolution twice, for he made verses in 1790, and wrote good poetry after 1830. Of the first of these lessons he has left us full record.

After saying

> " Let us . . .
> Leave this unknit republic to the scourge
> Of her own passions,"

he repeated the words of Daniel,

> " Unless above himself he can
> Erect himself, how poor a thing is man " ;

thus he laid bare the secrets of failure not of the French Revolution only, but also of all such revolutions ; and then, in respect of the future, he added—

> "We live by admiration, hope, and love,
> And even as these are well and wisely fixed
> In dignity of being we ascend."

One other aspect of Tennyson's four great predecessors must be carefully borne in mind in any attempt to estimate the relation in which they stood to their own time and to his ; neither Byron nor Keats announces that high conception of poetry and the poetic function which we associate with many great poets, and which possessed Tennyson almost as much as it possessed Milton. Neither Byron nor Keats could have said with the fervour of Shelley,

> "Drive my dead thoughts over the universe,
> Like withered leaves, to quicken a new birth."
> *Ode to the West Wind.*

> " I will be wise
> And just, and free, and mild, if in me lies
> Such power ; for I grow weary to behold
> The selfish and the strong still tyrannize
> Without reproach or check." [2]
> *Revolt of Islam.*

---

[1] See pp. 54, 74, 75, 107, 109, 324, 360.   [2] Cf. Tennyson's "The Poet."

Nor with Wordsworth,

> " I would give utterance in numerous verse
> Of Truth, of Grandeur, Beauty, Love, and Hope,
> And melancholy Fear subdued by Faith."
>
> *Recluse.*

From such a passage as this last we may learn what
Wordsworth was to Tennyson. We might almost hear
Tennyson's reply,

> " So did he speak ;
> The words he uttered shall not pass away. . . .
> No—they sank into me, the bounteous gift
> Of one whom time and nature had made wise."
>
> *Recluse.*

Such were Tennyson's predecessors, foremost figures in
the great poetic era of Revolution ; their writings enrich
the years that lie near the beginning of the nineteenth
century, some five-and-twenty on either side.

The lull that followed the Revolution storm was of
short duration. The very year of Tennyson's first volume
was the year of the second French Revolution and the
second English Revolution ; the year of the " Three Days "
in Paris, and of the appearance of Lord Grey as Prime
Minister in England and champion of the Reform Bill.
It was the year of the opening of the Liverpool and Man-
chester Railway. Mr. Huskisson, who met his death on
that occasion, had recently brought forward the first
notions of Free Trade, which the beginnings of steam
navigation were soon to do much to develop. It was the
year of Lyell's " Principles of Geology," and of Comte's
" Cours de Philosophie Positive." Keble's " Christian
Year" had been printed in 1827 ; in 1829 Catholic Eman-
cipation had become law ; and forthwith O'Connell began
to agitate for the Repeal of the Union. The position of
the Irish Church was called in question in 1831 ; and in
the same year the Corn Law Rhymes of Ebenezer Elliott

preached more powerfully than from any pulpit a new doctrine for the poor:

> " It is the deadly Power that makes
> Bread dear, and labour cheap."

At this time rick-burning was rife,[1] and Hunt and Cobbett were filling the new-forming mind of the masses with ideas of social equality, while the most autocratic of European nations, "that o'ergrown Barbarian in the East"[2] was absorbing Poland. The year of Tennyson's second volume passed the Reform Bill, brought out "Tracts for the Times," proposed to emancipate slaves, saw Faraday's experiments in Electricity, and heard George Combes lecture on popular education.

Thus we find in the years of Tennyson's first two volumes something more than the germs of "all the wonders that would be :"[3] political reform, social reform, religious reform; the retreat of old religions before the invasion of new religions, religions of inquiry, doubt, negation, emotion, art, philosophy; and, most marvellous, most potent of all, the "Fairy tales of Science"[4] that were now being told on every hand. Truly a great poet was crossing the threshold of a great age.

We need not follow him through that age; for its roots lie, all of them, in the years just described; and the history of the next sixty years, in their relation to Tennyson, may almost be summed up by a mention of the two Titanic forces taking birth that were to influence his life and work more powerfully than all the rest together—new religious inquiry and the doctrines of Evolution.

But we in our year of 1895 may look back and see those sixty years of future as they lie in the tract of the past Let us survey them from the poet's standpoint in the second Locksley Hall. It is something like Words-

[1] To " Mary Boyle," viii. ix. x.   Also " The Princess," iv. 363-367.
[2] Sonnet, "Poland."
[3] " Locksley Hall," couplet 60.
[4] *Ibid.*, couplet 6.

worth's case over again ; some enthusiasm for a mighty present, followed by distrust and disappointment, but not by despair; and then the final faith—" Onward." [1]

PART III.—CHARACTERISTICS OF TENNYSON.

Although the characteristics of a great writer often colour his writing to such an extent that when dealing fully with his literary work we describe the whole man, yet it is useful to regard them apart ; and, further, to arrange them under separate heads, provided we understand that the distinctions are more or less arbitrary, and that qualities assigned to some special department may at any time cross their borders.

I.—PERSONAL. Of Tennyson's form and feature nothing need be represented here ; his fine head is familiar to all who possess his poems ; and this is but a guide-book to be taken up by those who are travellers through that region of wonder and delight known as " The Works of Tennyson." A more accessible full-length portrait of the poet might, however, be desirable.

What is true of a man's physical frame is also true, but in a less degree, of his habits and his character ; they will vary at different periods of life. Nor is the testimony of friends always to be relied upon. When we have read Mr. Theodore Watts assertion that " Tennyson had that artistic egoism which enabled him to work upon his own lines in defiance of all hostile criticism," we are confronted by Mr. Knowles, who assures us that Tennyson was hurt by criticism as a sensitive child might be hurt by the cross look of a passing stranger ; and the same authority repeats Tennyson's own remark, " The Reviews stopped

1 See the last poem of the last volume, " The Death of the Duke of Clarence," lines 14-17 (page 856 in the one-volume edition) ; and in " Locksley Hall Sixty Years After," couplet 140.

me." Among this and similar conflicting evidence, we cannot do better than rest content with the testimony of three great men who knew him in his youth, manhood, and age, respectively. Arthur Henry Hallam, " My other heart, and almost my half self," [1] writes of his friend in 1832, " I think you would hardly fail to see much for love as well as for admiration." Next, Thomas Carlyle, most keen to observe character, spoke of him in middle life as "a true human soul to whom your soul can say ' Brother.' " The third tribute shall be that of Robert Browning in the year 1889,—" I have loved you dearly."

Turning now for a moment to look at the poet as he appears in his poetry,—and, we must add with some emphasis, in his prose—we seem to discover a somewhat slighter man. To those who have gazed long and lovingly he will now and then betray a foible or disclose a weakness. These minor blemishes are fully considered in an Appendix to this chapter, p. 49.

To the foregoing remarks we may now add a suggestive hint as to Tennyson's character first supplied by Hallam in 1832. " His nervous temperament and habits of solitude give an appearance of affectation to his manner, which is no true interpretation of the man, and wears off on further knowledge." We may fairly adopt this as a final estimate in regard to any personal weakness that may be detected in the poet's work, merely making the reservation that, as explained in the Appendix, it applies somewhat less closely in this literary connection.

II.—RELIGIOUS. Given a general vagueness incidental to the idealizing tendencies of an imaginative writer,[2] Tennyson's religion, as we gather from his works, was a religion of transition. If he had been asked to state the

---

1 " The Princess."
2 There are exceptions. Milton's trumpet, even in poetry, gave out no uncertain sound ; nor did it spoil his organ music ; it was as the trumpet-stop in an organ. So clear was never so musical.

fundamental doctrines of Christianity, first, when " Poems
by Two Brothers" were published, and again, "more
than half a hundred years"[1] later, when he wrote the
stanzas to Mary Boyle, his two statements would have
seemed strangely at variance.   For if we may judge from
the "Poems by Two Brothers," his views in 1827 were the
"happy views" of poem xxxiii. of "In Memoriam;" and
in the volume of 1889 will be found the poem to Mary
Boyle, which contains the following stanza :

> " What use to brood ? this life of mingled pains
>   And joys to me,
> Despite of every faith and creed, remains
>   The mystery."

But the transitional quality of Tennyson's religion was
not uniform ; it included oscillation and regression ; and
if we now rapidly follow the course of his religious
opinions as it runs through the long series of his poems,
we must first bear in mind the fact that with one
or two exceptions we have no means of ascertaining a
precise date.   The year on the title-page of a volume
serves as a limit in one direction only.   For example, in
the "Demeter" collection, "Crossing the Bar" is printed
last of all the poems,[2] but the date of its composition
may have been earlier than that of such other pieces as
"Vastness," "By an Evolutionist," and "To Mary Boyle."
We could not even speak of all poems in the last volume [3]
as representing the thought of the poet not earlier than
the date of the volume which preceded it ; it contains, for
example, " Mechanopilus," which is referred to the time of
the first railways.   Therefore the following quotations
which illustrate what have been called oscillation and
regression of religious opinion must be read with the
caution due to absence of exact date.

---

[1] " To Mary Boyle."
[2] It is now placed at the end of the one volume edition of Tennyson's poems
[3] " The Death of Œnone, Akbar's Dream, and Other Poems."

The "early heaven and happy views" may be said to have received their first shock at the university, where the inquiring minds of many associates set Tennyson also inquiring; and in the manner habitual to him throughout his career as an author, he takes occasion to utter through the lips of a fictitious character just so much as he chooses of his own emotions, and the result is "The Supposed Confessions of a Second-rate Sensitive Mind." It would seem that the epithet "second-rate" has its origin in another characteristic of Tennyson, already noticed, and called by some critic "unfortunate modesty;" and Hallam well says of this poem, "The mood portrayed is rather the clouded season of a strong mind, than the habitual condition of one feeble and second-rate." It is the mood, we may add, which at some time or other has clouded nearly every other strong mind from that day to this.

In this poem references to Scripture and to many points of Christian doctrine included within "happy views" are made in a manner totally different from that in the "Poems by Two Brothers." The poet has begun the battle of nineteenth-century uncertainty; he has begun to fight his doubts. ("In Memoriam," xcvi.)

In many other poems of the earlier volumes, the Bible is quoted partly through "childly wont and ancient use," partly in a spirit merely artistic; examples would be the "latter fire" of "The Kraken," the "strange angel" of "To ——," the "Like Stephen's" of "The Two Voices;" to which may be added

"There is a hand that guides."—*Princess.*

But these and many others like them must be passed by.

Meanwhile, as in "The Two Voices," Philosophy has been called in as an ally by both sides; and Evolution, newest and most terrible of combatants, is soon to lead the vanward of the army of doubt. We now reach "In Memoriam," the most important poem for our purpose, for it is also the most personal ; but on the side of doctrinal Christianity one quotation will be enough, because of its comprehensiveness ; it is the line in which the poet speaks

> " Of comfort clasp'd in truth revealed."

This doctrinal recognition of the Bible is unequivocal.

The next lines to be quoted show extremes meeting— the " early heaven and happy views " strangely assorting with a faith that " cares not to fix itself to form." It is a well-known passage,

> " There lives more faith in honest doubt,
> Believe me, than in half the creeds."

We are so accustomed to these lines now as to have difficulty in recognizing the years—not farther back than 1827—when to ninety-nine in every hundred of persons calling themselves Christians, they would have sounded blasphemous. Amid the consternation they caused, Bible texts would have been brought to bear upon them— " Blessed are they that have not seen, and·yet have believed "—and so forth.[1]

In " In Memoriam " also we find the first expressions of what some would call " Higher Pantheism," " Christian Agnosticism," and much more. But, before leaving the poem it is important to examine the introductory stanzas, which bear the latest date. The first of·these contains the word " believing "—almost the only instance of its use by Tennyson after the first period of " obstinate questionings." But, against one use of the creed-word in these stanzas, we have to set " thinks " in the third stanza, " seemest " in the fourth, " trust " in the sixth, and again

---

[1] Within the experience of the present writer, these remarks apply to years much more recent than 1827. It is well even now to contrast the two famous lines quoted above with such a later expression as the following in "Vastness" : " Faith at her zenith, or all but lost in the gloom of doubts that darken the schools."

" trust " in the tenth.[1]   Nor does the more dogmatic term occur again in " In Memoriam."

It is the same in " Maud,"—a religion liberal, and of compromise ; old and new meet with as little clashing as may be.   " We are puppets ; " "the drift of the Maker is dark ; " " He that made it will guide ; " " sullen seeming Death may give more life to Love ; "

> " Arise, my God, and strike, for we hold Thee just " ;

> " But the churchmen fain would kill their church
> As the churches have killed their Christ."

Tennyson's views of the human and the divine nature of Christ are also variable and comprehensive.   A good example of this tendency to compromise is furnished by the foregoing quotation when read side by side with the well-known line of " In Memoriam," " Ring in the Christ that is to be."   " Killed their Christ " means " Crucified the Son of God afresh, and put him and the religion they preach to an open shame by reason of their sloth, their worldliness, their anything but Christly lives." [2]   But in the line from " In Memoriam" the word "Christ" is less personal—"men have long called themselves Christians, but Christ's kingdom is not fully established yet ; his subjects are Christian chiefly in name, not in deed, in life ; we still have to look forward for a Christian community worthy of the name—'The larger heart, the kindlier hand'—the man who may be worthy even of Christ's second coming :

> " Whereof the man that with me trod
> This planet, was a breathing type." [3]

References to the efficacy of prayer are sometimes conventional and sometimes real ; those in the " Morte d'Arthur" are probably real because of their early date ;

---

[1] The stanzas themselves are fully explained in the Appendix to Chap. IX.
[2] Cf. "sabbath-drawlers of old saws," in " Sonnet to J. M. K."
[3] " In Memoriam," Epilogue, 38.

the similar expressions in "Harold" may perhaps be regarded as mere literary adornment.

Still more noteworthy, proceeding from the lips of Tennyson, are two lines connected with the "Idylls of the King." The first is in the "Dedication" to the Prince Consort, dated 1862,

> "Till God's love set Thee at his side again,"

and the other is the address "To the Queen," dated 1872,

> " And fierce or careless looseners of the faith."[1]

Nothing quite so definite as the first will be found again; and the second is evidence that to the last Tennyson clung to or looked kindly on "the old faith."

In the Arthurian poems, again, all the opposing elements appear still interspersed with scriptural allusions; positivism, agnosticism, monotheism, pantheism, doubts concerning God and love, faith in God and love; doubts concerning immortality, belief in immortality; and they will all be found over and over again, together with Bible references, in the poems contemporary with and that followed the "Idylls of the King." One consideration has yet to be added: the poems towards the close of the conflict speak oftener of trust in God, and Love, and Immortality.

From a survey of his poems, dramatic and personal, it would therefore seem that Tennyson's religious opinions have constantly varied, and could never well be regarded as absolutely definite; as a consequence, his writings are not altogether unlike those other writings, of prophet or evangelist, which may be cited to their purpose by men of very different shades of belief and thought, from dogmatists to philosophers. To these conclusions, which have been drawn from the poet's writings, there may now

---

[1]   " The old faiths loosen and fall, the new years ruin and rend."
                                                    SWINBURNE.

be added a very important item of personal testimony. In the " Nineteenth Century " for January, 1893, Mr. Knowles writes concerning Tennyson ; " He formulated once and quite deliberately his own religious creed in these words: ' THERE'S A SOMETHING THAT WATCHES OVER US ; AND OUR INDIVIDUALITY ENDURES : THAT'S MY FAITH, AND THAT'S ALL MY FAITH.' "

The connection between Religion and Ethics will vary, but it is nearly always close ;[1] even in this age of scientific analysis it is closer than we imagine. But if for a moment we may speak of a poet's ethics as apart from his theology, then assuredly not one voice in the whole civilized world would question the opinion that the influence of Tennyson's writings in respect of the highest conception of morality ever formed amongst men is not less than that of any other poet.

III.—POLITICAL AND SOCIAL VIEWS. Like his religious opinions, but in a less degree, these were transitional and tending to a compromise. There was in Tennyson a firm but not exactly dogged clinging to old forms and the past, and there was some disposition to make " the bounds of freedom wider yet."[2] But change, though necessary and healthful, was to be " nor swift nor slow." These words are to be found in the poem " Love thou thy land," stated to have been written about the year 1833, but not published till 1842. And so far off from this as the " Demeter " volume of 1889, almost the same words occur in a poem called " Politics " :

> "Up hill ' too-slow ' will need the whip,
> Down hill ' too-quick,' the chain."

In most of his views, therefore, Tennyson was cautious and temperate,

---

[1] See p. 37.
[2] " I believe in progress, and I would conserve the hopes of man."—Tennyson, in a letter to Aubrey de Vere.

> " Turning to scorn, with lips divine
> The falsehood of extremes."

He was too cautious, perhaps, ever to be sanguine. There were exceptions, however ; sometimes a political prejudice or a social conviction would overpower his poetry, as when he allowed the roar of the cannon to break in upon the music of " Maud," or when in the two " Locksley Halls " and " The Promise of May " the cries of prophet and preacher rose higher than the chanting of the poet.

Like Shakespeare and Chaucer he had a contempt for " the crowd," and not always so good humoured and kindly as theirs ; for his was an hour

> " When more and more the people throng
> The chairs and thrones of civil power ; "[1]

He showed great distrust in the crowd of " raving Paris," as we read in " The Princess," conclusion,

> " Yonder, whiff ! there comes a sudden heat ; "

And though the poet replies as for himself,

> " Maybe wildest dreams
> Are but the needful preludes of the truth,"

yet the protests against the " blind hysterics of the Celt " are twice raised in " In Memoriam ; " and so late as 1886, in " Locksley Hall Sixty Years After," we hear his final judgment—" Celtic Demos rose a Demon." In the same poem, while convinced that democracy is having its way, he tells us what that way seems to be—" Demos end in working its own doom."

Of course, like most of the poets of the fifty years behind him, or of those at his side, he has some confidence in the progress and higher destinies of the human race ; looks humanly forward to a time " When each shall

---

1 " In Memoriam," xxi. ; see also cxiii. These poems appear to have been written in or about the year 1848, as they refer to the Chartist movement at home and the various revolutions abroad.

find his own in all men's good : " (though here may be noticed most of all the wavering and occasional back-sliding that we have already associated with his religious opinions); and he looks even politically forward to a time when those distinctions, and prejudices, and animosities, and murders hitherto sanctioned by the dreadful, it necessary, name of " National " shall be swept away by humanity in its onward march ; or if not quite to this, at least to an epoch of Ethnocracy, as we may call it :

" There the common sense of most shall hold a fretful realm in awe."
Locksley Hall (65).

But there is little in Tennyson nearer to democracy than this ethnocracy ; to him, as to Carlyle, history has been " the biography of great men," and the death of that history is wept over in " Locksley Hall Sixty Years After " :

" Poor old History passing hence."

Greatness is the measure of the man ; those horn-handed breakers of the glebe do not count in the world's records. One still strong man in a blatant land is his best conception of government, present or future. He did not mix with the people in his life, nor with the people did he make his grave. Greatness was the measure of the men who bore his bier. When the poor and the oppressed are mentioned in his pages, it is not with the hopeful sympathy accorded to them in these latter days by many enlightened minds. Enoch Arden, the most heroic soul among all Tennyson's men and women, is one of the English working folk ; but Enoch Arden stands almost alone. As we read the poet's writings through, we feel that his interest and sympathy is oftener with the men of many acres. From first to last the rustic squire, for example, is a favourite type ; sometimes, as in " Maud," being earthly, he is re-buked, but in " Locksley Hall Sixty Years After " he appears at his best,[1] while the people have sunk to their lowest.[2]

Like Shakespeare's—perhaps too much like Shakespeare's—was Tennyson's patriotism. It was insular, and was often the patriotism of great men. It was left to our English poet to write a magnificent ode on the death of the Duke of Wellington. It was left to a French poet to breathe as in mournful protest a requiem over the thousands of brave English peasants who died where they had won that soldier's battle. This could hardly have been otherwise; nor does it lessen our debt of gratitude to the bard, who, by his splendid songs to the glory of our country, bids us remember how we came to be

> "This old England . . .
> Which Nelson left so great,"
> *The Fleet.*

and further reminds us how alone under existing conditions we may still stand together if need be against the world, and exclaim, "we are a people yet."

Peace hath her victories no less than war, and the splendid ode sung at the opening of the International Exhibition follows immediately on "The Charge of the Light Brigade." Was this juxtaposition of the two poems intentional?

At least it brings home to us the fact that this greatest of poets laureate could silence in due season the long accustomed strains of valour or battle, and hymn the newer praises of national amity and social love.

His views of war may be put briefly. Having referred to the notion that the existence of evil may be traced to worlds before the man, he adds that man

> "Needs must fight
> To make true peace his own."
> Epilogue to *Charge of the Heavy Brigade.*

This recalls the famous saying, "War is the natural state

1 Couplets 120 and 134.   2 Couplet 48.

of man," which is true or false according to the meaning infused into the word natural, the simple truth being that war is the natural state of man in a given state ; when the beast has been worked out, war is the unnatural state of man. This fact was not altogether lost sight of by Tennyson. In "Locksley Hall," before the blight fell on him, he looked triumphantly forward to a time when the war drum should throb no longer.

Later, the time when war shall cease seems to recede farther into the future—

> "Far, how far no tongue can say" . . .—*Exhibition Ode.*

> "Will it ever? late or soon?"
> *Locksley Hall Sixty Years After.*

Of commerce he believed perhaps too much at first, and too little afterwards. In "The Princess" "Commerce and Conquest" are "two crowned twins" destined to achieve the freedom of the world. In "Maud" the tone is more reserved ; in the "Exhibition Ode" his song is worthy of the occasion ; the progress of the human race will be advanced by the united industry of the nations, and the merchant ship is to be "the fair white-winged peacemaker." From this point, however, commerce is thought less of as a factor in the world's progress. It is no longer coupled with conquest, but in "Locksley Hall Sixty Years After" the vision of the "Exhibition Ode" is seen once more ; commerce and peace are now the two crowned twins, and rightly :

> "Robed in universal harvest up to either pole she smiles
> Universal ocean softly washing all her warless Isles."

But again, the vision is seen very far off :

> "Warless? when her tens are thousands, and her thousands millions,
> then—
> All her harvest all too narrow—who can fancy warless men?"

Equal in importance to the religious and social movements of the age, and closely related to each, is the great scientific movement, of inception on the one hand, where practical results are concerned, and of revolution on the other, where it enters the region of philosophic thought. If science has given us almost a new physical life, scientific inquiry has swept away systems of mental and moral philosophy as old as thinking man. The doctrine of evolution, we might say, has compelled mankind to begin mental life over again. From its principles, as from a single vigorous stem, all branches of modern knowledge are outspread.

Therefore in such poetry as Tennyson's, which is the very voice of the age, both these amazing products of the age must be represented.

The "fairy tales of science" found a ready listener in Tennyson. In "The Two Voices" we read:

> " Before the little ducts began
> To feed thy bones with lime . . . "

The two stanzas originally at the beginning of "A Dream of Fair Women" are one long figure taken from ballooning, a triumph of science that is introduced yet more skilfully into "Locksley Hall."[1] Gas is mentioned in "The Palace of Art," first edition, and, in the same poem, some omitted stanzas express "the joy wherewith the Soul contemplated the results of astronomical experiment;" and throughout his career, like Shakespeare, the poet makes good poetical material of such contemporary marvels; as, for instance, the conjectured planet in the lines "To H.R.H. Princess Beatrice." The latest example of this practice, and perhaps the most interesting of all, will be found in the opening lines of "St. Telemachus," where a graphic description is given of the wonderful sunsets that shortened our winter some twelve years ago.

But science was much more to Tennyson than occasion for poetical ornament: he expected from it as much as

[1] Couplets 61-63.

from commerce and conquest;[1] he was so enthusiastic that the progress of science seemed slow to him—as slow as civilization itself;

> "Science moves, but slowly, slowly, creeping on from point to point:
>
> Slowly comes a hungry people. . . ."

A temporary distrust expressed in the same poem passes away when he reflects that after all there is more enjoyment "in this march of mind In the steamship and the railway" than could be found in the islands at the gateways of the day. In "Maud" the distrust grows deeper, for "The man of science himself is fonder of glory, and vain, An eye well practised in nature, a spirit bounded and poor;" and by the year 1865 we have had "Science enough and exploring, Matter enough for deploring."[2] The rest of the story is short, and most of it will be told elsewhere in this volume. It is a sad story of disillusion and despair:

> "Till the sun and moon of our science are both of them turned into blood."[3]

And as will be shown in the chapter on "In Memoriam," Tennyson is never more sadly earnest than when he bids these "days of advance" remember that science "is the second, not the first."

Evolution he regards throughout with a caution due to the magnitude of the subject, its numberless yet vast issues. It does not enter his poetry until after the publication of "The Vestiges of the Natural History of Creation," in 1844. The date of some of the poems in "In Memoriam" may be determined by a reference to this book. There is just a little of teleology in "Locksley Hall," and sometimes the poet identifies teleology with evolution. "The Princess" introduces the cosmogony of La Place, the new theory of human development, and

---

[1] "In Memoriam," xxi. 5 ; lxxxv. 7 ; " Epilogue " 36 ; see also "Locksley Hall," 59 and 60-65.

[2] From the poem " 1865-1866."   [3] "Despair."

the doctrine of design in nature. But "In Memoriam" devotes whole poems to these and kindred subjects.[1] To sum up, the poet accepts the fact of evolution as regards the individual, and with some equanimity, though he does not attempt to explain the birth of the human soul, which is in reality a paramount difficulty when viewed from any such standpoint ; and as regards the evolution of mankind as a part, or of the universe as a whole, the bewildered hope of Tennyson is perhaps no less touching than the despair of Lucretius, stern, complacent, or magnificent :

> "Forward, backward, backward, forward, in the immeasurable sea,
> Sway'd by vaster ebbs and flows than can be known to you or me."

> "Sic igitur mundi naturam totius aetas
> Mutat, et ex alio terram status excipit alter ;"

though Tennyson, as usual, after serving as counsel for the prosecution pleads with equal earnestness for the defence—

> "Only that which made us meant us to be mightier by and by" ;

and thus in some sense he preserves a balance between blind optimism and arrogant pessimism.

It was much the same with the great Woman's Rights question ; the poet is mediator or umpire between contending parties rather than a partisan. This is well seen in one of the characters in "The Princess ;" for the King of the North is created to give fuller expression to the Biblical or primal opinions of the "fat-faced curate" in "Edwin Morris :" "God made the woman for the use of man." Yet the "Hard old king," after converting into poetry the well-known Scripture, "Thy desire shall be to thy husband, and he shall rule over thee,"[2] after coming

---

[1] liv., lv., lvi., cxviii., cxx. Some of these poems therefore appear to have been written later than 1844. So also cxxiii. and cxxiv. Many of them derive material from the Bridgewater Treatises of 1833-36 ; others are indebted to Lyell's "Principles of Geology."

"Man to command and woman to obey,"

near to repeating the savagery hinted at in "Locksley Hall," "a little dearer than his horse," [1] yet includes within the same speech sentiments that are the poet's own best convictions; "Man with the head and woman with the heart;" or again, "The bearing and the training of a child Is woman's wisdom." The first of these opinions is attested by almost all the women in Tennyson's poetry: the second may be found in "In Memoriam." [2] From all this we learn that the poet in his zeal as moderator sometimes weakens his position as dramatist. And with regard to all these important cases—religious, political, social, industrial, or philosophical, we may say in conclusion that they have been brought in for hearing time after time during some sixty years before an intellectual court in which Tennyson sat as judge. Doubtless the position of advocate would have been much more effective for a poet; but it would not have been so safe for the nineteenth century.

Tennyson erred—if he erred at all—on the side of freedom that grows out of law and bears fruit of order. And if we may embody another figure in a concluding remark, it should be added that during the past fifty years the function of Speaker in our House of Commons has more than once rivalled the function of the orator; and never was a speaker more needed in the parliament of thought, if these fifty years are, as the poet has described them, years of

> "Men loud against all forms of power—
> Unfurnish'd brows, tempestuous tongues—
> Expecting all things in an hour—
> Brass mouths and iron lungs."
>
> *Freedom.*

IV.—MAN, NATURE, ART. (*a*) *Man and Nature.*—
These two subjects of poetry are sometimes kept apart

[1]
> "She's yet a colt—
> Take, break her: strongly groom'd and straitly curb'd."

[2] xl., stanza 4   see also Chapter VII.

but we have the best of both when both are blended. Man is made man by virtue of his environment ; but, what is not so readily acknowledged, that environment in some sense owes its existence to man.

We need not do more than touch philosophy on the surface, and pass at once to a comprehensive definition of the third term in our heading—Art is man, or nature, or both, idealized.

But the subject of Art must be reserved for the next division of this section. We have here to consider some of the relations between man and nature as they appear in the poets.

The opening paragraph above may seem trivial, but it contains the root of all that is to follow ; and possibly it may not be usual to consider man as a subject of poetry, apart from nature. Yet a brief estimate of the extent to which human existence is reproduced by this poet or that, may not be uninteresting. Shakespeare, of course, stands first ; in one of his plays, say Henry V., there is more of our real English life than in any single work of any other writer. In these days of the steamship and the railway— and, we may add, the thousands of novels that sketch every type of character from every grade of life—it is easy enough for a poet to bring all mankind into his pages ; so much the more marvellous is the dramatic comprehensiveness of Shakespeare. But after Shakespeare, Tennyson may rank among the best who have left us large legacies of idealized English men and women ; he has created a delightful modern society to which all are admitted ; in which all may find friends who will never fail them ; to whom they may withdraw from a world too often coarse, or wearying, or unkind ; and in whose company they may multiply and prolong their days.

After this hasty glance towards that better and wonderful world peopled for us by the poets, we return to the subject of man and nature.

The artificial school of verse-makers[1] whose dealings are with the understanding, limit their rhetoric to man; nature, if present at all in their verse, is as parsley primly placed around cold meat—conventional, a matter of course, and not to be eaten. But in imaginative work like Shakespeare's, nature is as the wholesome salad, or the refreshing fruit of the feast, to be eaten and to be enjoyed.

In regard to the presentation of the natural world in poetry, Shakespeare is easily first. Certainly he never uses nature except as related to man; as the background of the human picture; but he is so spontaneous, so fresh and so true, that the flowers he has plucked and placed in his verse still breathe their early fragrance and glisten with the morning dew. No poet approaches him here.

Burns and Scott and Chaucer and Thomson and Matthew Arnold might next be mentioned; Tennyson is not far behind these. He paints our England minutely, beautifully, and lovingly, only not so freshly.

"If not so fresh, with love as true;" and for this we thank him deeply. As we turn his pages, the open loveliness of English landscapes, the more secret beauties[2] of insect, leaf, and flower—the countless common glories among which we tread with hurrying feet—all these he paints; and they are ours only because he has painted them. England is lovelier, all English life is richer, because he has lived amongst us.

Like the other poets named above, Tennyson mostly sketches his figures first, and then fills in his canvas with landscape. But, as already hinted, he loves to limn Nature for her own sake too, and sometimes, though rarely, her charms are all his picture. And he can paint all nature; not homely England alone. And, what is more, like Shakespeare and Milton, he can paint what he has not seen. Shakespeare may surpass him in the power of

[1] See pp. 8 and 9.   [2] Pp. 73 and 211.

describing scenery with the mere aid of the imagination ; and Milton must surpass him in the divine faculty of seeing "things invisible to mortal sight." He could not have the broad strong sweep of brush that has filled some of the pages of "Paradise Lost"

> "With many a frozen, many a fiery Alp,"

things fearful and wonderful and vast ; he could not have wrought into living beauty

> "All that bowery loneliness,
> The brooks of Eden mazily murmuring ;'

for this work of Titan and of Angel was intrusted only to a mortal who was blind ; who, compassed about with darkness might espy the secrets of the Abyss, as through the night we other mortals see our heaven beautiful with stars.

But in the Arthurian poems Tennyson has more than rivalled Spenser in depicting a world visionary yet real—more real, more beautiful, and more enduring than the world of living man.

Also he has given us glimpses, vivid and splendid, of

> " Larger constellations burning, mellow moons and happy skies,
> Breadths of tropic shade and palms in cluster, knots of paradise. . . .
>
> Summer isles of Eden lying in dark-purple spheres of sea."

The last word brings before us another of his triumphs. Shakespeare may always be excepted ; but who else like Tennyson has woven verse of the sound and colour and spirit of the sea? Only Swinburne, perhaps, for the sea was his "green-girdled mother."

Then there are the nature-worshippers ; poets who break away from their human relationships and share Nature's life ; who pant forth her praises till their voice becomes her voice. Such was Shelley—

> " He is made one with Nature ; there is heard
> His voice in all her music ;"

Such was Shelley when he sang to the west wind :

> "Be thou, Spirit fierce,
> My spirit ; be thou me, impetuous one ;"

or Byron, when he mused by the ocean :

> " I love not Man the less, but Nature more
> From these our interviews, in which I steal
> From all I may be. . . . ."

or Wordsworth, who would "bend in reverence to Nature," who "stood by Nature's side"—

> " Nor was this fellowship vouchsafed to me
> With stinted kindness. . . .
> Mine was it in the fields, both day and night,
> And by the waters, all the summer long. . . . "
>
> *Prelude.*

or such, again, was Keats who, to be alone with Nature, would

> "Fade far away, dissolve, and quite forget . . .
> The weariness, the fever and the fret
> Here where men sit and hear each other groan."

In our day, when scientific thought is again making a god of nature, such poets are the more entitled to a share of sympathy and admiration. But none of these was Tennyson. Like Shakespeare and Æschylus and Euripides and Sophocles (dramatists certainly, but they took their bent), like Homer and Virgil and Dante and Milton and Chaucer, and many other great and serene souls, he was human, and he never forsook his humanity. Possibly he held to the doctrine with which this section opened, " we have the best of both when both are blended."

(*b*) *Tennyson as Artist.* If poets such as Browning, Swinburne, Matthew Arnold, or William Morris were being considered under this head, we might approach the subject at once ; but before speaking of Tennyson as an artist in verse, it will be best to take a rapid survey of the principles of art. The poet's own views embrace a prospect extensive enough for the purpose of this short section, in which, as in the former one, philosophy may here and there be touched on the surface, but never sounded to its depths.

Tennyson's theory of the nature and function of art is popular rather than artistic or profound, yet it serves excellently as a starting-point for a whole treatise. In " The Palace of Art," for example, the poet has laid foundations on which both ethical and æsthetic structures may be built up in many a modern fashion. Though addressed in the first instance to an artist,[1] the poem was afterwards dedicated to an unprofessional friend ; at least, the word "artist" was removed. By this change the poet may have thought that he would be making a more general appeal, and one that would reach all men of culture.

For the ethical lesson of " The Palace of Art" is one that should be learnt by every educated man or woman who forgets that

> "There's nothing we can call our own but love."

It may be learnt by the poet himself if he remains " orbed in his isolation." We might almost venture to say that Tennyson had built his own little Palace of Art—hedged around with shrubs of laurel.[2] Other poems besides "The Poet's Mind" discover a tendency towards aloofness ;[3] or shall we merely say that he was jealous of his high vocation? In "Maud" the man of science was pronounced fonder of glory, and vain ; and if we may judge from the spirit of the age, this palace building is quite as common among the devotees of science as among the worshippers of art.

In "In Memoriam" a whole poem[4] has been inserted as a warning against the tendency to love knowledge for its own sake ; and a place is found in " The Palace of Art," especially in omitted stanzas, for the scientific

---

[1] "You are an artist, and will understand
Its many lesser meanings."

[2] "The Poet's Mind," p. 89.   [3] See p. 137.   [4] cxiv.

enthusiast who has broken with the affections and the responsibilities of our common humanity. But what the poem specially condemns is our modern tendency to turn to a merely selfish æsthetic account the most solid virtues known amongst men ; to live above and away from the "darkening droves of swine," those humbler human brethren of the plain : to shut ourselves up in a Palace of Art where we may feast in our isolated ease on artistic dishes made yet more delectable by sweet spices extracted from despised and mutilated memorials of human achievement and goodness. Such an one is the Soul in Tennyson's poem ; and for her, except repentance be timely, the worm that dieth not is surely waiting. She does repent, however, and is saved.

But, according to Tennyson, it fares worse with another type of one-sided human life. Concerning the youth in "The Vision of Sin" who built himself a palace of the flesh, the poet anxiously inquires, "Is there any hope?" And the answer is given in a language that no man understands.

There are yet other palace-builders in the volume that contains "The Vision of Sin' ; St. Simeon Stylites, St. Agnes, Sir Galahad, build for themselves their palace of ecstasy ; and this is the fairest of all ; but

> "There's nothing we can call our own but love ;"

these therefore are not free from blame ; they all have "shut Love out," and "in turn shall be Shut out from Love."

In the dedication to "The Palace of Art," from which the last quotation was made, the following passage will be found :

> "Beauty, Good, and Knowledge are three sisters
> That doat upon each other, friends to man,
> Living together under the same roof,
> And never can be sunder'd without tears.
> And he that shuts Love out, in turn shall be
> Shut out from Love . . . ."

Whatever may be its philosophical value—and this we shall endeavour to ascertain—the passage is remarkable because in 1882, just fifty years after its appearance, Matthew Arnold found it worth repeating almost verbatim. At the opening of the Josiah Mason Institute at Birmingham, Professor Huxley had declared that science of itself could furnish a liberal education. In an article combating this opinion, Matthew Arnold contended that science alone was by no means sufficient for the powers and needs of complete mental life.[1] " Human nature," he asserted, " is built up of three powers, a power for Beauty, a power for Conduct, and a power for Knowledge ; and they cannot be isolated." [2]   To return to Tennyson's statement, the " Love " of the last line quoted is really included in his " Good " of the first line ; and this again is the equivalent of Matthew Arnold's " conduct." [3]

Having suggested this slight modification, we proceed to examine the subject of art on the lines laid down by Tennyson.

The use of language endowed us with thought on the one hand, but also, in great measure, with the higher feelings and abstractions on the other. If we now speak of these higher feelings as being either moral, or merely emotional, we have a threefold division of mental life; and although the boundaries between these divisions are always debateable, yet the intellectual, the emotional, and

[1] Or, as Tennyson words it in the Dedication to " The Palace of Art," " the perfect shape of man."

[2] It is interesting to notice the same threefold division in " In Memoriam" (cii.), where the poet represents the maidens of his dream as singing " of what is wise and good and graceful."

[3] Possibly the physical life might have been taken into account, as in its relation to " The Vision of Sin." Life, we might say first, is physical as well as mental ; it is better that the soul should subdue the body, than that the body should weigh down the soul (" Vision of Sin ") ; but our physical being demands due recognition in any examination of complete human life. It is with the mental life, however, that we are chiefly concerned in the above.

the moral life are sufficiently distinct as a graspable growth of contrast. Next it will be seen that they correspond with the three divisions of Tennyson or Matthew Arnold ; for knowledge is the substance of the intellectual life, beauty of the emotional, and goodness of the moral. Further, science may be regarded as the minister and the expression of knowledge, art as the minister and the expression of beauty, while from one point of view religion will be recognized as the minister and the expression of a morality that extends through and beyond human experience into the regions of the infinite and the eternal.

Thus far we have been following the lead of the poet in our endeavour to discover the province of art, and the poet's habitation therein ; but at this stage we must make a short excursion by ourselves.

In the former section, art was defined as "man, or nature, or both, idealized." But the definition was left incomplete, because its completion involved a short inquiry into the history of the human mind.

As a general term for the advance made by man in his progressive self-adjustment to his surroundings, we may conveniently employ the word truth ; truth, then, is the measure of man's success in realizing and harmonizing with the exquisite fitness of things.[1]

But truth has its special aspects. In one of these it appears as the record of successful attempts made by the

---

[1] The statement on page 30, "that environment in some sense owes its existence to man," may now receive some explanation. It is possible that man's environment is more indebted to man than man to his environment ; because man's mind not only registers the facts of its environment, but also by a potential principle inherent in life and evinced in reaction, it relates and interprets these facts ; thus it reveals itself, builds up its own nature, and out of its progressive experience creates an ideal of further progression. As to the question whether man's environment may be said to exist apart from the intelligence that perceives it, we answer that each has called the other into existence, and each for existence depends upon the other. No wonder that Tennyson gives a prominent place to "Circumstance" in his poetry. (See under poem "Circumstance," p. 95 ; also p. 275, footnote.)

human intelligence to realize and establish harmonious relations between itself and the external world ; and the ideal of this objective or intellectual truth is set forth in Tennyson's well-known poem, "Flower in the crannied wall." In a second aspect it appears as a record of the successful attempts made by the human will to establish similar relations between itself and its actions—or what is ultimately the same thing—society ; and the ideal of this subjective or moral truth finds perfect expression in Shakespeare :

> " To thine ownself be true,
> And it must follow, as the night the day,
> Thou canst not then be false to any man."

Thirdly, when these efforts to realize life to the uttermost are put forth by the emotions, then the harmonies established constitute emotional truth, more commonly known as beauty.[1] Thus, beauty is in the region of feeling what intellectual truth is in the region of cognition, and moral truth in the region of volition.

This, then, is beauty ; one product of the many harmonious relations established between man and his surroundings by a potentiality of realization implied in consciousness ; and art is nothing more than the attempt to realize more of these harmonies through some emotional medium ; and thirdly, to idealize is merely to go beyond

---

[1] Therefore, as in the former note, the sense of beautiful that appreciates and the thing beautiful that is appreciated, have each of them called the other into existence, and each for existence depends upon the other. "The thing beautiful" is the object or the idea that has been placed in harmonious relation to our emotions ; beauty therefore in its first aspect is strictly relative.

As to the question whether an object may be beautiful in itself, we have postulated for man's intelligence an independent interpreting principle called into action by the external world ; similarly there may exist in this external world of stimuli something beyond and above stimulus ; but of this we have no knowledge. Further, because there is no limit to the harmonies of relation that remain to be established between emotion and environment, it follows that absolute beauty is unattainable. The same holds good of intellectual and moral truth

one's fellows in these progressive attempts to interpret the subjective world of society, and the objective world of nature, history, fact. The ideal of the savage will shock a modern European ; the ideal of the modern European in any of these departments of self-expression will doubtless be a cause of compassionate astonishment to " the crowning race." On the other hand, to vitiate any one of these approximations to the ideal,[1] is to destroy harmonies already established under that head.

Although very much remains to be stated, we are now in a position to complete our definition of art in the former section by adding the words, "through an emotional medium." Also we have learnt to regard Tennyson's threefold division of mental life as correspondent to the three aspects of one great reality—truth. And, finally, a point of view has been gained from which we may discover the "many lesser meanings"[2] of "The Palace of Art," and other poems by Tennyson, and more clearly to recognize the truth of his assertion :

> " Beauty, Good, and Knowledge are three sisters . . .
>
> And never can be sunder'd without tears."

With respect to the latter, we have learnt from Shakespeare and from some principles of ethics, that no self-realization or self-expression can be consistently and progressively self-regarding unless it has reference to the interests of the whole human family ; and since art, science, and morality are modes of self-realization and self-expression, it follows that each of the three embraces the general progressive good of mankind ; and therefore none of them is independent of the others, for none may neglect a power which works equally with itself for the general good. For example, the ideal moralist must avail himself of the kindred powers of knowledge and beauty ; in order to be generous he must first be wise. As to the

---

[1] Beauty, for example ; p. 40, footnote.   [2] See note, foot of p. 34.

relation between beauty and morality, Tennyson tells us in his poem, " In the Children's Hospital," that flowers " freshen and sweeten the wards like the waft of an angel's wing ; " and in regard to statuary, he points out in " The Princess " that

> " To look on noble forms
> Makes noble thro' the sensuous organism
> That which is higher."

Similarly, the artist and the thinker must work with the general good in view : they may never " shut Love out." [1]

We notice next in Tennyson's poem that the " soul," the "glorious Devil," loved Knowledge for its beauty ; and if Good, Good only for its beauty.   By this we are reminded of an expression much in vogue, " Art for art's

---

[1] We may here briefly consider such " lesser meanings " as the following:

> "Authors, essayist, atheist, novelist, realist, rhymester, play your part,
> Paint the mortal shame of nature with the living hues of Art."

A little further on (" Locksley Hall Sixty Years After ") we read

> "Have we risen from out the beast, then back into the beast again?"

That is to say, if we were right in admitting the progressive nature of morality, and our obligation to it, a return to the past will probably be immoral.   In ages dating nearer to man's " coarsest satyr-shape," we might expect in a poem the fleshly fever of Bacchanalian worship, or in sculpture, a Priapus.   Unfortunately, in his straining after effect, the artist often betrays a tendency towards such retrogression.   And this is what the poet implies in the words "Reticence," " Reverence," "naked," " Zolaism," in the context of the couplet quoted above.   As to the " realist," what is true of literary language is true of any other artistic mode of presenting form or fact ; it may be striking from excess of ideality or from excess of reality. Chiefly by virtue of contrast, the realist secures his effect of pleasing surprise by a mere copy of the fact, as in " Robinson Crusoe "—a work that may be contrasted with the ideality of the " Faerie Queene."   But the realist pointed at by Tennyson secures his effect of surprise, more or less pleasing, by copying facts that are unfamiliar because through the tacit consent of a progressive morality they have long been regarded as improper subjects for art.   In " Robinson Crusoe," for example, a number of the occurrences of our daily life are left unrecorded in deference to the higher purposes of art. Certainly, the modern realist claims only *some* of this " mortal shame of nature " ; to be consistent, he should surely claim it *all !*

sake ;" and we are often given to understand that a conscious moral aim is injurious to art.

The real truth is contained in a former paragraph, where art has been considered as a means to an end—the general good, towards which it contributes jointly with science and morality. If in the pursuit of art the mind aims at the higher good, the work of art will be of the highest order as well as of the highest perfection. If, on the other hand, the artist aims only at artistic effect, he will probably fall short of that mark because he did not aim above it. This explains the statement, "all really great schools of art have been inspired by religion." [1]

The foregoing considerations seek to establish the truth of Tennyson's doctrine as quoted at the outset ; but they may also explain the many half expressions of his whole truth that are met with in modern literature. The following are examples :

"Beauty is truth, truth beauty."—KEATS.

"The seal of truth is beauty."—CHARLES TENNYSON TURNER.

"To see things in their beauty is to see things in their truth."

MATTHEW ARNOLD.

"Knowledge is the parent of love ; wisdom, love itself."—J. HARE.

"True knowledge leads to love."—WORDSWORTH.

"Utter knowledge is but utter love."—TENNYSON.

"Moral beauty is the basis of all true beauty."—RUSKIN.

"Beauty is a kind of goodness."—HUXLEY.

In conclusion, therefore, the first and the highest aim of art is moral ; and it was this aspect that was most clearly perceived by Tennyson. He had an eye and a soul for beauty, but he was not an artist "That did love Beauty only ;" and to him beauty was "a kind of goodness."

Like him in this respect among great poets were Milton and Wordsworth ; among lesser poets might be added

[1] This most important truth may be stated in another form. Art, Science, Morality, are not antagonistic until one or more of the three makes an attempt to dominate another or the others.

Cowper and Longfellow; a characteristic utterance of each
would be as follows :

Of Milton :—"Poetical powers are the inspired gift of
God."

Of Wordsworth :—"The purpose of this highly-gifted
being is the expression of truth."

Of Cowper :—

> "I . . . tell them truths divine and clear,
> Which, couched in prose, they will not hear."

Of Longfellow :—"The poet, faithful and far-seeing."

In speaking of Tennyson as an artist, we have chosen
to deal first and most fully with his characteristic view of
the subject as set forth in one of his well-known poems.
It remains briefly to notice one other aspect of art, and
Tennyson's relation thereto.

To help us in this branch of the subject, we must con-
struct a more explicit definition of art. "Art is truth
expressed, by emotion, in a form of beauty." Milton,
both in theory and practice, holds a high conception of
beauty. Wordsworth sometimes stopped at truth.

In Tennyson's well-known poem "The Poet," metaphor
and imagery are often confused ; but we gather that the
poet in his theory attaches more importance to truth
in poetry than to beauty ; yet, as a fact, no artist in verse
has laboured harder than Tennyson to attain perfection
of beauty. For this he deserves our gratitude. How
essential to poetry is this element of beauty may be learnt
from the lines of Cowper quoted above, or from such
a line as this other in which Goldsmith apostrophizes
poetry :

> "Aid slighted truth with thy persuasive strain."

But this seeking after truest beauty belongs not to a
poet, nor to poets ; rather it is a passion to all artists who
are worthy of the name.

Much that appertains to the subject of Tennyson as a literary artist will be met with in the following pages. The late Laureate's position among poets is glanced at in the chapter on the " Idylls of the King." In the same chapter an attempt is made to estimate his qualities as epic poet. His dramatic powers are considered in Chapter XIV. His special gifts as a writer of ballad and song, of philosophical poetry, narrative poetry, idyll, monologue, are recognized in their appropriate places. Of Tennyson as a lyric poet generally, something is added in the second Appendix to this chapter, and a third Appendix indicates what may perhaps be regarded as the one slight blemish upon work so extensive, so various, and so good as that of Tennyson.

V.—HUMOUR. Much has been said of late on the subject of humour in Tennyson ; to some he appears almost destitute of this faculty : others trace rich veins of it in poems generally regarded as serious. Possibly something would be gained by a fuller inquiry into the nature of humour ; but this cannot be effected without some reference to the kindred faculty of wit. Wit may be regarded as a play of fancy addressed to the intellect ; whereas, humour is a play of imagination addressed to the emotions ; and just as imagination includes but transcends fancy, and emotion includes but transcends thought, so humour includes but transcends wit.

Wit is a product of the intellect, either alone, or aided by only so much of emotion as may serve to give point to the expression ; and this emotion will be of a low order, or even of the lowest—the emotion for example with which we regard a pantomime, as compared with that we feel when listening to a sonata by Beethoven. Humour, on the other hand, is far less dependent on the intellectual faculties ; imagination, fine emotion, sympathy, and a high moral sense are largely concerned in its production.

Wit is too often the heartless laugh of talent : humour

in its highest form is the "Olli subridens" of a godlike genius who sees through human life, and who therefore flashes a smile even on the tears of its tragedy.

In fact, any resemblance between wit and humour must be traced to the means by which the two forms of self-expression are produced : though shading off into one another, yet, broadly speaking, in purpose and effect they are unlike. In each case we may discover juggling of words and of thought ; but while this juggling is often the end of wit, it is but the beginning of humour. The great humorist, so far as he avails himself of the baser instruments, uses them strictly as a means to a noble purpose, until at last the stage fool is at once the impersonation of the highest morality, the profoundest wisdom, and the most touching pathos— for such is the fool of the world's masterpiece—King Lear.

The pivot of the subject is the word "play" in a former paragraph. A genius will almost certainly possess the power to "play," whether in regard to wit or humour, but he may not always have the inclination. Some joyous souls there are, Shakespeare and Chaucer, for example, who never lose the godlike faculty of smiling. With others it is intermittent. Others again, like Milton, must suppress it almost throughout their life. How was it with Tennyson ? Matthew Arnold seems to speak of him as one who "takes dejectedly His seat upon the intellectual throne." There is some truth in this. "Tears, idle tears" may be regarded as the poet's most passionate utterance of a ruling passion. But Tennyson was many-minded ; and he wore his nature lightly enough to laugh in due season. We must, therefore, expect to find in his writings a proportionate amount of humour.

The best poem for the purpose is "The Princess." There in abundance are wit and humour and all the gradations between. We may begin with the mere verbal

quibble. "They . . . would call them masterpieces : they master'd *me*." This was the highest humour that the puny Gama might aspire to, and his son's intellect is upon the same level. " I thought her half *right* talking of her *wrongs*." From these low beginnings of wit we may pass to such delicate humour as the following :

> " Scarce had I ceased when from a tamarisk near
> Two Proctors leapt upon us, crying, ' Names ; '
> He, standing still, was clutch'd ; but I began
> To thrid the musky-circled mazes, wind
> And double in and out the boles, and race
> By all the fountains : fleet I was of foot :
> Before me shower'd the rose in flakes ; behind
> I heard the puff'd pursuer ; at mine ear
> Bubbled the nightingale and heeded not,
> And secret laughter tickled all my soul.
> At last I hook'd my ankle in a vine,
> That claspt the feet of a Mnemosyne,
> And falling on my face was caught and known.
>   *The Princess,* IV. 239-251.

To this may be added such other passages in the same poem as IV. 189, 190, and IV. 206-8. As an instance of the poet's gift of refined irony, mockery, banter, nothing could surpass " The Spiteful Letter " ; and of poems essentially humorous the finest are " Will Waterproof's Lyrical Monologue " and " The Northern Farmer—Old Style."

Further it may be noticed that Tennyson's humour in such poems as " The Princess " and " The Northern Farmer " is not only delicate and subtle, for it broadens, deepens, softens into the beneficent smile of Shakespeare, and Chaucer, and those other demigods of verse who regard human things

> " With larger, other eyes than ours
> To make allowance for us all."

It is perhaps unfortunate that some of the best examples of Tennyson's humour are not dramatic, but mono-dramatic,[1]

---

[1] This fact alone, as will often be noticed in subsequent chapters, makes any comparison with Shakespeare misleading. Apart from the enormous gain of a dramatic environment, "The Northern Farmer" stands before us

and are bound up with the verbal play, as in the poems in dialect. "The Northern Farmer" and the rest are, some of them, wonderfully sympathetic, humorous studies of that ruder life to which a higher civilization looks back every now and then with the fondness and regret of a Cromwell for his sheepfolds ; and others again are sketched from a newer world with the same kindly and matchless insight ; but dialect is a sort of falsetto, not always reliable as a test of humour ; like parody, it produces the most striking effect with the least expenditure of effort.   Many young poets cover their faces with this mask of dialect—from Shakespeare, let us say, to Rudyard Kipling—they laugh or they screen their beardless chins behind it. It gave Burns an enormous advantage : " Her 'prentice han' she tried on man ;" this rhyme, and therefore this line (and you will find other instances in the same song), would have been forbidden to the artificer in literary English. Therefore we are not so greatly struck by humour in dialect form ; [1] and we may further repeat that it seems to lose in monologue just a little of the perfection to which it attains in drama proper.

VI.—As Poet Laureate.   The office of Poet Laureate is often an invidious one, and it has been held in suspicion and scorn by great poets themselves. But Tennyson filled it admirably.   As was noticed before, one can hardly fancy him saying of his perfect life—or of any part of it—O that I might live it over again ! What a rare fortune was this to fall to the lot of any mortal man ; and it is true of his poet laureateship ; he discharged it to perfection.   It was pleasant, no doubt, to have a great Queen for patron, and a great era of the people to sing to ;

---

as a statue that the artist has chipped and chiselled during half a generation. Falstaff on the other hand lives and moves amongst us ; is of our flesh and blood ; and his being is spontaneous as our own. Further, we may notice that in his dramas Tennyson's humour is rarely successful.

[1] These views are fully explained in the note on "The Northern Farmer."

for all that, it is no easy matter to acquit oneself well in this job-work of poetry. Like the hero in Byron, whose love was not to be commanded, so the poet is coy and difficult to win ; when he writes to order we hardly expect to find him at his best ; and in any case we have misgivings concerning the verse so produced. Yet Tennyson's duty work is of great excellence, and of itself would form an interesting and valuable volume. How graceful and courteous, yet how wise and dignified is the address to the Queen which is prefixed to the 900 pages of rare poetic wealth which he chooses to call his " poor book of song." It combines the advice of a privy councillor with all the respect and none of the flattery of a courtier. And such are most of the addresses to royalty. And among the other themes set apart for the poet who has won the laurel, what excellence again. His patriotic ballads are the finest and the noblest of their kind ; the " Ode on the Death of the Duke of Wellington " is worthy of " the last great Englishman." Or, again, what could be more fitting to the occasion than the " Ode sung at the Opening of the International Exhibition " of 1862 ; how different the history of the following thirty years might have been if they could ever have taken to heart the gospel of industry here preached. Whatever the position of Tennyson may be among the poets of the world, both the Crown and the people of England give him special thanks and honour for the services he has rendered as Poet Laureate.

And what comes next ? a slighter age, and no poet ?

> " A simpler, saner lesson might he learn
>   Who reads thy gradual process, Holy Spring ; . . .
> Thy scope of operation, day by day,
>   Larger and fuller, like the human mind."

Let us not say with one critic that Tennyson is the last of the Laureates, nor with another that 'poetry is played out.' Rather let us believe with Matthew Arnold that the future of poetry is immense ; that as long as human life retains the common instinct of self-preservation, it will care to reverence and to cherish the high poetic traditions and powers of its humanity.

Most appropriate here are the words of M. Taine : "The poet is for ever young. For us, the vulgar, things are threadbare. . . . On the other hand, the poet is as the first man on the first day."

The poet is for ever young, but our earth is not for ever ; and "Symbols, like all other terrestrial garments, wax old." And these wondrous word-symbols of poetry, they may outlive a picture, a statue, music ; but they too must pass away. Is there no hope beyond this world for poetry, the divinest thing human in this world ? Let us ask of the great master who has sung of worlds before this world. We ask him not in vain ; the answer comes as from the region of the immortals :

> " If the lips were touch'd with fire from off a pure Pierian altar,
> Tho' their music here be mortal, need the singer greatly care?
> Other songs for other worlds ! the fire within him would not falter ;
> Let the golden Iliad vanish, Homer here is Homer there."

Our Singer now is there—there where we find him worthier to be loved. There let us leave him, deeply thankful that he dwelt so long amongst us, reverently convinced that in benign influences of wisdom, love, and beauty, he dwells amongst us still.

APPENDICES TO CHAPTER I.

Appendix I.

(Abridged from " New Studies in Tennyson.")

"This question of occasional weakness in Tennyson's work gives me an opportunity of introducing the subject of Plagiarism, which some reviewers deal with in rather a summary fashion ; and they show but little respect for Mr. Churton Collins ; though why writers who, like Mr. Collins, dwell sometimes upon the 'letter that may be falsehood' should, *of a course*, be dead to the 'spirit that quickeneth,' I do not quite see. And here let me repeat, 'it is not that I love Tennyson less, but that I love Shakespeare and Milton more ;' and here let me add, 'that I love truth most.' Having the truth, therefore, as my motive, I proceed briefly to acquaint you with my impressions of Tennyson as a plagiarist.

"I should first remark that plagiarism is a relative term ; that is to say, a small poet is much more liable to the charge of poaching in the preserves of literature than is a greater poet. For example, when, in ' In Memoriam,' Tennyson recalled Shakespeare (Hamlet) :

> ' And from his ashes may be made
> The *violet* of his native land,'

he was not careful so much as to change the name of the flower. Our latter-day poet knew his powers and his consequent rights, and no man need trouble himself to dispute them.

"But when at the outset of my studies I discovered that many of the most important additions and improvements in later editions of Tennyson's poems might be traced to

Shelley, Milton, Wordsworth and others, I was set thinking: for there is some sort of difference between a suggestion from another writer that appears as an organic growth, and the same suggestion when it occurs as an interpolation. My reflections, however, ended by acquitting our poet on the ground of general greatness. But when, in the year 1884, I read the Laureate's letter to Mr. Dawson,[1] I was again set thinking ; and it was not without considerable effort that I disburdened my mind of its doubt. You may know the French proverb, ' Qui s'excuse, s'accuse ; ' well, it is certainly true of this letter [2]—written, as the poet tells us, ' quite contrary to my custom.' The most notable fact about the letter is that it consists in great part of apologies, which appear forced or inconsistent. There is included a very characteristic exposition of plagiarism, and some of the other remarks have an uneasy significance and appear to be uncalled for. Those who care to read for themselves will probably regret that such a letter should have been written, and they will assuredly be possessed by the conviction that the poet remains much greater than his occasional lapses into explanatory prose might seem to imply.

"Akin to this defect is the tendency common to some other poets to indulge in self-depreciation, to be a little careful about early poems, to point to their early date, to date them indefinitely, and so forth. We have, for example, ' The Dead Prophet,' 182—, the last figure being omitted, though it is possible that the omission may be due to a difficulty in assigning the date ; we have in the prefatory notice to ' The Lover's Tale,' ' 19th year,' ' omissions and amendments that would have been made,'

---

[1] See pp. vii-xiv in " A Study of Tennyson's Princess," by S. E. Dawson, published by Dawson Brothers, Montreal. (Second Edition.)

[2] " As of plagiarism generally ; all poets must borrow to some extent—the imitative, reflective, literary poets most of all. It is not the borrowing, but elaborate and scarcely plausible excusation that we should complain of."

'misprints of the compositor.' Again, in the note pre-
fixed to 'The Window,' *whose almost only merit is
perhaps* that it can dance to Mr. Sullivan's music.'[1]
So the 'Morte d'Arthur' was introduced to us as 'faint
Homeric echoes, nothing worth.' 'Becket' was 'not in-
tended in its present form to meet the exigencies of our
modern theatre.'

"To sum up, I recollect scarcely any reference made by
the poet to his poems[2] that does not appear artificial,
over-sensitive, or unnecessarily apologetic. I have already
noticed the 'genius and geniality' in the 'Tiresias' dedica-
tion. It is surely strange that such an artist should have
cared to gild refined gold. But, as a last word here, I
may tell you that Tennyson when writing prose was like
Garrick off the stage—'acting.'

"Akin, again, are the poet's lamentations over the dis-
advantages of time and place and race :

> ' What hope is here for modern rhyme. . . .'

> ' A tongue-tied poet in the feverous days . .

days of hurry and worry that will not let a singer compose
at his will like

1 Perhaps the drift of these remarks will be better understood if this
quotation is examined more closely as a typical one. In the original edition
the Dedication of "The Window" read as follows : "These little songs,
whose almost sole merit—at least till they are wedded to music—is that they
are so excellently printed, I dedicate to the printer." Nothing can be more
striking as an example of Tennyson's occasional ostentatious self-depreciation
than his carefulness to retain in a totally different context the words here
printed in italics.

2 " Since this Lecture was delivered, I have read Mr. Knowles' Reminis-
cences, 'Aspects of Tennyson, II.,' 'Nineteenth Century,' January, 1893.
Here I find careful note of the fact that the respective poems of the three
brothers may never be identified ; that none of the authors had been beyond
their native county ; that of twenty-six misprints, the publisher would
correct only seven ; that the mad scene in ' Maud ' was written in twenty
minutes, and had been accounted the finest thing of the kind out of Shake-
speare. Profoundly interesting is the reference to the construction of 'In
Memoriam.' In the same article the reader will meet with other kindred
and significant remarks, especially those on adverse criticism."

> ' Old Virgil, who would write ten lines, they say,
>   At dawn, and lavish all the golden day
>   To make them wealthier in his readers' eyes.'

"Many similar passages I could quote to you, but I
forbear; and we shall all be relieved by remembering
that our poet is said to have spent a day over a few lines
of ' Maud ;' and let us be deeply thankful that, apart from
these apparent exceptions, his genius was patient and
dignified."

APPENDIX II.

(From " New Studies in Tennyson.")

"Even in this department of lyrical poetry, in which
expression ranks comparatively higher, I cannot, like some
reviewers, allow Tennyson an absolute supremacy.   Cer-
tainly Shakespeare and Keats are mentioned as compeers;
and the lyrics of Tennyson (like those of Keats) are
' Perfectly beautiful, let it be granted them ; where is the
fault?'   But they do not always thrill you ; sometimes
they lack force, fire, passion ; sometimes they are sweet,
even to softness, and betray that element of weakness
pointed out in a former lecture.   Tennyson has written
' O that 'twere possible,' and 'Early Spring,' but Shelley
has written the 'West Wind' and the 'Skylark.'   Surely
Shelley deserved some phrase of mention—we will not
speak of honour—from the reviewer's pen.   If I might
select one poem in our literature in which all the best
elements of lyrical poetry seem to be represented, that
poem would be Shelley's ' Ode to the West Wind.'   Now
this is a lyric, and mere perfection of form might give it
some rank, but notice the many other high qualities that
unite to place it amongst the very finest of its kind.
There is the personal element strongly pronounced—a
wonderful charm in a lyric—you have all felt it in ' Cross-
ing the Bar ;' there is prolonged and fine, mighty and
prophetic emotion and thought; there is fiery passion

and deepest pathos ; there is imagery abundant and lovely and wonderful ; and as to the manifold music—listen to the large free movement, now calm for very fulness, now tumultuous as the tempest ; the absolute ecstasy of the song bird ; the wild or plaintive or passionate melody ; the long cadences of melancholy sweetness—think of these and all those other elements, just enough reduced to perfect form by just enough of perfect art—and then believe with me that in the poetry of the lyre Tennyson has another rival besides Keats. Shakespeare, as I endeavoured to show in my former lecture, should be no rival at all."

APPENDIX III.

(From "New Studies in Tennyson.")

"Tennyson's chief weakness—if I may be allowed the paradox—is 'weakness'; even in his charm we often find a softness which sometimes suggests want of strength, and is akin to effeminacy. Bulwer Lytton was not alto-gether at fault when he called our poet 'School-Miss Alfred,' and spoke of him as 'out-babying Wordsworth.' This, for example, is a babyism of Wordsworth's :

> 'One morning, raw it was, and wet,
> A foggy day in winter time. . . . .'

And this, though of later date than Bulwer's criticism, may stand for the out-babying by Tennyson :

> 'I stood on a tower in the wet
> And New Year and Old Year met. . . . .'

The following line, I think, occurs in the Arthurian poems :

> 'What go ye into the wilderness to see ?'

And this in the 'May Queen ':

> 'I thought to pass away before, and yet alive I am. . . . .

"These lines are quoted partly as examples of general

weakness, and not altogether as illustrating weakness in 'charm.' ' What go ye into the wilderness to see?' is biblical to excess ; metrically weak also.

" Much of the 'Conclusion' of the 'May Queen' is below the standard of the other two parts ; and this first line,

'I thought to pass away before, and yet alive I am,'

with its forced inversion and vowel repetition at the close (especially when we have regard to the rhymes of the first couplet), is by no means the strongest of its company. The expression, ' I thought *to pass* away,' may be dialectic; but we are more familiar with ' I thought thy bride-bed *to have deck'd*, sweet maid ' (Hamlet). The following examples are chosen from a later poem, ' The Princess ;' Canto V., lines 60-65 ; also lines 78-102 ; VI. 131 ; VII. 21 ; and some of these again find resemblances in such a passage as lines 338-357 in ' The Coming of Arthur.'[1] Others will be noticed as we proceed from the first volume where, in such a poem as ' Adeline,' they are very abundant, to the last volume where, in the dedication of ' The Bandit's Death " to Sir Walter Scott, they are slightly apparent.

As to the source of much of this weakness in Tennyson, especially as it appears in his first two volumes, we may find it in the earlier work of Keats—the poet to whom also he stands indebted for so much of his charm.

" Sometimes this occasional weakness is due to mannerism, verbal or metrical. An author is said to be guilty of mannerism when he employs a striking expression of his own, or a known rhetorical device so often as to offend good taste ; or when he employs it consciously, and for the purpose of producing a forced and isolated effect, rather than unconsciously, and as subserving the main

---

[1] It is further instructive to compare this speech of Bellicent with the "baby-words" of Clymene in the "Hyperion" of Keats. But the very slight weakness in this passage of Keats is more than partly intentional.

artistic purpose of his work.   One example will illustrate this.   The poetical use of the verb *hang* in such a line as

> 'I *hung* with grooms and porters on the bridge,
> > *Godiva.*

or in

> 'Who but *hung* to hear
> The rapt oration flowing free,'
> > *In Memoriam.*

occurs in 'The Princess' no fewer than nine times, and this frequent recurrence of the word has a tendency to weaken the style both of parts and of the whole.

"The reader must not too readily trust the impression produced on his mind by any isolated passage or example. This word would not have been put forward as suggestive of mannerism but for the fact that it is one among a large number of instances.   Only by taking into consideration as nearly as possible the whole of a poet's work can we expect to form a reliable opinion on such points. 'Parts,' says Dr. Johnson, 'are not to be examined till the whole has been surveyed.'"

CHAPTER II.

"POEMS BY TWO BROTHERS," "TIMBUCTOO," "THE LOVER'S TALE."

"POEMS BY TWO BROTHERS," 1826-7.

THE title-page of this interesting volume is as follows :—
"Poems by Two Brothers. ' Hæc nos novimus esse nihil.'
—*Martial.* London ; Printed for W. Simpkin and R.
Marshall, Stationer's-Hall-Court, and J. and J. Jackson,
Louth, MDCCCXXVII." The contents are 102 short poems
covering 228 pages. None of the poems are signed, though
initials were added in the original manuscript. These again
were removed before the book was published. In the re-
print of 1893, the poems are signed with the initials A. T.,
C. T., or F. T. (four poems), standing for Alfred, Charles,
and Frederick Tennyson respectively. Poems quoted in
this notice are signed A. T. In the preface to the new edition
the reader is informed by the present Lord Tennyson that
the identity of the poems cannot be relied upon, as his
uncle Frederick could not be certain of the authorship of
every poem, and the handwriting of MS. is known not to
be a sure guide. In this edition, moreover, a few poems
—not of any importance—have been added ; they formed
part of the original manuscript of 1827, and are signed
A. T. ; and they are followed by "Timbuctoo." As to

the original volume of 1827, we are inclined to wonder why it did not contain the "Ode to Memory," which is said to have been written "very early in life," and which is superior to anything in that volume.

In many respects the book bears a striking resemblance to Byron's "Hours of Idleness." It displays the same boyish affectation, self-depreciation, pedantry; there is the same or a greater abundance of classical quotations and allusions; notes of all kinds, explanations, volunteered information, apologies. Both books adorn their opening page with modest Latin. Byron makes the announcement that his poems were composed by "A minor"— "who has lately completed his nineteenth year"; some of the pieces dated from his fourteenth year. The authors of "Poems by Two Brothers" tell us that their verses were written "from the ages of fifteen to eighteen" (Charles was in his nineteenth year, Alfred in his eighteenth), "not conjointly, but individually, which may account for the difference of style and matter." In the "Advertisement" of disparagement from which these words are taken, occurs the very same figure employed by Byron in his self-depreciatory preface; "I have passed the Rubicon," says Byron, "and must stand or fall by the 'cast of the die.'" "We have passed the Rubicon," the young Tennysons write, "and we leave the rest to fate."

This preface in "Poems by Two Brothers" is succeeded by some introductory couplets of similar purport——

> "Ye who deign to read, forget t' apply
> The searching microscope of scrutiny,"

and these again find many parallels in Byron's prose prologue. It may be too early to detect in this volume signs of the sensitiveness to criticism which afterwards became almost a disease to Tennyson, but as in Byron's case, so in this, some characteristics of the future man may be traced back to boyish pages; where also we shall probably discover the first faint signs of genius. They will be very faint, however; the "Hours of Idleness," though not a precocious production, gave greater promise of poetic power, and secured a proportionate share of criticism.

"A good poet's made as well as born." Next to the influence of the "Hours of Idleness," this will probably be the strongest impression felt by an admirer of Tennyson who reads for the first time " Poems by Two Brothers." That the poet is " born " in Cicero's sense or Ben Jonson's could scarcely be conjectured from the first collection of the verses of Alfred Tennyson. Such a fact would have to be learnt from his later productions. Here we have perhaps the most unpoetical experiments in poetry that were ever gathered together in such quantity and proceeding from authors of such subsequent repute. One of the most striking features of "Timbuctoo," " The Lover's Tale," and the volume of 1830, is the enormous advance in poetic power which is displayed by each of them, an advance quite out of proportion to the interval of time that had elapsed since Tennyson contributed his share to the volume of 1827. Certainly "Timbuctoo" and "The Lover's Tale" are blank verse, which may account for something, and there is not any blank verse in " Poems by Two Brothers." In nearly all the pieces the young artists have to contend with rhyme.[1]

Yet, and this is another interesting feature of the volume we are now considering, an attentive eye and ear may discover the prototype or detect the musical germ of many a later masterpiece. We have the first of the Lilians and Adelines and Madelines in "Did not thy roseate lips outvie;" and it may be as well to mention here that these portraits of women seem to have been suggested, at least in part, not only by such sketches as

---

[1] To write very good blank verse is, of course, the highest achievement in this kind; but in blank verse something less than very good, a beginner may often display poetic powers that must be suppressed in rhyming verse.

Byron's "Marion," but also by various other writers, among whom would be Horace and Skelton.

Most important, however, and profoundly interesting, and not to be found in Byron's volume, is the first indication of that minute and emotional description of natural scenery, some of it near home,[1] which charms us in "Mariana" and "The Dying Swan"—

> " Damp and dank
> Hang the thick willows on the reedy bank ;
> Beneath, the gurgling eddies slowly creep
> Blackened by foliage, and the glutting wave
> That saps eternally the cold grey steep, . . ."

and in many poems, such as "The Dell of E——," we meet with sketches so famous and familiar in after pages—

> "High hills on either side to heaven upsprung,
> Y-clad with groves of undulating pine,
> Upon whose heads the hoary vapours hung,
> And far, far off the heights were seen to shine
> In clear relief against the sapphire sky." [2]

In "Persia" there is preluding of "Timbuctoo," "The Hesperides," and "The Lotos Eaters." It is in such fragments as these that we may get a first glimpse of Tennyson. But what some of us may perhaps look for, we shall not find, an early indication of the mystic side of Tennyson's being ; his affinities with other existences and other worlds than ours. In "Memory" there is regret for the past—

> "Memory, why deceive me
> By thy visions blest,"

but they are not the visions of "Tears, Idle Tears," "The Two Voices," "In Memoriam," "Far, far away," "The Ancient Sage," and yet other poems of later years.

There is much evidence, however, of deep seriousness

---

1 "In Memoriam," lxxix.
2 "Dying Swan," "Œnone," "Lotos Eaters."

and early earnest religion. Indeed the prevailing tone of verse is thoughtful, not with the thoughtfulness of a boy, but with the wisdom of manhood or the melancholy of age. But this no doubt is partly due to the influence of Byron ; and when the young poets bemoan "the vices of life," or look back on their past with disappointment or with fond regret, as the case may be, they can point to such lines as the following in the "Hours of Idleness :"

> "I loved, but those I loved are gone ;
> Had friends—my early friends are fled. . . ."

> "Weary of love, of life, devour'd with spleen,
> I rest, a perfect Timon, not nineteen."

Byron is the chief inspiration of "Poems by Two Brothers ;" but many other poets lend stray notes ; such are Moore, whom all boys love ; and romantic Scott, and Pope, who, strange as it may seem, is often the boy's poet ; and to these some contemporary versifiers may be added. There is also much ransacking of the classics ; indeed, literary materials are brought from many and strange lands, and the range of reading displayed in "Poems by Two Brothers" is perhaps greater than that which is discovered by the similar but more powerful volume, the "Hours of Idleness," of twenty years before.

"TIMBUCTOO," 1829.

Though not included in Tennyson's collected works, "Timbuctoo" will always be associated with the poet's name and fame. It is very often regarded as nothing more than a specimen of "prize poetry ;" and the date assigned is 1829. But Tennyson was not the man to write poetry to order within a limited space of time ;[1]

---

[1] See "Ode on the Death of the Duke of Wellington."

and when first advised to compete for the Chancellor's
medal he is said to have demurred. At the request of his
father, however, he yielded; but he had bethought him of
an earlier poem in blank verse, " The Battle of Arma-
geddon ; " this, re-cast, might serve the purpose. One
line from " The Lover's Tale "—" A center'd glory-circled
memory," and three good ones from the " Ode to
Memory," lent their aid to the venture. It has already
been noticed that "Persia," in "Poems by Two Brothers,"
may be regarded as the herald of " Timbuctoo."

In the " Cambridge Chronicle and Journal " of June 12,
1829, the award was made known as follows :

" On Saturday last the Chancellor's gold medal for the
best English poem by a resident undergraduate was
adjudged to Alfred Tennyson, of Trinity College."

The poem was printed in " Prolusiones Academicæ " of
1829, reprinted with Hallam's " Timbuctoo," in 1834,
again reprinted with the change of one word [1] in 1859
in a volume of Cambridge prize poems, and it is now
included in the recent edition of " Poems by Two Bro-
thers," 1893.

The subject of Timbuctoo is well set forth in the fol-
lowing passage from Hallam's poem :

> " Not all youthful joy has past away . . .
>   A City stands
> Which yet no mortal guest hath ever found.
> Thou fairy city . . . I would not wish thee found ;
> Perchance thou art too pure . . . a splendour in the wild."

Tennyson rebuilds to music the splendid city of a
dream. Musing on the past when Atalantis was " A
center'd glory-circled memory " and Eldorado a paradise
to which "men clung with yearning hope," he exclaims,

> " Wide Afric, doth thy sun
> Lighten, thy hills enfold a city as fair ? "

Suddenly a seraph stands by his side, and his eyes are

---

[1] " *Cones* of pyramids " was substituted for " *peaks* " of pyramids.

opened to behold "within the South " the "crystal pile " of Timbuctoo. The seraph then explains his mission, to "play about man's heart a thousand ways," and make him feel and know mysteries of loveliness, things higher than he can see ; yet, he continues, " The time is well nigh come When I must render up . . . to keen Discovery this glorious city, my latest throne." That might well be the poet's mournful conclusion, for, as Shelley says, " Those cruel twins, error and truth," have "left us nothing to believe in worth The pains of putting into learned rhyme."

Arthur Hallam writing to Mr. Gladstone, September 14, 1829, said of Tennyson's " Timbuctoo," " The splendid imaginative power that pervades it will be seen through all hindrances. I consider Tennyson as promising fair to be the greatest poet of our generation, perhaps of our century." A remarkable piece of criticism truly, especially for a young man of eighteen.

One of the finest passages in the poem is the brilliant simile beginning

> " Like dusky worms which house
> Beneath unshaken waters, but at once
> Upon some earth-awakening day of spring
> Do pass from gloom to glory, and aloft
> Winnow the purple, bearing on both sides
> Double display of star-lit wings, which burn
> Fan-like and fibred with intensest bloom,
> Even so my thoughts, erewhile so low, now felt
> Unutterable buoyancy and strength
> To bear them upward through the trackless fields
> Of undefined existence far and free."

Moreover, in the last four lines we have the first expression of Tennyson's tendency to a kind of trance involving a loss of personality, which however, seemed " no extinction, but the only true life." Tennyson describes the phenomenon to Mr. Knowles in these words : " Sometimes, as I sit here alone in this great room, I get carried

away out of sense and body, and rapt into mere exis-
tence."[1] As we have seen, no reference to this subject
could be found in " Poems by Two Brothers," but it is
here, and in other lines of "Timbuctoo," so ea ly as 1829;
and it is presen' in nearly all the longer poems to follow,
its fullest expression being found in poems cxxii and xcv. of
" In Memoriam." One aspect of this " movi ig about in
worlds not realized " is fully dealt with in the commentary
on " Tears, idle Tears."[2]

Milton, Keats, Shelley, and Wordsworth all enter into
the composition of " Timbuctoo ;" but Shelley is the most
important vitalizing force ; the fertility of imagination, the
rapid movement of the verse and the splendid imagery
are especially his. Still, the poem is due to Tennyson,
and besides being excellent work it is the source to
which we trace back the streams of greater excellencies
that flow through the " Idylls of the King," " The Prin-
cess," " Lucretius," and most of the other works in blank
verse. This Tennysonian close, for example, unless a
little too imaginative, will suggest Dora :

> " And the moon
> Had fallen from the night, and all was dark : "

Here is a cadence that will be heard in " Lucretius,"

> " And thick night
> Came down upon my eyelids, and I fell."

And this Miltonic trick of verse is often overdone by
Tennyson :

> " As when in some great city where the walls
> Shake, and the streets with ghastly faces thronged. . ."

The word "shake," owing to the pause immediately
following, takes to itself about half the collective weight
of accent in the whole line. Then, as might be inferred
from the rapid movement of the verse indicated above,

---

[1] " Nineteenth Century," January, 1893.   [2] Chapter VII., Appendix.

the lines often run without a break into one another until with the aid of the pause a medial line structure is effected within the terminal, and becomes a dominant measure of greater complexity and greater beauty.[1] It is the manner of young poets under less enlightened conditions to measure line and thought or limb of thought with the same instrument of measurement, and thus unconsciously they avoid much of the trouble of blank verse making. But then, of course, the lines they turn out are all, or most of them, end-stopt and monotonous, like many of the early lines of Shakespeare. Not in this respect only, but in a multitude of others, Tennyson (and this is true of Browning and Swinburne, and Matthew Arnold and most other modern poets) seems to have overleapt the period of mere experiment or tentative practice in blank verse ; and these remarks apply equally to another long poem in the same metre, "The Lover's Tale," which was written about this time.

"THE LOVER'S TALE," 1827-8.

This poem, written, as Tennyson tells us, in his nineteenth year, *i.e.*, between August 6th, 1827, and August 6th, 1828, and, therefore, before the poet went to Cambridge, was not given to the public until 1879, when it appeared, with "The Golden Supper" as Part IV., in a volume of ninety-five pages. Originally it had been printed as the last poem in the volume of

---

[1] Other characteristics of the verse are an abundance of slurred syllables ; these also quicken the movement ; and there are "feminine endings," which add to its variety. This subject is treated more fully in the first Appendix to Chapter III. The "did" tense (Chapter III., Appendix ii., p. 107) occurs frequently ; the word "rapt" is used twice ; so is our famous "distinct." Many phrases appear, which are employed afterwards, such as the "wild unrest" of "In Memoriam."

1833, but was withdrawn, perhaps, as being too long for the volume, or more probably, because its author was frightened by recent adverse criticism and regarded the poem as imperfect. Nevertheless, a title-page being added, it was published as a small volume of sixty pages, but was immediately suppressed. Of the few copies that had been presented to friends all were recalled except one, now preserved in the Rowfant Library. It was from this copy that the poem was pirated about the year 1868, and in consequence Tennyson determined to include it with a brief third part, and the Sequel, in "The Holy Grail" volume of 1869. But again the poem was withdrawn, only the Sequel being printed. This is known as "The Golden Supper."

If "The Lover's Tale" in its present form was written before Tennyson entered Trinity College, and within a year of the 1826-7 volume, it is a most remarkable work, especially when we understand that the author contemplated omissions and amendments, and that it was marred by the many misprints of the compositor (see Prefatory note). It is more remarkable than "Timbuctoo" of 1829, more remarkable than most of the contents of the 1830 or 1833 volumes as originally published, and only less remarkable than Browning's first poem. By a curious coincidence Browning's "Pauline" was published in 1833, the year in which "The Lover's Tale" was printed. And if we admit, what is only reasonable, that Tennyson's poem was under revision up to the time of its appearance in print, we shall be able to compare between the two young poets, who for more than half a century were to be rivals in such a rich renown. Browning was twenty-one on May 7th, 1833, and Tennyson was twenty-four on August 6th of the same year. Viewed in the light of these dates, "Pauline" has a still greater advantage over "The Lover's Tale;" for, as we venture to think, when viewed in any other light it appears to be a greater poem, and a poem of more certain promise.

Another striking coincidence between the two poems is the influence of Shelley in each. Line for line, there is not in all literature a wealthier storehouse of imagery, imagination, and passion than Shelley's "Epipsychidion." From this especially, but also from his writings generally, both poets have derived much inspiration and much material.

The characteristics of "The Lover's Tale" will reveal themselves to all who read it together with its sequel, "The Golden Supper," which appeared as an independent poem in "The Holy Grail" volume of 1869. Parts I. to III. which form the early poem have a certain charm in the very exuberance, freshness, and swiftness of youth ; sometimes an overwrought fancy as of the later Elizabethans checks the impetuous imagination of Shelley ; or again the stream of story is lost amid a wild luxuriance of imagery

> "Of eglantines, a place of burial
> Far lovelier than its cradle."

The rush of the verse seems to save the poet from some of the weaknesses that appear in most of his early work ; but such a figure as the following :

> "Cries of the partridge like a rusty key
> Turned in a lock,"

would have been excluded from his well-considered early work. In "The Golden Supper" all faults disappear ; we may miss some of the freshness of youth, but we enjoy the excellence of art.

CHAPTER III.

"POEMS, CHIEFLY LYRICAL, 1830; OR, JUVENILIA."

"To the Queen."

THESE dedicatory stanzas were first published in 1851, the year in which Tennyson was presented as poet laureate at the Queen's levee in Buckingham Palace. They were then one more in number, for the following was omitted in subsequent editions:

> "She brought a vast design to pass
> When Europe and the scatter'd ends
> Of our fierce world did meet as friends
> And brethren, in her halls of glass."

The stanza has defects, the expletive "did meet," for example. In other respects it is below the standard of the rest. And if we may trust the impressions of Carlyle, the exhibition of 1851 was not notable enough to be singled out from the events of the reign. Of the exhibition of 1862 Tennyson wrote later, "The world-compelling plan was thine," and this time the credit of the vast design is transferred to the Prince Consort. Almost every line of the original dedication has been altered; the first two words, "Revered Victoria," fully attest the enormous value of even the slightest changes made by Tennyson in the indefatigable industry of his genius.

One other emendation may be noticed :

> "And if your greatness and the care
> That yokes with splendour yield you time
> To seek in this, your Laureate's rhyme,
> For aught of good that can be there."

This earlier reading of the third stanza points to a time when the poet wore the wreath uneasily. And in the original MS. it was preceded by another from which we receive the same impression :

> "Nor should I dare to flatter state,
> Nor such a lay would you receive
> Were I to shape it, who believe
> Your nature true as you are great."

In 1889 this MS. was sold for £30. It contained the well-known footnote addressed to the publisher (Moxon), part of which ran as follows :—"Ought not all the *yous* and the *yours* and the *hers* to be in capitals?" To the poem in its present perfection, a reference will be found on p. 47.

"Poems, Chiefly Lyrical, 1830 ; or, Juvenilia."

In 1830 Tennyson came before the public with "Poems, Chiefly Lyrical," a small volume of 154 pages, and containing 53 short poems. This was succeeded in 1833 by another volume of about the same size, containing 30 poems, mostly short ones.

Every educated Englishman is familiar with the names of most of the poems that appeared in these first volumes ; but unless he happens to possess the books as originally published, he will form a very false estimate of Tennyson's earlier poetic achievements. Taking the two volumes together, it will probably be no exaggeration to say that their value as compared with the value of the poems that represent them in recent editions is not more than one third. For the presence, in the two early books, of poems afterwards rejected, lowers their value by about one of the thirds,[1] and the other third of deducted value is accounted for by readings since corrected. This fact should be borne carefully in mind by every student of Tennyson, namely, that the two groups of poems in modern copies headed "Juvenilia"[2] and "The Lady of Shalott and other Poems," are far from being representative of the poet's handiwork at the periods to which they respectively refer.

Further, the volume of 1842, in which many of the pieces comprised within the two groups just mentioned appeared in a revised form, contains a notice concerning the four poems "You ask me why," "Of old sat Freedom," "Love thou thy land," and "The Goose;" this notice is to the effect that these added pieces were written, with one exception, in 1833; but again we must remember that as they did not appear in print until 1842, they also received the benefit of the poet's maturer pains.[3]

Since, therefore, these two groups are corrected up to 1842, and yet the one group is still called "Juvenilia," and since both groups are practically regarded as representing the volumes of 1830 and 1833 respectively, we seem to have before us a double task; the first to treat the "Juvenilia" and "The Lady of Shalott" poems as

---

[1] A poet's genius at any given time is measured almost as much by what he rejects as by what he retains.

[2] A title adopted by Byron for one of his early poetic ventures. It may also be noticed that the "Juvenilia" contains poems that did not appear in the volume of 1830, and in "The Lady of Shalott" group are some poems not published till 1842.

[3] These remarks apply also to "The Two Voices," which, although first published in 1842, was originally dated 1833.

they originally appeared ; the second to deal with them in their improved forms as poems published not earlier than 1842. Or perhaps it may be possible to adopt the middle course of examining each version of a poem as we review the groups seriatim, taking also a passing glance at the rejected poems.

The equity of some such course will appear from many considerations. For example, in editions of twenty years back, we find "The Lady of Shalott" poems in their amended form described as "Poems published in 1832." That description is now wisely omitted ; then why should not the title "Juvenilia" be omitted also? Further, the other title, "The Lady of Shalott and other poems," is a little misleading, for it has a tendency to carry the reader back to 1833.

This chapter would therefore be headed more exactly "The Poems of 1830, together with such of these poems as were published in an improved form in 1842."

Why the title of the volume published in 1830 should have been "Poems, chiefly Lyrical" does not appear from its contents ; for strictly speaking, all are lyrical, more or less. Possibly the poet had in his mind the early volume of Wordsworth and Coleridge, the celebrated "Lyrical Ballads" of 1798, especially when we remember that Arthur Hallam was to have been joint contributor with Tennyson. Or the poet may have intended to imply that "The Lover's Tale" and many other long pieces were in hand, or some of these were originally to have been inserted, such as the "Unpublished Drama written very early," a chorus from which is included in the volume. Or again, we may interpret the title by citing Tennyson's remark to Mr. Knowles, "I soon found that if I meant to make any mark at all, it must be by shortness, for all the men before me had been so diffuse, and all the big things had been done." "Timbuctoo," a fairly long poem, had been forced, as we may say, into print ; and " The Lover's Tale," though actually included at the end of the volume of 1833, was withdrawn before the book was published. Such, appa- rently, was the poet's determination to publish only short poems, and " to get the workmanship as perfect as possible." [1]

And for so young a man, the workmanship of this and the succeeding volume is very fine indeed. It would not be easy to name a poet who wrote better verse at such an early age. The well-known remark of Coleridge in 1833, " He has begun to write verses without very well under- standing what metre is " admits of only a partial explana- tion. Coleridge tells us that he " had not read all the poems ; " nor did Tennyson accept the elder poet's advice " to write for the next two or three years in none but one or two well-known and strictly-defined metres." Possibly, as will be seen further on, some explanation will be found in the fact that the young poet often refused to write in metre at all.

On the other hand, if Coleridge had complained that Tennyson's early poetry was fair enough in form but wanting in spirit ; if he had noticed the weakness of poetic impulse as compared with experimental word painting and wealth of amassed material, and that many of the experiments were of a puerile, or trifling, or effemi- nate, or dilettante kind ; if he had noticed further that the relation between form and thought was inorganic, like that of clothes to body, not organic like that of body to soul—had he quoted a line from " Three Sonnets to a Coquette,"

" The form, the form alone is eloquent,"

we might have understood him better ; for many poets of the same age have been more poetical, have put more spirit into the form of their poetry ; there is too much—

---

[1] Remark to Mr. Knowles; " Nineteenth Century," January, 1893.

far too much—of the cunning phrase-maker, and too little of the singer in the first volume.

How different it might be, will appear from these lines of Byron :

> " As on the beach the waves at last are broke,
> Thus to their extreme verge the passions brought
> Dash into Poetry, which is but passion,
> Or at least was so ere it grew a fashion."

Most of the poetry in this, and much in the succeeding volume, is " a fashion." That is the gravest fault we can find with it. But this fault is not without a redeeming charm ; and how often have we wished that the early passionate utterance of Shakespeare, Byron, Shelley, might have clothed its strength with more beauty.

The following, in the order of their importance, are some of the special features presented by the fifty-three poems of the volume of 1830.

(*a.*) *The extraordinary inequality of the pieces,* some of which are weaker than any in " Poems by Two Brothers," while a few display a striking originality and a poetic faculty and charm considerably in advance of " Timbuctoo" and " The Lover's Tale." Inequalities in the same poem, *e.g.,* " The Ode to Memory," will also be noticed.

(*b.*) Two poems will be remembered as most fully representing this new charm so suddenly and unexpectedly introduced into poetic art—" Mariana " and " The Dying Swan." Of each of these the germs may be found in the quotations from " Poems by Two Brothers " on p. 59. The lines in " Mariana,"

> " A sluice with blacken'd waters slept,
> And o'er it many, round and small
> The cluster'd marish-mosses crept, . . ."

may be compared with the first quotation, " Damp and dank," etc., and with the second, " High hills on either side," etc., the following lines from " The Dying Swan " :

"Some blue peaks in the distance rose,
And white against the cold-white sky,
Shone out their crowning snows. . . ."

These two poems are the most original and the most delightful pieces in the volume. Next to them "Oriana" might be mentioned as possessing a little of their charm, and next to "Oriana," "Claribel."

Having looked into the poems to discover the source of this charm, we seem to find it in a new, often minute, and always emotional description of nature ; the emotion being lent partly by the earnest poet, partly by some individual animate object, generally a human being, which is placed in a pathetic situation and made to impress its pathos on all its surroundings ; whether the scene is sketched first, or the individual, the result is the same ; nature is interfused with the animate emotion. This will be more fully explained in the separate notice of each poem. In "Claribel," for example, the emotion expressed in the first line impregnates the whole. We may recognize the same effect in the first line of Gray's Elegy.

(*c.*) This is the pictorial element, chiefly. But along with it and as part of it, we hear a new music of verse, made of a blending of all past beauty of sound in song, and like the other element taking witchery from the human emotion. The impression of originality which we receive from these two elements in Tennyson is due first, of course, to the poet himself, in his earnest relation to his work, as explained in the note on "Claribel,"[1] but also to careful workmanship and a close attention to the best models and materials of former artists. In his most effective work, gems of former poets, sometimes re-cut or re-polished, will almost certainly be found set cunningly amongst his own.[2] It may be added that among Tennyson's forerunners, the poet who has most nearly succeeded

---

[1] P. 79.   [2] See also p. 96.

in producing this kind of poetry is Coleridge ; after him, Keats may be mentioned.

There is yet another new music of poetry in this volume, chiefly in blank verse, the main feature of which is its arrangement, body of sound, and movement ; it may be heard in the three lines quoted from "The Dying Swan," [1] or in blank verse in the opening lines of "The Sea-Fairies," and in such lines as the following in "The Mystic" :

> "Four facèd to four corners of the sky. . . .
> For the two first were not, but only seemed
> One shadow in the midst of a great light."

The last line is the ancestor of many hundreds in poems to come : [2]

> "And the new sun rose bringing the new year." [3]

This new verse is often weighty with finely modulated vowel sound, the nearest thing to it in earlier literature being the "Hyperion" of Keats.

(*d.*) *The number of poems irregular in metre,* or having no metre at all ; formless poems, such as most of the sketches of women—in fact, a large proportion of the pieces in the volume.

These formless poems are most of them novel, and they are not often imitated in after years. There are but three or four even in the volume that follows so closely on this, and there are none in the volume of 1842. They are not formless, however, quite in the sense in which most of the writings of Macpherson, Tupper, and Whitman are formless. They possess such symmetrical elements as feet, lines, and usually rhymes. But while one type of foot is mostly preserved throughout, the sequence of the rhymes, and the length and the sequence of the lines are not reducible to rule.

---

[1] P. 73.

[2] The chief peculiarity is in the last two feet ; they are, first Pyrrhic, second Spondaic.

[3] Last line in the "Idylls of the King."

This increase of variety often threatens not to adorn but to destroy the element of uniformity ; and we are sensible that the poet is securing for himself an unfair advantage. (See the first Appendix to this Chapter.)

(*e.*) *Influence of the poetic past :*—Minor contemporary poets are not so frequently present in this new verse. Of the past, Byron has ceased to be a potent influence ; Shelley is less a power over the poet than he was in "Timbuctoo" and "The Lover's Tale," but he is well represented, especially by material from "The Witch of Atlas." Keats appears ; and he will be more clearly recognizable in the next two volumes. Milton, Wordsworth, Coleridge and Shakespeare are met with here and there : but to complete the list of poets, Latin and Greek as well, whose echoes blend delightfully with this new music, would be impossible. And Tennyson drinks of other waters than those that flow from the familiar Hippocrene ; to take one example from the beginning of the volume ; the epithet "crimson-threaded" attached to "lips" in "Lilian" may be derived from "The Song of Solomon," iv. 3, "Thy lips are like a thread of scarlet."

(*f.*) Next to this careful hoarding and use of the literary treasures of the past—and it will be still more noticeable in subsequent volumes—we may mention the storing up of poetic materials, studious nature-painting, word-painting, phrase-making, elaboration of poetic diction of all kinds.[1] No poet ever amassed and prepared his materials so extensively, carefully, and systematically as Tennyson.[2] It should surely be the despair of all who

---

[1] Compound adjectives, poetic detail often repeated, excesses, as of -èd final (probably caught from Keats), pet words, perhaps archaic—"light and shadow," "marish," and the like.

[2] And no poet exhibits the fact so patently. Perhaps one illustration selected from a large number may serve to make this clear. The word *ivy-tod*, of doubtful grace, but employed by Spenser and Coleridge, was dismissed (p. 120) from "The Miller's Daughter" of 1833, and reappeared in "Balin and Balan" of 1885.

come after. Also there is abundant experiment in metre and numberless other poetical devices ; the most striking attempt being the many formless poems of which mention is made on p. 74. Apart from this, thought is often exquisitely adjusted to form, mood to imagery and music ; the natural world to its human habitants.

(*g.*) *The Effect of the Impulses of the Day*, and of new surroundings, especially Cambridge life, on the poet's habits of thought. This is illustrated by such poems as "The Mystic," "A Sonnet," "The Supposed Confessions of a Second-rate Sensitive Mind," "To ——" "The How and the Why," and by one or two patriotic poems ; for example, "The English War-Song," and the "National Song."

(*h.*) *A Tendency to draw Characters or Humours*, and sometimes to endue them with a portion of his own individuality.

(*i.*) *Restricted Views of Art.* See especially "The Poet."

(*j.*) *A Subtler Use of the Classics.* This is touched upon in (*e*).

The above list of special features of the volume which inaugurates Tennyson's remarkable career does not aim at being exhaustive. Many other poems might have been selected as giving some evidence of a new power or beauty in poetry, such as "The Ode to Memory," "Recollections of the Arabian Nights," "The Sea-Fairies," "The Poet," "The Sleeping Beauty": and the sometimes laboured, often musical, but always artificial sketches of women form a novel and pleasing group. Further, we are left with a general impression of fine imagination allied to sobriety of thought, of sympathy with nature, a marvellous power of depicting and idealizing natural objects, a refined devotion to truth as well as to beauty, and a musical inventiveness and charm that subdues all those other elements unto itself.

The poems will now be considered seriatim. As explained in the Preface, the numbers in brackets give the page of the one-volume edition.

(2) " CLARIBEL " by its title illustrates Tennyson's preference for fine-sounding literary names that contain some remote allusion. Thus he adds to the beauty of his work. Often the poem or scene comes first, and the name second, as in the case of " Fatima." " Claribel " has been made poetical by Spenser (" Faerie Queene," II. iv.) and Shakespeare (" Tempest "), though we need not always seek to identify Tennyson's name titles.

In this poem we find a curious compound word "low-lieth " ; also it is interesting to note that the following single words in the original edition, "roseleaves," " oak-tree," "thickleaved," "clearvoiced," are now written as compounds ; this means that the artist is anxious to adopt every possible device whereby a given number of words shall produce the most striking effect. Here also are favourite words and expressions ; " ambrosial," "thick-leaved," "inward," "athwart," "slumbrous," "runnels," "hollow." [1] The "lintwhite" and some of the former words occur in poems suppressed—portions of the second " Mariana " may be instanced. Some, such as " inward " or "inner" are very frequently used ; "with an inner voice," for example, in " The Dying Swan." As implied in some of our former remarks, a whole volume might be written on Tennyson's collecting, hoarding, and economizing of words, phrases, and images from nature ; there is nothing quite like it in the history of any other poet.

We may now add that to point to this fact is not to dispraise Tennyson ; in such careful study of poetical material of all kinds we have already discovered not a little of the magical beauty of his compositions ; but at present he has not become expert enough to disguise devices or

[1] From other poems the list may be increased by " marish," " mellow," "round," "circumstance," " use," " level," " counterchange," " poplar," and many more. " Broad-based " in the " Address to the Queen " and the " Arabian Nights," is ''the broad-based pyramids'' of " Poems by Two Brothers ;" then it appears in " Pyramids broad-based" of " The Gem " of 1831. In " The Supposed Confessions " it is varied to " broad-imbasèd."

to conceal effort. In "Claribel," for example, the over-fanciful compound "low-lieth" spoils the effect of the other words with a similar archaic ending.

This poem, which is placed first in the volume, is in many respects a typical production, and therefore must receive a proportionate share of our attention.

Tennyson calls "Claribel" "A Melody." What the poet means by the term may be guessed rather than discovered. Probably he would wish us to reverse the well-known expression "Songs without Words"—music, that is to say, which is almost articulate, and style his poem "words musically inarticulate," or word-music. Whatever intellectual basis the melody may possess, will be seen in the following paragraph. But first we may notice the time element—eve, noon, midnight—with which we are so familiar in the two "Marianas" and kindred poems; and remember also the constructive principle already suggested of rise, culmination, and decline. Finally, we may characterize "Claribel" as a beautiful requiem of nature over humanity, borne in upon us by

> "Some gradual solitary gust
> That comes upon the silence, and dies off,
> As if the ebbing air had but one wave." [1]

The poem has already been referred to in the Introduction to the volume of 1830, under the heads of emotional description of nature and emotional music, which blend in one new and delightful effect of charm. Sometimes we

---

[1] Nature is seldom used in this way by Tennyson. It is so in the serenade in "Maud," but that suits the excited lover ; is appropriate also to the lover in "The Talking Oak." Cf. also "The Brook," and the human sympathies of the sea in "Enoch Arden," and "Sea Dreams." The sentiment of "Claribel" may also be compared with the following stanza omitted from Gray's Elegy :

> "There, scatter'd oft, the earliest of the year,
> By hands unseen are show'rs of violets found ;
> The redbreast loves to build and warble there,
> And little footsteps lightly print the ground."

may discover the secret of Tennyson's charm by observing the process of building or reconstruction, as in the "Palace of Art;"[1] sometimes, but only in part, by removing the musical and pictorial elements, and comparing the residuum with the original. Treated thus " Claribel" would be reduced to some such prose as the following :—" Caroline is buried near an oak tree, a grove, a river, a smaller stream, and something like a cave. The spot is marked by a stone overgrown with moss." Or the bare fact might be stated in four words, " The girl is buried." If we now reverse the process and erect on this low foundation the whole fabric of music and vision, we shall find the practice delightful and instructive. If next we seek to establish within our minds the subtle relations existing first between the spirit and the form of the work, and secondly between the architect and the building as of creator to his creation, we shall probably expect to grasp the charm itself. But there we should stop ; for to grasp the charm, could we ever do it, would be to destroy the charm ; it would be like taking the heart out of a nightingale to get at the secret and the source of song.

Hence the words " in part " which are employed above. This exercise nevertheless, both analytical and synthetical, is useful and even necessary to the student and the lover of poetry ; and it is the same with all the other arts.

(2) "NOTHING WILL DIE." (3) "ALL THINGS WILL DIE." Many poets have set themselves to balance the *pros* and *cons* of life ; and according to the later Tennyson, the second scale is oftener the lowest ; yet, latest of all, he holds them even. There is something like this in Milton's " L'Allegro " and " Il Penseroso "—the order of

---

[1] This study, especially of emendations. is very important.

the poems in each case being the same, and seeming to discover a tendency toward the graver aspects of our existence. In Shakespeare the corresponding pieces are " Henry V." and " Hamlet." By-and-by in Tennyson the opposing forces meet in one poem,—" The Two Voices," or " In Memoriam," or " The Ancient Sage." Besides other poets, Shelley and Barry Cornwall may be recognized in " Nothing will Die," and Wordsworth in " All things will Die."

(3) " LEONINE [1] ELEGIACS." This exercise becomes interesting when compared with the experiments in quantity on p. 243 [2] (" Hexameters and Pentameters"). Making due allowance for the rhymes, these elegiacs are the " longs and shorts " of a schoolboy who scarcely knows how ill they look in their foreign dress ; and the later " Experiments " prove that the writer felt how exceedingly difficult it was to force the classic metre into English, but prove also that if it could be done, he could do it. As in " Claribel " and the " Marianas," a time element may be noticed ; but this poem has other affinities with the first " Mariana," as will be mentioned later.

(3) " SUPPOSED CONFESSIONS OF A SECOND-RATE SENSITIVE MIND." Hallam complains that the title has " an appearance of quaintness, which has no sufficient reason, and seems incorrect." " The mood," he continues, " is rather the clouded season of a strong mind than the habitual condition of one feeble and 'second-rate.'" The justice of this remark has been noticed elsewhere (p. 17). We here see something of the poet himself in the first stage of the religious uncertainty described in " In Memoriam " by the words " Perplext in Faith " (xcvi).

[1] From Leo or Leoninus, canon of the Church of St. Victor, Paris, twelfth century, who wrote many such. The end of the line rhymes with the middle.
[2] Complete Works, one vol.

> " It is man's privilege to doubt,
> If so be that from doubt at length
> Truth may stand forth unmoved of change. . . ."

> " Ay me ! I fear
> All may not doubt, but everywhere
> Some must clasp Idols."

The poem comes of contact with university life and thought, and gives evidence that Tennyson was beginning to share in the new ideas about religion. These ideas took the form either of destructive criticism, or of a new constructive, earnest, and practical Christianity. Tennyson adopts something of both.

At present we have glanced at five poems only ; but these are enough to show us what will appear more plainly as we proceed, that much of the poetic material employed bears the stamp either of Tennyson or of some other poet ; that is to say, reading almost any half dozen consecutive lines, we are able to say this is Tennyson's work, or, this is a modification of some other poet's work.

One or two passages in the " Supposed Confessions " are noteworthy. The sketch of infancy is remarkable chiefly because it gives no hint of antenatal existence. Interesting, on the other hand, is the appearance thus early of the following figure :

> " As from the storm
> Of running fires and fluid range
> Of lawless airs, at last stood out
> This excellence and solid form
> Of constant beauty."

The lines descriptive of the dying lamb have a wonderful fulness of detail. In sentiment they are something akin to the following from Pope's " Essay on Man," Epistle i. 81-86 :

> " The lamb thy riot dooms to bleed to-day,
> Had he thy reason, would he skip and play ?
> Pleas'd to the last, he crops the flow'ry food,
> And licks the hand just rais'd to shed his blood.

O blindness to the future ! kindly giv'n,
That each may fill the circle mark'd by heav'n.'

Being of a considerable length, the poem presents many peculiarities of imagery and diction, one or two of which may be mentioned. "An image with profulgent brows" appears in "A Fragment" as "A perfect Idol with profulgent brows." There also will be found "the slumbrous summer noon" of the eleventh line, but in "A Fragment" summernoon is printed as one word. Tennyson's characteristic use of the verb "draw" occurs twice in the poem ; twice also the word "hollow," which is perhaps his special favourite at this early period, and indeed for a long time to come : it appears in "hollow air ;" and "hollows of the fringed hills." The constantly recurring "inward" of "Claribel" and "Mariana" is here also. "Hating to" and "proof" are used again in the Sonnet to J. M. K. Other examples will be referred to in subsequent notes, but a considerable proportion will be left unnoticed. This is true in most other instances ; and sometimes, as in the case of the former poem, and even of such characteristic compositions as "Recollections of the Arabian Nights" and "Eleänore," the limited space of the present volume precludes the introduction of a subject which the reader should nevertheless keep carefully in view.

(6) "THE KRAKEN." The monster is either sea-serpent or octopus. "Faintest sunlights flee About his shadowy sides" . . . recurs in "Lucretius" as "How the sun delights To glance and shift about her slippery sides. . . ." The poem is a kind of sonnet of fifteen lines, with the climax at the tenth instead of the eighth. It contains some skilful lines, and some that resemble Shelley, "The dull weed some huge sea-worm battens on."[1]

---

[1] "Prometheus Unbound."

(6) " SONG." Here the " crisp waves " and the " ridges " of " The Supposed Confessions " re-appear as the " crisped sea " and the " ridged sea." The latter—the " enridged sea " of " King Lear," IV. vi. 71—occurs in " The Sea Fairies ;" and it may be compared with the "ridged wolds " of the " Ode to Memory ; " while the former becomes the " crisped Nile " of " A Fragment," and after frequent employment in poems published and unpublished may be seen as " the crisping white " in " The Holy Grail." " Mellow " may be noticed ; also the compounds " down-carolling," " low-tinkled."

(6) " LILIAN." Begins and ends with " fairy Lilian ; " rises like a fountain from a small jet of water, towers pretty and musical for a moment, then falls back into the jet. Here again is " pleasance ;" and the compound words in proportion to the length of the piece are very numerous—ridiculously numerous. It is astonishing that such a cunning artist should betray a lack of taste like this. The piece is also rather weak. Certainly the compounds suit the light sketch ; but " innocent-arch " and " cunning-simple " and some others are effeminate. Compounds are perhaps the most effective of all epithets ; they really compress a clause into a word. All good poets use them ; young or inferior poets sometimes abuse them ; at present they are so treated by Tennyson ; but they never were by Milton ; they were by Rossetti, who speaks of " soul-winnowing hands," and a " soul-sequestered face." Shakespeare is first under this head of compound epithets ; his are so fresh, forcible, appropriate, beautiful. In Shelley they are often splendid ; in Keats they sometimes resemble Tennyson's, as in " purple-stainèd mouth : " but Keats had a way of his own of strengthening and beautifying epithets, small or common ones, monosyllables—

" Where palsy shakes a *few sad last gray* hairs."

"And *winding mossy* ways."

"In *faery* lands *forlorn.*"

all which examples are from the same poem.[1]   The poem
of Tennyson's in which these double-edged adjectives are
seen to best advantage is " Recollections of the Arabian
Nights ;" but, as before noticed, he sometimes yokes
together two independent words by the mere means of
the hyphen ; and then, instead of securing his desired
effect, he defeats it.   In this poem " baby-roses" adds to
weakness and diminishes beauty.   Similar in the " Arabian
Nights " are " citron-shadows," " boat-head," " myrrh-
thickets."   Such strenuous striving after effect may be
the characteristic of a school of poets, but is not often
met with as an isolated case.

(6) " ISABEL." is perhaps the best of the portraits of
women, and the portrait of the best woman.   Here we
will notice the sounded éd final, such a marked character-
istic of the earlier work of Keats and Tennyson :

"Were fixéd shadows of thy fixéd mood
Reveréd Isabel, the crown and head." . . .

There are some half dozen others, and they help to
spoil the poem.   They are greatly in excess.   On the
other hand, the only example in " Mariana "—gnarled—
is beautiful.   Also in " Isabel " we seem to discover a line
of prose that could scarcely be intentional :

" A clear stream flowing with a muddy one."

(7) " MARIANA."   In the volume of 1833 is a lyric
entitled " O Love, Love, Love ! " to which is prefixed
a quotation from Sappho that suggests the source of
some of the lines, and guides us to classic originals for
most of the others.   In a later edition the title of the
poem is changed to " Fatima," and a new stanza is added

---

[1] "Ode to a Nightingale."

which makes mention of a "city's eastern towers" (*i.e.*, waiting for sunrise), "burning drought," and a "long desert to the south." This stanza having been added, the poem was ready for a central human figure, and the honour of the situation was conferred on Fatima. Somewhat in the same way, the background of "Mariana" may have been sketched, if only mentally, before the figure of the foreground was painted in, especially as Sappho again suggests some of the situations. The poet perhaps has brooded over some moated grange near his birthplace. Further, some of the scenery with the same predominance of detail over general features, has been met with in "Poems by Two Brothers." If he has sought a human occupant for his ideal abode, a chance line or two in Shakespeare supplies the want. It has already been mentioned that in "Leonine Elegiacs" we have a poem in many respects like "Mariana," but one in which evening alone is sketched; all that is wanting is some suitable name for the mournful lover who waits in vain for his Rosalind. Further, as "Mariana" suggested (for reasons to be given later) another landscape to sketch, so "Mariana in the South" probably lent the additional stanza to "O Love, Love, Love," and demanded for it a name.

This painting of nature so that every detail is made subservient to a human emotion, is to be met with in a fragmentary form in many poets from the times of Sappho herself; but Tennyson was the first to elaborate such pictures. Observe how we read desolation in every aspect of the scene long before we reach the desolate figure—the garden was neglected; the broken sheds looked sad; the grange was lonely. Indeed, the refrain which introduces the human being who is the subject of the composition is by far the weakest part of it, and from this point of view the poem might have been called "The Moated Grange" rather than "Mariana." So the three opening stanzas of

Gray's Elegy bespeak the subject. In that poem, too, is the time element, the daily round. Mariana was sad at evening, midnight, morn; but evening, as in the last stanza, and in similar passages by other poets, was the saddest of all.

Few changes have been made in this masterpiece; one or two deserve mention. The last line but four in the last stanza read originally:

> "Downsloped was westering in his bower,"

a worse line with something of Milton in it. In the first edition many of the compounds—"marishmosses"—were without the hyphen; some elisions, "up an' away," "i' the pane," have judiciously been altered. The metre is original and fascinating. A few other interesting particulars will be reserved until "Mariana in the South" comes to be considered. A note on the use of the poetical past indefinite in this poem will be found at the end of the Chapter (Appendix II.).

The portrait of Mariana may have been taken from the "Isabella" of Keats; or from Sappho—

> δέδυκε μὲν ἀ σελάννα
> καὶ Πληἳάδες, μέσαι δὲ
> νύκτες, παρὰ δ'ἔρχετ' ὥρα,
> ἔγω δὲ μόνα κατεύδω,

or from Henryson's "Testament of Cresseid":

> "On this wyse, weiping, scho maid hir mone . . .
> Weiping, scho woik the nicht fra end to end."

(8) "TO——." This is another evidence of the interest taken by Tennyson in the new religious energies of the day. We are reminded of the poem "To the Rev. F. D. Maurice." The epithet "clear-headed" is unfortunate, perhaps the most unfortunate in the volume.

(8) "MADELINE." In the former poem we had "ray-fringed;" here is "sun-fringed;" here also "light and

shadow," and a host of others, especially fanciful compounds. Outwardly the most striking feature of the two poems is their abundance of the tricks of diction already referred to. It is the determination to be brilliant that destroys the lustre.

(9) "THE OWL" has something Shakespearean about the first part.[1] The poem exhibits Tennyson's fondness for animate nature. Hereafter in "The Swallow Song," "Maud" and "The Throstle" he will repeat in verse the notes of other and sometimes sweeter birds.

(9) "RECOLLECTIONS OF THE ARABIAN NIGHTS." A brilliant series of poetical magic-lantern slides that move before us to a music equally brilliant; probably there is no more striking achievement of musical word-painting in the language. Something of the manner is caught from Coleridge; much of the material is Shelley's; but the ensemble is original and beautiful.

(11) "ODE TO MEMORY." Another characteristic poem, though due to many poets in its parts. It has been noticed incidentally on pp. 57, 72, 76. Some of the descriptive passages would be excellent if they were not overstudied; they can scarcely be disembarrassed of their own effort or of their burden of borrowed beauty. Nevertheless the Ode is thoughtful, well constructed, full of promise, and, again, in its entirety, original.

(13) "SONG." This must be regarded as the worst poetry we have yet met with; the refrain especially is weak.

(13) "A CHARACTER." Five stanzas of Wordsworth's "A Poet's Epitaph," beginning "Physician art thou," are

---

[1] Song at the end of "Love's Labour's Lost."

most probably the groundwork of Tennyson's "Character."
Other suggestions may have been supplied by Shake-
speare, " 1. Henry IV.," I. iii. 30-68, where, after the
fight, Hotspur is pester'd with a popinjay ; and where
Jaques recounts his meeting with the fool (" As You
Like It," II. vii. 12-42). The latter passage may have
furnished the expression " Lack-lustre eye." Striking
resemblances may also be found in the sketch of Achilles
in " Troilus and Cressida," Act II., Scene iii., such as

> " He doth rely on none . . .
> In will peculiar, and in self-admission,"

which may be compared with,

> " And stood aloof from other minds
> In impotence of fancied power ; "

or again,

> " He that is proud, eats up himself ; "

with

> " Upon himself himself did feed ; "

and again,

> " Possess'd he is with greatness,
> And speaks not to himself but with a pride
> That quarrels at self-breath,"

with

> " And trod on silk, as if the winds
> Blew his own praises in his eyes."

The piece, therefore, may be regarded as an "experi-
ment ; " and its manner reminds us of the satire in " Sea
Dreams," which also seems to have been suggested by
Shakespeare.

(13) "THE POET." Of the " Intellectual All-in-all " [1]
sketched in the former poem we are told

> " Yet could not all creation pierce
> Beyond the bottom of his eye."

---

[1] Wordsworth, " A Poet's Epitaph."

Such an one would "botanize Upon his mother's grave," but no blossom there could fill his heart with thoughts too deep for tears ; his "lack-lustre dead blue eye" might never penetrate beyond the sordid fact. But the Poet, according to Tennyson, is primarily a Seer.[1] And again, in "The Poet's song" :

> "He sings of what the world will be
> When the years have died away."

This poem has already been referred to.[2] It remains to be repeated here that Tennyson's conception of "The Poet" is not exactly artistic. Thought has precedence over emotion, morality over beauty. It is much the same in "The Palace of Art." Had he been musician, or painter, or both, had he possessed Browning's appreciative fondness for those arts,[3] he might have done more justice to the singer as such, and have claimed for him first—or demanded of him first—the faculty of song. In other words, he would have distinguished between the emotional beauty of the artist, and the moral or intellectual beauty that the great artist shares with less comprehensive souls. The greater includes the less ; the poet must be a singer first, as was Tennyson. Fortunately his theories did not affect his practice ; Wordsworth was less happy with his theory of over familiar and therefore "unnatural" poetic diction. To Wordsworth, moreover, something is owed by this stately poem, and something to Milton.

(14) "THE POET'S MIND." Suggested, it is said, by the disparaging remarks of some university friends. It is strangely earnest. It may be compared with the equally earnest thought of "In Memoriam," xciv.

---

[1] See especially the second stanza.   [2] See pages 42 and 76.
[3] Music he was fond of, but not with an artist's fondness. Very significant is the remark in "The Foresters," that a Saxon has no soul for music. Tennyson was of Norman descent.

The remarks made upon the preceding poem apply also to this protest, which, however, is as youthful in aspect as "The Poet" was mature.

(15) "THE SEA FAIRIES." This is the first of several poems, mostly classical in subject, and often appropriately modernized, which give expression to a feeling old-world in its first aspect, but soon claimed by a modern humanity. εἰς πόσον ἆ δειλοὶ καμάτως κ'εἰς ἔργα πονεῦμες ; "Let us eat and drink, for to-morrow we die,"—such are earlier statements of this particular feeling :

> "Were it not better done, as others use,
> To sport with Amaryllis ;"

such is the form it assumes in "Lycidas ;" and in Tennyson's next volume we shall find it splendidly developed in "The Hesperides"[1] and "The Lotos-Eaters:"

> "Is there any peace
> In ever climbing up the climbing wave ?"

Besides the very original blank verse at the beginning, a lyrical movement equally Tennyson's own, appears in this musical and richly coloured composition. Some of the imagery finds resemblances in Shelley :

> "The Nereids under the green sea,
> Their white arms lifted o'er their streaming hair,
> With garlands pied, and starry sea-flower crowns."
> *Prometheus Unbound.*

As to the subject of the poem, a first suggestion may be found in the following lines :

> Δεῦρ' ἄγ' ἰὼν, πολύαιν' Ὀδυσεῦ, μέγα κῦδος Ἀχαιῶν,
> νῆα κατάστησον, ἵνα νωιτέρην ὄπ' ἀκούσης.
> *Odyssey,* XII. 184-5.

(15) "THE DESERTED HOUSE." These verses contain but little poetry. They appear to have been written while the poet could still possess his "early heaven."[2]

---

[1] See p. 143.   [2] "In Memoriam," xxxiii.

(16) "THE DYING SWAN." No poem in the volume is free from affectation in respect of diction. In "The Dying Swan" these blemishes are less frequent than usual; but, as it is a well-known composition, they shall be mentioned in detail.

"Under-roof," "under-sky," an "inner" voice, "adown," "took the reed-tops," "took the soul;" of these latter two the prototype is the well-known passage in "Cymbeline:"

> "Daffodils
> That come before the swallow dares, and *take*
> The winds of March with beauty."

And in Milton, "*Took* with ravishment. . . ." But such uses of the verb "take" are mostly classical,—"Quaeque mihi sola capitur nunc mente voluptas"—and Tennyson may have being tasting the waters higher up the stream of song. The opening description of the second division of the poem has already been noticed as existing in part in the "Poems by Two Brothers" and elsewhere. "At its own wild will" is in Wordsworth's sonnets. Noticeable also are "marish," "marish-flowers." "Joy hidden in sorrow" occurs often, from "Poems by Two Brothers" to "The Gardener's Daughter":

> "Which perfect joy, perplext for utterance,
> Stole from her sister, sorrow,"

or "In Memoriam":

> "In the midmost heart of grief
> Thy passion clasps a secret joy."

To these may be added "Afar," "anear;" "tumult of their acclaim" may be compared with "Is wrought with tumult of acclaim" ("In Memoriam"). The "creeping mosses" are often met with; also "the wave-worn horns"— the "horned flood" of "In Memoriam," and, in a different application, the "horned valleys" of the "Supposed Confessions of a Second-rate Sensitive Mind." All the above words or phrases are used frequently by the poet, especially at this early period ; some, such as "under," "inner," "marish," so often that they become something more than mannerisms. As a further remark on a subject of such peculiar interest, we may say that they evidence—and there are more striking examples in other poems—the most studious collecting of poetical curiosities on record. Most poets make a note of this phrase or that, and perhaps store up choice words and images from nature ; but no poet has made such systematic use of them, or experimented with them so repeatedly. In this poem, short as it is, some are employed twice over : "took," for example. We might account for the repetition of "under" and "marish," but not of "took." Tennyson never quite freed himself from this foible of word worship or this fault of repetition ;[1] it will be apparent to every careful student of the poet. On the other hand we must remember that our English tongue owes not a little of its wealth and power and beauty to these very researches and experiments.

It is partly because such mannerisms are fewer, less obvious, and less obtrusive, that "The Dying Swan" is a notable poem ; nor has it undergone much alteration. But there is very much more to say. The poet's treatment of nature was explained on p. 73 ; but again there is much to add, and it should not be in the form of explanation. Many years ago, when the present writer had read the usual schoolboy's Latin, Greek, English, and French poetry, he cherished in his memory a fair share of poetical surprises. But one day he chanced upon a quotation from "The Dying Swan" in Chambers's "Encyclopædia of English Literature," and among his "surprises" the emotion of that moment became henceforth perhaps the most memorable.

The poem is indeed a remarkable one. Together with "Mariana" it proclaimed the advent of a poet original,

---

[1] See note on Mannerism, p. 54.

enchanting, and possibly great. The second section of the poem is the finest, as it is also the most characteristic piece of poetry in the volume of 1830.

But the Pre-Raphaelite first section is also very fine ; under the spell of the emotion symbolized, its realism becomes transformed into an ideal beauty that transcends all reality. Following these, the third section swells in a full crescendo, till it closes with a flood of music.

(16) "A Dirge."

" Thou diedst, a most rare boy, of melancholy.'

The remainder of the scene from which this line is taken (" Cymbeline," IV. ii. 208) may have suggested Tennyson's " Dirge." " Thou thy worldly task hast done"[1] corresponds to " Now is done thy long day's work." Other resemblances, especially in the flowers,[2] may be left to the reader. The poem is not very good ; "folds thy grave" is rather a strained expression, and there are other weaknesses. Here is "light and shadow" once more. The occasional change from trochaic to iambic measure is well managed.

(17) "Love and Death" is a poem generally admired. The sentiment is partly

" Our weakness somehow shapes the shadow, Time,"
Princess.

which, in " The Mystic," reads thus :

"One shadow in the midst of a great light,
One reflex from eternity on time ;"

Which again is Shelley's (" Adonais ") :

" The One remains, the many change and pass ;
Heaven's light for ever shines, earth's shadows fly ;

---

[1] Line 260.
[2] " Long purples" (printed as a quotation in 1st edition) are well known in " Hamlet "

> Life, like a dome of many-coloured glass,
>   Stains the white radiance of eternity,
>   Until Death tramples it to fragments."

The expression " what time," so much affected by minor
poets (in imitation of Milton's anglicised Latin), does not
occur often in Tennyson ; only—if we remember rightly—
in " The Princess," and in some minor or cancelled poems.
" Gathering light " is " Colligit ignes " of the " Georgics "
i. 427 ; the word "vans," found also in an inferior sonnet
of the 1830 volume, is used by Milton and others.
" Lustrous " occurs as a stock word, as do " sheeny,"
and " parted," and " eminent." The poem is built up of
fifteen lines, linked by rhyme, and having a climax at the
ninth.

(17) " THE BALLAD OF ORIANA " is effective, but
weak occasionally. It is a most difficult poem to read
aloud because of the frequent refrain. It appears to have
been suggested by other ballads written to memorize the
death of Helen of Kirkconnel, who threw herself in front
of her lover, received the bullet aimed at him by a rival,
and then died in his arms. Tennyson's version is not so
simply pathetic as the best of the Helen of Kirkconnel
ballads :

> " Curst be the heart that thought the thought,
> And curst the hand that fired the shot,
> When in my arms burd Helen dropt
>   And died to succour me ;"

so in Tennyson, " O cursed hand ! O cursed blow !"
And his " O breaking heart that will not break," is like
the fragment in " Troilus and Cressida :"

> " O heart, O heavy heart,
> Why sigh'st thou without breaking."

All nature, as usual, mourns with the mourner ; this is
very well done, and some of the lines are wonderfully
graphic in their condensation ;

> "When the long dun wolds are ribb'd with snow "

The high sounding name "Oriana" is not unknown in literature. Farquhar uses it for one of his characters in "The Inconstant." Queen Elizabeth was called Oriana in some contemporary madrigals.

(18) "CIRCUMSTANCE." This word, as we have seen,[1] was becoming an object of anxious interest to the poet. No wonder that he should have eased his heart by expanding the terrible abstract term into concrete poetical form. The poem has admirers, and is often quoted ; but it is not very remarkable. As to the word itself, it appears in "The Mystic" as "wayward vary-coloured circumstance," in the "Supposed Confessions" as "the grief of circumstance," and it will be conspicuous so late as the "Lines to the Duke of Argyl,"—"This ever-changing world of circumstance." The thought has some slight affinity with the doctrine of "Dualisms" :[2]

> "Two children lovelier than Love adown the lea are singing,
> As they gambol, lilygarlands ever stringing :
> Both in blosmwhite *(sic)* silk are frockéd . . .
> Like, unlike, they sing together
> Side by side,
> Midmay's darling goldenlockéd,
> Summer's tanling diamondeyed." [3]

(19) "THE MERMAN—THE MERMAID." Like "The Sea Fairies," these poems are vivid and musical. They may be called trifles in the volumes of Tennyson, but they would look more than pretty in the pages of a lesser poet. They exhibit his accustomed wealth of diction, in which they often resemble Shelley and Keats ; and they have much witchery of sound. Also they are disfigured by some of the blemishes so incident to this volume ; among their mannerisms may be noticed the word "inner."

(20) "ADELINE," (21) "MARGARET," (22) "ROSALIND,"

---

[1] See p. 37. The word is similarly used by Keats.
[2] One of the poems of this volume which were not republished.
[3] These lines are printed as above in the first edition.

(22) "ELEANORE." Of these, "Adeline" alone belongs to the volume of 1830; the other three appeared first in 1833. In "Adeline" we hear echoes of former poets; "Breathing Light (with its capital, to make the more of it) against thy face," occurs more than once in Shelley: "And move like winds of light";[1] "Nor unhappy, nor at rest" may be compared with Scott's "Were neither broken, nor at rest." This poem has been mentioned on p. 54, as furnishing numerous examples of Tennyson's occasional weakness in poetic style.

(22) "ELEÄNORE" recalls Shelley more than a dozen times, and many other poets, ancient and modern, enter into its elaborate composition. But in a volume such as the present, the subject of parallel passages like that of poetic diction must be dealt with incidentally rather than systematically; the reader is to be kept in mind of the existence of parallelisms, rather than supplied with an exhaustive list of them. Yet nothing is more conducive to a thorough knowledge and, finally, an appreciation of Tennyson, than attention to these constructive details. The same holds good with several other poets, notably Milton and Virgil. One resemblance to another poet may serve as an example of the rest; "Tresses unconfined" occurs in Byron's "Maid of Athens." As regards diction, "Eleänore" is almost as rich in picturesque words, phrases, and imagery as the "Arabian Nights." And we must bear in mind its date, 1832.

The poems describing women are generally regarded as mere exercises or fancy sketches. But there is little doubt that many of them are taken from real life, and some at least are a half expression of "love first learned in a lady's eyes," of which some poems no longer published also seem to give evidence.

[1] "Adonais.

(21) "MARGARET" gives us just a little of the "perfume of the cuckoo flower," which in "The May Queen" makes the sense faint with its sweetness. But in this poem its fragrance is hardly perceptible. Here again are "amber" and "mellow," and the rest; and the figure "sit between joy and woe" is a familiar one. "Burning brain" and some other expressions are in Shelley.

(22) "ROSALIND" was for a time withdrawn from publication. As the poem stands it is not without spirit, and is well adapted to the character. In the original a note was added, which, like a similar note in "The Palace of Art," enables the poet at once to reject and to retain a portion of his poem:

"Perhaps the following lines may be allowed to stand as a separate poem; originally they made part of the text, where they were manifestly superfluous."

This note is followed by thirty-three lines containing much that is interesting: "Full-sailed before a vigorous wind;" "full-sailed," probably from Shakespeare's sonnets, appears often; in "Eleánore," for example, and the "Supposed Confessions." In "The Princess" we read "That sail'd Full-blown before us," which is a curious variation. The lines:

> "Fresh as the early seasmell blown
> Through vineyards from an inland bay,"

are another reminiscence of Continental scenery;[1] and the passage

> "Because no shadow on you falls
> Think you hearts are tennisballs
> To play with, wanton Rosalind?"

testifies to the good taste of the poet who withdrew the piece. Some might fancy there was too much of "The Skipping Rope" in the last quotation. Eleánore

---

[1] See Introduction to next chapter.

is the last portrait hung in Tennyson's gallery of fair
ladies.   Horace and Byron have been indicated as
furnishing models for the later poet ; also Skelton, with
his verses to Maistresses Margery Wentworth, Isabell
Pennel, and Margaret Hussey.   To these poets many
others might be added.   Like Rosalind, Skelton's Mar-
garet Hussey is compared to " faucon Or hawke of the
toure."

(24) "MY LIFE IS FULL OF WEARY DAYS" is found
in the volume of 1833.   There it is addressed " To——."
The line " Ring sudden scritches of the jay," in which
we have another but not so fortunate example of bird-
notes, originally read " Ring sudden laughters of the jay."
" Laughter " was to be reserved for the wood-pecker—" As
laughters of the wood-pecker." [1]   These verses are spoilt
by the over-subtle pathos of the closing couplet, which
really amounts to bathos.   On the other hand, how suc-
cessful is the fall at the end of the " Lady of Shalott,"
" He said, she has a lovely face ; " successful also, spite
of the rhyme, is the last line but one of " The Lord of
Burleigh " : " In the dress that she was wed in."

(24) EARLY SONNETS.

(24) I. " To——."   Published in 1833.   This is after-
wards compressed into two well-known stanzas in " The
Two Voices," 127 and 128—" Moreover something is or
seems," etc.   The familiar phenomenon is referred to
in other poems, such as " In Memoriam," xliv.   See
also Appendix to Chapter VII.

(25) II. " To J. M. K." (1830).   This was John Mitchell
Kemble, at Cambridge with Tennyson, afterwards so well
known as an authority in early English literature and

---

[1] From " Kate," in the volume of 1833.   Also in " The Princess," the
note of this bird is compared to laughter (" Prologue," 210-211).

history. He was intended for the church, but devoted his life to literary work. Here is Tennyson's sympathy with the new stir in the church, referred to on p. 81.

(25) III. Published in 1833. This sonnet is badly constructed; the third line is especially poor. Two figures from the sea partly neutralize one another. It may be interesting to note the old spelling "it's" in the original. Faulty as it may be, three of its lines will commend themselves to all:

> "Mine be the power which ever to its sway
> Will win the wise at once, and by degrees
> May into uncongenial spirits flow."

(25) IV. "ALEXANDER." Mr. Collins remarks that the allusion to the naphtha pits shows that the poet had been reading Plutarch's "Life of Alexander." As in "Persia,"[1] some rhythmic music is derived from proper names.

(25) V. "BUONAPARTE." Published in the 1833 volume. It may be counted among the patriotic poems. The figure at the close is characteristic; several of the earlier sonnets and short poems end in a similar manner.

(26) VI. "POLAND." Tennyson does not take much to heart the fortunes of other lands than England; but in the volume of 1833 there are two sonnets on the subject of Poland. This one is entitled "On the Result of the late Russian Invasion of Poland," and the other is "Written on hearing of the outbreak of the Polish Insurrection."

(26) VII., VIII., IX. These sonnets, bearing the title "Three sonnets to a Coquette," first appeared in

[1] "Poems by Two Brothers."

" A Selection from the Works of Alfred Tennyson," pub-
lished by Moxon in 1865.   Whatever their actual date,
they are a striking contrast to the others that surround
them.   With these they claim kindred only in respect of
the figures at the end of VII. and IX.   Having due re-
gard to the subject, we may yet pronounce their manner
to be wholly different.   Though not full-bodied nor trumpet-
toned, they are as original as they are beautiful.   The
last sonnet we were examining was slightly Miltonic, but
not good.   These resemble nothing in all preceding
literature ; they are new in many ways, in delicate grace,
perfection of form, but, most of all in the movement of
the verse.   That is as much Tennyson's own as the verse
of " Tithonus," or a dozen other pieces that might be
mentioned ; only here, lest the sweetness should cloy, a
discord breaks up the cadence at the close of the series.
Five of the lines consist of monosyllables finely modulated.
One of the similes is very beautiful :

> " Sadder than a single star
> That sets at twilight in a land of reeds,"

and may be compared with Wordsworth's

> " Fair as a star, when only one
> Is shining in the sky."

These sonnets found many imitators, but they have seldom
or never been surpassed in their special excellence.

(27) X.   This is the second of two sonnets in the 1833
volume.   The first opens with the lines :

> " O beauty, passing beauty ! sweetest Sweet !
> How canst thou let me waste my youth in sighs ? "

And this second sonnet continues, " But were I loved. . ."
It has been retained as much the better of the two ; and it
ends with the usual Tennysonian figure.   Although superior
to some of the others, it should be compared with the former
three : it will hardly fail to make their perfection more

apparent. In those there was no redundant syllable to destroy the superb grace of movement ; no such line as "All the inner, all the outer world of pain," lines that may be found frequently in the sonnets of Mrs. Browning, for example. The figure "Fresh-water springs come up through bitter brine," is employed in an improved form in "Enoch Arden" :

> "And beating up through all the bitter world,
> Like fountains of sweet water in the sea."

(27) XI. "THE BRIDESMAID." This is going to the other extreme. There were halting lines in Sonnet X., but it was fairly good : here it is difficult to discover strength or beauty. "The couple" alone would condemn the work, even if the second line had not condemned it already.

This ends the series of poems styled "Juvenilia," most of which, though sometimes in an altered form, were published in the volume of 1830. A few comments will now be made on those poems of the 1830 volume, that are not included among the "Juvenilia." Of these the number is considerable ; no less than twenty-two of the original fifty-three contained in "Poems, chiefly Lyrical," having been rejected. The opinion has already been put forward, that a poet's genius is to be measured not only by what he retains, but also by what he rejects ; and since some of these remaining twenty-two pieces are astonishingly weak, we can afford to be less severe on the unfortunate critics who failed to discover the greatness even of a poet who could write "Mariana" and "The Dying Swan" ; and, strange to say, this is equally true of the next volume.

It may be well to state here a general fact to which attention should be directed ; a poem or some portion of a poem is often found to be omitted, apparently because it contains a too obvious imitation of some other poet.

Such, for example, might be the case with a sonnet of some merit, in which—in the manner of Keats—

> "All night through archways of the bridgéd pearl,
> And portals of pure silver walks the moon,"

like which the poet's soul must

> "Turn cloud to light, and bitterness to joy,
> And dross to gold with glorious alchemy."

There is something of Shakespeare in the last line. And in the line

> "An honourable eld shall come upon thee,"

"eld" looks like Byron's property. Other and more obvious cases will be mentioned in succeeding chapters.

Also it is interesting to notice the very large number of phrases in these rejected verses that subsequently find a place in later poems ; from the line "When the first matinsong hath wakéd loud," the poem "Memory" supplies material to "Love and Duty" and "In Memoriam." In "The Grasshopper," the passage "Thou hast no compt of years, No withered immortality," makes "Tithonus" the richer—

> "Me only cruel immortality consumes ;
> I wither slowly. . . ."

And "The Mystic" with its "Daughters of Time, divinely tall," adds a grace to the "Dream of Fair Women :"

> "A daughter of the gods, divinely tall."

From the poems afterwards published as "Juvenilia" many mannerisms were expunged, such as "blossom-starréd shore" from "The Poet's Mind"; and we therefore expect to find in the condemned poems a larger proportion of these experiments or tricks of style. Of the sounded "éd" final the most remarkable example is that quoted on p. 95 in the extract from " Dualisms," where other curiosities of diction will be found, as also a recollection of Keats' " Mid-May's eldest child."

Probably the most characteristic fragment of diction to be met with in these experimental poems is the following line from " The Mystic,"

> " Keen knowledges of low-embowéd eld,"

which, however, is not so bad as the metaphysical poet's

> " Knowledge's first mother is invention."

Here we meet with Byron's "eld" again. Of course, "eld" belongs to other poets, to Keats, for instance, as in "crazéd eld"; but it was affected by Byron in his earlier verse.

An account of these poems seriatim would be extremely interesting, but it must be left for a larger work. Among the most important are " The Mystic," already referred to, which contains another reference to the condition of trance into which Tennyson seems occasionally to have fallen (pp. 62, 63) :

> " He often lying broad awake, and yet
> Remaining from the body, and apart
> In intellect and power and will, hath heard
> Time flowing in the middle of the night,
> And all things creeping to a day of doom."

Another is " The Sleeping Beauty," a very good beginning of what was afterwards to become a beautiful poem in the volume of 1842. " Hero to Leander " is a striking reproduction of Shelley's erotic verse, with an admixture of Keats. The book ends with οἱ ῥέοντες,[1] which, though ostensibly ironical, contains such lines as

---

[1] A nickname given to the Heraclitean philosophers who maintained, as one of their doctrines, that all things were in a state of perpetual change or "flux," or "becoming." These old-new philosophies really commended themselves to Tennyson in many of their aspects; hence the words "ostensibly ironical" above. In this connection the poem may be compared with "The Mystic" and others.

> " But if I dream that all these are,
> They are to me for that I dream,"

which was afterwards to become, in " The Higher Pantheism,"

> " Dreams are true while they last, and do we not live in dreams ? "

And the argument at the close, "Argal—this very opinion is only true relatively to the flowing philosophers," is not so good as Byron's

> " When Bishop Berkeley said there was no matter,
> And proved it, 'twas no matter what he said."

APPENDICES TO CHAPTER III.

APPENDIX I.

The high pleasure of art is found in a more even contest between the forces of irregular emotion and the laws of regular expression ; in a nice adjustment of impetuous thought to well-defined art form. If we cannot discover some law in obedience to which every portion of the art structure is harmoniously adjusted to every other portion and to the whole, then the symmetrical element is destroyed, and the work ceases to be a work of art. (See also the remark on Form in Drama, in Chapter XIV.)

Of course this law will operate with more or less stringency, according to the period, temperament, and environment of the writer ; it will vary as fashions vary, and for exactly the same reason. It will vary even in the same individual. Let us take Shakespeare for an example. As noticed already on p. 64, when he begins to write blank verse he does not exactly count syllables or accents on his fingers, but he does this ; as far as possible he makes sentence or phrase coincide with the line ; and thus the thought helps to measure the line, and saves the beginner much anxiety and trouble. He makes his foot of a uniform pattern; in each line he pauses at the natural place—after the second foot; for there is no middle in a line of five feet; and the strong stress which marks the pause will be laid on the shorter first portion of the line, much as it strikes the earlier syllables of an English word.

By means of these and many other devices that could be mentioned he "measures" his verse with the maximum of certainty and the minimum of trouble; but the resulting uniformity is dangerously near to monotony. This is the opposite extreme; a too rigid application of rule. He will on occasion write such uniform verse even when he has mastered his art, but then we shall always recognize both his purpose of effecting a contrast and the beauty of the expedient. Passing on, however, to such a play as "The Tempest," we have before us blank verse so varied in its structure that the old devices of formal foot, regular pause, and end-stopt line are altogether disguised,—but not destroyed; the most obvious of structural elements, the very lines themselves, headed by their capital letters, almost give place to new lines that reach from pause to pause (and the pauses may occur anywhere); and so with the other structural elements. But amid all this variety we never fail to recognize if not the old law, at least what may be called a "law within the law." Such poets as Macpherson, Tupper, and Whitman abuse the licensed play of variety within uniformity; and many others at times assume a freedom that perplexes rather than pleases.

These remarks apply with as much truth to the structure of poems themselves as to the structure of their parts. The "Ode," which is considered in Chapter VIII., is not often successful in English; Gray set a rigid example which few or none could follow: but these irregular poems of Tennyson's first volume seldom exhibit such symmetry of form as will rank them with the " Ode." They are more like some of the lyrics in " Maud," which from one point of view might be regarded as an unsuccessful compromise between chorus and drama, but were probably suggested by the song Dryden wrote for the madhouse scene in " The Pilgrim."[1] We may therefore assign to the irregular poems of this volume the remarks which will be found in the chapter on " Maud," adding, however, that the very important symmetrical element of rise, culmination, and decline is observable in the construction of some of the pieces, such as " Claribel" and " Lilian."

Appendix II.[2]

" In order to realize the surpassing excellence of Tennyson's workmanship, we may compare his song, ' Home they brought her warrior dead,' with the following lines on the same theme in 'The Lay of the Last Minstrel,' canto i., section 9 ; and even when we have made in favour of Scott all necessary allowances, we shall probably be astonished at the superior finish and taste displayed in the work of the later poet.

> ' But o'er her warrior's bloody bier
> The Ladye dropp'd nor flower nor tear !

---

[1] Entitled " Of a Scholar and his Mistress, etc."—

> "Look, look, I see—I see my love appear"
> (" And I see my Oread coming down.")

> " For like him there is none "
> (" There is none like her, none.")

And the metrical movement of " Come into the garden, Maud," is found in the speech of Phyllis,

> " Shall I marry the man I love."

[2] From " New Studies in Tennyson," pp. 68 and 69.

Vengeance, deep-brooding o'er the slain,
　　Had lock'd the source of softer woe ;
And burning pride, and high disdain,
　　Forbade the rising tear to flow ;
Until, amid his sorrowing clan,
　　Her son lisp'd from the nurse's knee—
"And if I live to be a man,
　　My father's death revenged shall be ! "
Then fast the mother's tears did seek
To dew the infant's kindling cheek.'

"Just now I was directing your attention to the genius
displayed by Tennyson in refining upon the excellences
of former poets, especially those of this century, and in
bringing them nearer to men's lives in a poetry of
striking originality ; but I forebore to point out, from the
many thousands, some one constituent element of that
originality, because any such example would serve equally
well to illustrate my present subject. From among the
five or six hackneyed turns of expression in these lines by
Scott, I will select for your guidance this one, viz., 'did
seek.' Now, such a poetical past indefinite tense may,
according to conditions of date, context, and the rest, be
either a beauty or a blemish, and chiefly on this account ;
the law by which the comely hat of one year is con-
demned as the hat hideous of another year, operates also
in the region of poetical devices. In our earlier literature
this 'did' tense, though perhaps employed to excess in
Spenser and the immature writings of Shakespeare, is
usually in good taste. Milton makes it beautiful in
Lycidas ; Pope condemns it ; by his time it has become
'out of fashion.' Yet Gray uses it with peculiar grace ;
smaller poets at the end of the eighteenth and the begin-
ning of the nineteenth centuries rendered it repulsive ;
some leading poets of the same period employed it with
indiscretion ; though well adapted to his manner, it is
sometimes a blemish in Keats, from whom it may have
descended to Tennyson ; it is a blemish in this passage
from Scott ; but when Tennyson revived its use, it was

again made to produce the effect of 'pleasing surprise.' In these lines from Mariana in the Moated Grange, it is charming—nay, bewitching :

> ' When thickest dark *did* trance the sky . . .
> For leagues no other tree *did* mark . . .
> The poplar made, *did* all confound . . .'

"Nothing, again, could be more beautiful than the employment of this word in the 'Lotos-Eaters,' although there it is appropriate rather as echoing Spenser and Thomson. On the same principle we justify and admire Mr. Swinburne's revival of not systematic, but abundant alliteration."

CHAPTER IV.

THE VOLUME OF 1833, OR, "THE LADY OF SHALOTT, AND OTHER POEMS."

THE date of this volume is sometimes given as 1832, for it was published in December of that year ; but the title-page reads, "Poems[1] by Alfred Tennyson, London : Edward Moxon, 64, New Bond Street, MDCCCXXXIII." It contains thirty poems, mostly short ones, which, together with a long note beginning on p. 121, fill up the volume of 233 pages.

Of this second collection of poems the most striking characteristics are the evidence of foreign travel, the increased influence of Keats, and an extraordinary inequality of workmanship. Nevertheless, the poet advances to a greater perfection some of the best qualities of the former volume; more elaborately, as in "The Lotos-Eaters" and "Œnone," he clothes an universal emotion in a classic dress ; the romantic ballad, richly wrought, is an important feature ; he begins to treat moral questions in an allegorical manner and with greater earnestness, as in "The Palace of Art" ; and, lastly, as in "The Miller's Daughter" and "The May Queen," he sings of the affections and the home and simple country life and scenery as only an English poet could, and more sweetly than any other English poet ever did.

[1] The words " Chiefly Lyrical " are now omitted

(27) "THE LADY OF SHALOTT." This poem, which stood sixth in the volume of 1833, will serve to illustrate the foregoing mention of inequality of workmanship. Some poets, like Swinburne and Browning, seldom write a weak line ; others, like Tennyson, and spite of the fact that " His worst he kept, his best he gave " will now and then give the people of their worst. As if to show how weakly he could still write, he ended the first stanza of " The Lady of Shalott " as follows :

> "The yellowleavèd waterlily,
> The greensheathèd daffodilly,
> Tremble in the water chilly
>   Round about Shalott."

Tennyson never looked younger than that. The only difference is the change of accent from acute to grave.[1] The following lines also occur in the original edition :

> " Though the squally eastwind keenly
> Blew, with folded arms serenely. . . ."

there also the brilliant figure of fire-flies, used with much effect by Shelley, adorns one of the stanzas. It is to be met with again two or three times in the early poems of Tennyson, notably in " Locksley Hall." About seventy of the lines in " The Lady of Shalott" have undergone change ; others judiciously omitted are such as these :

> " She leaneth on a velvet bed,
> Full royally apparallèd ; "

and again,

> " No time hath she to sport and play."

But, with not more than one other comparison of the text, we shall understand that the earlier poem wanted not only the strength and finish[2] of the 1842 version, but also much of its charm. And the same is true of other poems of the 1833 volume, notably "The Miller's Daughter," which was almost entirely spoilt by the first stanza alone.

---

[1] Acute in 1830, grave in 1833.   [2] The rhymes, however, remain imperfect.

Similarly it was the last stanza of " The Lady of Shalott " that most of all killed the charm of the poem :

> " They crossed themselves, their stars they blest,
> Knight, minstrel, abbot, squire and guest.
> There lay a parchment on her breast,
> That puzzled more than all the rest,
>   The wellfed wits at Camelot ;
> *'The web was woven curiously*
> *The charm is broken utterly,*
> *Draw near and fear not—this is I,*
>   *The Lady of Shalott.' "*

From the earlier version, however, we learn—if it is necessary to learn it—the much quested " moral " of this brilliant romantic ballad :

> " She knows not what the curse may be ;
> Therefore she weaveth steadily,
> *Therefore* no other care hath she. . . ."

It is the " eclipsing curse of birth " into a world wherein a capacity for higher enjoyment implies a capacity for higher pain.   It is put into these two pathetic lines from " Lancelot and Elaine " :

> " Being so very wilful you must go. . . .
> Being so very wilful you must die. . . ."

In its wider application the principle is set forth in " In Memoriam " :

> " 'Tis better to have loved and lost
> Than never to have loved at all."

For

> " She lives with little joy or fear," [1]

but to this must be added

> " Like a beast with lower pleasures, like a beast with lower pains." [2]

On the other hand, could mankind reverse the fourth stanza of Part II. in " The Lady of Shalott," and see the lovers in the moonlight first, and after that see the dark-

---

[1] " The Lady of Shalott," 1st ed.

[2] See the whole of Poem xxvii., " In Memoriam."

ness and the funeral pall, there might be less of heart-breaking. So much for "the moral" shut within the bosom of this rose.

The last stanza of the new version, besides being more excellent in every way, brings Lancelot to look on her; brings, therefore, the whole poem nearer to the "Idylls of the King," and gives us another glimpse of the poet as he is at work on his great subject in the years 1833-1842. We seem to gather that during this interval the idyll of Elaine was under contemplation:

> "And Lancelot later came and mused at her. . . ."

Among other correspondences, the web that was woven curiously becomes in "Lancelot and Elaine" "The silken case with braided blazonings," and the parchment that lay on her breast is the letter that Arthur in the later legend spied in her hand.

The poem of 1833 has more in common with the "Mariana" group; but there is this difference in either version; nature changes with the mood or the situation of the figure it surrounds. In Part III. the advent of Love is announced by a sun that dazzles through the leaves and flames on the armour of Sir Lancelot; his emblazoned shield sparkles amid the yellow harvest—and so on with every stanza; and it was "All in the blue un-clouded weather." If a figure is employed, it will be of the purple night and starry clusters, or it will be a brilliant meteor. How changed is everything when the curse is come; as we read Part IV. it almost seems that earth felt the wound.

But without staying to notice other special artistic features of the poem, we must briefly remark that in form, sound, and colour it is splendidly wrought; of things that are at once new and beautiful it has enough, we might almost say, to found a whole school of poets—as it has done in part. Rossetti's manner may often be traced to the magical influence of this ballad, as may some of Swinburne's music.

The "Lady of Shalott," as every one knows, is afterwards to be "The lily maid of Astolat." Sir Francis Palgrave tells us that the poem was founded upon an Italian romance. That some sort of prototype was found for it more suggestive than Malory is certainly probable ; but we may well be content in this instance to accept Tennyson's great gift with a thankfulness that does not care to inquire further how it came into his possession.

(29) "MARIANA IN THE SOUTH." According to Shakespeare, the Moated Grange was situated near St. Luke's in Vienna ; but, except for a vineyard, there is very little scenery in "Measure for Measure." The names and the sentiments are Italian mostly—" I had as lief be a list of an English Kersey" says one of the speakers.

The scenery of "Mariana" in the earlier volume appears to be English, and often of the county of Lincolnshire, if we may judge from such a line as :

"And glanced athwart the glooming flats,"

and from some passages in the "Poems by Two Brothers."

Now, Tennyson has been travelling to the Rhine and to lands of vineyards since he wrote the first "Mariana ;" this we gather from "In Memoriam"[1] and "O Darling Room ;" also we know that he spent some time in the neighbourhood of the Pyrenees ; hence he was brought in mind of the fact that vineyards were not to be found in England ; accordingly he composed another "Mariana" poem, putting in what "southern" scenery he could.

And he makes the most of this southern scenery. First of all, the line quoted above reappears in "The Gem" for 1831,

"Looking athwart the burning flats."

This is Egypt, further south still. Tennyson was fond of

[1] lxxi. and xcviii.

the more or less indefinite " South ; " it occurs again and
again in his verse.   " Fatima " looks

> " Athwart the burning drouth
> Of that long desert to the south,"

and thus suits the poem to her name.   This recalls the
" level " of the second line of " Mariana in the South."
As suggested elsewhere, the second stanza in " Fatima "
from which two lines have just been quoted may have
been left over from this " Mariana."   But to identify
all the scenery of the poem would be impossible.   For
example, an olive in the first edition becomes a willow
in the second.   Very interesting is the " dry cicala " of the
last stanza, seen by the poet in the Pyrenees ; [1] and often
mentioned by earlier poets ; in " Œnone " it appears
along with the lizard,[2] as it does in Shelley : [3]

> " The cicale above in the lime,
> And the lizards below in the grass,"

although the lizard was probably suggested by Theocritus.
We shall find the lizard also a little further on in the
earlier version of " Mariana in the South."

To sum up, the first " Mariana " had been a success ;
Tennyson, who might have felt the original English
setting inappropriate to a lady placed in the south by
Shakespeare, takes the opportunity of resetting the theme,
and in southern scenery, especially as he himself has
been travelling " south."   Mr. Churton Collins finds a
resemblance to Sestini's description of a " hapless wife
pining forlorn amid the torrid horrors of the Maremma."
This is very probable : in either version of " Mariana in
the South," there is more of the Maremma landscape than
any other.

[1] " In the Pyrenees, where part of this poem was written, I saw a very
beautiful species of cicala."—TENNYSON, *in note on* "Œnone."

[2]   " The lizard, with his shadow on the stone
              Rests like a shadow, and the cicala sleeps."
                                        (Old version.)

[3] " Hymn of Pan."

The only relation that Tennyson establishes between the two " Marianas " is contained in the note he attaches to the second " Mariana," viz., " See ' Poems, Chiefly Lyrical.' " But from the poem in its earlier form much more is to be discovered, too much, we fear, for our space. We have already seen that the poet identifies much of the scenery of " Œnone " with the Pyrenees, and the presence of the same cicala in " Mariana in the South " refers that detail also to the Pyrenees. This is true of many other poems in the volume of 1833. Else-- where Tennyson tells us that " veils of thinnest lawn " in the " Lotos-Eaters " was suggested by the Pyrenees.

The following is part of the first stanza of " Mariana in the South " as originally published :

> " Behind the barren hill upsprung
>   With pointed rocks against the light,
> The crag sharpshadowed overhung
>   Each glaring creek and inlet bright,"

which is less like the Maremma; a vineyard also is introduced. Moreover, the lizard appears in this version, but in a dream :

> " The lizard leapt : the sunlight played."

Other passages support the conjecture of Mr. Collins :

> " Down in the dry salt-marshes stood
> That house darklatticed."

And other lines of the stanza possess an interest that makes them worth quoting :

> " Not a breath
> Swayed the sick vineyard underneath,
> Or moved the dusty southernwood."

For many other purposes a study of original versions is necessary to a full or even an appreciative knowledge of Tennyson. The reader would find the word " runnel " of " Claribel," the oft repeated figure, " the large leaves talked with one another," and perhaps as many as a hundred other lessons in poetical composition on the one hand, and—what is also important—lessons in the gradual evolution of Tennyson's grace, perfection, unutterable charm.

In its present form, "Mariana in the South" is in some respects a better poem than its predecessors; nothing in the volume of 1830 bears comparison with the superb second and third stanzas;[1] and to do Tennyson justice, they are not so much altered from the original as are many other parts of the poem. The scenery is more "made up," but it is very effective. A variation on the metre of the first "Mariana" was tried in this second poem, but subsequently abandoned, and rightly. At present the two poems are nearly alike in metre.

(30) "THE TWO VOICES." This poem of 154 stanzas was published for the first time in the volume of 1842; it was then dated 1833, but the date was subsequently removed. The form of the verse is to be found in the "Ode on the Death of Lord Byron" in "Poems by Two Brothers," and there it is more appropriate, though of course employed with less skill. The stanza serves well enough for a Threnody or a Litany; but it does not make very good poetry; least of all in such a long poem as "The Two Voices," where we find many awkward or halting lines— "To which the Voice did urge reply," "Which did accomplish their desire," "Should that plain fact, as taught by these;" or, for a whole stanza, what could be flatter than the following :

> "It spake moreover in my mind :
> 'Tho' thou wert scattered to the wind,
> Yet is there plenty of the kind.'"

Here and there the verse becomes poetry—sometimes

---

[1] With "her melancholy eyes divine," cf. Keats' "her maiden eyes divine."—*Eve of St. Agnes.*

very good poetry; such would be the five stanzas be-
ginning "The highest mounted mind;" and there are
others, especially near the close; and no doubt the
poet thought the triplets admirably adapted to his sub-
ject: and of course he manages the metre as well as
can be. For all that, the poem is dull, and drags, and
is often weak; and this irrespective of the argumentative
and heavy subject. It is easy to turn, by way of com-
parison, to real poetry, in what may be called a companion
poem. In "The Ancient Sage" there is nothing that
resembles a weak line:

> "The plowman passes, bent with pain
> To mix with what he plow'd;"

or if it is not enough to call attention to a representative
line or two, we might substitute the twenty lines in which
these two occur, or the succeeding lyric of sixteen, and
ask whether, as poetry, these are not worth the whole of
"The Two Voices." Only the rhymed lines have been
compared; but much would remain to be said in favour
of the blank verse of the later poem.

As to the subject matter of "The Two Voices," that is
somewhat better than the manner, though much of it
streams on to us from the Flowing Philosophers them-
selves. But first, there is no reason why good—or even
bad—philosophy should not make good poetry. Almost
any material, when duly idealized and tinged with emotion,
is a fair subject in poetic art. Nothing at first sight could
appear less inspiring than the pursuit of agriculture or
the atomic cosmogony of Democritus; yet the "Georgics"
are based on the first of these, and the great poem of
Lucretius deals largely with the other.

"The Two Voices" takes us back to "Nothing will
Die," "All things will Die," and "Supposed Confessions
of a Second-rate Sensitive Mind."

Not only in "L'Allegro" and "Il Penseroso," but also
in "Comus," we find Milton "making choice" between

many things, choice between cavalier gallantry and
Puritan austerity, for example, or between pomp of ritual
and purity of character. His rule of life had to be chosen
rather than discovered. With Tennyson it was very
different :

> " Shall we not look into the laws
> Of life and death, and things that seem,
> And things that be, and analyze
> Our double nature, and compare
> All creeds till we have found the one—
> If one there be ? "

This passage from the "Supposed Confessions of a
Second-rate Sensitive Mind" could hardly have been
written by Milton ; but we seem to hear it spoken aloud
despondingly, or cheerfully, or manfully, or defiantly as
the case might be, not by Tennyson alone, but also by
Maurice, and Browning, and Carlyle.[1] From one point of
view, as we have seen already, Truth is an everlasting
seeking ; and this truth was the only rule of life possible
to these eager souls, cast as they were by a somewhat
violent wave of the Great Deep upon the shore of this
nineteenth century.

Many other names might be added of great men who
were born into the world about the same time, and did
battle, each in his own way, with the spiritual, social, and
intellectual disorder of their day. Such were Newman,
Gladstone, and Ruskin.[2] And later, when the century
had half run its course, the typical words quoted above
from the "Supposed Confessions" had to be said over
again—and again despondingly, or cheerfully, or man-
fully, or defiantly, or all these in one—by Matthew
Arnold, and Kingsley, and Clough, and George Eliot.
Nor do these names by any means exhaust the list ; the
poem of "The Two Voices" is the commonest symptom
among sufferers from the malady of the age ; and few

---

[1] Maurice, born 1805 ; Browning, 1812 ; Carlyle, 1795.

[2] J. H. Newman, born 1801 ; Gladstone, 1809 ; Ruskin, 1819.

really earnest men and women have escaped that malady. They all have " renewed the quest ; "[1] their truth was an everlasting seeking.

Into the nature of their seeking or its results this is not the place to inquire ; perhaps the best that they have left us may be found in one line of Matthew Arnold's " Thyrsis "—

> " Roam on ! the light we sought is shining still."

At any rate we must not expect to get a new and complete system of moral philosophy out of Tennyson's poems. We read Lucretius not in order to discover how worlds are made and unmade, but to steep our souls in mournful beauty. The merit of " The Two Voices " must be sought in the yearnings and the strivings of the heart of a great poet. Whatever consideration the grave doubts and answers there proposed seem to call for, will best be given to them in the notes on " The Ancient Sage," which was written as the result of fifty more years of doubting and answering.

Meanwhile it may be suggested that those who would gain for themselves some general knowledge of Tennyson's philosophy, should study the following poems as a group :—" The Two Voices," " In Memoriam," " The Higher Pantheism," " De Profundis," " Despair," " The Ancient Sage." There are others ; but these are most akin ; indeed any one of them will be found to repeat and occasionally to modify theories set forth in the others.

For example, from one point of view, " The Two Voices " may be regarded as " Despair" and " The Ancient Sage " thrown into one. We meet with a man " full of misery "—almost the words used by Tennyson in the prefatory note to " Despair." A first voice advises death as

---

[1] " The Scholar-Gipsy," by Matthew Arnold.

the only remedy for ill.   Against the more than twelve
several persuasions and arguments of this " dull and bitter
voice," the afflicted man advances many of the counter
arguments of " The Ancient Sage."   When the voice
urges, "What were you before birth ?   Nothing !   Then
die, and return to nothing" (107-111), it is met with a
rejoinder of many stanzas (112-128), some of which
embody the " Passion of the Past," which is so eloquently
repeated in the later poem.

"The Two Voices" concludes in a manner which at
first sight is more poetical than convincing ; but as stated
already, the point will be considered more fully on a later
page.   "This antenatal Past," the Voice resumed, "this
walking of the soul from state to state is but a dream ;
your pain is your only reality."   "You have missed your
mark " is the reply (130); "you attempted to shut me out
from the future as well as the past ; what I want is not
death, but more life."   The voice might have objected
that this past and future was not proven ; but it merely
added mockingly "Behold, it is the Sabbath morn."   "On
to God's house the people prest. . . .   One walked be-
tween his wife and child ;" and while the man who had
fought with his despair was looking at this picture of love,
a second voice came to his ear and whispered of "a
hidden hope."

A brief analysis of the poem will be found in an Ap-
pendix to this chapter.

(36) "THE MILLER'S DAUGHTER."   Again there is
very much to be learnt from a comparison of the earlier
version with the present ; the following originally stood
as the first stanza of the poem :

> "I met in all the close green ways,
>   While walking with my line and rod,
> The wealthy miller's mealy face,
>   Like the moon in an ivytod.

> He looked so jolly and so good—
> While fishing in the milldam-water,
> I laughed to see him as he stood,
> And dreamt not of the miller's daughter.'

Such a stanza may fairly be described as a compound of the very worst of Wordsworth, Cowper, and Campbell. Again,

> "Oh ! that I were the wreath she wreathes,
> The mirror where her sight she feeds,
> The song she sings, the air she breathes,
> The letters of the book she reads."

The fifteenth stanza of the original seems to have been omitted partly because its last four lines just quoted bear a close resemblance to some others in a chanson of Ronsard, which also supplies most of the song, " It is the miller's daughter." Ronsard, moreover, enlarges on various Greek originals.

The following may be noticed as one example of the process by which Tennyson refines his poetic metal ; the line in the song, "About her dainty dainty waist," was in the earlier copy " Buckled about her dainty waist." The change reminds us of Browning's :

> "O the little more, and how much it is,
> O the little less, and what worlds away."

The improvements made in this song alone are perhaps as many as fifty. This is the more remarkable, because it really is intended to be "A trifle" which nothing of poetic art but only "true love spells ;" such a song as might have been written by " the long and listless boy " himself. The marvel is, that although so carefully elaborated, it gives us just that impression still. Another secret of the poet's art is revealed by the first edition. The song "Love that hath us in the net" is another trifle that true love and not true art is supposed to spell : for example, with one exception all the rhymes are alike, and that again, is exactly the sort of verse we should expect from such a lover, who was a "rhymester" in his youth, and "over-garrulous in age." In the earlier version another song took its place, but this had the same characteristics, especially in regard to the rhymes.

Tennyson's unguarded manner is well exhibited by the line "Rosecheekt, roselipt, half-sly, half-shy," or by "silver-paley," as an epithet of the cuckoo flower. Finally, the original abounds with all those interesting peculiarities noted elsewhere, and it can hardly bear any comparison with the version of 1842.

This poem, as now perfected, needs no praise ; it is one of Tennyson's many masterpieces, and, again, is strikingly original. It has often been said of human character as presented in the verse of this poet or that— "How perfectly life-like ; these men and women are as familiar to us as the light of day ; and this life, we live it." In "The Miller's Daughter" there is something more. An introductory note on "Nature in Tennyson"[1] gives expression to the opinion that in art we have the best of man and nature when both are blended. In this poem the blending of the two is so perfect that to conceive of either as apart from the other is almost impossible ; to use a formula already found convenient, "each seems to have called the other into existence, and each for existence depends upon the other." This comes of Tennyson's close and sympathetic study of particular scenery in his native land ; combined with the assiduous practice begun long before in adapting every aspect of external nature to the particular forms of human life which it environed in his poetic picture. This, in its new perfection, is perhaps the chief charm of "The Miller's Daughter," and of many poems to follow. Other beauties of the poem were pointed out on p. 109. As a final remark we may say that had "The Lady of Shalott"

---

[1] See p. 29, section iv.

and "The Miller's Daughter" appeared in their present form in 1833, they might have been regarded as the most astonishing efforts ever put forth by a young poet. But whatever their date, it is still remarkable and admirable that two poems so novel, and so totally unlike, should be included in the same small volume. If "The Lady of Shalott" might have founded a school of poets, so might "The Miller's Daughter." A new wonder and delight was added to romance by the first of these poems, and to our common life by the second.[1]

(39) "FATIMA." The ultimate form of this poem seems to have been suggested by the two " Marianas," which in many respects it resembles. Originally it was called "O Love, Love, Love," and was preceded by the follow-ing quotation :

> Φαίνεταί μοι κῆνος ἴσος θεοῖσιν
> Ἔμμεν᾽ ὤνηρ—

which takes the reader to Sappho's celebrated ode ; but Tennyson's verse may be further indebted to Greek litera-

[1] The following stanzas omitted from the early version possess great beauty, though some of it is spoilt by the mannerism "under-air," and the difficulty of the "whispering," spite of the second stanza :

> "Remember you the clear moonlight,
> That whiten'd all the eastern ridge,
> When o'er the water, dancing white,
> I stepp'd upon the old millbridge ?
> I heard you whisper from above,
> A lutetoned whisper, 'I am here !'
> I murmur'd, 'Speak again my love,
> The stream is loud : I cannot hear.'

> " I heard, as I have seem'd to hear
> When all the under-air was still,
> The low voice of the glad new year
> Call to the freshly-flowered hill.
> I heard, as I have often heard
> The nightingale in leavy woods
> Call to its mate, when nothing stirred
> To left or right but falling floods."

ture, for Ibycus and Tatius are mentioned by Mr. Churton Collins as entering into its composition ; and some slight resemblances are to be found in Ovid's " Sappho Phaoni."

The piece, therefore, is patchwork ; and not the least curious bit of pattern is the second and additional stanza which, as already mentioned,[1] determines the locality, and seems appropriate to the title. The merit of the poem is considerable ; the four rhymes followed by three produce a fine effect of intense and prolonged emotion ; indeed, music, imagery, passion, all are remarkable, and more than worthy to be the inspiration of Mr. Swinburne. Seldom does Tennyson allow himself such a passionate utterance ; perhaps only in " Love and Duty," and the stanzas in " The Tribute." [2]

(40) " ŒNONE." Those who compare the earlier with the later versions of Tennyson's poems, will probably be struck by the frequency with which an added beauty may be traced to another writer. This fact was referred to in the remarks on Plagiarism.[3] Many instances might be given, such as " Large Hesper glitter'd on her tears," in the last stanza of " Mariana in the South ; " it replaces " Large Hesper overshone The mourning gulf," and it resembles " No light could glimmer on their tears " in " Hyperion."[4] Such resemblances are numerous in the new edition of " Œnone ;" the best known line in the whole poem, "And at their feet the crocus brake like fire," which was added in the 1842 copy, can be traced in part to Homer ; and with some certainty ; for in its company came other flowers not in the earlier version ; and the figure at the end of the line may have been suggested

---

[1] P. 114.   [2] See Chapter X.   [3] P. 49.

[4] Judging from this very common characteristic of emendation in Tennyson, we may fairly conjecture that in many instances some beautiful expression in another poet was the sole occasion of the emendation. And all this again would be due to the immense accumulation of past poetic wealth which Tennyson always had within easy view.

by Wordsworth's " Flowers that set the hills on fire." [1]
The reference to Homer is made much clearer by the fact
that the lines in the context,

> "And o'er him flowed a golden cloud, and leaned
> Upon him, slowly dropping fragrant dew,"

are almost word for word with two lines in the context of
the Homer—

ἐπὶ δὲ νεφέλην ἕσσαντο
καλὴν χρυσείην· στιλπναὶ δ' ἀπέπιπτον ἔερσαι.
Iliad, XIV. 350, 351.

This example must be regarded as a typical one ; and we
will now dismiss the comparison between the old and
the new version by remarking that with the exception
of "The Palace of Art," the "Œnone" of 1833 fails
more than any other poem of its final perfection in 1842.

The blank verse is very remarkable ; though almost
the first we have met with, it is excellent, and something
new. Stateliness of movement, fulness of sound, are its
chief characteristics. These effects are produced partly
by a careful employment of open and closed vowels, partly
by avoiding a weak tenth syllable ; the lines, though not
necessarily end-stopped, have weight enough at the close
to give emphasis to the turn of the verse, and majesty to
the whole rhythm.

The poem, which seems to have been suggested by
Theocritus and other classical writers, and still more
closely resembles Beattie's "Judgment of Paris," is said
to have shaped itself in the poet's mind while he was
in the Pyrenees ; accordingly, the first draft is filled
in partly with Pyrenean partly with other scenery,
some of it imaginary. In the revised version, as was
noticed in the case of "Mariana in the South," there
is less of the Pyrenees and more of imaginary land-
scape. The same is true of "The Palace of Art."

---

[1] Compare also the χρυσαυγὴς κρόκος of Sophocles ("Œd. Col." 685).

Many bits of natural description from " Poems by Two Brothers " are worked into the sketch of the valley. In this way the poet secures a more perfect correspondence between the solitary figure and the scene of her sorrow —the ruin'd folds, the fragments tumbled from the hills— than if he had gone with his pigments to Mount Ida and brought home on his canvas some real and revolting incongruity. As it is, earth hearkens to her cry, the stream is loud because of her wrongs, the very stars of heaven are trembling above her.

" Œnone," " Hesperides," " The Lotos Eaters," and " Ulysses " are classical in outline, but mostly modern in sentiment. Just as in Shakespeare we meet with long passages that are really excrescent from the true dramatic growth, so in " Œnone " the speech of Pallas is the speech of the nineteenth century poet himself ; it breathes of his sobriety, his love of order and law, his wisdom and —a word that cannot be written without apology—his goodness. There is little enough of the Greek in it.

The story of " Œnone " is summed up in one line of Ovid, " Sustinet Œnonen deseruisse Paris." But the one line stands between two Epics. For the mortals, or even the demi-gods of Greek tragedy, were as flies whom the high gods killed for their sport ; and behind the stage of saddened nature on which Œnone plays her short, pathetic part, a banquet of the gods is spread, and Strife, the Abominable, throws among them the fatal apple.

Œnone had the gift of prophecy. This effective element Tennyson does not introduce as Œnone's ; it would take away from the pity of her sorrow ; but she will talk with the wild Cassandra, and hear her tell how the noise of battle is ringing in her ears. And we who also listen can dimly forecast the ten years war in Troy, and all its mighty issues.

(44) THE SISTERS. This ballad is very slightly altered

from the form it took in the volume of 1833. The out of vogue elision in "turret an' tree" has been rectified. Byron, as we should remember, is still in the poet's mind. The well-known lines in "The Miller's Daughter,"

> "There's somewhat flows to us in life
> But more is taken quite away,"

were a reminiscence of

> "There's not a joy the world can give like that it takes away;

and in this poem,

> "I kiss'd his eyelids into rest
> His ruddy cheek upon my breast"

is **very** much like Byron's ("The Bride of Abydos")—

> "Come, lay thy head upon my breast,
> And I will kiss thee into rest."

Tennyson's poem recalls some of the old ballad form, and some of the old ballad spirit, and adds a perfection unknown to both ; but the subject is improbable, and not so attractive as that of Oriana.

(44) "THE PALACE OF ART." For the Introduction, "To ——, with the following poem," and the ethical teaching of the poem that follows, see *Tennyson as Artist*, pp. 33-43.

Probably no poem by Tennyson has received such careful revision as "The Palace of Art." It stands as the antithesis of those fresh and forceful poetic masterpieces with which we are so familiar in Shakespeare and many other Elizabethans, in Scott, Byron, Shelley, and Burns. However composed, their work has at least the appearance of freshness. Tennyson himself in "Will Waterproof" trusts that after his libation to the Muse he may not find it necessary to

> "Add and alter, many times
> Till all be ripe and rotten."

From the first, Tennyson was an imitative poet, and these also are the poets who elaborate. Yet if they succeed in removing all marks of painstaking, their work has a value and a charm of its own, second only to the charm of impetuous passion and swift creative power. As yet, painstaking has been apparent everywhere, but sometimes in a degree so slight as to be scarcely a blemish. And we regard its presence almost with satisfaction when we reflect how important this very trifling with words and phrases and rhythms has been to a genius like Tennyson's ; but for this the world could never have wondered at the flawless beauty of "Tithonus," "Come into the garden, Maud," "Tears, Idle Tears," "Early Spring," and other poems too numerous to mention.

In "The Palace of Art" of 1833 more traces of European travel are discernible than in the improved copy. Rejected fragments are reserved to be made more beautiful in future poems ; among the pictures on the arras "Venus . . . . glowed double on the blue ; " in "The Princess" she becomes "a double light in air and wave ; " and the "streaming crystal" that flowed from her sides in this later poem, was in "The Palace of Art" the property of another figure. Here too we have the explanation of the woods that shook and the colour that danced above the flood in "The Princess ; " for we catch "The gleam Of that great foambow trembling in the sun."

> "She lit white streams of dazzling gas
> In moons of purple glass"

will be met with again in "The Princess" as

> "Two sphere lamps blazon'd like heaven and earth,"

a new and ingenious scientific device, worthy to remain though the vulgarized gas must go. But the gas, when first introduced, was good poetic material, like Milton's artillery.

Again, "The Halicarnassëan" becomes "The Carian

Artemisia strong in war." We have not exhausted the phrases transferred to " The Princess ;" and a large number are left to be traced to other poems. Many other interesting lessons must be passed by. And it cannot be too often repeated that a study of these poems as first published is most useful if not essential to a knowledge of Tennyson ; and the subject might well fill a volume.

Next we notice the poet's remark (appended as a note to stanza 14 in the original) : " When I first conceived the plan of ' The Palace of Art,' I intended to have introduced both sculptures and paintings into it ; but it is the most difficult of all things to *devise* a statue in verse. Judge whether I have succeeded in the statues of Elijah and Olympias."

Now Tennyson had drawn many pretty but artificial verse portraits of women ; next, as in this poem, he reproduces pictures in verse ; these, not being regarded as originals, but as copies, are admirable ; on the other hand, the portraits of women had to be regarded as originals, and therefore were less successful. Of course, the pictures are original, " devised " by the poet; but they are supposed to be pictures, imagined as such, before they became verse. To create in the mind a piece of sculpture is very much harder than to call up in imagination a painting ; harder also to reproduce the colourless, one-element form in verse. To describe sculpture, as Byron did, would be comparatively easy. This seems to be the poet's meaning. But his note serves a double purpose ; it not only apologizes for any imperfections that might be discovered if his improvised sculpture were compared with Byron's well-known descriptions ; it also gives him an opportunity of bringing his two statues into public view ; there was no appropriate place for them in the poem ; and they were adroitly set up in a note.

Two other notes in the original are of sufficient interest to be included in this survey ; the first is as follows :—

" If the Poem were not already too long, I should have inserted in the text the following stanzas, expressive of the joy wherewith the soul contemplated the results of astronomical experiment." It was pointed out on a former page, that Tennyson preaches to himself as well as to others : this habit he shares with many great masters, including Shakespeare. At first his enthusiasm for science was almost a passion, and sometimes in his earlier poetry it was a rival of love, as in " Locksley Hall." In this part of the poem especially we hear the poet speaking to himself :

> " Regions of lucid matter taking forms,
>   Brushes of fire, hazy gleams,
> Clusters and beds of worlds, and bee-like swarms [1]
>   Of suns, and starry streams."

" These world-wonders," he would say, " I am over-inclined to worship ; you will find them all in some form or other in my earnest verse." The same view may be taken of other branches of knowledge excluded from the revised edition, but displayed with a purpose in the first.

The next note is explanatory of an expression that may have perplexed many readers of the later editions of the poem—

> " Plato the wise, and large-brow'd Verulam,
>   The first of those who know."

These were originally,

> " Bold Luther, largebrowed Verulam,
>   The king of those who know."

To the last line the following note was added :

> " Il maëstro di color chi (*sic*) sanno."—DANTE, *Inf.* iii.

This then is not so much Tennyson's deliberate estimate of Bacon, as a convenient phrase from Dante. Bacon's was a mighty intellect, but he is scarcely entitled to the rank of king. That Tennyson felt this seems clear from the change made in the new edition, where Plato is put

---

[1] C. the similar figure in " Locksley Hall," and Shelley's "The Cloud."

by the side of Verulam ; "first" is substituted for "king," and "The first of those who know" may apply to both Plato and Verulam.

In the version of 1833, more of the "moral" is given :

> "And being both the sower and the seed . . . became
>   All that she saw."

> "Full of her own delight, and nothing else,
>   My vainglorious, gorgeous soul. . . ."

> "In deep or vivid colour, smell, and sound,
>   Was flattered day and night."

The stanza adopted in this poem is generally regarded as an invention of Tennyson's, but it was used by Vaughan. An example will be found in the Appendix to Chapter VII. It is not such a pleasing variation from the elegiac quatrain as the stanza employed in "A Dream of Fair Women," because the shortened second line spoils the effect of the three accent cadence at the close.

The scheme of the poem may have been supplied by G. Herbert's "The World,"—

> "Love built a stately house. . . ."

In Herbert's poem, the palace was razed to the ground,

> "But Love and Grace took Glory by the hand
> And built a braver palace than before;"

in Tennyson it is to be left standing for future occupation by the repentant soul and those to whom that soul was bound by love.[1]

Other sources may be found in Ecclesiastes, ii. 1-17. Of the poem generally it may be said that originality, wisdom, and beauty are somewhat marred by a stiffness due in part to the stanza adopted, partly to a lingering suspicion of artificiality which the most studied elaboration failed to remove. The landscapes "copied" each into a stanza are new effects in poetry, and quite astonishing in their condensed truth and beauty. One of the best is the bit of English scenery—

---

[1] Towards the end of the poem the Soul herself becomes part narrator.

> " And one, an English home,—gray twilight pour'd
>   On dewy pastures, dewy trees,
> Softer than sleep,—all things in order stored,
>   A haunt of ancient Peace."

As a rule, the shorter the poem, the more perfect should be the rhymes. This rule was violated in " The Lady of Shalott." Here the slightly imperfect rhymes, " trees" and " Peace," almost add a grace to the stanza. The beautiful expression, "softer than sleep," occurs in Shelley; and either poet may have had in mind Virgil's "somno mollior herba."

(49) " LADY CLARA VERE DE VERE " was printed for the first time in the volume of 1842. " The gardener Adam" of this edition was subsequently changed to " The grand old gardener;" but the newer phrase proved ambiguous, and therefore in 1875 the original reading was restored. Notice how suitably this poem follows " The Palace of Art," for it administers another rebuke to selfish pride: not pride of intellect and imagination, but pride of birth. True pride of birth is in " The Princess :" —" Our place is much ; we two will serve them both." In other words, noble birth imposes the obligation of high-minded principles and noble actions.

The poem is very good, and is worthy of special notice for the numerous examples it affords of the wisdom of many set forth in a beautiful and permanent form by the wit of one ; as for instance in the well-known line,

> " 'Tis only noble to be good."

(50) " THE MAY QUEEN." " The May Queen" and " New Year's Eve" belong to the volume of 1833, but the " Conclusion" did not appear till 1842. The first two parts underwent only slight alteration. One curious change was made in " New Year's Eve," where " The blossom on the blackthorn" takes the place of the older

reading, "The may upon the blackthorn." It is just possible that the poet had been confusing the hawthorn and the blackthorn; yet—and judging from other passages—this is scarcely probable. He may have intended the association of the two shrubs to be a conventional one, such as is not unknown in country places. Yet again, if so, why the alteration? He has well changed " I shall hear ye when ye pass " to " I shall hear you when you pass."

How the stanza of " The May Queen " grew out of two quatrains of such a poem as " The Talking Oak " may be discovered by a glance at the first stanza of the " Conclusion." This is little more than eight lines of " The Talking Oak " rolled out two into one, omitting the alternate rhymes. We shall notice something similar in the history of the couplets of " Locksley Hall." In this iambic case, however, many extra syllables were needed to quicken the movement when the measure was adapted to a light theme, as in " The May Queen " ; and other changes were introduced, such as a trochaic or monosyllabic fourth foot—" The night winds come and go, mother, upon the meadow-grass " ; " To-night I saw the sun set : he set and left behind."

In the introduction to this chapter, some reference was made to the originality and beauty of " The May Queen." As in " The Miller's Daughter " (especially the last stanza) the effect is mainly produced by richness and novelty both of material and method disguised beneath an impression of the most perfect simplicity. We will take the following as an example :

> " When the flowers come again, mother, beneath the waning light
> You'll never see me more in the long gray fields at night ;
> When from the dry dark wold the summer airs blow cool
> On the oat-grass and the sword-grass, and the bulrush in the pool. '

And first, in regard to the material ; if we look closely into the stanza, we shall notice two pairs of epithets, both entirely new, viz., "long gray," as descriptive of "fields,"[1] and "dry dark" as descriptive of "wold" : next, of the objects of nature themselves some will be new, but mostly simple enough to be unobtrusive : for example, the wold, the oat-grass, the sword-grass, and the bulrush ; and, thirdly, the occasion of the whole stanza is novel, yet most appropriate ; it is all in "the waning light." Next, as to the method : but this subject is inexhaustible ; nor is it so clearly exhibited by a single stanza ; it will perhaps be enough to point out that the bare sentiment is expressed by the words, "You'll never see me more" ; but by reason of the amplitude of choice and the skill in choosing them ; by their arrangement ; by the tone they take from the context ; and by the subtle sadness of the music, the very large proportion of materials from the natural world which go to make up the stanza are so charged with the emotion of the articulate sentiment that although inarticulate they express it over again with an infinite pathos ; and, last of all, care has been taken that all these elements shall produce an impression of simplicity and naturalness.

Yet, as is the case with "The Lord of Burleigh," the balance between pathos and bathos is so even that the jarring of a single word would destroy the equilibrium ; and we are not quite sure that the "Conclusion" altogether escapes this danger.[2]

(54) "THE LOTOS-EATERS." Two poems in the volume of 1833, "The Hesperides" and "The Lotos-Eaters," are related to "The Sea Fairies" of the former chapter. These two stand side by side ; but eventually "The Hesperides" was withdrawn, and gave up some of its beauty to "The Lotos-Eaters" ; gave, for example, the word "full-faced" from the following line :

"But when the full-faced sunset yellowly ;"

for the line in "The Lotos-Eaters" "Full-faced above the

[1] Cf. the "long dun wolds" of "Oriana."   [2] See also pp. 54 and 98.

valley stood the moon," read thus in the first edition—
"Above the valley burned the golden moon." Besides
these changes, the latter part of the more fortunate poem
was re-written ; and "The Hesperides" was rejected
possibly on account of a few slight weaknesses, but more
probably because its resemblances marred the single
beauty of "The Lotos-Eaters."

That a poet should make alterations in his published
work, even many times, is a matter partly [1] for admiration
and advantage, partly for disapprobation and regret. In
this respect of new editions, literary art stands almost alone.
When we buy a picture that has been hung in the Royal
Academy, we take it for granted that the painter has done
with it. But masterpieces of literary art, sold as such,
should not be subject to continued remodelling ; for the
purchaser may be inclined to murmur, "Your work was
either ready for sale, or not ; and if not, you might have
kept it until it was ; you were either deficient in some
critical faculty, or you forced unfinished work upon the
public and compelled them to buy over again." To this
imaginary charge Tennyson has made himself much more
liable than any other poet ; and under this head it will
be interesting to compare him with such other modern
poets as Browning, Swinburne, Longfellow, Wm. Morris,
M. Arnold, D. G. Rossetti.

But, to adopt the homely phrases of this argument, and
twist it back upon itself a little, the lover of poetry who
had the good fortune to buy "The Lotos-Eaters" of 1833
received full value for his money. "Nihil tetigit quod
non ornavit" must be quoted once more as we write of
Tennyson ; but after this, few of us will greatly care to
hear the familiar Latin again.

Three sonnets were mentioned a short time back, as pos-
sessing an excellence unknown to the sonnet before : this
time it is the Spenserian stanza with whose murmuring

[1] See p. 167.

> " She had lulled him fast asleepe
> That of no worldly thing he care did take,"

and to whose music :

> "'Gan all the quire of birds
> Their diverse notes t' attune ; "

but the five stanzas at the beginning of " The Lotos-Eaters" breathe a murmuring or a music more melodious even than Spenser's on The Idle Lake or in the Bowre of Blisse.

Very fine also is the musical effect of the closing section as it is found in the improved version. Tennyson had at least an ear for the music of verse ; and the description of " the nerve-dissolving melody" in the second section of " The Vision of Sin " which may be compared with the section before mentioned, seems to show that the Laureate was more of a tone poet than we are sometimes disposed to admit.

The main subject of " The Lotos-Eaters" occurs in the "Odyssey ;" a good deal has been suggested by Bion and Moschus, and in English literature, Spenser's "Fairy Queen" and Thomson's "Castle of Indolence" have furnished additional motive and material. Indeed so many poets are laid under contribution that the poem is almost "a posy of other men's flowers," and "little more than the string that binds them" is Tennyson's ; but the bond is a cestus of no common magic.

It is impossible to speak of " The Lotos-Eaters," however briefly, without repeating what must be delightfully obvious to all, the skill with which the poet has placed his languid dreamers where earth, and heaven, and the sea, and the very gods themselves are one languid dream. But in the self-indulgent repose of the Lotos Land the comrades of Ulysses were not permitted to linger :

τοὺς μὲν ἐγὼν ἐπὶ νῆας ἄγον κλαίοντας ἀνάγκῃ—

this is the voice of Tennyson ; and we shall soon hear it again in " Ulysses " :

> "How dull it is to pause, to make an end,
> To rust unburnished, not to shine in use,
> As tho' to breathe were life."

And thus, a moral emerges from this beautiful poem.

(56) "A DREAM OF FAIR WOMEN." Like "The Miller's Daughter," this poem was quite ruined by the opening lines since removed. Some of these must be repeated, because they tend to support a former opinion, hazarded in these pages, that the poet may sometimes build for himself a Palace of Art. The first two stanzas describe "a man that sails in a balloon;" they tell how he waves his flags to *the mob* below, from where his balloon "Glows ruby-like . . . . Filled with a finer air":

> "So, lifted high, the Poet at his will
> Lets the great world flit from him, seeing all,
> Higher thro' secret splendours mounting still,
> Selfpoised, nor fears to fall,
>
> "Hearing apart the echoes of his fame. . . ."

Very interesting in their relation to the "Princess" are the following stanzas:

> "In every land I thought that, more or less,
> The stronger, sterner nature overbore
> The softer, uncontrolled by gentleness
> And selfish evermore:
>
> "And whether there were any means whereby,
> In some far aftertime the gentler mind
> Might reassume its just and full degree
> Of rule among mankind."

The stanzas in the present edition, beginning, "The smell of violets" repeat a thought expressed in a very inferior song on page 142 of the 1833 volume:

> "Who can tell
> Why to smell
> The violet, recalls the dewy prime
> Of youth and buried time?"

Both passages are important, for though their violet does

not bring back all the glory and the dream of Wordsworth's
" Pansy," [1] yet when read in conjunction with the last two
stanzas of the poem they are found to forecast the " yearn-
ings that can never be exprest" of " Tears, Idle Tears."
A great many improvements were made in the 1842
version of this poem, the most notable being the lines :

> " The bright death quiver'd at the victim's throat,
>   Touch'd. and I knew no more,"

which are a very fortunate variation on the grotesque
earlier reading :

> " One drew a sharp knife thro' my tender throat
>   Slowly—and nothing more."

The variation, as is so often the case, seems to find a
parallel in some former poet. [2]

"A Dream of Fair Women," besides being suggested
by Chaucer's "Legend of Good Women," " bears a close
resemblance to the Trionfi of Petrarch." Like " The
Lotos-Eaters," it owes very much to other poets.

The poem, though often brilliant, has none of the
naturalness of "The Miller's Daughter" or "The May
Queen ; " in style it most nearly resembles " The Palace of
Art," and gives an impression of stiffness. As yet, the
only characters the poet has sketched without any show of
effort are those we met beside the mill-dam, or on the
village green. These women in the " Dream," however,
are better drawn than the Adeline group ; they gain
by being historic, and they have dramatic touches.
Jephthah's daughter and Cleopatra are splendidly
painted, and made still more vivid by contrast and sur-
roundings ; Cleopatra especially is a portrait so striking
and full of colour and of motion withal, that we find our-
selves convinced of the superiority of words to pigments
in some departments of pictorial art.

---

[1] See Appendix to Chapter VII.   [2] Sophocles, " Electra," 1395.

It may be added that the Fair Women whom the poet has honoured in this highly-wrought poem are Helen of Troy, Iphigenia, Cleopatra, Jephthah's Daughter, Fair Rosamond, Margaret Roper, daughter of Sir Thomas More, Joan of Arc, and Queen Eleanor. Cleopatra had fascinated his imagination and made some of his best poetry in "Poems by Two Brothers." Fair Rosamund and Eleanor play an important part in his "Becket."

(61) "THE BLACKBIRD" was first published in 1842. In the first edition the last stanza but one read as follows :

> " I better brook the drawling stares,
> Now thy flute-notes are changed to coarse—
> Not hearing thee at all.   . ."

The poet seems to have had his eye on the object while writing his verses ; in spite of some blemishes they are fresh and natural.

(62) "THE DEATH OF THE OLD YEAR." This is the last poem but one in the volume of 1833.

It is just in Tennyson's early manner ; remains unaltered, and contains nothing that is not his own ; unless if it be not to consider too curiously, we faintly hear among the verses the merriment and infinite jest of Yorick, and the quips of Hal with Falstaff, whose nose at death was "as sharp as a pen" (stanzas 4 and 6). The subject has several times entered into Tennyson's poetry. Here it is treated with a pleasing fullness and picturesqueness.

(62). "TO J. S." These beautiful verses fitly closed the published volume of 1833, which, as originally prepared for the press, ended with "The Lover's Tale." J. S. is the James Spedding who was one of Tennyson's circle at Cambridge, and afterwards became a kindly reviewer of the poet's work. Until his death in 1881, Spedding continued to be one of the laureate's intimate friends.

This poem also remains nearly in its original form, but with that remark our notice shall conclude. All Tennyson's early poetry is open to a criticism both interesting and valuable ; but the verses to J. S. seem too sacred for scrutiny, whether intellectual or æsthetic. There will be few enough among the readers of this book who have not felt the terrible inadequacy of words to comfort the bereaved ; and they will surely derive consolation from the thought that our great poet who addressed to his afflicted friend these stanzas, not exquisite alone, but also most earnest in sympathy, should yet exclaim, "'Twere better I should cease."

(63). "ON A MOURNER" was first printed in 1865, in the same volume that contained "Three Sonnets to a Coquette." In this collection it naturally follows the verses to J. S. There is some interesting study of nature, unmistakably Tennyson's, in the poem ; and lofty thought. The figure and allusion in the last stanzas produce an effect already noticed ; [1] in this case, however, emotion seems to lose too much by the neutralizing close.

(64) "YOU ASK ME WHY, THO' ILL AT EASE," (64) "OF OLD SAT FREEDOM ON THE HEIGHTS," (64) "LOVE THOU THY LAND," and (66) "THE GOOSE" did not appear till 1842, though stated to have been written in 1833. (66) "ENGLAND AND AMERICA IN 1782" was first published in the cabinet edition of 1874.

The five poems form a group devoted to political and social topics. Tennyson had little sympathy with the reforms that were being effected, and sometimes with eager haste, during the years that followed close on 1830 ; and he often cast an anxious glance across the narrow

[1] See p. 100.

seas[1] where raw haste was again proclaiming herself
half-sister to delay. The friend to whom the first poem
is addressed seems to have had less sympathy than the
poet with the great democratic movement of the age ;
Tennyson will not forsake England unless a society that
calls itself free shall happen to have made the individual
its bondslave.[2] The stanzas are based on a speech of
Spedding's in the Cambridge Debating Hall in 1832.

The next poem, (64) " OF OLD SAT FREEDOM ON THE
HEIGHTS," expands two lines in the foregoing :

> "Where Freedom slowly broadens down
> From precedent to precedent : "

And in the history of Freedom a very important place is
assigned to Great Britain. The last two lines admirably
describe Tennyson in his office of moderator.

[1]   " God bless the narrow seas,
        I wish they were a whole Atlantic broad."
                              The Princess.

[2] It will be convenient at this point to notice the charge brought against
Tennyson of remaining averse to the creed of Collectivism. The claims of
the individual to recognition are at no time less important than the similar
claims put forward on behalf of the community. But the epoch of Tennyson
exhibits a tendency towards communistic or socialistic extremes ; and again
it appears reasonable to admit that the laureate's neutral position was safest
and best. That it was a fairly neutral one might be gathered from the
eightieth couplet of " Locksley Hall Sixty Years After : "

" When the schemes and all the systems, kingdoms and republics fall,
    Something kindlier, higher, holier—all for each and each for all,"

though in such a passage as the following in " Merlin and Vivien," the indi-
vidual receives something less than his due—

    " But work as vassal to the larger love
    That dwarfs the petty love of one for one."

The relative importance of individualism and collectivism is admirably
stated in the following extract :

" Individuality, that is to say, conscience, applied alone, leads to anarchy ;
society, that is to say, tradition, if it be not constantly interpreted and
impelled upon the route of the future by the intuition of conscience, begets
despotism and immobility. Truth is found at their point of intersection. It
is forbidden, then, to the individual to emancipate himself from the social
object which constitutes his task here below, and forbidden to society to crush
or tyrannize over the individual."—MAZZINI, *Essays.*

(64) "Love thou thy Land" is again an expansion of the last two lines of the poem preceding, some of the reflections being due to Spedding. It would be difficult to find so much political and social good sense anywhere else in literature. In one respect at least these verses are worth all the writings of Burke; for while the old may easily look back to them with fond or bitter regret, the young may as easily learn them by heart, and become furnished not with opinions but, what is much more important, with the best foundations on which to build up opinions. Our age advances very rapidly, and the little poem was written many years ago; but if all boys and girls before they left their teens could be brought to absorb its few stanzas, we might look forward with more confidence to the future.

(66) "England and America in 1782" dates English freedom from Hampden. The third stanza in "Of old sat Freedom," speaks of the "grave mother of majestic works" as god-like in respect of dominion, and king-like in respect of polity.

The real truth will be found in the fourth stanza of the same poem, "The wisdom of a thousand years Is in them." Whatever measure of freedom England may possess, her people have achieved it; freedom is not conferred by a government nor even bought with the blood of a patriot.

(66) "The Goose" is a lively allegory of commerce and free trade. "Alfred," said Fitzgerald, "cannot trifle. . . . His smile is rather a grim one." There is just a little truth in Fitzgerald's remark, and we may fairly admit that in "The Goose" the poet smiles grimly; but the poem is much cleverer than anything else of the kind in the first two volumes.

We have now reached the last of the group headed "The Lady of Shalott and other poems." It may be convenient at this point to select from this group those pieces that were published, mostly in a much inferior form, in the volume of 1833. They are the following :— "The Lady of Shalott," "Mariana in the South," "The Miller's Daughter," "Fatima" (as "O Love, Love, Love") "Œnone," "The Sisters," "To ——," "The Palace of Art," "The May Queen," "New Year's Eve," "The Lotos-Eaters," "A Dream of Fair Women," "The Death of the Old Year," "To J. S." To these must be added (from "Juvenilia,") "Margaret," "Eleanore," "Rosalind," and four sonnets.

As the volume contained thirty pieces, there are yet several not included in the foregoing list. Of these by far the most important is " The Hesperides," a beautiful creation which has been noticed on p. 134. The following lines will be sufficient to show the many resemblances that this poem bears to the " Lotos-Eaters."

> " Father Hesper, Father Hesper, watch, watch, night and day,
> Lest the old wound of the world be healèd
> The glory unsealèd,
> The golden apple stol'n away,
> And the ancient secret revealèd.
> Look from west to east along :
> Father, old Himala weakens, Caucasus is bold and strong.
> Wandering waters unto wandering waters call ;
> Let them clash together, foam and fall.
> Out of watchings, out of wiles,
> Comes the bliss of secret smiles.
> All things are not told to all.
> Half-round the mantling night is drawn,
> Purplefringèd with even and dawn.
> Hesper hateth Phosphor, evening hateth morn."

Another of the lady portraits, " Kate," has some merit, and the lines " To Christopher North," otherwise Professor Wilson, possess a personal interest. Wilson had attacked Tennyson and some of his friends in a critique of the 1830 volume published in " Blackwood's Magazine "

for May, 1832. Tennyson was sneered at as " the pet of
a cockney coterie." The following is part of the poet's
reply :

> " When I learnt from whom it came,
> I forgave you all the blame,
>   Musty Christopher ;
> I could *not* forgive the praise,
>   Fusty Christopher."

This is smart and amusing ; but Tennyson was too great
to make capital of any such bickerings ; and although to
the last he never lost his extreme sensitiveness to criticism,
his future references to critics are usually more graceful, or
good-humoured or dignified.

One other poem in this volume of 1833 deserves
mention, but not on account of its merit, for its weakness
is phenomenal ; one might almost say it was thrown in
among the other pieces as a *morceau délicat* for some
hungry critic ; and critics were often ravenous in those
days. The mere title of the three stanzas, " O Darling
Room," is a commentary in itself ; we should like to
discover that the poem was of very early date, but,
strange to say, it was written on Tennyson's return from
the Continent in 1830.

> " For I the Nonnenwerth have seen,
> And Oberwinter's vineyards green,
> Musical Lurlei ; and between
> The hills to Bingen have I been,
> Bingen in Darmstadt, where the Rhene
> Curves towards Mentz, a woody scene.
>
> " Yet never did there meet my sight,
> In any town, to left or right,
> A little room so exquisite."

Besides the poems of the volumes of 1830 and 1833,
three pieces have to be noticed that were contributed to
" The Gem," a Literary Annual, in 1831. In the first,
" Anacreontics," the two lines

> " And drooping daffodilly,
> And silverleaved lily "

are evidently the precursors of

> " The yellow-leavèd waterlily
> The green-sheathèd daffodilly "

which we have seen in the first edition of " The Lady of Shalott." Otherwise the poem is not remarkable.

Much more interesting is " A Fragment." Though perhaps rather more Miltonic in style, it may be regarded as left over from " Timbuctoo." In its thirty-one lines we find the usual proportion of jewels re-set in after years :

> " Farsheening down the purple seas. . . ."

> "The great Pyramids
> Broadbased amid the fleeting sands, and sloped
> Into the slumbrous summernoon.'

> " Awful Memnonian countenances calm
> Looking athwart the burning flats. . . ."

> " Breathes low into the charmed ears of morn
> Clear melody flattering the crisped Nile."

The third of these pieces, a short lyric entitled " No More," will be found in the Appendix to Chapter VII.

In the same year, 1831, Tennyson contributed a sonnet, " Check every outflash, every ruder sally," to " The Englishman's Magazine " for August. In 1833 it was reprinted in " Friendship's Offering." As a sonnet it is not excellent, but it describes the valley where " first I told my love." The first three lines lend a sentiment to the Lotos eaters—

> " Speak low, and give up wholly
> Thy spirit to mild-minded melancholy,"

and in " The crispèd waters whisper musically," we recognize some of the poet's favourite phrases.

In the year 1832 two sonnets were published, " Me my own fate to lasting sorrow doometh," in " Friendship's

Offering," and "There are three things which fill my heart with sighs," contributed to "The Yorkshire Literary Annual." The first of these, like the sonnet "Check every Outflash," seems to strike a personal note—

"But yet my lonely spirit follows thine ; "

and the second reads like a reminiscence of the continental tour with Hallam—

"Of late such eyes looked at me—while I mused . . .
In old Bayona nigh the southern-sea."

APPENDIX TO CHAPTER IV.

A SHORT ANALYSIS OF "THE TWO VOICES."

Stanza (1) Death is the only remedy for ill. (2) But . am so wonderfully made. (3) So are dragon-flies. (6, 7) But man is better than they. (8-11) Man is not the highest life ; and of men there are plenty better than you. (12) Yet no two men are alike. (13, 14) But who will miss you? (15) What hope of answer or redress? (16, 17) Death is the only remedy for ill. (18, 19) I might do better in the future. (19) No ; your disease is past cure. (20, 21) "So many worlds, so much to do, So little done, such things to be !" (22-24) For all that you must die, and know little of the wonder that will be. (25, 26) Yet —for one hour—I strive— (27-33) Truth will never be found—and least of all by you. (34) A selfish death is dishonour. (35-39) A loathsome life is worse. (40-52) Might I not do some good before I die? (53-67) Good intentions ; but they fade with life away ; and truth flies faster than men may follow. To die is best. (68-75) But some have done well. (76) It was mere chance.

(77-80) Death may be worse than life. (81-88) The dead are at rest. (89-105) Yet in that sleep of death what dreams may come. Our yearning for immortality is the one sure proof of immortality. (106-111) Where were you before birth? To begin implies an end. (112-128) Eternal process moving on, From state to state the spirit walks. (192) Mere dreams ; your pain is real. (130-133) But you cannot tell me what death is, nor what might become of my soul. Not death but better life is the world's desire. (134) "Behold, it is the Sabbath morn !" (135-154) "There's nothing we can call our own but love."

CHAPTER V.

THE VOLUME OF 1842, OR, "ENGLISH IDYLLS AND OTHER POEMS."

I. INTRODUCTORY. After the year 1833 no poetry was published by Tennyson until 1837, when he contributed the stanzas " O, that 'twere possible" to " The Tribute," and " St. Agnes " to " The Keepsake." Again he kept silence until 1842. In that year his famous third volume was given to the public.

During this interval of nearly ten years he had not been idle. In a letter to Aubrey de Vere, Monckton Milnes writes : " Tennyson composes every day, but nothing will persuade him to print, or even write it down." The last statement must not be taken literally ; part at least of " In Memoriam" was lovingly written and re-written at intervals between the years 1833 and 1842 ; many of the earlier poems were re-cast ; and by the end of the period the poet had prepared for the press the wonderful volume which is the subject of this chapter.

It was accompanied by a volume i. in two parts ; the first containing a selection from the volume of 1830, and the second from that of 1833. The two parts are entitled, (I.) Poems (published 1830) and (II.) Poems (published 1832). At the end of Part II. the following note appears :

" The second division of this volume was published in the winter of 1832. Some of the poems have been considerably altered. Others have been added, which, with one exception, were written in 1833." [1]

Volume II., which contained the new pieces, is also entitled " Poems ; " and the title of the two books together is, "Poems by Alfred Tennyson. In two volumes. London : Edward Moxon, Dover Street. MDCCCXLIII." The contents of the second or new volume are, " The Epic," " Morte D'Arthur," " The Gardener's Daughter," " Dora," " Audley Court," " Walking to the Mail," " St. Simeon Stylites," " The Talking Oak," " Love and Duty," "Ulysses," " Locksley Hall," " Godiva," " The Two Voices," " The Day-Dream," with its nine divisions, "Amphion," " St. Agnes' Eve" (the St. Agnes of 1837), "Sir Galahad," " Edward Gray," " Will Waterproof's Lyrical Monologue," " Lady Clare," " The Lord of Burleigh," " Sir Launcelot and Queen Guinevere," " A Farewell," " The Beggar Maid," " The Vision of Sin," " The Skipping Rope," " Move eastward, happy earth, and leave," " Break, break, break," " The Poet's Song." At the end of the volume the following note occurs : " The Idyl of 'Dora' was partly suggested by one of Miss Mitford's pastorals ; and the ballad of 'Lady Clare' by the novel of ' Inheritance.' "

II. FIRST ASPECT OF THE VOLUME—" LOCKSLEY HALL" (98). Possibly nothing better could be chosen as suggesting the most remarkable characteristic of Tennyson's third volume of poems than the well-known passage in Shakespeare's " As You Like It"—

> "*Jaques.* Yes, I have gained my experience.
> *Rosalind.* And your experience makes you sad."

Shakespeare was probably about thirty-five when he

---

[1] "You ask me why." . . . "Of old sat Freedom." . . . "Love thou thy land." . . "The Goose."

wrote "As You Like It;" a little older when he created "Hamlet."

Turning to "Locksley Hall," we find a very similar passage, although referred to the future :

> " He bears a laden breast
> Full of sad experience."

And there are many passages in the same poem, not so verbally alike, but of the same import, and pointed to the present.

Judging from the date, 1842, Tennyson was about thirty-three when he wrote "Locksley Hall," and we may suppose he was some ten years older when he created the nameless hero of "Maud," that poem "slightly akin to "Hamlet." [1] Like Shakespeare's Prince of Denmark, and this more modern Hamlet of Tennyson's "Maud," the disappointed lover in "Locksley Hall" finds that "the time is out of joint." [2]

Now, although, as will be explained in the chapter on "Maud," the age of the Prince of Denmark seems to grow maturer, like his character, as he plays the tragedy through, yet an average estimate would make him only a little younger than the author of "Hamlet." In the same way [3] the hero of "Locksley Hall" is only a little younger than the author of "Locksley Hall." Amy, moreover, is something like Ophelia, in life but not in death. Maud slightly resembles Ophelia in life and in death.

"Locksley Hall," therefore, is Tennyson's "As You Like It," wherein another Jaques is the forerunner of another Hamlet. But Tennyson's poem includes many passages suggestive of Hamlet ; let us, therefore, call it also "the first draft of 'Hamlet,'" and "Maud" the revised and enlarged tragedy.

[1] See Chapter X.
[2] "Locksley Hall," couplet 67. "Hamlet," I. v. 188. "Maud," I. i. 6, 8, 9. And we are tempted to add, not one of the three seemed the sort of man "to set it right."
[3] See the first Appendix to this Chapter.

From this point of view "Locksley Hall" is the most important poem in the volume, and the one to be studied first.

III. "LOCKSLEY HALL:" SUBJECTIVE. [1] The poem before us is a long soliloquy; one actor comes upon the stage, and pronounces one long speech; for the

[1] Although the terms *subjective* and *objective* have become a little worn with usage, they are nevertheless convenient; and a few prefatory remarks may serve to explain their application to the subject of the present section.

We are sometimes too ready to believe that an artist must be altogether impersonal, objective; that he is a being indifferent towards his creations, and apart from them; that the poet-singer, for example, is

> "Not a whit
> More in the secret than yourselves, who sit
> Fresh-chapleted to listen."
>
> ROBERT BROWNING.

As usual, the truth lies midway between two extremes. "Poetry," says John Stuart Mill, "is overheard." That is to say, the poet speaks to himself, or from the lips of his characters; his utterance is oracular, indirect; and those who would know the secrets of his heart must listen with a most sympathetic and long-accustomed ear: and they must listen to all he has to say.

To all; that is a very important point. He who would form an independent opinion of the personal element in any one poem or passage, must begin by knowing all that the writer has written. If possible, he should not miss a single line the poet has penned. He should examine verses unpublished or withdrawn, for these have a peculiar power of casting light. He should notice changes made in later editions; he should become familiar with the poet's habit of expressing himself in any one dramatic piece by carefully studying his other monologues, mono-dramas, and dramas: in short, as far as possible, he should know the whole work, and the man from his work. Hence he may expect to find that opinions vary, and that his own opinion will be subject to modification as he pursues his studies year after year.

Of course some poets, Milton and Byron, for instance, are more personal than others; but none can be regarded as impersonal throughout. Shakespeare's biography may be read in his works; or, in a shorter form, by the aid of "A Midsummer Night's Dream," "Hamlet," and "The Tempest," studied in connection with the Sonnets.

Again, some forms of poetry are more personal than others. In the ordinary lyric, the poet is expected to overflow with his own emotion; in epic and narrative he is a story-teller, but he may tell the story so as to suggest something quite apart from it, or he may make occasional reflections of his own, or, even put them into the mouth of one of his characters; and this is true, though in a less degree, of the drama.

other characters, for plot, for change of scene, we have to trust, and often in vain, to his descriptions. What, for example, could be vaguer, more unlikely, more un-dramatic than the first and the seventy-third couplets of "Locksley Hall?" Tennyson calls such poems "*Dramatic* Monologues;" but is the one character a *dramatic* character at all? he is merely a portrait made to speak. The difference between such a character as he is repre-sented, or as he represents himself, and the same character in drama proper, where he plays his *part*, is the difference between the portrait and the life. Character is developed or discovered only by contact with character, and life by the environment of life. As it is easier to draw the one character, the portrait, than to draw life, so Shake-speare in some of his earlier plays created only one character, and allowed the rest of the *dramatis personæ* to remain puppets. For the same reason Tennyson's dramatic attempts are for many years limited to the monologue.[1] He has called "Maud" a "monodrama;" it is strictly speaking a monologue. All that is added to the monologue is a lyrical scene-shifter,[2] if we may so phrase it.

These monologues are peculiarly adapted to a subjective treatment. Through the lips of his one "character," who, to suit his purpose, will usually be overdrawn, the poet may safely utter his own more daring thoughts, his stronger emotions; and then, whenever convenient, he will call his character to correction.[3]

---

[1] "The Princess" might to some appear an exception, but the question as to whether the story is told consistently will be discussed in Chapter VII.

[2] Change of mood, as well as change of scene or incident, are often announced by a new lyric with a new form.

[3] In drama proper, on the other hand, it is much more difficult for the writer to project himself into a character. Except in the temporary dramatic suspension of the soliloquy (and not then necessarily), so incessant is the action of each character on all the others, and so directed to subserve the dramatic issues, that any conscious modification of this action on the part of

In order to determine between the subjective and objective elements in such a poem as a monologue, we first ascertain the poet's general tendency by glancing at the whole of his work. In Tennyson's case the examination leads us to expect a personal motive. Then we ask, " under what circumstances was the poem written ? Is it accompanied by other poems having a similar motive ? " For ten years Tennyson has been almost silent ; " Much has he thought, much suffered." [1] We may therefore expect to find some poem standing in the same relation to his 1830 and 1833 volumes, as Shakespeare's " Hamlet " to " Love's Labour's Lost." He has lived long enough and sadly enough to begin to find fault with life.

Now we inquire of other pieces contemporary, or nearly so, with " Locksley Hall." To begin with, the first song in " Audley Court " is just another smaller " Locksley Hall." In " The Epic," the realm of religion is invaded by science, and there is a " general decay of faith Right through the world." In " Walking to the Mail," they that loved " At first like dove and dove were cat and dog " ; the man, we are told, was " Vexed with a morbid devil in his blood, That veil'd the world with jaundice " (we may note the same figure, " jaundice," in " Locksley Hall ") ; he had married, ten years before, the daughter of a cottager. And what was the result ? she " sour'd To what she is." " Like breeds like, they say. Kind nature is the best " (all this is in " Locksley Hall "). In the same poem is mention of " A Chartist pike " ; " the raw mechanic's bloody thumbs " that " sweat on his blazon'd chairs : " of the " two parties "—" those that want and those that have,"

the author is destructive of dramatic effect. Drama then ceases to be an organic growth, actual life ; it becomes merely a representation of life by means of painted bricks cunningly pieced together. Unconsciously to himself, however, as often in Shakespeare's case, the creator's intense and ruling emotion may be expressed in his creation as far as some one leading character is concerned.

[1] Letter of Margaret Fuller, August, 1842.

which "still divide the world"—"The same old sore."
To this we may add the six lines beginning

> "His nerves were wrong. What ails us who are sound."

"Edwin Morris" (printed in 1851) furnishes equally significant material,

> "Something of a wayward modern mind
> Dissecting passion."

Our space does not permit fuller quotation ; but those who glance at the poem will discover another Ophelia, another Maud, who "Moved Like Proserpine in Enna gathering flowers." And here we may quote from "Maud," "What is it he cannot buy" ;[1] for the lady is sold for £60,000, to "slight Sir Robert with his watery smile." Trustees and aunts and uncles preach down the daughter's heart.

"St. Simeon Stylites," though sufficiently objective, is placed before us as a man who thought he found his highest duty in forsaking his highest duty. Another poem—of which we scarcely dare to speak—"Love and Duty"—says of Duty, "O this world's curse." That duty seemed to lie in sacrificing true love upon the altar of untrue marriage, or, more exactly, an alien love on the altar of lawful marriage. "The Golden Year" (printed in 1846) despairs of "the feverous days." The better days to be are "not in our time, nor in our children's time." And the poem concludes, as in "Locksley Hall," with a plea for action in the present : "Howsoever these things be . . . I go."[2] Ulysses moreover, when we meet with him, is yearning "to seek a newer world."

It should here be stated in passing that there is little of religion in "Locksley Hall" and in many of the other poems that group themselves around it ; that subject is

---

[1] See "Maud," Part I. X. ii. Also reference to this passage on p. 160.
[2] "Locksley Hall," 95 and 97.

fully dealt with in the desperate struggle between "The Two Voices"; also in "In Memoriam."

To resume the former running comment, we may next notice that "The Day Dream" pleads with utility in behalf of beauty;[1] and that in "Amphion" the poet asserts

> " 'Tis vain ! in such a brassy age
> I could not move a thistle."

Possibly if "Will Waterproof" had been drinking water instead of port, we should have had a very different sketch of the times : even as it is, not everything looks rosy through the roseate wine. And just because the flagon (that held a pint) is empty,

> "With self at strife
> I take myself to task,"

a proceeding which is continued through some five stanzas.

The poem "To ——, after reading a Life and Letters" (printed 1849), doubts whether the times are such as make the poet's name worth the winning. "Lady Clare" tells us how Lord Ronald was rewarded for being true to true love. "The Lord of Burleigh" likewise stooped, but he played true love false—just ever so little. "King Cophetua" was more fortunate with his beggar maid.

The lines, "Come not, when I am dead" (printed in 1851), grow in meaning if read with the following passage on which they appear to be based :

> " Here lies a wretched corse : of wretched soul bereft !
> Seek not my name : a plague consume you wicked caitiffs left !
> Here lie I, Timon ; who, alive, all living men did hate :
> Pass by, and curse thy fill ; but pass, and stay not here thy gait."
> *Timon of Athens.*

A somewhat similar sentiment finds expression in Shakespeare's sonnets. Over these Tennyson brooded often at this period, as we gather from "In Memoriam."

---

[1] " Science grows, and Beauty dwindles."
Locksley Hall Sixty Years After.

"The Vision of Sin" forms a fitting climax to this long array of poems that deal, most of them, and more or less directly, with the mystery of evil.

All the foregoing poems used to be regarded as belonging to the volume of 1842. They have therefore been grouped together. "Break, Break, Break," might be added ; but, sacred to the memory of Hallam, it finds a place in the chapter on "In Memoriam." The lonely melancholy of "A Farewell" may also be mentioned ; it probably belongs to the year 1837, when

> "Leaving these, to pass away,
> I think once more he seems to die."
> *In Memoriam*, c. y.

Glancing now at other poems near enough in date to be regarded as contemporary with the volume of 1842, we first notice the mournful and remarkable stanzas contributed by Tennyson in 1837 to "The Tribute —A Collection of Miscellaneous Unpublished Poems by Various Authors." They are well known as being the nucleus of "Maud," and they are fully treated of in Chapter X.

"Tears, Idle Tears" must next be mentioned ; its tenderly regretful music flowing from the illimitable years, found a place in "The Princess" in 1847, but it was probably of earlier date. It is fully considered in the Appendix to Chapter VII.

Some short poems published a little later,[1] patriotic and war-like, give further evidence of influence exerted by contemporary events ; as also do the subjects of war and patriotism generally, which will be mentioned in the chapter on "Maud." Meanwhile, the questions to be dealt with as arising out of "Locksley Hall" are chiefly social. They appear again in the "Enid and Nimuë" of 1857, the "Idylls of the King" of 1859, and the "Sea Dreams" of 1860. When we reach "Aylmer's Field" of

[1] "Britons, guard your own" (1852); "The Third of February" (1852); "Hands all Round" (1852) ; "The War" (1859).

1864, we hear the curse first pronounced in "Locksley Hall" upon "the social wants that sin against the strength of youth," repeated with terrible emphasis :

> "He believed
> This filthy marriage-hindering Mammon made
> The harlot of the cities : nature crost
> Was mother of the foul adulteries
> That saturate soul with body."

At "Aylmer's Field" we pause ; it is the latest of the longer poems that have links with "Locksley Hall" ; and to complete the list, we now add the earlier long poems of the period, "The Princess," "In Memoriam," "Maud." The four "Idylls" might well be cited in this connection ; but we will leave them in the region of romance, and briefly show how closely the other four are related to "Locksley Hall." This must be done very generally ; possibly by a single quotation. From "The Princess," for example, we might choose the very short passage "Ourselves are full Of social wrong." "In Memoriam" includes most of the topics of "Locksley Hall" ; the quotation chosen shall be similar to that from "The Princess :" "Ring out old shapes of foul disease" (cv). As to "Maud," a just comparison between that poem and "Locksley Hall" would require a separate chapter. The poems are probably separated by a narrower space of years than the dates 1842 and 1855 seem to imply. Each ostensibly is a love story in which love is undone because the guardians of love have

> "Two eyes for your banker,
> And one chilly glance for yourself ; "

and in each poem the moody hero exclaims "Frailty, thy name is woman," and is then tempted to add, "Man delights not me, nor woman neither." [1] Strange characters both, but for the fact that none could better play the part

---

[1] "Thanks, for the fiend best knows whether woman or man be the worse."
Maud, I. iv. 19.

of mouthpiece for the poet. The lover in "Maud" also resembles the unheroic prince in "The Princess," who is redeemed by love after terrible illness ; loses, for example, his "haunting sense of hollow shows," as the lover in "Maud" loses to some extent his "old hysterical mock-disease." But to return to "Locksley Hall" and "Maud." There is the same outcry in each against almost exactly the same social abuses : and the same distrust in Science, though this is more decided in the later poem ;[1] there is the same consideration[2] of the possible benefits of commerce : of the more possible benefits of war ; of patriotism as the moving spring of noble life. In each the love motive is often overmastered by some other, such as patriotism, or war. In "Maud," for instance, as will be seen in Chapter X., although Maud looks down from the regions of her rest and cheers her lover, yet the complete cure of the "disease" is left to a patriotic war ; and very strange indeed is the effect of the close of the poem. So in "Locksley Hall," the chief and the final hope of noble life is contained in the two words, "I go,"[3] to which we are bound to add, with your merry comrades ; and, we may suppose, to fight somebody somewhere. But this most interesting comparison between Tennyson's first and second "Hamlet" must not be carried further. It remains to glance again at the fourth long poem, "Aylmer's

---

[1] Compare—

"There methinks would be enjoyment more than in this march of mind,"
Locksley Hall, 83.

with

"But these are the days of advance, the works of the men of mind ; "
Maud, I. i. 7.

in the first we have only the expression of doubt ; in the second of ironical conviction.

[2] Also in "The Princess," "Those two crowned twins, Commerce and Conquest."

[3] "Let it flame or fade" at the end of "Maud" corresponds exactly to "Howsoever these things be" at the end of "Locksley Hall."

Field " : from which may be quoted a passage appropriate not only to the more important but also to the lesser of these many "poems of circumstance," as they might almost be called ; in all of them we may fairly say that Tennyson

> "Dash'd his angry heart
> Against the desolations of the world." [1]

And now, in the face of such overwhelming evidence, which will be considerably strengthened in the chapter on " Maud," we may reasonably conclude that the chief motive of " Locksley Hall " is to be found in that part of the subject matter which was contemporary ; which had been accumulating for many years ; which for many years had invaded and pervaded the poet's life ; which found expression, more or less full and distinct, in almost all the poems he wrote at that period.

But what of the second " Locksley Hall "?—was that written under the same circumstances ? Precisely, is our reply. It bears the same relation as the first " Locksley Hall " does to the time in which it was written, and the poems near to it in date. The fitting character could be created at any time ; and in " Locksley Hall Sixty Years After," Tennyson gathered together the sadder topics of the day, the sombre reflections scattered among many contemporary poems, and then once more

> " Bore down in flood, and dash'd his angry heart
> Against the desolations of the world."

Whatever he may have been in actual life, Tennyson is seldom joyous in his poetry ; there he thinks deeply, feels soberly, takes the time seriously.[2]

IV. "LOCKSLEY HALL," OBJECTIVE. At the risk of weakening our argument we place this inquiry in the second place, thus securing a fuller advantage to a generally received opinion. But to regard " Locksley Hall "

---

[1] " Aylmer's Field," 633, 634.

[2] " His also habitual gaze at life in its deeper aspects, which else would almost have overwhelmed him with awe."—MR. KNOWLES *of Tennyson.*

as a work of impersonal art is exceedingly difficult ; the subjective motive cannot be lost sight of long together. Nor can we view it aright under this head without including within our range of vision the companion poems, " Maud," " Aylmer's Field," " Locksley Hall Sixty Years After." It will be best to sketch the story first, and then examine the leading characters.

It is a well-known story, as noticed in the former section ; it is told by Tennyson several times over. It finds a place, though with a difference, even in " Locksley Hall Sixty Years After " :

> " Jilted for a wealthier ! wealthier ?"

A man and woman have known each other perhaps since they were boy and girl together. The result is love. The currents of their being flow on in one fair strong stream. But as long ago as Shakespeare's time,

> "The course of true love never did run smooth,
> But, either it was different in blood . . .
> Or else it stood upon the choice of friends."
>
> *Midsummer Night's Dream*, I. i. 134.

A " choice " determined by a too eager regard for gold, and a too light regard for the intensest and the holiest emotion of human life. If the girl is weak, she forsakes her lover and marries a fortune ;[1] if she is strong, she remains true, and dies ; and this with more or less of heroism ; for often the fashion of it looks clandestine in a day like ours.

Such, in brief, is the story of " Maud," " Aylmer's Field," " Locksley Hall," and some other poems near the date of 1850.[2]

---

[1] Was Amy so much to blame ! "Amy loved me, Amy fail'd me ; Amy was a timid child."

[2]   "These had been together from the first ;
      They might have been together till the last."
                              Aylmer's Field, 713, 714.

This is the tale as told by " Maud," " Locksley Hall," and " Aylmer's Field." There is no such pathos of relation between the lovers in " The Gardener's Daughter."

The subject, however, as introduced into " Locksley Hall Sixty Years After " is different ; the woman is not weak, but vicious, " A worldling, born of worldlings."

" She that holds the diamond necklace dearer than the golden ring " (11).

In this later poem, moreover, the lover is said to be " of easier, earthlier make."

Our brief consideration of the theme as such has now brought us to the border of the former section, for the fact that the poet tells the story with a purpose more conscious than a mere art motive, is here again forced upon us, first from the frequency with which he tells it, and next, because the moral of " marriage-hindering mammon" may always be read in some irrelevant passage.

In " Locksley Hall " and " Maud " a remedy is proposed for wounded love ; in the former it is a prospect of progress due mostly to science ; in " Maud," where the poet's faith in science has been shaken, it lies in the energizing of a nation by war. In " The Princess," we may add, which dates between the two,

" The sport half-science, fill me with a faith . . ."

while again, in " In Memoriam," science fills the poet with a doubt ;

" A higher hand must make her mild
If all be not in vain."

In " Aylmer's Field " the poet's best hope seems to be expressed by the saying " marriages are made in Heaven." [1]

And lastly, in " Locksley Hall Sixty Years After," no hope is left in science or commerce ; none is suggested by war ; none by the present anywhere, except in a goodness itself exceptional ; what other hope there may be is withholden in the future.

[1] Line 188.

From the story we turn to the characters ; as a general statement at the outset, we may say that most of them spoil the story. " Locksley Hall" and " Maud" contain some of the finest poetry ever written about early love, and in each poem love is slain by the very hero himself. The poet who could write :

> " First love, first friendship, equal powers
> That marry with the virgin heart "

would hardly do fair justice to " first love : " his lovers are extravagant ; those they love are disappointing. The hero of " Locksley Hall" stultifies his position ; he is the sport of moods which " vary Mostly for the worse":

> " The fires of youth, the follies, furies, curses, passionate tears." [1]

The moods of Maud's lover vary yet more for the worse. One has hardly the patience to point them out. As to " Aylmer's Field," the lover there does not make himself a lunatic ; and why ? simply because his brother acted as Tennyson's spokesman, and spoke to the extent of some hundred and fifty lines, and spoke pretty plainly. That is just the difference : in " Aylmer's Field " the poet had no motive for making the lover a caricature. We look on to " Locksley Hall Sixty Years After ; " in this poem, as in " Locksley Hall " and " Maud ", there is only the one character through whom the poet may find utterance for impatient long-pent emotion, and therefore that character is again a caricature.

Tennyson, say some, allowed the lover to rave and exaggerate in " Locksley Hall," in order that he might represent him in " Locksley Hall Sixty Years After" as a man whom time had made wiser, kinder, and more worthy to be loved. But surely Time, the physician, never had a more unsatisfactory patient ; it would be much easier to show that sixty years had made Amy's

---

[1] " Locksley Hall Sixty Years After " (20).

lover sixty years older and not a year wiser.[1] Certainly he does caution his grandson in reference to the past,— "Youthful jealousy is a liar," but of himself in that present he confesses,—

> " Heated am I ? you—you wonder—well, it scarce becomes mine age— Patience ! let the dying actor mouth his last upon the stage."

> " Cries of unprogressive dotage ere the dotard fall asleep."

Lovers of Tennyson take not so much exception at the cries of the dotard ; but they bear it ill that two of the otherwise most entrancing love poems in our literature, "Locksley Hall" and "Maud," should be made to ring false because of the unaccountable moodiness of the lover, a moodiness—and here again we return to the former section—that after all is accountable when we regard the character as an exponent of the poet's own opinions.

The lover in "Locksley Hall" is inclined to believe[2] that "woman is the lesser man"—"Here, at least, where nature sickens, nothing ; " and a contemporary poem speaks of the "Wayward modern mind, Dissecting passion." The first of these doctrines, we are sure, is not entirely Tennyson's own ; the second, he entirely condemns:

> " Your modern amourist is of easier, earthlier make."

For he held by an older doctrine, and himself could look back upon the time[3]

> " When passion first waked a new life through his frame."

Then why did he not leave us at this maturer period a poem of young love at once passionate and sane ? Because he was so engrossed with his Hamlets.[4]

---

[1] Edith, to whom the work of redemption was left conjointly with Time,— " Nurse of ailing body and mind " (Couplet 26)—does not seem to have been much more successful.

[2] Couplets 75, 76, 77.

[3] As in the sonnet "Check every outflash . . ." (p. 145).

[4] "The Gardener's Daughter" and the new version of "The Miller's

But Shakespeare, who was dowered with the love of this love, left us more than one such poem. And it is curious that his notable play without a heroine is the play that passionately idealizes a friend. Just for a little he lost his faith in woman; he forsook Ophelia for Horatio; but he never did it again. And from Romeo and Juliet to Ferdinand and Miranda, what lovelier pictures were ever drawn of love? Let us be tremblingly thankful that love—this love [1]—was made immortal by Shakespeare.

V. CONCLUSION. Although Tennyson must seem to have spoilt the impression of these three monologues, "Maud" and the two "Locksley Hall's," by too much suspicion of motive, they are nevertheless remarkable poems. And although he does not say enough about the good that is brought forth of evil, and seems sometimes to forget his own maxim,

> " It is better to fight for the good than to rail at the ill,"

yet there is left in them enough of wisdom and beauty to charm us into grateful admiration. Nor does the leading character in "Locksley Hall" lose altogether his individuality or his attractiveness. He is young enough to have a future before him, and buoyant enough to have some belief in it. To praise the poem in detail would be impossible here, even if fifty years of praise had not made praise something like presumption. It will be enough to say that "Locksley Hall" is one of Tennyson's greatest

---

Daughter " might at first seem exceptions; yet these give not the passion of young love, but merely recollections of love in age. "Love and Duty" is a mystery; "The Talking Oak" a lovely trifle. Further, it is a very notable fact that in all these poems the speaker is a man ; and further, as will be seen in "The Princess," the man's attitude is always patronising—never naturally passionate. Hence also Tennyson's women are never heroic like Shakespeare's.

[1] We do not forget our gratitude to Tennyson for the love he made immortal ; the love of a friend in " In Memoriam," and in " Rizpah " the love of a mother.

successes ; one of the most original, most fascinating, most popular short poems of our time.

It was a poetical surprise and delight, one of those fortunate poems that everybody reads, and concerning which some one tells you with enthusiasm, "I shall never forget the first time I read it." Of these "fortunate" poems Tennyson has written a remarkable number. Shakespeare and Milton in our literature, and some five or six masters of song in other literatures are of course excepted when we make the assertion that it is impossible for any man, reader or critic, to keep fairly in mind the beauty, originality, variety, and extent of the poetic treasures bequeathed to his fellow millions by this one poet. The maker of a book about Tennyson may be pardoned if now and then he puts aside the weights and measures of judgment, and pauses merely to admire.

VI. OTHER ASPECTS OF THE VOLUME OF 1842. THE REMAINING POEMS :—The later explanatory title, "English Idylls and Other Poems," points to a second important characteristic of the volume of 1842. The term "idyll," which is so largely employed by Tennyson, meant in the original Greek, "little picture." In the sense of little pictures of life it was applied to the bucolic and love poetry of Theocritus, which deals chiefly with the life of shepherds, and mostly uses pastoral scenery for the background of the picture. This poetry, which was essentially natural, found many imitators, such as Virgil. It then lost its naturalness, admitted political, moral and philosophical elements ; and in the hands of many English writers of pastoral verse became an insipid jingle of artifice and convention.

The modern idyll seeks chiefly to expel artifice and restore nature. Southey, accepting a hint from the German idylls, wrote eight eclogues, which may be regarded as the precursors of Tennyson's idyllic poems. Some of Crabbe's tales are idyllic, as also are some of

Wordsworth's.   Tennyson, however, has widely extended the province of the idyll, so that it includes such various compositions as the "small sweet Idyl" of "The Princess," and the epical series of Arthurian poems.

One definition of the term "idyll" will be found on p. 201; and the following may serve as another; but a precise definition of this form of poetry in Tennyson seems impossible :—"An idyll is a picture in verse of the simpler, purer, and more natural life that is always associated with the country ; and the scenes amid which that life is laid will interpret and harmonise with its emotions."

Such are most of the idylls in this volume ; and we may therefore expect a certain number of poems developing in various directions the type already introduced in "The Miller's Daughter" ; poems of modern English life, fresh, simple, and of pure affection ; and made one with everything that is beautiful in nature.   Of these the best example is "The Gardener's Daughter."

Modern English life is also represented in poetry of a conversational half-idyllic character, such as "Edwin Morris" and "Walking to the Mail."   These pieces are strikingly novel.   In "Will Waterproof's Lyrical Monologue" Tennyson's fine faculty of humour appears for the first time ; and in "Morte d'Arthur," the book further affords an earnest of the Arthurian idylls.

This volume of 1842, containing as it did so much that was new and at the same time magnificent, easily established Tennyson's position as a poet of a very high order. Moreover, although most of the poems were to undergo a good deal of revision, they were on the whole much more highly finished than those of the former volumes : and, what was also important, with the exception of "The Skipping Rope," they offered little that could provoke hostile criticism.

Finally, the poet had profited greatly by criticism and by ten years of toil ; in the new poems the mannerisms that were so painfully abundant in the two earlier volumes become less frequent, and in some cases disappear altogether ; there is less straining after effect, and more of the serious business of poetry ; melody does not so often attempt to free itself from matter ; the whole volume is pervaded by yet higher refinement, truth, seriousness, nobleness ; and, to return to the former section of this chapter, if Tennyson's experience has made him sad, it has also made him a greater poet.

Nor must another important cause of his somewhat sudden renown be forgotten ; it has already been remarked that the volumes of 1830 and 1833 which now reappeared as " Volume I.," were increased in value threefold. But to measure poetic value in any such definite way is not enough ; it would be easier and probably truer to say that the revised edition of the earlier poems was almost as new and remarkable as the additional volume of 1842.

Three volumes, therefore, we might almost say, were now sent forth at once : and with these Tennyson could challenge all or most of the poets his contemporaries, among whom, though some had almost ceased to write, were redoubtable names, such as Wordsworth ; and the following list of possible competitors, formidable or otherwise, is not uninteresting:—Southey, Landor, Leigh Hunt, Monckton Milnes, Browning, Elizabeth Barrett, Lytton, Sir H. Taylor, Mackay, P. J. Bailey, Sterling, Hood, Campbell, Ruskin.

(67) "The Epic,"—(68) "Morte d'Arthur" (see " Idylls of the King," Chapter XI.).

(72) "The Gardener's Daughter ; or, The Pictures."—The second of these titles seems to suggest the motive of the poem. The subject of the idyll is " A Rose in Roses ;" that is to say, the poet wants to paint a beautiful woman in suggestive and equally beautiful

surroundings. Compared with what he intends to accomplish now, his former sketches, with one or two exceptions, are a mere jingle of words; among the exceptions are The Miller's Daughter, Aphrodite, and Cleopatra. Further, the whole picture as in " The Miller's Daughter," is to be suffused with the glow of young love. What story will suit? it must be of the slenderest, for he intends to paint rather than articulate ; then he had better borrow incidents from actual painting, and thus disguise his intent, or draw a parallel to it. Hence the pictures ; hence the artist story-teller, for he may enlarge the pictorial element as he proceeds ; hence, as a further disguise, the second artist, who paints his pictures also. But the story is a little improbable, and after all too evidently a makeshift ; yet, in its kind, this poetry is matchless. We have a picture, let us say, rather than a poem ; modern poets have often succeeded in expressing emotion, too subtle for definite thought, by a kind of word-music ; here, instead of articulate emotion we have word-painting. Naturally, therefore, rhyme or quick movement will be out of place where a pictorial effect is aimed at ; it is too obviously musical ; and we have stately blank verse accordingly.

But the poem has other perfections, and too numerous to mention ; it has also some of the faults with which we are familiar ; and other poets are laid under contribution much as in the earlier volumes. Of these the chief is Milton. For example, " Paradise Lost," iv. 268-270 :

> " That fair field
> Of Enna, where Proserpine gathering flowers,
> Herself a fairer flower . . . "

may be compared with " A Rose in Roses." That the passage was in Tennyson's thoughts might be seen from another imitation in " Edwin Morris," " Like Proserpine in Enna gathering flowers." " Leaves that tremble round a nightingale," would be Milton's " Airs, vernal airs,

Attune the trembling leaves." While under the spell of such beauty as lives in every line of " The Gardener's Daughter," we do wisely to remember the yet more abun-dant and more enchanting beauties of " Paradise Lost."[1]

(77) " DORA."—Tennyson's bent is towards simplicity ; yet his worst faults appear in his simpler styles. His chief weakness is weakness ;[2] and this weakness will naturally assert itself in such simple poems as " Dora," where self-consciousness of manner has not been altogether refined away. "' Locksley Hall Sixty Years After" has twice the strength and much of the beauty of " Locksley Hall " ; " The Ancient Sage " is worth a score of " Two Voices " ; " Lucretius " can rival " Tithonus " and more than rival " Enoch Arden " ; and a stanza of " Rizpah " might to some seem a fair exchange for " Dora." " Dora " is a kind of poem about which we might say, that had the poet written that one only, it would have given us a dif-ferent impression ; the author of " Dora," and not Words-worth only, would have exposed himself to the amusing mimicry of the brothers Smith—

> " Papa (he's my papa and Jack's)
> Bought me, last week, a doll of wax,
> And brother Jack a top. . . ."

> " I saw them go ; one horse was blind,
> The tails of both hung down behind,
> Their shoes were on their feet."

The opening lines of " Dora," for example, read without context, might seem to hold bathos at bay ; but, looked

---

[1] The famous comparison,

> "That hair
> More black than ashbuds in the front of March,"

may seem more novel than exact. The ashbuds that adorn the brow or the early part of March, have a rusty and dusty brown-black appearance, which is more noticeable by comparison with Swinburne's figure for a lady's hair—

> " Clear now as the plume of a bright black bird."

[2] Page 53.

at 'more closely, and in connection with the rest of the poem, they are assuredly weak. To begin with, the repetition of any one set device in such a poem is enough to turn the scale. " With Farmer Allan at the farm abode William and Dora. William was his son,"—is good enough ; but towards the close we have, " And for three hours he sobb'd o'er William's child, Thinking of William." This reminds us too clearly of "farm" and "William," both repeated in the former passage. Again, the word "abode" is used a second time, perhaps intentionally, at the close ; but it is too special in its use, too biblical to bear such repetition. This judgment comes of a more general view : " yearned towards " in the first half-dozen lines is excessively biblical, as also is, " Then the old man was wroth," a few lines further on. To the remarks made upon the close of the poem may now be added a reference to the over-studied metrical prose of the last four lines. As to the repeated line, "And the sun fell, and all the land was dark," it would be majestic in its beauty in the " Idylls of the King ; " here its strain is of a mood much too high. If now we view these particulars (which might be increased almost indefinitely), as they appear in the poem as a whole, we are sensible that the style has not grown naturally out of the subject ; it is not what expression is to the features ; it is not as the spirit that irradiates the form.

The faults of " The Gardener's Daughter " were altogether different ; that was a much better poem ; weakness was rarely apparent ; there was a multitude of filed phrases that had been used before by the author, or would be used again ; some slight excess of natural description over motive and impulse—in other words, the poem was at times rather too objective to be the work of an artist in words ; and there was perhaps an unnecessary quantity of borrowed ornament. But the effort was as highly successful as it was novel

" Dora," as Tennyson informs us, was "partly sug-
gested" by "The Tale of Dora Creswell," in Miss
Mitford's "Our Village." One characteristic of the
verse would be anticipated by a consideration of its
simple style ; there is a very large proportion of mono-
syllables ; moreover the imagery is as plain as the style ;
and the vocabulary is essentially English.

(79) "AUDLEY COURT."[1] This idyll of plain modern
English life is both new and excellent. The story may
be partly if not wholly a means of introducing the songs,
especially when we remember the two songs in "The
Princess" that were sung at a picnic.[2] For these songs
are something almost if not quite new; they are blank
verse made fairly lyrical—to be made charmingly lyrical
in later volumes.[3] Already the second of the two antici-
pates the "Swallow Song" in "The Princess." At the
end is another well-known Tennysonian close, follow-
ing and making appropriate a bit of description other-
wise somewhat long, somewhat too emotional, but, as it
stands, real, admirable, beautiful. Exactly the same
device may be noticed at the end of "The Princess,"
where a yet more highly-coloured description is toned
down by three matter-of-fact lines and their concluding
"home well-pleased we went." And, generally, it will be
noticed that in all these idylls a perfect correspondence is
preserved between the subject, and the scenery and
imagery that adorns it. Many of the figures in this poem
are plain but fresh, and "breathing of the sea." " Sharper
than an eastern wind ;" "as a thorn Turns from the
sea;" "The pilot of the darkness and the dream ;" "the
cliffs that guard my native land ;" " I might as well have
traced it in the sands ;" "the sea wastes all."

[1] See also p. 153.
[2] Viz., "Tears, idle Tears," by Violet, and "The Swallow Song," by
the Prince, Canto IV.   [3] See Chapter VII., Appendix.

(81) "WALKING TO THE MAIL." This is another
Idyll, conversational or half-dramatic in form, which
brings us close—perhaps too close—to modern ordinary
English life. The humour is a little broad, as might be
expected between characters who are recollecting school
or college days, when one of them was "As cruel as a
school boy."

To the motive of the poem some reference is made on
p. 153 ; it may be discovered partly in the line that con-
tains words in italics, "*He* left *his* wife behind ;" also,
"That was the last drop in the cup of gall." In other
words, the poet deals first with unhappier relations be-
tween husband and wife than those of the Lord of Bur-
leigh ; next, with "the same old sore" that "breaks out
from age to age." At the close we note the reversion
from earnest moralizing to "three pyebalds and a roan."

(83) "EDWIN MORRIS ; OR, THE LAKE" [1] was first
published in the seventh edition of Poems, 1851. In this
idyll, as befits the occasion, the theme of "Locksley
Hall" receives lighter—perhaps happier—treatment :

"She seems a part of those fresh days to me."

Again we have a poem quite new in every particular ;
and a pleasant addition it is to the stores of English
poetry. Nothing very powerful or grand, perhaps, but—
and so are they all—a wonder of minute beauty, fine
imagination, wise thought, perfection of form. As, writing
these notes, we turn the pages over to glance for the
hundredth time at this succession of pieces original and
matchless of their kind, we become almost bewildered at
the "full cell'd honeycomb of eloquence Stored from all
flowers ; " especially when we remind ourselves that there
are yet to be noticed "The Talking Oak," "Love and
Duty," "Ulysses," "Tithonus," and many more. From

[1] See also p. 154.

this slight poem alone what a selection of apt or charming quotations might be made ! what vividness of gesture-painting, for example, in the lines, " Again with hands of wild rejection—Go !" but to begin quoting is easier than to end ; our attention, as often, must be limited to the close of the poem ; not intentionally commonplace this time ; for the last three lines sketch the returning spring and summer that bring back little Letty; only three lines, yet the enchantment of spring [1] and the light and colour and warmth and slumbrous beauty of summer are in them ; and they do not contain one among the many thousands of hackneyed expressions which the average poet must make use of when describing those seasons. Everything in the three lines is new, or newly put, and put with ravishing effect.

(85) "ST. SIMEON STYLITES." " A man's charity is in proportion to his knowledge ; the greater knowledge, the greater charity." Therefore when Tennyson paints for all time such types of mediæval religion as St. Simeon of the pillar, St. Agnes, Sir Galahad, and the rest, he will do it with some sympathy of charity. " Thou wilt not gash thy flesh for him," says the preacher in "Aylmer's Field ;" "for thine Fares richly, in fine linen." Macaulay says somewhere, " It made them a sect ; it left them a faction." Even the ways of doing God service will change with the times ; and what is at first a virtue may at the last become a ridiculous form. The days have been when men who would worship must flee into the desert ; the world has been so lustful that he who would save his soul from his body must triumph over his body altogether ; and St. Simeon on his pillar not only drew safely nearer to his God, but also was lifted up before men who could learn self-sacrifice and holiness in no other way. Cer-

---

[1] " Prime " recalls Milton's line

" The season, prime for sweetest scents and airs."

tainly Tennyson makes a poem out of the situation ; but
not quite as the Soul in the " Palace of Art " turns to a
vain and selfish æsthetic account whatever the past had
treasured of nobleness, faith, truth, beauty, and love. He
does three things : as an artist, he sets before us an ideal
representative of this class of ascetics ; as a moralist, he
makes clear to us their mistakes ; as a wise man, he
makes us feel kindly disposed towards them, even as he
almost certainly does himself.

" St. Simeon Stylites" will be found in Gibbon's " De-
cline and Fall of the Roman Empire ; " in those pages he
meets with no sympathy. The poem is a very clever in-
tellectual study ; that is its chief art, and from that we
must derive our chief pleasure.[1]

(88) "THE TALKING OAK." Spite of Goldsmith's
" Edwin and Angelina," and many other poems in which
this ballad stanza could not be regarded as a complete
success, Tennyson was determined to try its qualities ;
and, as usual, was completely successful.

The poem itself is one of the most delightful in the
volume ; dainty, graceful, and intensely English. The
well-known figure, "The flower she touch'd on," is not
quite like Scott's

> " E'en the slight harebell raised its head
> Elastic, from her airy tread,"

for it is a "pathetic fallacy ; " and as such is appropriate
enough in a poem about a " Talking Oak."[2]

Those who know Tennyson as a metrist would expect

---

[1] At the same time, it may be questioned whether such poetry is of a very
high order. Let prose remain the recognized medium for expressing in-
tellectual thought, and let what we prize most in poetry still be music, picture,
emotion, imagination. Or, if extremes are being dealt with, let us not be
blamed if, from the two forms of poetic excess, we choose a "harmonious
dance of words upon the brink of nonsense," before the rigid verses of un-
adorned reason.

[2] See also footnote, p. 78.

that in a poem of this length, some variations would be introduced in the rhythm of the short-lined and rather rigid stanza ; and such is the fact. " Like a golden butterfly," " The berried briony fold," are among the most important, and they are more daring than usual. As an example of condensed poetical material drawn from the past, we would select " All starry culmination drop Balmdews." This, unravelled, would make some half-dozen lines of prose. The figure, or part of it, occurs very frequently in Tennyson's poetry : " And balmy drops in summer dark Slide from the bosom of the stars."[1]

(92) " LOVE AND DUTY." (See also p. 154.) This poem seems to call for a good deal of criticism. Did the poet choose the subject as he chose the fragment of " Sappho " (p. 123), merely to exercise himself in the utterance of passionate love ; or was the subject prescribed for him ?

In either case the sentiment rings false. Among the many hard sayings of the Bible there is one to the effect that the man who has lawfully bound himself to one woman, and therewithal dwells fondly in his thought on another woman, is disloyal to the first. In other poets —especially if modern—the discrepancy might not be striking ; but one of Tennyson's greatest poems, the " Idylls of the King," tells how a kingdom fell in ruins because of the violation of the injunction " To love one only, and to cleave to her." And this doctrine, as will presently be seen, is maintained in all his other poems that deal with the relations between men and women. The subject is treated more fully in the notes on " The Wreck."

But apart from this moral aspect of the situation, how condescending is the attitude assumed by the man ; he

---

[1] " In Memoriam," xvii.

will take care of himself in his own way, but the woman **is** to do what he tells her, which amounts to little more **than** a vague looking forward.

The poem bears some resemblance to the "Farewell to Nancy" of Burns. Browning in "Evelyn Hope" and Swinburne in "The Triumph of Time," without contravening the most exacting morality, work out, each after his own method, a problem of love unfulfilled. In Tennyson's poem, if the words "behold thy bride" are not to be taken in their usual sense, the passion exhibited grows out of all proportion to motive. It will perhaps be best to abandon this part of the subject as a problem not worked out, merely adding from "The Gardener's Daughter" a short quotation which seems appropriate to any possible solution—

> " Not easily forgiven
> Are those, who, setting wide the doors that bar
> The secret bridal chambers of the heart
> Let in the day."

Again, as regards the form of the poem, although the work is splendid, it loses a little from the obtrusiveness of borrowed beauty.

Once more, the last few lines may be chosen for comment—four of them. The effect, as ever, is very fine; emotion dies away into the loveliness of great nature. And the material employed is exquisitely managed ; but it is not so new as in the passage at the end of "Edwin Morris." There we found the classical variant "Then while ;" here it is the more familiar and less poetical "Then when." But some further important remarks under this head will be reserved for a second appendix to the present chapter.

(94) "THE GOLDEN YEAR." In this admirable poem, which was first published in the Fourth Edition of "Poems," 1846, the poet has much to say on his own account. As

an Idyll, it is conversational, like "Edwin Morris," "Audley Court," and "Walking to the Mail," and like these contains much wisdom and sound sense, flavoured with a little dry humour. The lesson we learn from "The Golden Year" is an important one in any age ; and in every age it has found some one to teach it ; but no age should know it so thoroughly as our own. "Act, act in the living present," has become one of the religions of the nineteenth century. Yet no one looks back upon the past with dearer regret than Tennyson ; and none more yearningly towards the future. He does both in this poem ; and then, for his own behoof as well as for the advantage of the world at large, he sets old James in our midst :

> "What stuff is this !
> Old writers pushed the happy season back,—
> The more fools they,—we forward : dreamers both."

The passage, "Shall eagles not be eagles, wrens be wrens?" may be partly explained by Richard III. i. 69-72 :

> "The world is grown so bad
> That wrens make prey where eagles dare not perch :
> Since every Jack became a gentleman,
> There's many a gentle person made a Jack."

(95) ULYSSES. According to the poet and the friends of the poet, "Ulysses" is a portrait of Tennyson ; but there were many Tennysons, or at least two ; and a better likeness of the author of "Far-far-away" will be found in "Tears, Idle Tears." Those two poems come straight from the heart ; the others, such as "Ulysses," may be "drawn from the spirit through the brain." If Ulysses is a "gray spirit yearning in desire To follow knowledge,' we also have it on the poet's own authority that "Tears, Idle Tears" was written to express yearnings for the past. "Ulysses" fitly follows "The Golden Year," and affords a striking contrast to "The Lotos-Eaters." The modernized Greek "works, and feels he works."

This is a noble poem in conception and in execution, although its Ulysses is no more that ancient King of Ithaca than the Arthur of the idylls is King of Britain. Of the earlier Ulysses a dim legend may be read in Homer, and hints gained from Virgil and Horace ; and these poets are represented in Tennyson's verse. But the more modern figure has taken shape in Dante's " Inferno" (xxvi. 94-126), and to Dante Tennyson stands most indebted. The blank verse of the poem is admirably adapted to the character " Strong in will To strive, to seek, to find, and not to yield."

(96) " TITHONUS." How different is the soft sweet plaintive rise and fall, line after line, of the music of this infinite mournfulness—

> " Immortal age beside immortal youth."

In manner, this exquisite poem resembles the soliloquies in such Greek plays as those of Sophocles. " Ulysses" was a striking sketch of character ; in " Tithonus" we have rather the study of an emotion and its circumstances. The subject is found in the Homeric Hymn to Aphrodite, and it is splendidly treated by Tennyson ; nor will we mar his perfect work by detaching any portion for comment. Only a few incidental notes are added. In the setting of this classic theme the poet occasionally uses classic material : " The gods themselves cannot recall their gifts" may be supplied by the poet Agathon as quoted by Aristotle :

> μόνου γὰρ αὐτοῦ καὶ θεὸς στερίσκεται,
> ἀγένητα ποιεῖν ἅσσ' ἂν ᾖ πεπραγμένα,

" While Ilion like a mist rose into towers " :—This mist in " Œnone" is " a cloud that gathered shape " : and in Milton—to be imitated afterwards by Pope—

> " Anon out of the earth a fabric huge
> Rose like an exhalation."

The legend, without the mist, is in two lines of Ovid :

> " Ilion aspicies, firmataque turribus altis
> Mœnia, Phœbeæ structa canore lyræ."

And in "Gareth and Lynette" the city of Camelot was built "to the music of their harps."

As the poem is perhaps the most perfect specimen of poetic workmanship in all Tennyson, it may be supposed to be a product of his maturest period ; and in fact "Tithonus" was not published until 1860, when it appeared in the "Cornhill Magazine" for February of that year. Very slight alterations have been made ; the first line originally read, "Ay me, ay me, the woods decay and fall," a Tennysonian weakness that would have seriously impaired the poem, especially as the exclamatory phrases occur again in line 50.

(103) "GODIVA." The story is famous, and English, and one often told, yet not altogether a pleasant one. Sir William Dugdale ("Antiquities of Warwickshire," 1656) dates it about 1057 : and he gives a full account of Godiva's heroism, and of the baseness and prompt punishment of Peeping Tom of Coventry. Drayton also in his "Polyolbion" (1613, 1622) gives the legend at full length. Moultrie and Leigh Hunt both made it the subject of a poem, and both their poems should be compared with Tennyson's "Godiva." Elizabeth Barrett is said to have preferred Leigh Hunt's version to Tennyson's.

The poem has remained unaltered. The blank verse is in the poet's best idyllic manner ; the local colouring is the chief merit of the piece. "His beard a foot before him, and his hair A yard behind," "Then fillipp'd at the diamond in her ear," "He parted, with great strides among his dogs," "Like a summer moon, Half dipt in cloud," "And all the low wind hardly breath'd for fear,"

" The little wide-mouthed heads upon the spout,"—all
these and many more adorn a well-told story.

(104) " THE DAY DREAM." " Such is this elegant and
commonsense society, refined in comfort, regular in
conduct, whose dilettante tastes and moral principles
confine it within a sort of flowery border." Having
sketched our modern English society in these words,
amongst others, M. Taine proceeds to take the measure
of its favourite poet and of his poetry ; " Does any poet
suit such a society better than Tennyson. . . . The
ladies have been charmed by his portraits of women ;
they are so exquisite and pure . . . His poetry is like
one of those gilt and painted stands in which flowers of
the country and exotics mingle in artful harmony. . . . It
seems made expressly for these wealthy . . . heirs of the
ancient nobility. . . . It is an eloquent confirmation of
their principles, and a precious article of their drawing-
room furniture."

M. Taine was often dazzled by his own brilliance, but
never so much as when writing his famous chapter on
Tennyson. Certainly there is some truth in these para-
graphs ; besides, Alfred de Musset filled all the room of
all the critic's love. But Taine allows Tennyson so little ;
" We think of that other poet, away there in the Isle of
Wight, who amuses himself by dressing up lost epics."
He might as well have thought at the same time of
Virgil dressing up lost epics in a Sicilian or a Cam-
panian villa, anywhere away from Rome. He could not
see the second Tennyson, a man not of the people perhaps,
nor yet tortured by passion nor by pain—but him we know
as The Ancient Sage, Ulysses, Lucretius, as the case
might be. Let us however admit that the first Tennyson
or his Day Dream was an article of drawing-room
furniture ; such also is a rose ; and as the thought rises
in our minds, we turn to the poem before us, and there

we find the poet's best defence, and a " moral shut Within the bosom of the rose " :

> " Liberal applications lie
> In Art like Nature, dearest friend."

Alfred de Musset may make the heart bleed with pity or truth or pain unknown before ; Robert Browning may fortify the soul as with strong new wine; but Alfred Tennyson may create in us the love of loveliness; and where we could neither be frightened into conviction nor preached into practice, he may entice us into nobleness :

> " In spite of all
> Some shape of beauty moves away the pall
> From our dark spirits."
> (KEATS, *Endymion.*)

The "Day-Dream" contains other morals, which each "may find According as his humours lead."

This graceful, delicate, and delightful poem grew out of the section entitled "The Sleeping Beauty," which appeared with some differences in the volume of 1830.

(108) "AMPHION" is another poem with a moral. This is quite another way of enticing us into nobleness. Probably there does not exist in all literature a more charming short poem than the one preceding ; as to the merit of its successor we must be in some doubt. It has been improved in form, and contains many humorous touches ; but the humour is somewhat heavy; and here again the poet's smile is "a grim one." Still, the poem is excellent work in many respects ; and but for the personal suggestiveness of the whole, might be regarded as a fairly clever performance. But altogether the impression it leaves on the mind is a doubtful one ; we can hardly say "Here we have the poet at his best."

It may be regarded as a privilege accorded to poets that they should despair of their time and place and race ;[1]

---

[1] See p. 51.

but Tennyson often comes near to abusing the privilege ;
and here in "Amphion" it is "a brassy age" in which
"I could not move a thistle." This is perhaps to be
regretted, for no poet has received greater reward or
greater honour than Tennyson. An age that purchased
10,000 copies of the "Idylls of the King" within six
weeks, proved itself to be no "brassy age ;" no poet
was so constantly supported by leaders of thought ; and
considering the unusual weaknesses that provoked
criticism in his first two volumes, he has been dealt with
by the critics most gently. He speaks of "months of
toil," but we hardly realize the advantages afforded to a
poet in these days of abundant editing, good printing,
and low priced literature—to a poet, moreover, who is
"heir of all the ages." In order to gain the same amount of
knowledge, Milton must have laboured twice as hard and
with discomforts innumerable. It is not strange that he
should have become blind. Certainly he hoped to find
"fit audience, though few ;" but it can hardly be said
hat he realized the hope.

A poet who knows his art so well as Tennyson will
employ double rhymes to give point to his humour ; and
they are well managed. Among the improvements,
spindlings" in the last stanza but one replaced "poor
things." The first four lines of the fifth stanza were
originally

> "The birch-tree swung her fragrant hair,
>   The bramble cast her berry,
> The gin within the juniper
>   Began to make him merry."

(109) "ST. AGNES' EVE." This, slightly altered, is the
"St. Agnes" of "The Keepsake" of 1837. Why the
title should have been changed in 1855 from "St. Agnes"
to "St. Agnes' Eve," does not appear. Was the change
due to the remark of a friend, "An iced saint is certainly

better than an iced cream, but not much better than a frosted tree. The original Agnes is worth twenty of her?" Possibly the figure in the convent before us is not quite that of the young girl of thirteen who suffered martyrdom during the persecution of Diocletian; yet, on the other hand, she is no Madeline, of whom it might be said,

> "They told her how, upon St. Agnes' Eve
> Young virgins might have visions of delight,
> And soft adorings from their loves receive
> Upon the honey'd middle of the night."

It will be best to regard her as another type of mediæval religion—the religion of the convent. She may be compared both with "St. Simeon Stylites" and "Sir Galahad." Again we are made to sympathize with the pure and beautiful enthusiast who has died away from all her human emotions, and become the bride for whom a Heavenly Bridegroom is waiting. What a fascinating religion the church of Rome gradually built up, whether for women or for men; and never before was the witchery of its ritual so wrought into verse. Wordsworth at his best, as in "Lucy," might scarcely match the music of these stanzas; their pictorial perfection he could hardly attain unto; every image is in such delicate harmony with the pure young worshipper, that it seems to have been transfigured by her purity, and in the last four lines the very sentences faint with the breathless culmination of her rapture.

(110) "SIR GALAHAD" is an ideal of chivalry as well as a type of religion. But from one point of view he is St. Agnes in the form of a man. Like hers is his stainless purity and his ecstatic devotion to an ideal that has usurped the dearer instincts of humanity. But the poem though full of lyrical splendour is not so good as the former; that was perfect in its sufficiency; this is imperfect in its opulence; there is somewhat of "high

action" in the art. But the blemish is very slight, and taking the knightly theme into consideration, we expect more of action, colour, and sound. In the first stanza are striking—perhaps too striking—assonantal and onomatopœic effects. It is a question whether in stanza five "the tempest crackles on the leads" is in keeping with the former line. A reference to this poem is made on p. 35.

(111) "EDWARD GRAY." This is a pretty homely ballad of the type of "Barbara Allen,"[1] but much refined. The sentiment is that of Shakespeare, "Two Gentlemen of Verona," IV. ii. 113-15 :

> "*Pro.* I likewise hear that Valentine is dead.
> *Sil.* And so, suppose, am I ; for in his grave,
> Assure thyself, my love is buried."

(111) "WILL WATERPROOF'S LYRICAL MONOLOGUE." Here Tennyson has struck a much richer vein of humour than in "Amphion." The volume of 1842 is another volume of experiments, and most of them are successful. Of the many disguises assumed by the poet when he intends to have a talk to himself and a talk with us at the same time, this much-contented rollicking eloquence of the flowing can, or the maudlin-morality that haunts the vacant cup, is of the happiest possible. Such a feast as this of humour and wisdom, wit and imagination, ethics and fancy, philosophy and common sense all served up with excellent poetry, was never spread before in that famous tavern. We have not the heart to be captious when we find our poet, in "a kind of glory," "unboding critic pen ;" or when he looks into the "empty glass" for "Hours when the poet's words and looks Had yet their native glow." And the one shadow of biographical regret that falls upon the poem sweeps away as we stoop to gather that exquisite violet of a legend—the

---

1 Percy's " Reliques."

Rape of Ganymede—which blows half-hidden among the chops and steaks.

(114) "LADY CLARE." This excellent ballad, which has been subject to a few amendments, is less modernized than "Edward Gray." See also the poet's own note, p. 149.

(115) "THE CAPTAIN" appeared first in the selection of 1865. It is not an excellent poem ; scarcely good enough to serve as a warning. And the incidents are improbable ; no enemy would riddle a ship that did not fire a shot in return. The metre, which is seldom at fault in Tennyson, is not so appropriate nor so well controlled as usual. Yet no one but Tennyson could have written the last four lines ; they contain in the second and fourth lines the most delicately adequate rhythmical discord ; and the imagery—as we have so often noticed at the close of other poems—is here seen and felt in its peculiar perfection.

(116) "THE LORD OF BURLEIGH." Visitors to Burleigh House are still shown a portrait which is said to be that of the Lady Burleigh of this pathetic ballad. She died in 1797.

The trochaic measure is prevented from degenerating into sing-song by such discords as " Her sweet face from brow to chin." A further remark on the metre has been made on p. 197, and the style is noticed on p. 134.

(117) "THE VOYAGE." The hidden subject of this beautiful allegory is one very dear to Tennyson.. It appears in " Ulysses," " To follow knowledge like a sinking star ;" in " The Two Voices," " He sows himself on every wind ;" in " The Princess," " O we will walk this world ;" in " Sir Galahad," " I leave the plain, I climb the height ;"

in " Locksley Hall," " Not in vain the distance beacons ; forward, forward, let us range ;" in " Freedom," "O follower of the vision, still In motion to the distant gleam ;" in " Locksley Hall Sixty Years After," " Follow Light ;" and it finds fullest expression in " Merlin and the Gleam." Many other poems might be added to the above list, and many other poets mentioned who never paused in their voyage over the ocean of life, but ever followed " one fair vision—like Fancy, like Virtue, like Knowledge, like Heavenly Hope, like Liberty,"—and, we may add, like ideal truth, beauty, and goodness.

> " Why faintest thou ? I wander'd till I died.
> Roam on ! the light we sought is shining still." [1]

Though of later date than 1842, the poem has much in common with the quotation from " Locksley Hall " above, as in the lines :

> " We loved the glories of the world,
> But laws of nature were our scorn ;"

which again appears in " In Memoriam," "Under whose command Is earth and earth's." (" Epilogue," 36.)

The voyager may pass beyond the horizon of life ; in " The Princess," the Prince continues, " And so Thro' those dark gates across the wild That no man knows ;" but here, as in most of the later poems, the poet ventures beyond the doors of death :

> " We know the merry world is round,
> And we may sail for evermore."

> " Eternal process moving on
> From state to state the spirit walks."
> *In Memoriam.*

So in " Merlin and the Gleam," the end was but the beginning, for

> " There on the border
> Of boundless Ocean,
>   Hovers The Gleam."

---

[1] See p. 119.

And as death drew nearer, this passion of "onward" grew stronger than ever in the heart of the poet ; we may learn it from the last line of his last poem :

"On, and always on ! "

But there was one among the voyagers, "'A ship of fools,' he sneer'd and wept " :

αἱ δ' ἐλπίδες βόσκουσι φυγάδας, ὡς λόγος.
καλοῖς βλέπουσαί γ' ὄμμασιν, μέλλουσι δέ.

" He saw not far ; his eyes were dim "—

ἐν ἐλπίσιν χρὴ τοὺς σοφοὺς ἔχειν βίον.

Apart from the allegory of earnest, lofty, and hopeful living, the poem was an occasion for vivid painting of sea and distant shore.

(118) "SIR LAUNCELOT AND QUEEN GUINEVERE." Three poems of the volume of 1842 take their subject from the Arthurian legends ; they are " Morte d'Arthur," " Sir Galahad," and " Sir Launcelot and Queen Guinevere." To the latter title we notice the significant appendage, "A Fragment." By this the poet seems to say, " I intend some day to build up the stories about King Arthur into a great poem ; meanwhile I am turning into verse one or two incidents here and there."— Romance has here inspired a most brilliant lyric ; better in some respects than " Sir Galahad."

(119) "A FAREWELL," probably to the brook so tenderly described in " In Memoriam " (ci.) It was in 1837 that the Tennysons left Somersby. Another poem in this volume, " Break, Break, Break," is to be associated with " In Memoriam."

In this beautiful lament such rhymes as "deliver" and "forever" lose all their discord. They are further sanctioned by the usage of many good poets.

'119) "The Beggar Maid":

> "Young Adam Cupid, he that shot so trim
> When King Cophetua loved the beggar-maid."
> *Romeo and Juliet*, II. i. 134.

According to Shakespeare, in "Love's Labour's Lost," the ballad of the King and the Beggar was not to be found; and, adds Armado, " I will have that subject newly writ o'er."

Two versions are now extant, one in a collection of old ballads, the other in Percy's "Reliques." Cophetua was a mythical king of Africa; Penelophon (according to Shakespeare, Zenelophon) was the name of the beggar-maid. We have again the figure of Godiva " Like a summer moon Half dipt in cloud." There is little enough of rough merit in the two older ballads; Tennyson writes with his customary grace and charm.

(119) "The Eagle," though a fragment, brings a fine bit of far-off nature delightfully near to us.

(119) "Move Eastward." Possibly this fragment is retained because it seems to correct a popular fallacy; it makes the earth go east; but the effect to the uninitiated is not poetically pleasing.

(119) "Come not when I am dead."[1] These verses were contributed in 1851 to "The Keepsake," edited by Miss Power.

(120) "The Letters." This poem appeared in the "Maud" volume of 1855. As a ballad of modern life it is not very effective. It looks like earlier work than 1855. "Gloom'd" and "athwart" are early favourites; "humm'd a bitter song" may be compared with "humm'd a surly

[1] See p. 155.

hymn" in "The Talking Oak"; "the wholesome human heart," with "Pray heaven for a human heart," in "Lady Clara Vere de Vere." The first four lines of stanza iii. are graphic; the second four are bad. "When gifts of mine could please"—"Dulces exuviæ, dum fata deusque sinebant." "As looks a father on the things," is not in Tennyson's best manner; "the public liar" sounds of "Maud." The last four lines in iv. are weak; "meanest spawn of Hell" in v. is effusive. "Like torrents from a mountain source" may compare with Shelley's

> "Confused in passion's golden purity
> As mountain springs under the morning sun."

"The very graves appeared to smile, So fresh they rose in shadow'd swell," are weak lines; nor are the remaining lines good.

(120) "THE VISION OF SIN" takes a very high rank among allegorical poems. It has undergone only slight alteration. Near the end were two additional lines:

> "Another answered, 'But a crime of sense?
> Give him new nerves with old experience.'"

In this poem we notice some fine metrical contrasts, such as those in "The Brook," and "The Ancient Sage." The jigging trochaic quatrains of section iv. are admirably adapted to the careless devilry of the speaker, but the excessive levity of the measure is judiciously tempered by such lines as "The chap-fallen circle spreads." There is a good deal that resembles Shelley, especially in section ii.; and the whole poem may have been suggested by his "Triumph of Life." Other poets, notably Shakespeare and Milton, seem to have lent their aid. Nevertheless, the work is both original and powerful.

The allegory is easy to follow; and as in "The Pilgrim's Progress," the allegorical character is not less interesting than the ethical lesson he has been created to teach. It is

just the opposite to the lesson we have been learning from
"St. Simeon Stylites" and "St. Agnes"; they attempted to
ignore the body; the youth in "The Vision of Sin" attempts
to ignore the soul.   And, thirdly, as was seen in "The
Palace of Art," there is in our time a tendency to live a
life of isolation in selfish intellectual pleasures.   All these
are wrong; and they are fatal, each in its degree.   Pos-
sibly this lust of the flesh is the most common of the three
failures to live the complete life; it is certainly the most
terrible and the most loathsome.   We have before us a
young man, vigorous and highly gifted, but already riding
hard and weighing down to earth the winged horse of his
soul.   We see him enter the palace gates of sensual
Pleasure; pleasure refined at first, but ever growing
coarser as his jaded appetite demands fiercer excitements.
At length his senses grow dull:

> "A heavy vapour, hueless, formless, cold,
> Came floating on for many a month and year;"

his whole being is becoming withered; and when again
we see him, it is as a gray and gap-toothed man, slowly
riding a worn-out hack; he alights at a ruined inn—the
close of a ruined life; he is as lean as death, miserably
and prematurely old, degraded yet shameless, tottering
yet malignant; then, drinking wine through "shrivell'd
lips," he sits mocking in the same breath both his God
and his fellow-men.   But his voice grows faint; the end
has come—what end?

The poet tries to penetrate the Divine purposes:

> "Below were men and horses pierced with worms";

but from the mystic mountain come voices as of spirits
who are contemplating the ruined life; the first spirit
pleads that sensual pleasure was its own punishment: for
it gradually destroyed all capability of pleasure.   The
second urges that with the loss of pleasure came hatred
of good; that passive self-indulgence ended in active

crime. But a third answers that the very desperation of the ruined man's last orgies proved that he was still troubled by a twinge of conscience. And in the earlier edition a fourth spirit would have him begin life over again with the advantage of this terrible experience. There is something like a glimmer of hope ; but the sentence of the Great Judge is not recorded.

(123) "To ——, AFTER READING A LIFE AND LETTERS." This poem appeared first as "To ——," in the "Examiner" of March 24th, 1849. Next it was printed in the sixth edition, 1850, and again with the second part of the title, and some slight alterations, in the eighth edition, 1853.

The tone of the poem has already been remarked upon ; we hear again the "laudator temporis acti." "The many-headed beast" of Pope and others is an ungracious expression. "Shakespeare's curse" had nothing to do with "days that deal in ana." "Nor king" ;—Tennyson himself has spoken feelingly of "That fierce light which beats upon a throne" ; in that light the Kings of thought must sometimes stand ;[1] and perhaps no poet has so successfully anticipated criticism as Tennyson. For all that, the poet will secure our fullest sympathy and respect ; when we have yielded him all that he claims, we shall shrink within ourselves at the thought of the enormous debt we owe him still—and for ever.

(124) "To E. L. ON HIS TRAVELS IN GREECE." These stanzas were first printed in the edition of 1853. They are addressed to Edward Lear, the landscape painter, and they refer to a book he had written, "Journals of Tours in Central and Southern Italy and Albania."

---

[1] Compare also Tennyson's praise of Wellington :

> "Whatever record leap to light,
> He never shall be shamed."

This and the former poem are written in the stanza of
" In Memoriam," which has a lighter movement in both,
especially in the second :—" By dancing rivulets fed his
flocks." The lines to E. L. are picturesque, and set forth
the poet's veneration for " classic ground."

(124) " BREAK, BREAK, BREAK." In the first stanza
of the fifth poem of " In Memoriam " the poet dwells on
the inadequacy of mere words to express emotion ; real
sorrow lies so deep within the soul, and is so sacred, that
to give it outward shape in language is little short of pro-
fanity. Moreover, as nature, the ample vesture of the
Deity, makes his presence felt to us, yet disguises his
form, so words may convince the world of sorrow, but at
the same time blur its very outlines.

There is some of this sentiment in " Break, Break,
Break ; " and before proceeding to a consideration of the
poem, one is forced to enlarge the poet's doubt, and
criticism will falter as it approaches such sacred loveli-
ness of sorrow.

Yet the mere sound of the poem, and the poignancy of
its anguish have such power to take captive our ear and
heart, that we sometimes miss the beauty half concealed[1]
within it. Few of Tennyson's productions are so spon-
taneous as this ; yet it is more than a mere cry of despair ;
for in none does nature so eloquently express what words,
and even melody can only conceal. Five times the poet
abandons the disguise of speech, and paints his sorrow
in a vivid picture. Before us lies the sea, powerless to
tell its sobbing trouble to the shore, as wave after wave
of utterance dies broken on the cold grey stones. On
the shore the children are playing ; what could they know
of death ? Out on the bay the sailor boy is singing in the
happy activity of life ; in the offing are ships returning

[1] " In Memoriam," v.

from a prosperous voyage, and sailing on majestically to the neighbouring port—four pictures in one ; and in these the poet expresses more eloquently than in any words the sense of desolation made yet more desolate by contrast with joys it cannot share. In " In Memoriam" the corresponding emotion may be discovered in one heartbroken line,

> " The noise of life begins again " (vii).

The fifth picture is of the sea breaking hopelessly at the foot of crags that seem to spurn it from its desire ; so death stands inexorable between him and all that he loved.

This pictorial rather than articulate representation of grief occurs frequently in " In Memoriam ;" examples are furnished by such poems as the sixth, seventh, eighth, eleventh, twelfth, fourteenth, fifteenth, sixteenth, nineteenth and twentieth. Indeed " Break, Break, Break" naturally takes its place along with these, in one of which, the eighth, occurs the expression " a vanish'd eye," and in another, the tenth, " a vanished life," expressions that claim kindred with " a vanished hand." Also we may compare

> " O for the touch of a vanish'd hand
> And the sound of a voice that is still,"

with a passage in the thirteenth poem of " In Memoriam,"

> "And, where warm hands have prest and closed,
> Silence, till I be silent too."

(124) "THE POET'S SONG." In this poem we have presented to us another characteristic view of the poet's function :

> " Longius et volvens fatorum arcana movebo."

> "The marvel of the everlasting will,
> An open scroll,

> Before him lay." [1]

---

[1] " The Poet."

But Tennyson has looked into the twain eternities ; and the poet who could hear a whisper " from o'er the gates of Birth," might well, and more clearly than other men, hear the same whisper from the other distance :

> " A breath
> From some fair dawn beyond the doors of death."

The imagery again is characteristic ; vivid, and fresh, including also something of the past ; " gates of the sun," like the " gates of the east " of Hyperion and the " eastern gate " of L'Allegro, is common poetic property ; " waves of shadow " may be compared with the " waves of wheat " in " In Memoriam " (xci) and Thomson's " Summer," " Sweeping with shadowy gusts the fields of corn." The wild swan is a favourite with Tennyson ; in the " Princess " we read of " The leader wild-swan in among the stars."

The group " English Idylls and Other Poems," which ends here, includes all the poems of the 1842 volume except " The Skipping Rope." This very light piece of twelve lines has been omitted in all editions subsequent to the 6th (1850).

ADDENDA TO CHAPTER V.

Three other poems which have not been republished may receive mention here. In the winter of 1845, Sir E. B. Lytton published anonymously " The New Timon : a Romance of London." In this poem, which was partly narrative and partly satirical, he took occasion to denounce Tennyson in such couplets as the following :

> " The jingling melody of purloined conceits,
> Out-babying Wordsworth, and out-glittering Keats.
> * * * * *
> Let School-Miss Alfred vent her chaste delight
> On ' darling little rooms so warm and bright.' "

He further attacked the poet because a pension of £200 a year had just been granted to him by Sir Robert Peel :

> "Tho' Theban taste the Saxon's purse controuls,
> And pensions Tennyson, while starves a Knowles."

Tennyson replied with pardonable bitterness in "The New Timon and the Poets," a poem of eleven stanzas signed "Alcibiades," which appeared in "Punch," Feb. 28th, 1846. The fourth stanza is as follows :

> "And once you tried the Muses, too ;
>   You failed, Sir : therefore now you turn
> To fall on those who are to you
>   As Captain is to Subaltern.

But the next number of "Punch" contained five more stanzas by Tennyson, headed "Afterthought ;" and these stanzas, which placed him in a position of unassailable dignity, are now included among his published poems under the title of "Literary Squabbles." It should be added that in after years the relations between the Laureate and Lord Lytton were the pleasantest possible.

The second of these omitted poems—"Here often, when a child, I lay reclin'd,"—was contributed to "The Manchester Athenæum Album" in the year 1850 ; and the third consists of three stanzas published in "The Keepsake" [1] for 1851. The last stanza is weak, but the first two possess some interest :

> "What time I wasted youthful hours,
> One of the shining wingèd powers,
> Show'd me vast cliffs, with crowns of towers.
>
> As towards that gracious light I bow'd,
> They seem'd high palaces and proud,
> Hid now and then with sliding cloud." [2]

In the third stanza the poet is encouraged to make his upward way to these beautiful abodes, for the path, though difficult, is "free to all."

---

[1] Edited by Miss Power. London : David Bogue.
[2] A fragment of imagery to be compared with many other passages, such as "The soft white vapour streak the crowned towers." *The Princess.*

APPENDICES TO CHAPTER V.

APPENDIX I.

Notes on "Locksley Hall."

(*a.*) The hero of "Locksley Hall" is usually regarded as a boy; and the poem is said to express "a boy's resentment for imagined wrongs." As a fact the recollections of youth are placed some years back, and they breathe of ardent hope; but the whole poem is the expression of almost disenchanted manhood. The speaker of this long soliloquy ought to be nearer thirty than twenty. By a poet's licence Tennyson in "Locksley Hall Sixty Years After" assigns the same date to two events:

"Here we met, our latest meeting, Amy, sixty years ago."

The speaker on this occasion is eighty years old; therefore, when he parted with Amy he was twenty.

But again, Amy lay "dead in child-birth . . . sixty years ago."[1] This could hardly have been.

The impression we receive on reading "Locksley Hall" is that the man who was twenty when he left Amy to go and enlist in the army, has returned after a lapse of some years; he uses the expression "as of old;" talks of turning "that earlier page" "before the strife" ("the strife" occurred when he was twenty); and he further comments on his noisy lamentation over the lost love as follows:

"Shall it not be scorn to me to harp on such a moulder'd string?"

The lowest limit of age should be twenty-five. This leaves only five years wherein Amy's love will falter, will be given to another, whom she will wed; and some time thereafter she will die. Her lover in the same interval

---

[1] Couplets 18 and 19.

has to learn that she has failed him ; has then to become a soldier ; to return again after an apparently long interval to the scene of love ; and when that scene awakens the old love again, he scorns himself for harping on " a mouldered string."

Unless we bear in mind some such approximate age of the hero, the several acts of the drama are liable to become confused. Nor is it easy to follow the speaker through the abrupt turnings in his reminiscences. As also in " Locksley Hall Sixty Years After," these sudden transitions may be in keeping with the character, but they demand the reader's close attention.

(*b.*) Much of the charm of " Locksley Hall " is due to the metrical movement. The ordinary stanza of four trochaic tetrameters is arranged in two lines ; and the removal of the double rhymes strengthens at the same time the hands of the artist, and the material he moulds. It was a happy thought thus to transform the weakest of English measures into an impetuous sea-sounding rhythm. Yet in " The Lord of Burleigh," by making only a slight variation, Tennyson uses the old weak stanza with such art that with perhaps one or two exceptions, weakness is wrought into the simple sweetness of pathos.

(*c.*) It is always interesting to observe from time to time how poetical dainties of the past become " imbedded and injellied "[1] in Tennyson's rich and ample pasties. This is more noticeable in the earlier poems. Some of them almost resemble Gray's well-known "mosaic ; " " Locksley Hall " is one. You open an old Shakespeare at random ; on the left hand page you read, "all that look on him love him ; " though Tennyson's "Whom to look at was to love " is closer to the "But to see her was to love her " of Burns. Then on the right hand page you see a well-known passage which appears to hint that " Woman is the lesser man," as in the lines—

[1] " Audley Court."

> " Alas, their love may be called appetite,
> No motion of the liver, but the palate ; "

these, besides their other similarities, seem to furnish the word "motions" in couplet 75 of "Locksley Hall." But this is "Twelfth Night," a play that deals with love ; and you turn to a less familiar part of the volume, a collection of fragments at the end ; yet here from the two pages you select "Love, whose month was ever May"[1] to compare with couplet 10 ; then the "treble-dated crow" on the other open page recalls the "many-wintered crow" of 34 ; though this is still more like the "annosa cornix" of the Horace whom Tennyson knew by heart. "Every door is barr'd with gold and opens but to golden keys" has a likeness to

> "The strongest castle, tower, or town,
> The golden bullet beats it down,"

on the same page.

"The many-wintered crow that leads the clanging rookery home" has some additional interest. A friend wrote to ask Tennyson why he first called the bird a crow, and then a rook ; the main part of the poet's reply was to the effect that he was not much concerned with the ornithological question, and that he merely avoided the use of the word "rook" twice in the same line. But he might have added the well-known passage in "Macbeth,"

> "The crow
> Makes wing to the rooky wood,"

where "rooky" is generally understood to mean "the haunt of rooks," or, "abounding in rooks."

Appendix II.

Note on "Love and Duty."

In the former appendix some random comparisons were made with Shakespeare. The following remarks on the

---

[1] This occurs also in "Love's Labour's Lost."

last four lines and one or two other passages in " Love and Duty," will include similar references to Milton.

" Matin-chirp " (last line but three) which is a variation on the " matin-song " of the " Poems by Two Brothers," and some later pieces, is represented in Milton by the " shrill matin-song Of birds on every bough." Tennyson's " full quire " reminds us of Milton's " The birds their quire apply." The lines

> " And morning driven her plough of pearl
> Far furrowing into light the mounded rack,"

will first suggest some lines in " The Princess,"

> " Morn in the white wake of the morning star
> Came furrowing all the orient into gold,"

and both passages may next be compared with Milton's

> " Now morn, her rosy steps in the eastern clime
> Advancing, sowed the earth with orient pearl."

" Far furrowing " recalls " Far-sheening " on p. 145 ; and we notice that the hyphen is omitted. Our most important comparison, however, is the last line,

> " Beyond the fair green field and eastern sea,"

which finds an interesting parallel in

> " The parting sun
> Beyond the Earth's green Cape and verdant Isles
> Hesperian sets."
> *Paradise Lost*, viii. 630-632.

In the next line of " Paradise Lost " we read, " Be strong, live happy, and love," which appears in Tennyson's poem a few lines back as " Live happy ; tend thy flowers," etc. ; and the two preceding lines in Tennyson,

> " Shall sharpest pathos blight us, knowing all
> Life needs for life is possible to will,"

are represented in the immediate context of Milton,

> " Take heed lest passion sway
> Thy judgment to do aught, which else free will
> Would not admit . . . to stand or fall,
> Free in thy own arbitrement it lies."

A few lines before in the Milton (587, 590) we read, "Love refines The thoughts, the heart enlarges," which corresponds to

> "Am I not the nobler thro' thy love?
> Yea, three times less unworthy! Likewise thou
> Art more thro' love."

These comparisons between "Love and Duty" and "Paradise Lost" might be more than doubled in number. At this time Milton seems to have gained yet greater power over Tennyson, and he may be said to have kept it for some twenty years longer.

CHAPTER VI.

ENOCH ARDEN, AND OTHER POEMS.

"ENOCH ARDEN." (125)

ORIGINALLY the "Enoch Arden" volume[1] was entitled "Idylls of the Hearth." A note on this title will be found in Chap. XI. In subject, form, and style "Enoch Arden" is more properly an Idyll[2] than any of the Arthurian Poems for which that title is still retained; they, strictly speaking, are heroic poems; but Tennyson called them Idylls chiefly because he hesitated to regard them as an Epic; and he changed the title of the present volume at the last moment probably because he felt that two volumes of Idylls following that of 1842 would be an excess, and

---

[1] The volume, "Enoch Arden, etc.," published in 1864, contained the following poems:—"Enoch Arden." "Aylmer's Field." "Sea-Dreams" (which had appeared in "Macmillan's Magazine" for January, 1860). "The Grandmother" (formerly "The Grandmother's Apology," in "Once a Week," July, 1859). "The Northern Farmer." "Tithonus" (which Thackeray had secured for the "Cornhill," Feb., 1860). "The Voyage." "In the Valley of Cauteretz." "The Flower." "Requiescat." "The Sailor Boy" (first printed in a miscellany, "The Victoria Regia," Christmas, 1861). "The Islet." "The Ringlet." "Welcome to Alexandra." "Dedication." "Attempts at Classic Metres in Quantity" ("Cornhill," Dec., 1863).

[2] A picture-poem, "Nature in the background, and in the foreground men and women of primitive manners and simple nobleness."

yet he must not give up his " Idylls of the King." [1]   Otherwise " Enoch Arden" is a narrative poem of humble life, like some of the " Tales" of Crabbe and Wordsworth.

In all the essential features of a moderately long poem, in design, construction, finish, and impression, " Enoch Arden" is excellent. It is probably more perfect than any other of Tennyson's poems of equal or greater length. " Lucretius" and the " Holy Grail" may be said to come nearest to it, and " Guinevere" next ; and it is more perfect than many of the shorter poems. For example, " Dora," another story of simple life, when placed by its side, is seen at a great disadvantage ; compared with this poem, the style of " Dora" is at once felt to be an artificial adornment, not a natural growth of beauty, and hence loses all its charm. The simplicity of " Enoch Arden" asks no undue attention to itself ; this and all other elements blend and are lost in one impression of perfectness.

As to the longer poems, " The Princess," " Maud," " In Memoriam," " Idylls of the King," it will often be found useful to test some of their qualities by the process of comparison with " Enoch Arden."

We need not apply to this poem the word " great ; " that epithet is reserved for works of grander scope ; in Tennyson, the " Idylls of the King" and " In Memoriam" and some of the Dramas would be called greater poems. But in its kind it is so great that the " Tale of the Prioress," told by Chaucer, is not touched in honour by its company. It has met with adverse criticism ; the story has been considered inadequate to the setting, overloaded with detail, and so forth ; but the verdict of time will almost certainly be favourable.

For no poem could be better suited to Tennyson's genius. It is long enough to produce an effect of creative

---

[1] See also Chapter xi.

power rather than creative prettiness ; yet not too long to embarrass the poet with complexity of plot, diversity of character, or extent of prospect. And besides restricted scheme and scope, there are other respects in which it is peculiarly adapted to his poetic powers and tastes, especially the simplicity of a theme arising from lowly life. Poets are not expected to make tragic passion out of "The short and simple annals of the poor." The treatment will, therefore, be Idyllic—a manner to which Tennyson was inclined, and not epic nor tragic ; the poem will take the form of an "Idyll of the Hearth." But simplicity in art, if absolutely natural, is beautiful and impressive by virtue of its striking perfectness ; and whether the simplicity be a result of unconscious art, as in the "Pilgrim's Progress," or of conscious art rendered practically unconscious by emotion, as in "Enoch Arden," such works have a double charm ; they will commend themselves to all classes of readers ; to the unlearned by their artlessness, to the learned by the instinct or the art which makes that artlessness real or apparent.

The subject of the poem is probably known to all who use this book ; if otherwise, they will scarcely neglect the first opportunity offered to them of reading one of the most truly pathetic stories in literature. It is not new in itself ; Crabbe's "Parting Hour," and A. A. Procter's "Homeward Bound" furnished the framework ; something also may have been suggested by Mrs. Gaskell's "Silvia's Lovers."

We are accustomed to regard the original materials of most of Shakespeare's plays as being honoured by their adaptation or absorption ; this is not always our view of borrowing, especially with later poets ; for the circumstances under which they borrow are changed considerably. But the question is fully discussed on p. 49. Here it may be profitable to notice the way in which Tennyson worked out his original. We may compare, for example, the well-known paragraph (663-677) beginning, "There Enoch spoke no word," with the following stanza in Miss Procter's ballad :

> " It was evening in late Autumn,
>   And the gusty wind blew chill ;
> Autumn leaves were falling round me,
>   And the red sun lit the hill."

The rough sketch here supplied to him, Tennyson does not alter ; he merely adds detail and colour.   But in the course of his poem he departs from the main lines of the earlier narrative ; in this the solitary mariner makes himself known to his wife and her new husband, gives the woman his blessing, and then goes forth again to the ocean, where he murmurs,

> " I too shall reach home and rest."

Tennyson heightens the pathos of the story by making Enoch resolve

> " Not to tell her, never to let her know."

This resolve some critics have questioned, perhaps needlessly ; and the other question, " Ought Enoch to have marred Annie's happiness by making known to her his return through Miriam Lane," scarcely calls for serious consideration.

We have said that the main feature of " Enoch Arden " is a natural simplicity ; for the story is one of simple village and seafaring life, and everything in the poem is in harmony with the subject.   The blank verse has none of the majesty of the " Passing of Arthur," nor the passion of " Lucretius," nor the free movement of " The Princess " or the Dramas, nor even the baldness of " Dora ; " it is natural, quiet, homely ; often conversational in its simplicity ; once it reaches tragic intensity, as in the lines 754-787, " Now when the dead man . . . and the boy, my son ; " and once is elevated to grandeur, in the description of the tropics, 568-595.

It may be noticed that the passage last mentioned is

the only one in which the poet is led away from man
to nature ; and even in this he is describing the home of
the "long-bearded solitary." That the rarer and grander
aspects of nature often cast a spell over Tennyson, is
abundantly evidenced by the "Recollections of the
Arabian Nights" (1830) and "The Voyage of Mael-
dune" (1880), and by many poems in the fifty years
between ; as also by some poems that come after. As
we have seen already,[1] some of the best lines in "Locksley
Hall" (couplets 78-82) are inspired by a vision of the
tropics ; and here in "Enoch Arden" the poet goes a
little out of his way to make this splendid sketch of the
island of eternal summer. He had been long accus-
tomed to describe parts of England and of other lands
that he had not seen, as may be gathered from "Poems
by Two Brothers," written by boys who had "never been
beyond their native county ;"[2] and, therefore, it is not
surprising that the splendours of this "Eden of all
plenteousness" should be represented even in such detail
as "The league-long roller thundering on the reef," with
which may be compared "In Memoriam," xxxvi (4) :

> "Those wild eyes that watch the wave
> In roarings round the coral reef."

Otherwise, as more usually with Tennyson, nature is a
pictorial illustration of the story ; and as in his other
poems, so in this, the natural scenery is marvellously in
keeping with the humanity of the piece. Finest of all is
the descriptive paragraph (663-677) already referred to,
the desolate November scene through which the deso-
late wanderer treads wearily to his doom. Again, how
often the sea fills up the human picture.[3] But nothing

---

[1] See p. 32. [2] See p. 51.

[3] Although space does not admit of a fuller quotation, passages such as
the following may be briefly indicated : "As the beacon-blaze allures The
bird of passage" (724), "For sure no gladlier . . ." (824-828), "there came
so loud a calling of the sea" (904), "Crying with a loud voice 'A sail ! A
sail !'" (907).

in this connection is more striking than the first paragraph of the poem ; it stands in the relation of dumb-show to the old drama ; every aspect of nature in these nine opening lines suggests some scene in the tragedy to follow.   There is something like this in the next poem, "Aylmer's Field," where the first paragraph of six lines dimly foreshadows the approaching Nemesis.

Another aspect of the simplicity of the poem is discovered by the poet's control of incident.   The situations are uncomplicated ; often they are made obvious by antithesis.   Philip at the outset is the counterpart of Enoch at the close ; as a boy his eyes are flooded with "the helpless wrath of tears" ; he loved in silence ; a sick father needed his care that autumn holiday, and thus he lent Enoch an opportunity of telling his love to Annie ; his self-sacrifice reached a climax when he saw the pair of happy lovers, read his doom, slipt aside like a wounded life, and had his dark hour unseen.

So is it throughout the story ; the bells ring merrily for Enoch's wedding ; they ring as merrily for the wedding of Philip ; in the hazel wood Enoch won Annie

> " Just where the prone edge of the wood began
> To feather toward the hollow,"

and when Annie yields to Philip, the poet places them not only in the same hazel wood, but

> " Just where the prone edge of the wood began
> To feather toward the hollow."

The characters are equally free from complexity. Annie, the pivot of these situations, also holds the balance between the two chief actors, and is colourless enough to add due colour to them.   Had she been ever so little heroic the piece would have been spoilt.

A supernatural element[1] appears in nearly all Tennyson's important poems—"The Princess," "In Memoriam," "Maud," "Locksley Hall," "Idylls of the King," several of the dramas, "The May Queen," "Aylmer's Field," and many others. In "Aylmer's Field" a telepathic communication of more scientific aspect[2] is in keeping with the more exalted personages and the story of higher life; in this companion idyll it will take the form appropriate to simple folk and a Puritan tradition; that of unconscious prediction, strange presentiment, the homelier marvels of a dream, and, most essential of all, a text of the holy Book to serve as a sign (491-2).

It is the same with all the elements that enter into the composition of the poem—style, tone, atmosphere, feeling, humanity, all blend in one harmony of simplicity; there is also concentration of narrative, avoidance of sensation, repression of false sentiment. And thus is produced that rare unity of impression spoken of in the second paragraph of this chapter.

Finally we ask, Is there any moral shut within the bosom of *this* rose? What ethical lesson may we expect to draw from the misfortunes of good and noble men? In "Aylmer's Field" Nemesis will overtake the transgressors, those parents who are too worldly-wise in seeking their own daughter's good; their house will be left unto them desolate. But this tragedy is without even the "dram of eale;"[3] there is no excess nor defect of any human passion that might have worked his doom for any. Here no one sins except life itself; and for the evil of bare human life Nemesis may in some sense be reserved.

---

[1] Arising partly out of his mystic temperament. See p. 62.

[2]   "Star to star vibrates light : may soul to soul
     Strike thro' a finer element of her own."

                      (Lines 578-583.)
Enoch Arden hears far away, "in the ringing of his ears," the pealing of his parish bells (609-611).

[3] Globe reading of Hamlet I. iv. 36.

This then is the moral.   On the scale of Infinity all is well.   But

> " Life, like a dome of many-coloured glass,
>   Stains the white radiance of eternity,
>   Until Death tramples it to fragments "

The laws that govern human life are doubtless the best under existing conditions ; but no law is so just as not to to be unjust in some of its applications ; and while the world is more and more the individual must often wither. The Lady of Shalott bought love at the price of death ; all humanity buys life at the price of death ; yet for all that we find it well to love and to live ; " it is indispensable to acquire the advantage ; it is lamentable to incur the evil."

Even if unrecorded on earth, the heroism of Enoch Arden, on the scale of infinity, would live and grow in strength and beauty for ever.   One of the greatest of England's poets was well content to rest his fame "with God." He is not the least of heroes who suffers in silence, and the glory of whose victories has been unsullied by human acclaim.

But since Enoch's self-sacrifice has been recorded on earth, we are permitted to read its " moral " more clearly. The very intensity of his pathos made him more perfectly noble.   He lifts the poor to the highest level of humanity ; he makes them worthy of the world's regard and reverence ; he is a pattern to rich and poor alike ; and the influence of his sublime fate has become " The sweet presence of a good diffused."

(142) "AYLMER'S FIELD."   The story told in this poem, which stands second in the Enoch Arden volume of 1864, was supplied to Tennyson by his friend Thomas Woolner, the sculptor.   It has some points in common with Words-worth's " Hartleap Well," in which a "grey-headed shep-herd " tells the poet why " the spot is curst." Tennyson's story is referred to on page 160.   The locality is probably the county of Kent, as may be judged from some of the

scenery. The "little port" that buried "Enoch Arden" is said to be Deal, in the same county.[1] The title "Aylmer's Field" is explained in the last ten lines of the poem, where we are told that the great hall—Aylmer's Hall—was "broken down" and that "all is open field." Here, as often in other poems, the last few bars repeat the opening phrases of Tennyson's music.

"Aylmer's Field," though it may be regarded as a companion idyll, is in many respects a great contrast to "Enoch Arden." Selfishness takes the prominent position formerly occupied by self-sacrifice ; unlovely figures in the high places of the world usurp the simply-noble village folk ; passion rages and destroys where emotion was refined and repressed ; and fitful, or turbulent, or overstrained rhetoric often takes the place of a style perfect in its oneness of simplicity.

"Aylmer's Field" is a more powerful poem than "Enoch Arden," yet less meritorious as a work of art. It is too unequal ; it has most of the faults whose opposites constitute the chief beauties of the other work. For example, "Enoch Arden" was a story, told as such, and with faultless art ; but in "Aylmer's Field" we have a story, and too much besides. It is a remarkable fact, but one only among several of the same kind, that in nearly all of his poems in which he takes occasion to speak for himself, Tennyson drags in some foreign nation. The French come on the scene to receive the poet's censure in "The Princess," "In Memoriam," "Aylmer's Field," "Locksley Hall Sixty Years After," and some minor poems ; in "Maud" it is the Russians ; and in "Locksley Hall" :

> "The jingling of the guinea helps the hurt that Honour feels,
> And the nations do but murmur, snarling at each other's heels."

---

[1] Some would place it in the Isle of Wight, some in Lincolnshire. But, as a fact, like Shakespeare's enchanted island, it is best left unidentified.

There is nothing about the French or the Russians or any other nation in " Enoch Arden." But this subject of motive in "Aylmer's Field," as apart from the story, has been discussed in a former chapter.[1]

Whatever may have been the details as given by Mr. Woolner, it is certain that some of the incidents in Tennyson's version are too near the verge of improbability. They would pass muster in a second-rate novel, but in a poem of such importance and of such magnificence of workmanship as "Aylmer's Field " they become a more serious blemish. Something similar will be noticed in " Maud." Like the style, the dramatic intensity of the poem is unequal ; the tragic issues are too momentous in proportion to the characters and the previous flow of passion or the nature and sequence of the incidents. " From Edith was engraven on the blade "—" redden'd with no bandit's blood "—terrors like these might adorn the end of some desperate lover in melodrama, or even of an Othello or a Brutus, but they are scarcely in keeping with " such a love as like a chidden babe After much wailing, hush'd itself at last ; " and the well-known sermon, a wonderful piece of declamation in itself, is surely too long and too loud for its setting.

On the other hand, as in " The Princess," nothing can exceed the beauty, or truth, or grandeur of the parts. The beauty alone must concern us here. "Aylmer's Field," " Enoch Arden," and " The Gardener's Daughter " set forth the peculiar loveliness of an English landscape or an English homestead with a truth and an effectiveness never attained, attempted, dreamt of before. Those who think this praise excessive may temper it by adding " In Memoriam," " The Miller's Daughter," and " The Brook," and then allowing the six poems to take the place of the three. Or they may add so many more that other poets

[1] See pp. 159 and 162.

will be surpassed by the mere number of Tennyson's loving and masterly sketches of his native land. To quote examples from "Aylmer's Field," where they are so abundant and so perfect, would be superfluous; but the pathetic descriptive passage at the close [1] may be mentioned as an example, first of realism in its more legitimate effects, and next of the poet's accurate observation of the humbler aspects of nature.

Turning now to the characters, we first notice that if Leolin had been made more heroic, he would have spoilt the tragedy as Tennyson was choosing to shape it. The part played by his brother has been explained on a former page.[2] We have no hero in this poem; and Sir Aylmer who, after Leolin, might have stood above the rest, has no redeeming feature, and is therefore almost a caricature. Iago was an inarticulate poet; but this would-be "villain" is absolutely colourless—or overdrawn, which amounts to the same thing. Tennyson is thinking, not of the human being, but of the social mistake which that human being is to hold up to the light for the time's behoof. One touch of natural affection brings him for a moment closer to humanity—but he was warm with wine:

> "She look'd so sweet, he kiss'd her tenderly,
> Not knowing what possess'd him."

Lady Aylmer — as often in Shakespeare — is the male character over again in the form of a woman. The Indian cousin has individuality, and his presence, though fitful, is always a pleasant relief. Edith, like Maud, is not a character; she is a beautiful vision called up by love, and made ours for ever by death. For such we set apart a shrine within the soul where the noise of common life may not be heard, nor the light of common day penetrate. And perhaps at some holier moment we gaze inwardly upon the vision till the heart beats more sweetly and

[1] Lines 846-853.   [2] See p. 162.

more calmly, and the blood flows through our being like a liquid joy.

And if now, as at the close of our reflections upon "Enoch Arden," we choose to draw a moral from the poem before us, it must be the moral of pity and fear deduced by Aristotle from all tragedy of wrong-doing ; but we must spread out our compassion and feel the fear in a way somewhat different from Aristotle's intention. Two young and beautiful lives that had been "together from the first," and who "might have been together till the last" are sacrificed to "marriage-hindering mammon." To these we give our pity ; against false pride and the worship of wealth we watch and pray. From their "narrow gloom" the wretched parents call to us in the very words of the broken-hearted poet :

> "As ye have lived, so must ye die ;—O Terror,
> Strike through these stubborn worldlings to the core ;—
> If heaven can little win your hearts from error
> Let hell do more."

(139) "THE BROOK." It may be presumed that Lord Tennyson arranged the list of contents prefixed to the one volume edition of his works. But it is not always easy to discover the principles that govern the arrangement. This group of five is called "Enoch Arden and Other Poems" ; but only two of the remaining four, "Aylmer's Field," and "Sea Dreams," were published in the "Enoch Arden" volume of 1864. "The Brook" appeared in the "Maud" volume of 1855, and "Lucretius" in the "Holy Grail" volume of 1870.

Besides "The Brook," the "Maud" volume contained "The Letters" of the former chapter ; also "The Ode on the Death of the Duke of Wellington," "The Daisy," "To the Rev. F. D. Maurice," "Will," and "The Charge of the Light Brigade" all of which are found in the group following "The Princess," and will be considered in Chapter VIII.

It will be seen in the table of contents above mentioned,[1] that the first four of the group, " Enoch Arden and Other Poems," are printed at the same distance from the margin, whereas " Lucretius " stands nearer to it.   This arrangement probably implies that the first four are a group of idylls.

Of the poems that were printed with " Maud " in the volume of 1855, "The Brook" is by far the best.   It should be compared with " Dora," and in the comparison, while " Dora " discovers itself perhaps altogether as an artificial imitation of Wordsworth's simpler style,[2] " The Brook " will appear the more perfectly original and successful ; it calls for comparison with Wordsworth, being almost as natural in its happiness as the poem of " The Brothers" is natural in its sorrow.   More than ever the scenic background sets off the human picture ; indeed, some portion of the natural scenery plays a human part in the foreground ; for the brook, the inarticulate presentment of eternity amid time, is made to chant in human tones its happy everlasting hymn.   This is a great advance on " The Talking Oak."   The story, too, is a delightful one delightfully told, which could not be well said of " The Gardener's Daughter."   As to the workmanship, the poet's complete mastery over his art is not contested by a single blemish.   Moreover, in this most perfect of all the idylls we find an easier yet subtler faculty of characterization, whether the type is rugged like old Philip,[3] or the bailiff,

---

[1] Prefixed to the one vol. ed. of " Tennyson's Works."

[2] It is a good plan to read Dora first, and then Wordsworth's Idyll " The Brothers," mentioned below.   The chief impression left on our minds by the former poem is that the poet is a good showman ; but by Wordsworth our souls are bowed down with pity at the pathos of life.

[3] Old Philip's constantly recurring phrase, " and so the matter hung," reminds us of " It stinted, and said 'Ay,'" of Juliet's nurse.   And Philip is just such another chatterer.

or delicate like Edmund and Katie Willows. We find also a finer grace of form and colour; the transcripts from nature for example, are more striking yet none the less apt, than in earlier poems; "Such a time as goes before the leaf, When all the wood stands in a mist of green"; "It has more ivy"; a remarkable example of isolated local colouring; "High elbow'd grigs"; "lissome as a hazel wand"; "In gloss and hue the chestnut, when the shell Divides threefold to show the fruit within";

> "By that old bridge which, half in ruins then,
> Still makes a hoary eyebrow for the gleam
> Beyond it."

> "Twinkled the innumerable ear and tail."

Nor have the various shades of emotion been so delicately blended as now; the poet does not fail to make audible "The still sad music of humanity":

> "Poor lad, he died at Florence quite worn out. . . ."

> "Poor Philip, of all his lavish waste of words
> Remains the lean P. W. on his tomb,"

and thus by contrast he heightens the harmonizing effect of the brook's glad eternal melody.

Tennyson delights to weave his story out of the happy sadness of memory; in "The Miller's Daughter" the old squire tells to his wife "Across the walnuts and the wine" the history she knows so well of their life of long ago; in "The Gardener's Daughter" the aged artist unfolds "the most blessed memory of his age"; and here by the brook, after twenty years of absence, Laurence Aylmer stands musing. The brook babbles as of old; the scene around him is unchanged; it restores the life of twenty years before. His thoughts return to the young poet brother who sang the song of the brook, with whom he parted on this very spot, and who went to Florence to die. Once more Katie Willows comes to him and tells him the trouble of her love ; and once more he lends a patient ear to old Philip's "daylong chirping." The sequel to all this is so happily and daintily wrought out by the poet that any further comment would imperil one of the finest effects in this kind of poetry.

The words "lucky rhymes" in the fourth line of the idyll are a little curious. They are most probably suggested by "lucky words" in the twentieth line of "Lycidas"; but Milton uses the term in the sense of "that wish luck," and Tennyson uses it in Cowper's sense of "though apt, yet coy." But it is possible that Milton's phrase was not present to him.

Originally the words "an Idyl" were added to the title, "The Brook." By this the poet implied that "The Brook" was the only poem of the kind in the "Maud" volume.[1]

(156) "SEA DREAMS." This idyll, as we have seen, originally (p. 201) stood third in the "Enoch Arden" volume of 1864. Like others in that volume it is fitly called an "Idyl of the Hearth." The story of "The Brook" was the flower of romance ; in "Sea Dreams" we have a meagre incident from the most homely life.

---

[1] Tennyson's sketch of "The Brook" may be compared with one in the twenty-fifth stanza of the "Hallowe'en" of Burns, where the picturesque "bickering" is found ; and the refrain, "men may come," etc., resembles the following inscription on a sun-dial :

> "Io vado e vengo ogni giorno,
> Ma tu andrai senza ritorno."

The word "waterbreaks" may come from one of Wordsworth's sonnets— "dancing down its waterbreaks." Cf. also his stanza :

> "Down to the vale this water steers,
>   How merrily it goes ;
> 'Twill murmur on a thousand years,
>   And flow as now it flows."

But as the brook which gave a name to the former poem entered like a joyous being into its composition, so the sea which appears with such significance in the title of this poem, also becomes a living presence that lends grandeur to the whole work. How much we may learn from the mere title of a poem is a fact often noticed in the present treatise, and there is no doubt that the main intention of the poet in regard to these two poems is to be discovered in their titles. In "The Brook" and "Sea Dreams" certain forms of nature are brought into closer relation with humanity, and endowed with an utterance more divine than human—"With Him there is no variableness, neither shadow of turning"—this is the voice of the brook. The other is the mighty voice of the ocean— "Thy judgments are like the great deep." And these judgments, as we learn from "Sea Dreams," are forgiveness and love.

This is another notable feature of Tennyson's idylls ; they range from the light and graceful picturing of human loves among fair scenes of nature to the picturing, through nature, of a love that is divine ; and "Sea Dreams," which is so sublime in its simplicity, fitly concludes the series.

Among the many important aspects of the poem is Tennyson's view of satire expressed in the lines, beginning "I loathe it." As to the satire itself,—"With all his conscience and one eye askew," the poet seems to say to us, "You see how I could write the well-known couplets if I chose, but I do not choose." The germ of this "old satire" may perhaps be found in Shakespeare's "Richard III." I. iii. 323-338 : for Gloucester, whose arm or back were askew, as was all his conscience, says,

> "I do the wrong, and first begin to brawl. . . .
> But then I sigh, and with a piece of scripture
> Tell them that God bids us do good for evil :
> And thus I clothe my naked villainy

> With old odd ends stolen out of holy writ ;
> And seem a saint when most I play the devil." [1]

No poet has described dream-life so fully and accurately as Tennyson.   In " The Brook " which we have just left, this realistic passage occurs :

> " As one before he wakes
> Who feels a glimmering strangeness in his dream."

" In Memoriam " contains many interesting studies from the world of dreams ; and this is true of other poems ; indeed, the subject is important enough in Tennyson's works to deserve separate treatment.

In this poem one dream is well conceived, and both are such as we " recollect Just ere the waking," [2] for each is caused by the noise that also breaks it.   The husband's dream is natural ; but the woman could not possibly dream out all that allegory.   Such a history of discordant creeds that become music " in the roll And march of that Eternal Harmony,"—this and other interpretations that might be offered, tend to show that the allegory, like the mad scene in " Maud," has too much

---

[1] The line
> "So false, he partly took himself for true,"

is like the passage in "The Tempest," I. ii. 100-102,

> " Who having unto truth, by telling of it,
> Made such a sinner of his memory
> To credit his own lie."

The line
> "And snakelike slimed his victim ere he gorged,"

appears with a variation in " The Princess,"

> "And dress the victim to the offering up."

The figure, "oily", occurs in "King Lear," I. i. 228,

> " I want that glib and oily art
> To speak and purpose not ;'

compare also the "oily courtesies" of "The Princess.*
[2] "Lucretius."

method in it.   Nor does the poet's own interpretation, though purposely distorted, remove the impression of improbability.   Further, the "loud-lunged Antibaby-lonianisms" of their Boanerges pulpiteer, or "The preaching man's immense stupidity," as Browning calls it, have little in common with the dream except "the ruin of a world."

The poet's power of gesture-painting already referred to is conspicuous in such lines as "And then began to bloat himself, and ooze All over with the fat affectionate smile That makes the widow lean"; this appears in "The Princess" as "oozed All o'er with honey'd answer." Still better known is the passage

> "Then my eyes
> Pursued him down the street, and far away,
> Among the honest shoulders of the crowd,
> Read rascal in the motions of his back,
> And scoundrel in the supple-sliding knee."

Equally familiar is the tender picture of domestic love which closes the poem.   But a word must be said about the characters ; we have met them all elsewhere—all but the woman ; she moves amongst the rest, a healing presence of forgiveness and love, till they too are subdued unto her loveliness ; and she can only be compared to that other Presence felt throughout the poem—the Ocean of Love itself.

(161) "LUCRETIUS."   "Lucretius" was first published in "Macmillan's Magazine" for May, 1868, and was sub-sequently reprinted as the last poem in "The Holy Grail" volume of 1870.

In many respects it is a remarkable work.   In no other has Tennyson's dramatic, or rather monodramatic, faculty expressed itself with such assurance and at the same time with such passionate force.   It is easily the most power-ful of all his shorter poems.   "Love and Duty" would rank next. Nor is there anything in the dramas that could be compared with its vivid dramatic portraiture.

Next, the incident chosen was a doubtful one for Tennyson to deal with, although he had previously written "Vivien." With some it would be a question whether these fleshly effects of a love potion are a fit subject for poetical treatment at all. In Matthew Arnold's "Tristram and Iseult," the magic cup is an occasion for nothing more serious than fine love poetry ; but the intermittent ravings of Lucretius, however they may be contrasted with his saner moods, carry us beyond the bounds of human experience, or at least of the human experience that lies within the region of legitimate art. We do not draw pictures of fowls that are moulting—though, after all, we might, for their condition is not exactly abnormal.

It has already been pointed out [1] that there are two ways of securing novelty of effect in art ; one is by introducing material sometimes regarded as abnormal ; such in modern literature would be the dialect of "The Northern Farmer," the social corruption of "Don Juan," the amorous maladies of "Poems and Ballads" (First Series), the daring nakednesses of "Leaves of Grass." This is the easier way ; and it may lead to notoriety instead of renown. The other, which is difficult, is the more literary method, noticed several times in this volume, where attempts have been made to guess the secret of Tennyson's early charm ; seen also in that medley of easy wit and unstudied pathos in "Don Juan," in the strong new music struck from the instrument of words in "Poems and Ballads" (First Series), and in the vigour and freshness and aptness of phrase of "Leaves of Grass."

Apart from this possible objection, "Lucretius" remains the masterpiece of Tennyson. It was also a masterpiece in regard to choice of subject—we are not now referring

[1] See p. 40, footnote.

to the philtre, but to the groundwork supplied chiefly by the great poem of the Roman writer. Indeed, we might almost say that the earlier artist left to Tennyson little more than the condensing and re-shaping of the work. " Tithonus " was a much more difficult study ; materials were meagre, the character was shadowy. But in the " De Rerum Natura " Tennyson had before him a living model ; this, being a great artist, he would reproduce in lifelike dramatic portraiture ; such a result would more certainly follow the reading of a work whose pathos penetrates the soul like some keen electric force. Tennyson is reported to have said to a friend, " I shall never write a good drama ; I have not enough passion." But we might almost say of his " Lucretius " that the poem is sometimes profound in its passion, and sometimes pants with it.

Also from the " De Rerum Natura " Tennyson naturally draws much of his material ; sometimes he is content with paraphrase or even translation. Other classical writers are occasionally called upon for contribution. But the incident of the love potion and the manner of death are not derived from sources strictly classical—a fact that lends weight to the objection noticed above.

" Tithonus " was Greek in manner, and but slightly modern in sentiment; " Lucretius," as would be expected, is Roman, and is infused with not a little of our century's pessimism. Avoiding details, which would be exceedingly numerous, and having regard only to the general effect of the poem, we may add that the darkness of its night is relieved by an implied remoteness. By re-writing the tragedy—not so much of the death of Lucretius, whatever that may have been, as of what may perhaps be called the tragedy of his poem—Tennyson has given it perspective : he would have us say to ourselves, " Thus the noble melancholy enthusiast of those dark Roman days thought and died " ; and there follows something like a moral : " Some say the night is father of the light." [1] For all that we may also detect in the laureate's great poem not a little of his habitual inclination to be fascinated by the dark,[2] as well as his *one* opportunity of letting "darkness keep her raven gloss."

[1] "The Ancient Sage."

[2] "For the drift of the Maker is dark."—*Maud.*

See also the remark of Mr. Knowles, p. 159, footnote. To this may be added Tennyson's own observation to Mr. Knowles concerning "In Memoriam," "It's too hopeful, this poem, more than I am myself." Yet in order to be strictly impartial, it seems best to believe on this as on many other occasions, that there were two Tennysons ; and these two may be discovered side by side near the end of the Fourth Canto of "The Princess," in the seventeen lines preceding the song "Thy voice is heard thro' rolling drums."

CHAPTER VII.

"THE PRINCESS."

I. "A MEDLEY." Shakespeare once wrote a play to be performed " on Midsummer day at night." This " midsummer " frolic of youthful fancy was delightfully adapted to the occasion ; but the author was careful to explain its incongruous elements and improbable incidents by the wording of the title ; therefore he called it " a dream." And in order to be sure that his audience would take him at his word, he seized every opportunity that the piece afforded him of reminding them of its dream-like character ; and at the conclusion, the speaker of the epilogue begged them to imagine that they had but

> " Slumber'd here
> While these visions did appear."

In the same way Tennyson calls his " Princess " "A Medley ;" repeats his description in a prologue, " This *were* a medley ;" tells us in the body of the work that "raillery or grotesque or false sublime" will now give place to a more heroic style ; and then, in an epilogue, after making the admission :

> "And drove us, last, to quite a solemn close,"

he adds with peculiar emphasis :

> " I moved as in a strange diagonal,
> And maybe neither pleased myself nor them."

In spite of the poet's most explicit statement, many commentators are at the pains to prove that " The Princess " is not " a medley ; " the real, they say, does not jostle with the ideal, nor mediæval chivalry with girl graduates, nor mediæval romance with modern science ; if they find that opposing elements do not serve the purpose of contrast, they endeavour to show that these elements harmonize, and thus they destroy their individuality ; in short, to quote from the play of Shakespeare above referred to, they everywhere "find the concord of this discord."

We prefer to take Tennyson, like Shakespeare, at his word ; "A Midsummer Night's Dream " is a dream ; and " The Princess " is a medley.

Whether as a work of poetic art " The Princess " ought ever to have been a medley, is a question that will thrust itself upon us when the story comes to be considered. This much, at present, is certain ; it is easier to write a medley than a work which exhibits throughout harmony of design and consistency of treatment.

If Tennyson had not called " The Princess " " A Medley," we might perhaps have rested satisfied with the severe criticism brought to bear upon his work by the poet himself after its first appearance in 1847. Yet the numerous alterations in scheme or in detail which were made in the subsequent editions, strongly support the previous part of this chapter. And finally, after all this revision, the appellation " A Medley " was still retained.

Few poets have made so many comments upon their writings as Tennyson. Not seldom his poems are disfigured by some "prelude of disparagement." Of these notes and apologies many have been suppressed ; but from " Poems by Two Brothers " to " Demeter," the tendency to self-depreciation is still noticeable. In " Morte D'Arthur " it seems to raise a technical question, "Why bring the style of those heroic times ? " and again, in " The Princess," " What style could suit ? " But the subject has been discussed in the first Appendix to Chapter I., and in another aspect it will be glanced at in the Appendix to Chapter XI.

II. "THE PRINCESS" COMPARED WITH OTHER POEMS. The following considerations are more important to our present subject. From the Appendix to Chapter XI. we learn to look for signs of hesitation in all Tennyson's longer poems—"The Princess," "In Memoriam," "Maud," and the "Idylls of the King." For the outpouring of his grief and love in "In Memoriam" the poet chooses no framework; not even a series of sonnets; he employs unequal groups of stanzas. "The Princess" and the "Idylls of the King" are seen to be tentative epics, while "Maud" is a tentative drama. To tell a story is, primarily, the easiest thing in literary art; therefore, for his first essay, "The Princess," Tennyson will choose the form of a story. But as the story of "The Princess" was lofty enough and long enough to grow dangerously like an epic, the poet hit upon the happy device of parcelling it out among several story-tellers, and in later editions he assigned to the ladies their important parts, the songs they sang between the various sections, whereby his poem gained greatly in consecutiveness and unity. King Arthur, "the grandest subject in the world," seemed to call unequivocally for epic treatment; but again the poet proceeded with caution, and pieced it out among more or less disconnected episodes. In "Maud," as noticed elsewhere,[1] a series of lyrics effect the rise and fall of the curtain, paint the scenery, develope the one character, and save the poet much management of incident; in fact, he thus contrived to get almost as near to drama as was possible without attempting what, after all, is the real life of drama—interaction of characters. Tennyson's own view of the dramatic qualities of "Maud"

[1] Chapter X.

is not entirely different from the foregoing :—" No other poem (a monotone with plenty of change and no weariness) has been made into a drama where successive phases of passion in one person take the place of successive persons." [1]

But it is not in design alone that Tennyson's longer poems show signs of weakness. Weakness hitherto has been concealed within shortness. Indeed, we could hardly expect to find the perfect workmanship of " The Palace of Art" in every paragraph of " The Princess." This again, being the first of Tennyson's longer poems, affords the most numerous examples of the weakness described in a former chapter. [2] There was always in Tennyson a tendency towards puerility together with that excessive refinement of phrase which really touches the borders of bathos. There is scarcely a considerable poem he has written that does not discover an example of this tendency. " Lucretius," the most consistently powerful of all his writings, and, even in metre, strong with the strength of its original, is probably the only exception.

III. OTHER FEATURES :—What then are the merits of " The Princess "? Briefly, they are those of Tennyson's other long poems ; the matchless beauty and the priceless wisdom of parts. Lovers of " In Memoriam " will not be blind to its occasional banalities nor deaf to its occasional discords, but they will know by heart more than half of the sections of the poem. When readers of " Maud " reach Parts II. and III., they may be surprised at the intrusion of intellectual elements into the exposition of emotion, but they will return to Part I. and read it again, and be more than ever convinced of its surprising loveliness and astonishing originality. Next, considering the magnitude of the work, it may be said that in the " Idylls of the King" weakness is rarer and excellence more

---

[1] " Nineteenth Century," January, 1893. [2] See pp. 53-55.

sustained than in any other of these four poems. As to
"The Princess," it may be a medley; but the medley
includes such a prodigality of beauties, that—if the state-
ment be not ungrateful—we run some risk of becoming
surfeited with sweets. There are many passages in "The
Princess" that surpass, line for line, almost any other
poetic work of the same kind out of Tennyson; and the
whole poem is so replete with what is wise and good and
graceful, that in this respect it may be compared with
"In Memoriam," but, as far as we are aware, with no
other poem in literature.

For a first example of particular passages, let us take a
paragraph of mock-heroic style, in which the sobriety of
Tennyson might not be supposed to excel. "The Rape
of the Lock" has been compared to "The Princess"—a
very unfortunate comparison for Pope; by the side of
"The Princess" the graceful form of Pope's famous poem
can no longer conceal coarseness of wit, meanness of
satire, finality of fancy, insincerity of artifice; it is the
perfection of pettiness.

But in Tennyson even the fireworks of fancy flash
against a moonlit heaven of imagination, and there is
nothing in "The Rape of the Lock," and surely, again,
there is nothing in all literature that can approach such a
delicate interweaving of the graceful and the grotesque as
will be found in a passage already quoted.[1]

Next, as regards word-painting, the description of the
tournament may be a little overwrought, but to match it
we go naturally to "The Idylls of the King." Of gesture-
painting the examples are admirable and abundant:

> "Thereat the Lady stretch'd a vulture throat,
> And shot from crooked lips a haggard smile"

is one among a dozen such. The small sweet idyl:
"Come down, O maid, from yonder mountain height," is

[1] P. 45.

of extraordinary excellence. As to the songs, they, of course, are matchless ; one of them, "Tears, idle Tears," is so wonderful that it must have separate notice.[1] Indeed, to describe a tenth of the minor beauties of "The Princess" is far from possible. Certainly, as hinted above, the poet's thoughts sometimes appear over-dressed ; and remind us of certain photographs in which the finery and not the person makes the picture. But on this very account of excess of ornament the poem offers the best material extant for the student of literary art. In regard to Humour, it will be found that the article on this subject in Chapter I. makes special reference to 'The Princess." Nature, in this poem, is mostly ornament, or the hand-maid of human emotion ; but how excellent is the poet's work in either case :

> " Not a thought, a touch,
> But pure as lines of green that streak the white
> Of the first snowdrop's inner leaves."

This remarkable climax, following close upon another, reminds us of

> " Chaste as the icicle
> That 's curdied by the frost from purest snow,
> And hangs on Dian's temple."

Chaste as a cold, bright point of ice ; not any ice, but ice curdied ; not by any other agency, but by frost ; not from water, but from the melted snow ; not any snow, but the purest ; the purest of the pure, for it lay on the roof of the temple of the goddess of chastity herself. So with the other ; pure as a fine line ; a line of green ; pencilled on white, the white of a snowdrop, of the "first snowdrop of the year ;"[2] and on the snowdrop's inmost leaves. The next quotation puts us in mind of the manner in which Victor Hugo makes nature interpose to sympathise with human emotions :

[1] Pp. 250-258.   [2] "St. Agnes' Eve."

> " Till notice of a change in the dark world
> Was lispt about the acacias, and a bird
> That early woke to feed her little ones
> Sent from a dewy breast a cry for light."

The change in the dark world suggests change—sweet change of dawn—in the darkened heart of the princess; in nature it is the dawn of love; of a mother's love for her offspring; such as the princess had dreamt of when she felt the helpless orphan hands about her breast in the " dead prime." All this comes out from the words, " her little ones." Before leaving the passage we may notice the poet's exactness. The dark world is the " dead prime," or the " dark summer dawns" of " Tears, Idle Tears,"— " For night is darkest just before the dawn." The change that was " lispt " is the breeze of morning trembling o'er the leaves,—the breeze that time after time [1] swept with its sweets across the lyre of Tennyson.

Hitherto we have spoken more particularly of the " graceful "; it remains for us to say that the " wise" and " good " are everywhere abundant; " Better not be at all than not be noble" is one among hundreds of such jewels of truth cut and polished by this most cunning of craftsmen. To sum up, we may pass from isolated passages, and refer to the last canto as containing within itself—not humour, for it is the " solemn close,"—but almost all other excellencies of poetry; and it contains nothing but such excellencies.

IV. THE SUBJECT. (*a*) *In its general aspect.* Originally male and female are often one physical being. The ideal individual man and woman of the future also form one being, physical, mental, and moral. Another ideal which has less regard for the individual, pictures the sexes as equal yet different parts of a community, each part finding its own in the other's good.

---

[1] "In Memoriam," xcv. "Maud," Part I. xx.i. 2, etc.

Of these two ideals, the second or collective, is the more modern ; and, at its best, seeks to include the first.

Tennyson, as we have seen in his politics, was an individualist. Therefore in his "Princess" the relation between the sexes is mostly individual—a relation which is expressed with striking felicity in the last line but one of his poem,

> " Accomplish thou my manhood and thyself."

This, then, is the first fact to be borne in mind by readers of "The Princess." For the more modern ideal they must turn to other writers.

The relation between men and women has varied from time immemorial. But from fable alone can we gather that the women ever had it all their own way ; as in the case of the "legendary Amazons" who, bee-like, had turned out the drones. Oftener, historically at any rate, the opposite has been reported—that man, like chanticleer, "Stoutly struts his dames before." Having glanced at these extremes we may sum up in one line the varying position of women in the past—"This hour a slave, the next a deity ;"[1] adding, however, that the slave position has been the more usual one.

In natural history, again, we find on a lower scale, examples of almost all the varying relationships between men and women ; it will be enough to say generally and very briefly, that maternal duties have made the female sex physically weaker, more passive, more patient ; adroit, gentler, more attractive.

Therefore what men have prized in women is tenderness, beauty, love ; what they have missed is, to use the idea of Milton, matchable conversation. All this is being altered now :

> " For in the long years liker must they grow."

---

[1] "The liver vein, which makes flesh a deity."—*Love's Labour's Lost*, IV iii. 74. "Superstition all awry."—*The Princess*, ii. 121.

Already women are less maternal, less wifely, less love-able : they have not been content with acquiring a more matchable conversation. Love must lose something ; something may be gained. But when a future Carlyle sketches his Blumine he must leave out one priceless sentence—" Not a caprice he could spare." Our remain-ing reflection will be a judicial one :—" It is indispensable to acquire the advantage ; it is lamentable to incur the evil."

(*b*) *In its relation to " The Princess."* The many women of Tennyson's earlier volumes are conventional ; but they are the best of their kind. There are the " innocent-arch " Lilian ; Isabel, " model of wifehood," " queen of marriage," " of finish'd chasten'd purity " ; there are Adeline, shadowy, dreamy ; Elëanore, serene, im-perial ; there are Madeline, perfect in love-lore ; Margaret, pale and pensive ; there are loving, laughing Leonora, wild Rosalind, gallant Kate ; and there is the smart *maîtresse de ses sens*, the lady of the skipping rope :

> *He.* " Nay, dearest, teach me how to hope,
>   Or tell me how to die."
> *She.* " There, take it, take my skipping-rope
>   And hang yourself thereby."

They are all delightful, all loveable ; but of none are we told that she was eminently intellectual. They would surely tell us of themselves, every one of them, that " men hated learned women ; " and the poet, when he drew them with such delight of daintiness, would surely be saying the same.

We next notice the importance thus early attached by Tennyson to love and marriage as the portion of women, to home as their sphere, and to maternity as their first duty :[1] the intellectual qualities, capacities and pursuits

---

[1]   " What every woman counts her due,
     Love, children, happiness."
         The Princess, iii. 228, 229.

are never allowed to take rank with these. For example,
when we read

> " The child shall grow
> To prize the authentic mother of her mind,"

we look closely at the word " authentic," and suspect that
the poet is postponing affection to intellect. But we are
to be undeceived ; no sooner has the princess made this
seeming plausible statement than she unwittingly testifies
to the enormous preponderance of one hour of " authentic "
motherhood :

> " I took it for an hour in mine own bed
> This morning : there the tender orphan hands
> Felt at my heart, and seem'd to charm from thence
> The wrath I nursed against the world."

And in "Locksley Hall," the "baby fingers, waxen touches"
are a far stronger rival to the lover than the man who took
away his love.   Whether before he writes " The Princess,"
or after, motherhood, and next to that, wifehood, is Tenny-
son's ideal of womanhood.   From countless passages
we learn the importance, the sacredness of a mother ;
and to a mother's love he concentrates the highest effort
of his tragic and lyrical genius—" Rizpah."

We have anticipated a little, but it was with the purpose
of showing that when Tennyson took up the great
Woman's Rights question, he was likely to deal with it
temperately :

> " Turning to scorn, with lips divine,
> The falsehood of extremes,"

a quotation, we may add, which can hardly be repeated

" Her office there to rear, to teach. . . ."
In Memoriam, xl.
To this it may be added that the line

" Who loved one only, and who clave to her,"

contains perhaps the chief moral teaching of the " Idylls of the King." A
further reference to this subject will be found in Chapter XV.

too often. The poet, therefore, will approach the subject from all sides, and with due caution ; according to his wont he will express various opinions, and among them his own, through the medium of various characters, in order, as it were, to hear how they sound when falling from the lips of others.

The questionings concerning woman's true position in the economy of nature confront us quite suddenly in Tennyson's poetry. "The Skipping Rope," which was mentioned as being the last of his early sketches of fair women, was given to the public together with "Locksley Hall" in 1842. We have already noticed [1] a passage in this latter poem, "Woman is the lesser man" as one that was uttered only half in earnest ; nevertheless it denotes a new attention to the subject ; and the passage beginning "Or to burst all links of habit . . .", in which the speaker will withdraw from a society whose women are weakness, and join himself to a healthier savage race, and woo a savage for his bride, is in many respects the counterpart of the plan of Princess Ida. But with this exception "The Princess" of 1847 is the first intimation of the extent to which the subject had occupied the poet's mind. Yet in "Edwin Morris," though not published till 1851, we have such an elementary statement of the question [2] as might justify a surmise that this poem dates earlier than "The Princess."

When a great writer has selected a subject, or has had it forced upon him, he makes himself acquainted with the literature that already bears upon that subject ; and thus he usually meets with suggestions for his own plan of treatment. Tennyson was often keenly alive to the burning questions of his day ; he could not fail to hear the outcries against injustice to women in the past, and the demand for reparation ; and when he had determined to

[1] P. 163.
[2] "God made the woman for the use of man," etc. See p. 154.

devote his learning and his genius to a consideration of their case, he began by sifting the evidence already brought forward in the pages of literature. For some of the results of his inquiries we may turn to the speech of Lilia in the Prologue to "The Princess": "Quick answered Lilia;" and her answer was to the following effect: "Women are not such inferior creatures; the marvel is that after 'six thousand years of wrong' they are not much worse; stupid customs still deny space and fairplay to their possibilities of nobleness; their chief want is education. 'It is but bringing up'; prohibition of education is the worst injustice done to them; and that terrible injustice they have suffered at the hands of man. But the time has come when right may sometimes raise its head; women may perhaps take of themselves what men have so unwisely and so ungraciously refused to give. Oh that she could 'build Far off from men a college like a man's:' there she would teach women 'all that men are taught.'" This, and more of the same purport Tennyson would read in his survey of literature; but, as we shall shortly discover, he would also learn, what did not occur to Lilia, that to teach women "all that men are taught" would be far from satisfying the aspirations of a right-minded woman. Passing over suggestions offered by the Spartan customs, by Plato's "Republic," by mediæval writers, and later by Ascham, Milton and others, we meet the first definite College project in The Female Academy of Margaret Cavendish, 1662. Next, Defoe, who whether sincerely or otherwise, was often a notable champion of the weaker cause, may be regarded as commencing the dawn.[1] Defoe proposed to establish a College for Ladies where they should learn subjects "suitable to both their genius and their quality." In his "Essay on Projects," 1697, Defoe wrote: "I need

---

[1] "The Princess," ii. 122.

not enlarge on the loss the defect of education is to women, nor argue the benefit of the contrary practice ; it is a thing will be more easily granted than remedied. This chapter is not an essay at the thing, and I refer the practice to those happy days, if ever they shall be, when men shall be wise enough to mend it."

The great cause continued to find champions ; Steele and Addison inaugurated the good work in the eighteenth century ; progress, though fitful, could be recorded as the century rolled on ; and in 1787 the celebrated Mary Wollstonecroft began her literary career with "Thoughts on the Education of Daughters."   Then, in the very year [1] of Tom Paine's "Rights of Man," she published her Rights of Woman.[2]   She asks in prose what Shelley and Tennyson, with equal wisdom, asked in verse,

> "Can man be free if woman be a slave?"
> *Revolt of Islam.*

> "If she be small, slight-natured, miserable,
>   How shall men grow?"
> *The Princess.*

Or, again, if woman "Stays all the fair young planet in her hands," ought not those hands to be trained for their important task ?   This valuable book set the example of a temperate and enlightened treatment of a subject fraught with sensation ; but the example of Mary Wollstonecroft was not always followed—not even by Shelley, whose contribution, however, has a value of its own ; and by the time that Tennyson in England shed over it the beautiful light of imagination, and Auguste Comte in France the strong light of truth, the question had become wellnigh lost amid darkness of extravagant ignorance.

The scheme of "The Princess," as Tennyson designed

---

[1] 1791-2.
[2] "Vindication of the Rights of Women, with Strictures on Political and Moral Subjects."

it, will probably be discovered if we place a passage in Johnson's " Rasselas " by the side of " Love's Labour's Lost." The Princess in " Rasselas " " desired first to learn all sciences, and then proposed to found a college of learned women in which she would preside, that, by conversing with the old and educating the young, she might divide her time between the acquisition and communication of wisdom, and raise up for the next age models of prudence and patterns of piety." That Tennyson availed himself of this hint is almost certain, because a little earlier in the context we read, " The princess thought that of all sublunary things knowledge was the best." " Knowledge, so my daughter held, was all in all," says Gama ; and Tennyson is very careful to point out this mistake in Ida's scheme. Again, Ida did first desire for " many weary moons " to learn a science, or sciences ; in the college were learned women, and Lady Blanche was one of the " old." In fact this passage, together with " Love's Labour's Lost," supplies more than the foundation of Tennyson's famous College. " The Princess " is a counterpart in opposites of Shakespeare's play ; there the plot turns on the withdrawal from the world of a king and three lords for the purpose of study ; they withdraw for a term of three years ; they bind themselves not for three years to see any woman ; and a princess and her three ladies play very much the same part as the prince and his companions in Tennyson's story. Minor resemblances between " Love's Labour's Lost " and " The Princess " are far too numerous for mention ; but no reader should omit to notice them.

V. THE STORY.—Except in the case of the numerous and abruptly-shifting scenes of " Maud," and in that of some of his less familiar poems, Tennyson's stories may be left to tell themselves. Our purpose in this review of "The Princess " will be to consider the story rather than re-tell it, to discover the significance of the characters, and point out the more important lessons to be learnt from the poem.

In regard to the main part of the story—the establishment and conduct of the College by the Princess, it would seem that Ida has been harshly dealt with by commentators ; and harshly and somewhat inconsistently by the poet. She is not really so much to blame as Tennyson, for his purpose, intends her to be. She has been accused of rejecting the opinion, the presence, and the support of men who wished well to her cause ; of trusting to mere knowledge for the redemption of women ; of regarding the isolation of woman from man as the best method of imparting that knowledge to her own sex, and as the only means of re-establishing a just equality with the other sex. She is further accused—and this is the gravest charge—of shutting out the natural affections. Her whole scheme for the betterment of women is generally regarded as a delusion, a folly, if not a fault.

In order to test the validity of these charges, we will at first proceed in the usual way, and merely inquire, " What do we really learn from the story ? " Remembering that our inquiry is a provisional one, we notice that the Princess asked " space and fairplay " for an experiment. She first took care that her own education should be such as might justify her position as head of the college. Others, whose age and learning commended them, shared her project.

But we must now inquire into the origin of that project ; what, according to Ida, was to be accomplished for women, and how was it to be accomplished ? Of this we have many accounts in the poem, so many that reference to each is impossible ; nor do they always agree. But we gather from them generally that Ida's view of the past history of women was " six thousand years of wrong ; " wrong in every age and nation ; such persistent wrong from man that she might well distrust all men ; and the

cure for these evils was to be "bringing up," in the words
of Lilia, or "equal husbandry" in her own words, as
quoted by Gama.

And now to return to the founding of the college. Ida
secured a staff of professors who, as far as we are told,
had "no links with men." Lady Psyche seems to be an
exception, for she had a brother ; but Ida had brothers
and a father. Her purpose was to "build a fold" far off
from men, and to which no man should be admitted—"on
pain of death"; that sounds ill, and it must be left for
future notice.

This fold she stored "full of rich memorial ;" nothing
was omitted that could influence her students for their
good.

But they were "not for three years to correspond with
home." Without regarding the ambiguous date of Ida's
experiment, we can point to many an institution of our
own times in which rules the same in kind, though perhaps
not in degree, for the space of three years, are enforced.
The Princess thought she would obtain better results if the
refining influences of her college could win their way with-
out interruption into hearts that, at the average age of
her students, were very liable to receive less favourable
impressions elsewhere ; and submission to these rules
was voluntary. She herself purposed "never to wed."
That was quite her own affair, and she was not the first
woman so to purpose. But she merely cautioned her
pupils against men who "rhyme themselves into ladies'
favours, and then reason themselves out again"—rogues
"of canzonets and serenades"—she does not even advise
them not to marry ; though if the authors of some modern
novels had been on her staff, she might well have gone
as far as that ; she first warned them against

> "Things whose trade is over ladies,
> To lean and flirt and stare and simper,"

but she also warned them against the same faults in them-
selves ; for Shelley's stanza continues :

> "Till all that is divine in woman
> Grows cruel, courteous, smooth, inhuman,
> Crucified 'twixt a smile and whimper ; "

and so the Princess continues

> "You likewise will do well,
> Ladies, in entering here, to cast and fling
> The tricks, which make us toys of men—"

so that, if they did wed, they might make better wives.
She avows no deliberate intention to isolate woman from
man, nor any systematic design of shutting out the affec-
tions ; her purpose " never to wed " was a grand one,
spite of the betrothal (which her father had some difficulty
in recollecting) :

> "Have we not made ourself the sacrifice ? "

and she was ready—she yearned—to face instant death

> "To compass our dear sisters' liberties."

The Princess might even be pardoned for her apparent
belief that mere knowledge would supply all the elements
of the higher education of her pupils ; she used Pope's
phrase, " Drink deep," and followed it with words of high
purpose. With such a woman to tend it, the drooping
flower of knowledge would in due time be changed to
fruit of wisdom. That is fairly certain from the promi-
nence she gave to art and moral teaching. We have
noticed[1] in an earlier chapter that at the opening of the
Josiah Mason Institute not many years ago, it was main-
tained that Science alone afforded a liberal education ;
and it required the genius of Matthew Arnold to prove
the contrary. That former doctrine Ida would never have
admitted ; for, as was mentioned in the same chapter,[2]
she dwells on the influence of the sculptor's art ; and

[1] See p. 36.   [2] See p. 40.

thereafter she urges her students, " Oh, lift your natures up ; let your minds be ennobled by looking on these noble works of art ; and further, they embody, idealized, all that is noblest in woman." And to this she adds, " Better not be at all Than not be noble." The drooping flower of knowledge has already changed to fruit of wisdom.

Another question now presses for space ; what, according to the story, were the weak points in Ida's scheme? Again the accounts vary ; and our conclusions must be brief, and hastily gathered up. We may begin with the subject last touched upon—knowledge. In the confession made by the Princess herself towards the end of the poem, we read that she " sought far less for truth than power In Knowledge." That is a very common mistake ; Knowledge is a means to an end. Some people rest in the means, as does the " man of science " in " Maud."[1] Ida at present was busied with the means of accomplishing her purpose ; but the dream " that once was hers " would soon have " raised the blinding bandage from her eyes," and bidden her behold the end. In her case the power that knowledge brought would itself have rendered a right use of knowledge possible. But quite apart from this question we must notice the exaggerated tone of all this confession :

> " It was ill counsel had misled the girl."

This is inadmissible on many grounds ; first because of the same dream that once was hers ; and then we have to set against it her own protest that in itself the institution was excellent ; that it fell through treachery :

> " Had you stood by us
> The roar that breaks the Pharos from his base
> Had left us rock."

She had " fail'd in sweet humility." This is subject to the same modification ; we are tempted to add, in the

[1] See p. 27.

words of the Prince, " True, she errs, But in her own grand way." She had failed ; her labour was but as a " block Left in the quarry" ; but it was goodly labour none the less. "There's a downright honest meaning in her," said Arac. The labour was noble, we add.

Certainly, the girls in the College "murmur'd that their May was passing" ; this is the best justification of the " three years " regulation. After these incidental remarks we will quote the chief apparent cause of Ida's failure : " She sees herself in every woman else." That is to say, had she been supported by others as noble as herself, her College might have been left " rock."

Our " provisional" inquiry has now been carried far enough ; we have proceeded, as stated at the outset, in the usual fashion, picking up, that is, as we have threaded our way through the Medley, facts or statements that recommended themselves to our purpose. The experiment is now at an end.

Suppose we adopt a different method, and test any one statement by its relation to the rest of the poem ; we shall probably be surprised to see what may result from a disregard of the famous but much abused unities of place and time. Ida's stern rule,

" Let no man enter in on pain of death,"

will serve for the purpose ; as an incidental example, it had to be reserved for discussion here. The Prince compared this deadly inscription on the gate to a scarecrow in a fruit garden. In our day the comparison might be just. But what were these days? Since we cannot identify them, let us put them back in a convenient past ; and then we find that the Princess had as much right to treat marauders in this way, as the heroic lady of the Prologue, who

" Arm'd her own fair head,
And beat her foes with slaughter from her walls."

And she was quite as capable of doing it ; and where

one woman could fight, so could more than one. If a quarter of her students were half like herself, it was no idle determination

> " To unfurl the maiden banner of our rights." ·

But all this hypothesis leads to the conclusion that the College, with its numberless modern concomitants, was established in the same remote past.

The theorem can now be stated thus : " Given an age, legendary or historic, in which women are fighters, in that age they will establish a modern College."

Let us now reverse the theorem. Ida establishes a College for women, quite modern in its essential concomitants. By-and-by she gets into all sorts of difficulties, and incurs the blame of every critic. But she was placed in those difficulties by a series of circumstances quite incompatible with the founding of the College ; a tournament was an impossibility, to say nothing of the " wasps" that "entered the good hive." This, stated as a theorem would be the converse of the former, and would lead us to a similar conclusion. For, as we can form no opinion of Ida's conduct except as it is related to the whole of its environment, and as that environment is an impossibility, it follows that to sit in judgment on Ida's conduct is an impossibility.

If now we put the question, " What brings about Ida's overthrow ?" we find ourselves in a position to answer : " It is ‘ The Medley.’ "

And returning for a moment to the popular mode of criticism, and putting the Medley—if possible—aside, we might continue with the reflection that, given space and fair play, the College would have been not a perfect but a useful institution, and that the lady superior was admirably fitted for her post.

This section will conclude with one other consideration, rather an important one, but again to be made irrespective of the real fact, the Medley. We feel that Ida has to plead guilty for very much more than her share. Her confessions, as noticed above, were unwarranted ; the Prince assumes an undue superiority, a patronizing air that seems out of place. No wonder Walter should have remarked, "I wish she had not yielded." The fact is that the catastrophe, especially as concerns Ida, was not duly brought about ; it was convenient to the poet but not inevitable to Ida ; it was not supported by events.

VI. THE CHARACTERS. Viewed through the obscurity of the Medley, the impossibility, that is, of making situations tally, the characters, if visible at all, are inconsistent. If we grant that they may be dimly outlined, then Ida is too heroic for conquest by a love that was underhand, even though that love was the agent of "great nature" ; and the Prince is too unheroic to take her sweet hands in his, though she resigns them to Love rather than to a lover. Here, we say, is another maudlin man come upon the poet's stage to show the audience how a woman can redeem him ! Edith, we have already conjectured, must have "spent a stormy time" with the "strange"[1] being of "Locksley Hall." Maud's marriage fortunately would be made in heaven ; Arthur's, unfortunately, was made on earth ; and Guinevere would have nothing to do with his "waste dreams," and so everything went wrong. And now this Prince of shadows, dreams, and weakness, has the audacity to talk as follows to a woman who is verily a maiden moon-glorifying a clown :[2]

> "Dearer thou for faults
> Lived over : *lift thine eyes ;* my doubts are dead,
> My haunting sense of hollow shows."

This is exasperating enough ; but when we come to the insolent condescension of the words

> "Approach, and fear not,"

we have lost all patience with the man.

---

[1] The words of Gama, spoken of Ida.   [2] V. 178, 179.

And we are wrong ; it is not the man, but the Medley.

What the poet has said and done is one thing, what he meant us to understand is another. But how are we to get at his real meaning ? Our best but not very satis-factory answer is, that his meaning must be sought most frequently in the very inconsistencies of his work, and for this reason : the necessity of explanation often gave rise to the inconsistency.

For example, the " weird seizures," the " haunting sense of hollow shows," is a trait added to the character of the Prince in the edition of 1851. And the poet meant it to emphasize the part played by nature in subduing the Princess ; also to make the Prince less heroic, and to serve as an apology for his being so ; to serve also as an apology for the character of the whole poem ; and more especially to make the work of redemption set apart for the Princess more important and more complete,[1] for her is reserved the doubtful privilege of making a man of him. If we grant that the Princess is least a woman when she boldly dares all these male thunderbolts that first gave and then treacherously withheld space and fair-play for her scheme, we may also notice that when she is least a woman so is the Prince least a man—he is "among his shadows," a condition suggestive, according to the King of the North, of " old women." But then, again, we have first to accept the important hypothesis that Ida was on those occasions least a woman, and this, as we have seen already, may be disputed. Therefore when the poet's meaning emerges it is usually from an inconsistency ; but even then it may not commend itself to all. Was it fair that Ida should be given over to " an old woman " in order that the reader might understand it was Nature and not the Prince who won her heart ?

[1] In regard to these " weird seizures " which are referred to on pp. 62, 63, 103, etc., it is interesting to note that in " The Princess " the poet always speaks of them in contemptuous terms, as befits their dramatic position.

The other characters are less baffling, though now and then the same dilemma distorts their features. Cyril, who is the incarnation of humorous common sense, displays to view his "solid base of temperament" perhaps too plainly when he is told off for the duty of reminding Ida that Love and Nature are more terrible than her strong will. The speech has nothing in it of Cyril as he appeared formerly, except the adroit finish : "Give *me* it ; *I* will give it her." But Cyril was "batter'd" when he spoke, and he pleaded out of love. Florian represents the relationship between brother and sister, Psyche the more important relationship between mother and child ; but that same relationship as between Lady Blanche and ·Melissa appears somewhat strained, and not on the part of the mother alone. Whatever the circumstances, Melissa was hardly justified in speaking of her mother as she did to perfect strangers, and she ill becomes the part assigned to her by the poet, that, namely, of "dragging in" her wretched father.

Lady Blanche is Ida's opposite. "Then comes the feebler heiress of your plan, And takes and ruins all." She explains the mistake of the Princess who "sees herself in every woman else" ; she is a foil against which every nobleness of Ida's sticks fiery off indeed. Other opposites are the Kings. He of the North impersonates unreflecting brute force, and it colours his view of women. Gama is the impersonation of insignificance and effeminacy, and his view of women is, like his character, insignificant. He remembers the betrothal of his daughter by "The year in which our olives fail'd" : and "Swamp'd in lazy tolerance," and beginning with a formal "We," he confesses, "We remember love ourself In our sweet youth," as though he had come nigh to forgetting what had affected him so lightly. Arac and Ida are heroic children of a weakling father ; but this points to a mother unusually noble, from whom all their nobility must have been derived—"When the man wants weight the woman takes it up." Arac is Ida in man's form, but only the form is great. He illustrates the contention " we are twice as quick," " Were we ourselves but half as good, As kind, as truthful," and generally that, other things being equal, " The woman is the better man."

It has been suggested already that motherhood, and next to that wifehood, is Tennyson's ideal of womanhood ; naturally, therefore, he will make his ideals govern the issues of the poem. And as one ideal requires a child for its expression, and children are implied in the expression of the other, he has introduced Aglaia as the embodiment of both. To her, then, as final arbiter all questions must be submitted, and she will adjust or re-adjust all relation-ships between the contending parties. This is a beautiful idea, to set Nature in their midst in the form of a little child ; and equally beautiful was the poet's kindred idea of allowing the voice of Nature to be heard from time to time :

> " Between the rougher voices of the men
> Like linnets in the pauses of the wind."

For the songs, like the little child, breathe of motherhood, wifehood, love ; of that love which is the poet's best solu-tion of the problem he undertook to solve. (P. 378.)

VII. THE TEACHING OF THE POEM. Although Ten-nyson's violation of the Unities compelled a suspension of judgment respecting the sequence of events and the conduct of the principal characters, there is less difficulty in appraising the sentiments expressed by the various speakers,[1] and in assigning his own to the poet. Not the least among the many excellencies of " The Princess " is the skill with which almost the whole history of opinion on the question in hand is distributed among the *dramatis personæ*. That history might be exhibited in a very

---

[1] But see also p. 28.

interesting form by a series of quotations beginning with the King of the North's " Man is the hunter, woman is his game," which takes us back to the customs of certain savage tribes, and ending with Tennyson's own summing up of the case in those two speeches[1] so wise and far-seeing in their eloquence that men and women of to-day, however advanced in opinion, will surely learn something from them ; will look, for example, towards the human being of the future, perfect in body, mind, and spirit, twain and yet one.

The poem fitly concludes with two other speeches. In the first[2] Tennyson describes his ideal woman, and from what has already been said we may be sure it is the portrait of a mother. It may be compared with Wordsworth's stanzas, " She was a Phantom of Delight," and with Milton's splendid lines in " Paradise Lost," viii. 546-559.

Although Tennyson has not addressed any poem to his mother, she is more than once reflected in his verse ; and she would be present in his thoughts as he made this wonderful sketch, probably the finest thing in the poem. "Happy he With such a mother!" That happiness appears to have been Tennyson's ; and if it falls to few, yet on all men who come after him the picture here drawn confers a possibility—imposes a duty—of happiness and nobleness.[3]

The other and remaining speech, though inconsistent, as we have seen, with the story—too patronising, for example, as addressed to one " The lifting of whose eye-

---

1   " Blame not thyself . . ."
and
           " Dear, but let us type them now. . . ."

2 " Alone, I said. . . ."

3 We have seen that Tennyson's women of an earlier date were not learned; even in this speech he says deliberately of the ideal woman,

       " Not learned, save in gracious household ways."

But later, as in " The Wreck," he seems sometimes to look into the future.

lash is my lord "—is nevertheless appropriate as a concrete presentation of the main contention of the poem, " My hopes and thine are one."

" Either sex alone is half itself." These words are found near the end of " The Princess." Tennyson's thoughts have all along dwelt rather on the individual and personal aspects of the subject ; to its social and political issues he gives but a passing attention, as in the lines

> " Millions of throats would bawl for civil rights,
> No woman named."

The political bearings of the question, such as they were at the date, would no doubt be regarded lightly by the poet, who may also have implied that a better social structure would soon and surely rise on improved personal foundations. For if woman, already the conservator of society, " set herself to man Like perfect music unto noble words," true marriage will become possible ; and true marriage, the poet thinks, means true society. But in our day the social development of woman carries the question some little distance beyond the limits of " The Princess."

Of the various family relationships in the poem that of the father is least distinct. Of the relations of friendship, that between woman and woman is placed in a most unfavourable light ; and by a curious, if not serious, anomaly, the poet, who rightly regards " either sex alone " as " half itself," speaks of a friend as " almost my half-self." The anomaly need not be tested arithmetically, nor even its bearing on the last speech[1] be considered ; it will become ethically apparent when " In Memoriam " is placed by the side of any poem consecrated by Tennyson to the love of woman. These notes on " The Princess " will therefore close with a brief inquiry into the poet's position as regards friendship and love, and thus they will form a

---

[1] " ' Nay, but thee,' I said. . . ."

connecting link between this chapter, whose subject was love, and the next chapter but one, which deals with friendship.

In " In Memoriam " we also meet with the doctrine,

> "First love, first friendship, equal powers
> That marry with the virgin heart : "

but the distinction between friendship and love is essentially real, however much they may at times seem to balance or to blend.

The two instincts that impel individuals to supply "felt deficiencies" are the sexual and the gregarious. Now, roughly speaking, love is a phase—more or less highly developed—of the first, and friendship a similar phase of the second. Next, as the sexual instinct is the more powerful, and the more important in the economy of nature, so the higher growths, associations, and sentiments of this instinct are superior to those of the other instinct. But the sentiments born of sexual love vary with the ages, chiefly because the relation of woman to man (mostly educational) has so greatly varied. And the passion of refined friendship preceded that of refined love, owing to woman's low position. Higher love, for example, scarcely ever existed in ancient times, say among the Greeks and the Latins; hence the appearance of friendship in ancient literature, the many literary monuments to friends in both ancient and modern literature, and the comparative absence of love. The physical basis upon which the edifice of love has been built, by no means detracts from the beauty of that edifice, nor could the mighty passion have risen from any stronger foundation.

We readily admit that even in the same epoch, and the same nation, and the same social grade, the passion of love will assume many different forms, for these exceptions, if rightly regarded, will support our contention that in love, as generally understood, we recognize the most entrancing, the most beautiful, the most spiritual, and the most permanent of human emotions. As to "First love, first friendship, equal powers," Moore may speak for us :

> " Who would not welcome that moment's returning
> When passion first waked a new life through his frame,
> And his soul, like the wood that grows precious in burning,
> Gave out all its sweets to Love's exquisite flame."

Of course, first love may also be first friendship, but the case is rare. And we may further admit that the passion of refined friendship does occasionally approximate to the passion of refined love ; yet they can never be equal or identical. The physical basis of love is to love what the root is to the tree ; and there is no such physical basis in friendship.

If further proof of love's supremacy were needed, we might accept it from Shakespeare, who best of all knew the human heart. Even he for a time (as mentioned in Chapter V.) confused the false love of woman with the true, as when he wrote his "Hamlet"; but to learn Shakespeare's real opinion on the subject we have merely to glance at this list of names—Juliet, Perdita, Helena, Miranda, Katherine, the two Portia's, Mariana, Isabella, Viola, Rosalind, Julia, Beatrice, Hermione, divine Desdemona, divinest Imogen; or his opinion may be given in his own words :

> " Love, first learned in a lady's eyes,
> Lives not alone immured in the brain ;
> It gives to every power a doubled power,
> And when love speaks, the voice of all the gods
> Makes heaven drowsy with the harmony."

Next would come the consideration of the relative importance of love and friendship in the establishment and the economy of society ; but for this, as for several other subjects arising out of the poem, especially the social position of women, no space could be found in the present volume.

APPENDIX TO CHAPTER VII

A LESSON FROM THE LYRICS.

"TEARS, IDLE TEARS."

(From "New Studies in Tennyson.")

From the Lyrics I choose the song, "Tears, idle Tears," partly because we do not expect to find much sediment of thought where the music has been evaporated out of this species of composition, and partly because so many of us have quoted the three words, " Tears, idle tears," without suspecting their meaning, or without caring to believe that they could have any meaning at all. Yet even the airy structure of song should rest on some solid foundation, and I shall endeavour to show that these simple stanzas may tell us much about themselves that is pleasant and profitable, and may be made to reveal not a little of the author's inner life.

But the author must be his own interpreter. This, which is so specially true of Shakespeare, is true of all other great poets. For example, we begin our process of interpretation in this case by quoting from Tennyson's "Timbuctoo" of 1829 :

> "I have raised thee nigher to the spheres of heaven,
> Man's *first*, last home ; and thou with ravish'd sense
> Listenest the lordly music flowing from
> Th' illimitable years."

Almost the same words, and many kindred thoughts, are to be found in the " Ode to Memory," which probably dates earlier ; and in the " Lover's Tale," written, as the poet tells us, in his nineteenth year, we meet with " The Goddess of the Past," " The Present is the Vassal of the

Past," and more to the same effect. And from these early poems we may turn to the last sweet and sad volume of all, and there, in the very last and most sacred poem of all, "The Silent Voices," we hear "a wind Of memory murmuring the Past."

Now search through the poet's work that lies between these limits, and you will discover almost countless passages suggestive of *deep musings and tender broodings over the past—and not the past of human life alone; for many of them are "echoes of some antenatal dream."*

Two or three of these passages I will select.[1] The first is a poem published in "The Gem," 1831 :

> "Oh sad *No more!* Oh sweet *No more!*
>   Oh strange *No more!*
> By a mossed brookbank on a stone
> I smelt a wildweed-flower alone ;
> There was a ringing in my ears,
>   And both my eyes gushed out with tears.
> Surely all pleasant things had gone before ;
> Lowburied fathomdeep beneath with thee, No MORE !

From "Locksley Hall " I choose :

> "Thou shalt hear the ' Never, never,' whisper'd by the phantom years,
> And a song from out the distance in the ringing of thine ears."

Here compare—

> "The earliest pipe of half-awaken'd birds
> To dying ears."

Numerous other such comparisons, with explanations, will be given in the larger volume.[2]

---

[1] Others have been noticed in preceding chapters of this book : for example, another passage from "Timbuctoo," p. 62 ; one from "The Mystic," p. 103 ; and lines from "A Song," of the 1833 volume, and "A Dream of Fair Women," pp. 137 and 138.

[2] These are not included in the present Handbook ; for since the above Commentary was written, the following explanation supplied by Lord Tennyson himself, has been published by Mr. Knowles ("Nineteenth Century," January, 1893) : "All such subjects (idealism, the state of trance, etc.) moved him profoundly, and to an immense curiosity and interest about them. He told me that 'Tears, idle tears' was written as an expression of such

For the antenatal recollections we may turn to the "Two Voices":

> "Moreover, something is or seems,
> That touches me with mystic gleams,
> Like glimpses of forgotten dreams,
>
> "Of something felt like something here,
> Of something done, I know not where,
> Such as no language may declare."

But the most important reference is this, to the "Ancient Sage":

> "To-day? but what of yesterday? for oft
> On me, when boy, there came what then I call'd . . .
> In my boy-phrase 'The Passion of the Past,'
> The first grey streak of earliest summer dawn, . . .
> Desolate sweetness—far and far away—"

And with that compare:

> "What vague world-whisper, mystic pain or joy,
> Thro' those three words would haunt him when a boy,
> Far—far—away?
>
> "A whisper from his dawn of life? a breath
> From some fair dawn beyond the doors of death,
> Far—far—away?
>
> "Far, far, how far? from o'er the gates of Birth,
> The faint horizons, all the bounds of earth,
> Far—far—away?"[1]

Moreover, this lovely song, "Far—Far—Away" resembles "Tears, idle tears" in many points, and not the least in its strange sweet sad charm.

Next the "In Memoriam" contains many references to the "eternal landscape of the Past." But I refrain from

---

longings. *It is in a way like St. Paul's 'groanings which cannot be uttered.' It was written at Tintern when the woods were all yellowing with Autumn seen through the ruined windows. It is what I have always felt even from a boy, and what as a boy I called the 'passion of the past.' And it is so always with with me now; it is the distance that charms me in the landscape, the picture and the past, and not the immediate to-day in which I move."*

[1] "The Soul . . . cometh from afar."—WORDSWORTH'S *Ode on the Intimations.*

further quotations from Tennyson, at least until I have called upon one or two other poets to aid me in the work of elucidation :

Wordsworth's "Ode on the Intimations of Immortality from Recollections of Early Childhood" must, of course, be mentioned first. In this we have an eloquent expression of these sweet and sad visions of the past, these yearnings for something better—above us—beyond us—Far, far away :

> "It is not now as it hath been of yore . . .
> The things which I have seen I now can see *no more*."

This expression *no more*, which occurs in the refrain of "Tears, idle tears," must detain us here. It is a great favourite with our poets ; so is "never more." Poe's account of his selecting the long *o* as the most sonorous vowel, in connection with the *r* as the most producible consonant, is over fanciful ; but we may readily believe that the refrain "Never more" created his well-known poem ; and this is true of refrains generally; they help to build up the lyrical structure.

A good example of this fact may be found in the first song of "The Princess," in which the significant bit of local colouring, "pluck'd the ripen'd ears" (see "Maud," Part II., i. line 3), was suggested by the refrain "with tears." *No more* appears again in the song, "Ask me no more" ("Princess"), and this latter sentence begins each of five stanzas in a song by Carew. These remarks on the words "no more" must close with two appropriate quotations, one from Byron :

> " No more, no more, oh nevermore on me,
> The freshness of the heart shall fall like dew,"

and one from Shelley,—

> "When will return the glory of your prime?
> No more—oh never more !"

The poet to be named next to Wordsworth will, equally

of course, be the poet last quoted. We might be sure
that for such a theme Shelley would supply material both
beautiful and abundant,[1] such as is found in the stanzas,
entitled, " Time Long Past":

> " There is regret, almost remorse,
>   For time long past."

Like the influences of love, the poet's rhythms—

> " Roll from soul to soul,
> And grow for ever and for ever;"

and the plaintive waves of Shelley's music seemed to
have rolled into the large heart of Tennyson, there to re-
verberate in echoes strangely sweet, deep, and far.

One other poet to be mentioned in this connection is
Henry Vaughan, whose lines " The Retreat," beginning—

> " Happy those early days, when I
> Shined in my angel infancy "

have much in common with Wordsworth's Ode. There is
also a beautiful stanza in Vaughan's poem, " Beyond the
Veil "—

> " And yet as angels in some brighter dreams
>   Call to the soul, when man doth sleep,
> So some strange thoughts transcend our wonted themes
>   And into glory peep."

In this search after the inmost meaning of " Tears, idle
tears," we shall not examine the context nor the song itself,
for these other two lines of inquiry are important enough
to be followed up separately ; and they lead to the same
conclusion. We may, however, notice that according to
the poet, the song "moans about the retrospect ;" that it
deals not with "the other distance, and the hues of pro-
mise." Here, again, reflection lifts the rod to silence
feeling ; Tennyson chides his Violet much as Shakespeare
rebukes a Hamlet, or a Brutus, when they echo some

---

[1] See also his " Speculations on Metaphysics," v. 4.

secret yearning that escaped in music from his soul ; and we understand that the author of " The Princess "—partly in his artistic design—will not make any frank admission such as that we have heard in " The Ancient Sage." The dramatic purpose of the song—and there is little enough of this—may be discovered in one line of the context, where we are told that some of the girls imprisoned in the College "murmur'd that their May was passing," and we may suppose that Violet gives expression to this regret.

I do not wish to imply that our great poet is in the habit of idly and uselessly "moaning about the retrospect ;" the rebuke of The Princess, also, is something more than dramatic, as we may learn from the " Golden Year :"

> " Old writers push'd the happy season back,—
> The more fools they,—we forward : dreamers both ! '

But for all this, the past and the far—

> " The devotion to something afar
> From the sphere of our sorrow,"

the lost, the gone—all these are a passion to him ; and a passion that must sometimes seek utterance. It is Wordsworth's case over again :

> " To me alone there came a thought of grief ;
> A timely utterance gave that thought relief,
>   And I again am strong."
>   *Ode on Intimations.*

Deep musings and tender broodings over the past—and not the past of human life alone, for many of them are " *echoes of some antenatal dream !* " I repeat these words (p. 251), for they suggest our next inquiry ; What was there in that past ? and what is it that is lost and gone ? According to Wordsworth, it is a kind of " celestial light " that " apparelled " all earthly objects until " Shades of the prison house began to close Upon the growing boy."

> " Such hues from their celestial urn
> Were wont to stream before mine eye,
> Where'er it wandered in the morn
> Of blissful infancy."
>
> *Evening Voluntary*, ix.

So it was with Tennyson. He was doomed to lose the light of "the million stars which tremble O'er the deep mind of dauntless infancy." He came amongst us, "trailing clouds of glory"; he became a man, only to see them

> " Die away,
> And fade into the light of common day."
>
> *Ode on Intimations.*

And now,

> " That type of Perfect in his mind
> In Nature can he nowhere find.
> He sows himself on every wind."
>
> *Two Voices.*

Yet ever and again he exchanges his grown-up Platonic faith for childhood's perfect sight, or the more perfect antenatal vision—as only a poet can.[1]

But I may not do more than touch upon any Platonic element in this marvellous song; I will only trust that the foregoing considerations will now enable us to paraphrase the famous first line—

> " Tears, idle tears, I know not what they mean."

In prose the author would speak to us thus :

" If you suppose that your poet's regret for the past is not very natural, very deep, and very real, then you know him scarcely at all."

[1] " This glimpse of glory, why renewed ? . . .
Which at this moment, on my waking sight
Appears to shine, by miracle restored."
Evening Voluntary, ix.

> " A height, a broken grange, a grove, a flower
> Had murmurs, Lost and gone and lost and gone ! [1]
> A breath, a whisper—some *divine* farewell."
>
> *Ancient Sage.*

Here we have the epithet *divine* of " Tears, idle tears."

> " Trailing clouds of glory do we come
> *From God*, who is our home."
> *Ode on Intimations.*

> "Dreams of the past, how exquisite ye be,
> Offspring of *heavenly faith*."

And in these quotations we may possibly find the source of that epithet ; something also not altogether alien in this :

> " What sight so lured him from the fields he knew,
> As where earth's green stole into heaven's own hue,
> Far—far—away ? "

I have done little more than conduct the student-lover of Tennyson to the threshold of this beautiful building of song ; but doubtless he will enter in and survey the glory of the interior for himself.   Therefore I take my leave of him with just one parting remark.   One of the chief reasons for the superlative excellence of " Tears, Idle Tears " will be found in the absence of rhyme.   This, and especially in so short a composition, gives the poet a great advantage, and enables him to unite the three elements of thought, feeling, and expression in an equal perfection. So perfect, indeed, are all these, that the absence of rhyme is not felt, and the poem has a melody of its own, which, as was implied above, is admirably adapted to the melancholy sweetness of the thought.   And the source of

---

[1] " But there's a tree, of many, one,
A single field, which I have looked upon ;
Both of them speak of something that is gone. . . .
The pansy at my feet
Doth the same tale repeat."

Ode on Intimations.

See also pp. 137 and 138.

this melody is found where the brook-like lightness, sparkle and passion of the lyric blend with the graver stream of blank verse.[1]

And now, little song, what shall be my word of farewell to you? I trust that you are very precious to all who read you, or sing you, or muse upon your silent music. If I were Shelley, I should "bid them own that thou art beautiful"; or if I were the laurelled singer who sang you with such ineffable charm, I might sing again—

> "What charm in words? a charm no words could give !
> O dying words, can music make you live
> > Far—far—away?"

---

[1] This lyrical blank verse may almost be said to have originated with Tennyson ; for though it may be found here and there in the poetry of former poets, they have seldom or never employed it in the definite lyrical form of "Tears, Idle Tears," and other songs by the same author. To some of these a reference will be made in Chapter XI., Section IV.

CHAPTER VIII.

"ODE ON THE DEATH OF THE DUKE OF WELLINGTON," AND OTHER POEMS.

FOLLOWING "The Princess" in the table of contents, and reaching as far as "In Memoriam," is a long series of poems composed at various times. The first six of these are patriotic or national—"Ode on the Death of the Duke of Wellington," "The Third of February, 1852," "The Charge of the Light Brigade," "Ode sung at the Opening of the International Exhibition," "A Welcome to Alexandra," and "A Welcome to Her Royal Highness Marie Alexandrovna, Duchess of Edinburgh." Then follow three of the best of Tennyson's character studies, "The Grandmother," "Northern Farmer, Old Style," and "Northern Farmer, New Style." The remaining poems of the series do not admit of classification, unless we mention the four philosophical pieces near the end.[1]

(218) "ODE ON THE DEATH OF THE DUKE OF WEL-LINGTON." The Duke of Wellington died on September 14th, 1852, and Tennyson's Ode was published on the day of his funeral, November 18th. The poet, therefore,

---

[1] "Wages," "The Higher Pantheism," "The Voice and the Peak," "Flower in the Crannied Wall."

would seem to have written in some haste ; further, he was toiling at a task suddenly imposed upon him. Nothing could have been more trying for Tennyson ; and the first draft of his "Ode," which appeared as a small pamphlet of sixteen pages, was certain to place him in an unfavourable light. Other poets of less repute had been faster writers ; and so much excellence was expected of the laureate by a nation accustomed to his highly-finished poetical work that they were naturally dissatisfied with this hurried performance ; nor was the form of the Ode, in which it was written, at all attractive.

We have seen [1] that Tennyson's mode of composition was generally slow and elaborate ; "Timbuctoo" might have lost him the Chancellor's medal had he not been able to work upon a poem already written. Having regard, therefore, to all the circumstances, we are not surprised that the Ode should have been disappointing, or that it should have been subject to frequent revision. A second edition, considerably altered, appeared in 1853 ; and further changes were made in the poem when it took its place in the "Maud" volume of 1855.

But, in spite of many imperfections, the Ode in its original form had considerable merit ; and Sir Henry Taylor's estimate of the earlier edition may safely be transferred to the finished work : "It has a greatness worthy of its theme."

Before attempting to consider the poem more fully, it will be advisable to inquire into the nature of its construction, and to say a few words on the Ode as a form of poetry. If we glance through the table of contents in the volume of Tennyson's poems, we shall find that the word "ode" occurs three times ; there are the "Ode to Memory," the Ode now under notice, and the "Ode sung at the Opening of the Exhibition." What, then, is an ode, according to Tennyson ? It is a short poem that gives honour to some personage, real or figurative, or celebrates some event ; it is irregular in every detail of structure, rhymes, lines, groups of lines ; the only element of symmetry being a correspondence between movement and style on the one hand, and emotion on the other, and a general observance of the principle pointed out in a previous chapter, of rise, culmination, and decline from beginning to end of the composition. This "Ode on the Death of the Duke of Wellington" has often been compared to some of the music of Handel ; but the comparison is neither very apt nor very just ; because in music the connection between emotion and form is much more vital, more identical, than it is, or ever will be, in poetry, which is therefore more dependent upon form.

The arbitrary character of the symmetrical element in this kind of ode is easily attested by the fact that the poet obeys no rhythmic law ; he is a law unto himself ; and his own law is indefinitely variable. For example, on revision of his Ode already published, Tennyson added and rejected a considerable number of lines ; and the point to be noticed is this : that by far the greater number of alterations were made not for the sake of the rhythm, but for the sake of the sense. The law of rhythm, therefore, must have been most elastic. On the other hand it will be argued that if the poet succeeds in giving shapely form to the mass of his units, however irregular these may be, he has achieved a great poetical success ; but we reply that opinions will differ in regard to the shapeliness of form ; it is always indefinite. And we cannot escape an uneasy sense of unusual license allowed to the poet in the construction and arrangement of the parts.

This much is certain ; these irregular odes are neither very abundant nor very popular.

Then there are the almost regular Greek odes, built of strophe, antistrophe, and epode, such as Gray mostly wrote. Yet these in their modern manner are scarcely

more pleasing ; chanted on the dancing stage of the
Greeks they were delightful ; but, shorn of their wings of
music, vocal and instrumental, even the words of Pindar
have lost much of their ancient power ; and in the pages
of English literature the so-called Pindaric Odes are flat
and formal ; they usually look as if built by rule and line,
and not by the creative energy of musical emotion.

As to the third class of odes, those that are composed
of similar stanzas, like most of the Odes of Horace, or
like Collins' "Ode to Evening," they either need not be
called odes at all, or we may also give the name to such
lyrics as Tennyson's Horatian lines to Maurice.

With the aid of this digression we may now review the
structural aspects of Tennyson's Ode.   The movement at
first, especially in 3 and 4, is like the tread of mourners ;
but from time to time it quickens, till the short lines—

> " In full acclaim,
> A people's voice "

at the end of 6, are breathless with an impetuous rapidity ;
from the opening of the 7th till the close, the march of the
measure is often stately and slow.   Next, the rise and fall
of emotion may be likened to the coming and the depart-
ing storm.   In the first three divisions the thunder mutters
distant and low ; in 4 and 5 it becomes louder and nearer ;
at the end of 6 the storm has reached its height ;

> " With honour, honour, honour to him,
> Eternal honour to his name ; "

it gradually declines in 7 and 8, but not without some loud
recurrent peals as at the end of 8—

> " With honour, honour, honour to him,
> Eternal honour to his name ; "

then in 9 it passes away, softly moaning itself to rest.

There is yet another characteristic of the ode, which is
abundantly illustrated by this one of Tennyson's.   The
sentiment will usually be noble and sustained, and the

style ornate and dignified. Tennyson's work, as in "The Princess," is often overloaded with ornament and disfigured by traces of effort or straining after effect ; but these faults are almost transfigured in an ode like the present, which is majestic rather than inspired or passionate, and adorned with all the accessories of funeral pomp and national ceremony.

It might be supposed that before approaching his subject, Tennyson would refer to the literature of ode and elegy ; the well-known opening of the sixth division, where Nelson is represented as asking, "Who is he that cometh like an honoured guest?" may be due to Tickell's lines on the death of Addison,

> " Ne'er to these chambers, where the mighty rest,
> Since their foundation, came a nobler guest."

But more would have been suggested by the panegyric poems of Claudian, from which, in his speech on the occasion of the Duke's death, Disraeli adapted the line, "Venerandus apex et cognita cunctis canities," which appears in Tennyson's Ode as "O good gray head which all men knew."

(221) "THE THIRD OF FEBRUARY, 1852." This is one of three patriotic poems contributed by Tennyson[1] to "The Examiner" early in 1852, the other two being "Britons, guard your own" (Jan. 31st), and "Hands all Round" (Feb. 7th). They were called forth by the action of Louis Napoleon, who on the 2nd of December in the preceding year had converted himself from President to Prince-President of the French Republic—or, rather, of a military despotism—and this in a manner that was underhand, selfish, and cruel. Both Lord Palmerston and Lord J. Russell thought it advisable to maintain friendly relations with the new French constitution, although the subject

---

[1] Under the Arthurian *nom de blume* of "Merlin."

was made the occasion of a dispute between them ; and
Tennyson's poem refers to a debate on the question in the
House of Lords.   It was natural that Tennyson should
regard the third Napoleon with distrust, for he was known
to be possessed of a vulgar ambition to imitate the career
of his great uncle, the first Napoleon.   Moreover, a long
neglect had rendered the defences of England weak at all
points :

> " Easy patrons of their kin
> Have left the last free race with naked coasts."

When in the poem Tennyson calls war " this French
god," he has set his thoughts on Bonaparte, who had more
than once made war on land merely to gloss over a defeat
at sea.   In the same stanza the line, " We dare not even
by silence sanction lies," resembles the language he
employs in " Maud," where he speaks of the Czar as " a
giant liar."   At that later time we were in league with the
French Emperor, an arrangement in regard to which
Tennyson was nevertheless silent, for, as might be gathered
from his sonnet on Poland, his hatred of Russian des-
potism was yet greater.

The poet's views of war and politics are much the same
in this poem as in " Maud " ; there we hear of " Peace in
her vineyard—yes ! but a company forges the wine," a
line which may be compared with the second stanza of
this poem.   His opinion, " O fall'n nobility " (and the
whole of stanza 6), is expressed in some lines omitted in
later editions of " Maud "—

> " What use for a single mouth to rage
> At the rotten creak of the State machine,
> Though it makes friends weep and enemies smile
> That here in the face of a watchful age
> The sons of a gray-beard-ridden isle
> Should dance in a round of old routine,
> While a few great families lead the reels."

In the chapter on " Maud " reference is made to the
" niggard throats of Manchester " in the last stanza.

(222) "THE CHARGE OF THE LIGHT BRIGADE." The last two lines of the former poem are a fitting introduction to the stirring Balaclava lyric :

> "And these in our Thermopylæ shall stand,
> And hold against the world this honour of the land."

It is magnificent, but it is not war : and we are well content that it should be only magnificent, for by such magnificence England became great. And peace is indeed desirable and not war, nor the song of war ; but by war we were welded into a nation ; there was no other way, whatever may be the way of the future. " No writing of mine," says Tennyson, " can add to the glory they have acquired in the Crimea " ; but we must not acquiesce in the laureate's modesty ; the glory of warrior never found a lovelier or a truer helpmeet than the glory of song ; and in order to correct the poet's estimate we have only to inquire, " Is there any Englishman who would wish Tennyson's ' writing ' to be unwritten ? " And lastly, it may have been a blunder, and the blunder gets into the poem, but—and these again are Tennyson's words : " It is one for which England should be grateful, having learnt thereby that her soldiers are the bravest and most obedient under the sun."

"The Charge of the Light Brigade" appeared in the "Examiner" for December 9th, 1854, with the following note : "Written after reading the first report of 'The Times' correspondent, where only 607 sabres are mentioned as having taken part in the charge." Next, it was included, with several alterations, in the "Maud" volume of 1855. Soon after this it was printed on a quarto sheet of four pages ; at the end was a letter by the author, from which an extract has already been made. The first sentence is as follows :

"Having heard that the brave soldiers before Sebastopol, whom I am proud to call my countrymen, have a liking for my Ballad on the ' Charge of the Light Brigade,' at Balaclava, I have ordered a thousand copies of it to be printed for them."

This popular poem, which should be compared with Drayton's "Agincourt," is a little open to criticism ; but those it honoured are nearly all among the dead ; and comments, however numerous and elaborate, might all end with the remark that it is a glowing tribute to military glory, for which, both the tribute and the glory, a whole nation may well be thankful.

(223) "ODE SUNG AT THE OPENING OF THE IN-TERNATIONAL EXHIBITION." This is one of the best of Tennyson's official poems. In spite of the distrust in commerce and peace due to the war fever in " Maud"—

> "No longer shall commerce be all in all, and Peace
> Pipe on her pastoral hillock a languid note,"

the merchant ship is here "the fair white-winged peace-maker"; and the fifth section, in which these words occur, recalls the enthusiasm of "Locksley Hall" (61, 64) and the trembling hope of "The Golden Year," as expressed in the last two stanzas of Leonard's song, "Fly, happy, happy sails." Yet more tremulously the same hope is repeated in "Locksley Hall Sixty Years After" (83, 85). And if the day for which Tennyson waited is yet "so far away," he has surely brought it nearer. If there is any-thing in poetry that must enter into the heart of every man who hears it, and beat with his blood, it is surely such lines as these :

> "Ah ! when shall all men's good
> Be each man's rule. . . ."
> *Golden Year.*

> "Till each man find his own in all men's good,
> And all men work in noble brotherhood."
> *Ode sung at the opening of the International Exhibition*

> "Follow Light, and do the Right. . . . . .
> . . . . . Love will conquer at the last."
> *Locksley Hall Sixty Years After.*

The "Ode" was sung at the opening of the International Exhibition, May 1st, 1862. In June it was printed in "Fraser's Magazine." In earlier editions the divisions were not numbered, and the fourth division ("Is the goal so far away?") was not included. This added portion repeats the lesson of "The Golden Year";[1] but it is further one of the many instances in which the poet chooses to temper enthusiasm with doubt.

(223) A WELCOME TO ALEXANDRA, March 7, 1863, printed by Edward Moxon as a sheet of four pages, was sold among the crowd. The five lines beginning, "Rush to the roof . . ." were added later. With other emendations it appeared in the "Enoch Arden" volume of the following year.

(224) A WELCOME TO HER ROYAL HIGHNESS MARIE ALEXANDROVNA, DUCHESS OF EDINBURGH, March 7, 1874. This, like the former, was printed on a single sheet; later it appeared in "The Times." It is not so spirited as the preceding; there is less of stirring poetry, but it has wisdom enough to make it a welcome addition to the collection of laureate poems.

(225) THE GRANDMOTHER. Browning seeks unfamiliar types of character; Tennyson paints those that are familiar. Browning's sketches are striking by reason of novelty and complexity, the difficulty involved in delineation, the intellectual strength and acuteness by which the difficulty is overcome. Tennyson's portraits are admirable because of their perfection; as usual with him, he chooses the simpler, less complicated subject, but he deals with it so elaborately, and leaves it so carefully finished,

---

[1] "Unto him that works," etc.

that his work is often more pleasing and more valuable than that of Browning. For one reader who appreciates "Caliban upon Setebos," there are perhaps a thousand who know such a poem as "The Grandmother" with a knowledge that is akin to affection.

This admirable study appeared under the title of "The Grandmother's Apology" in "Once a Week" for July 16th, 1859. It was accompanied by an excellent illustration by Sir J. E. Millais. In 1864 a place was found for it in "Enoch Arden and other Poems."

(228) and (231). THE NORTHERN FARMER—OLD STYLE AND NEW STYLE. These again are admirable studies ; in their rougher naturalness perhaps more striking than "The Grandmother." But they appear to be somewhat disguised under their garb of dialect ; we cannot always tell where drapery ends and statue begins. We are sure of the men when we see them ; we are uncertain about their speech ; it claims an undue attention ; there is something of artifice in the sound of it. The exactness of imitation need not be called in question ; indeed, the Irish dialect in "To-morrow" may be regarded as equally exact, and it ought to be equally famous ; but it is exposed to the same objections. By comparisons innumerable the reader can judge of the poet's literary language ; he cannot judge of this ; he only knows that it gives the artist an unlimited means of covering the face of weakness with the mask of strength, as he expresses the character through an unfamiliar and variable medium. The poet knows this too ; and just as the elocutionist will choose a piece in dialect to begin with, in order that he may gain confidence in himself and his audience, so the poet feels more secure with this disguise of dialect ever at hand.

Next, the medium is not natural to the poet ; he has not mastered it ; he must evolve it separately while he draws his character, and to the detriment of the drawing. In the proof sheets of " The Northern Farmer," Tennyson made a very large number of corrections ; and this was partly because of the strange raiment of speech in which he was dressing up the figure. But the most important consideration, already hinted at above, is stated more fully in Chapter I. under the head of Humour. Our attention is divided between the character and its environment, for we feel that, under existing conditions, the environment is something apart from the character ; we are aware that the poet has failed to create it in any vital connection with the character ; he would not think out his character in dialect ; some at least of the dialect could be stuck on afterwards ; and we are further aware that he trusts to it separately to produce an impression.[1] In the same way it is easier to draw a humorous than a serious character, and a comic character is easiest of all. Shakespeare, therefore, begins with comic characters ; he creates Launce, and Bottom, his earlier Falstaff, and Falstaff himself, at least before he finishes Hamlet ; but Hamlet he never finished. Nor was it until his powers were fully matured that he brought Iago on the stage.

(233) "THE DAISY." This tender and delightful poem of the "Maud" volume of 1855 tells us how the poet while in "the gray metropolis of the North," found between the leaves of a book a daisy gathered by him on the Splugen in 1851. He was then travelling abroad with his wife, whom he had married the year before, and this finding of the daisy gave the poet an opportunity of going over the foreign scenes again in his lightly moving verse. Other reminiscences of continental travel sketched with the same swift grace, occur in " In Memoriam." " The

---

[1] Hence it would appear that poems in dialect scarcely come within the province of literary art ; and only a brief notice can be assigned to them in this Handbook. P. 219.

rich Virgilian rustic measure Of Lari Maxume" is explained by a reference to Virgil's Georgics, ii. 159.

(234) "To the Rev. F. D. Maurice." The Rev. Frederick Denison Maurice, who had been one of Tennyson's friends at Cambridge, and is sometimes known as the founder of the Broad Church School, had recently been obliged to resign his professorship in King's College because of the undisguised liberality of his religious opinions. Hence the lines, "Should eighty thousand college councils," etc. Tennyson, who hated intolerance of all kinds, sent to Maurice by way of sympathy this characteristic letter, which is dated January, 1854. The stanza employed in this and the former lyric is light and musical; and the easy grace and superb finish of the poem itself suggests a comparison with Horace, even before we note the many turns of thought where Horace blends with Milton.[1]

(235) "Will" (1854). Here also are thoughts from Horace, Odes, III. iii.—the first eight lines; and the figure "who seems a promontory of rock . . . ." will be found in the tenth book of the Æneid, 693-696. The line of Shakespearian elements[2] in the second stanza, "Or seeming-genial venial fault" can hardly escape censure as being over fanciful, although the sound was doubtless intended to emphasize the sense. The chief merit of this formless but sturdy little poem seems to be the remarkable figure at the end of it, which, apart from the suggestion of a rhyme for "fault," is likely to have a history. Compare with this poem "All Life needs for life is possible to will;"[3] also Smiles' variation of Addison :

> " 'Tis not in mortals to deserve success,
> But we'll do more, Sempronius, we'll command it.'

---

[1] Sonnets to Mr. Lawrence and Cyriack Skinner.
[2] " So seeming just," " a venial slip."   [3] " Love and Duty."

(235) "IN THE VALLEY OF CAUTERETZ." In this mournful and tender poem we have the reminiscence of another continental tour. In 1861 Tennyson revisited the Pyrenees, and stayed at Mont Dore-les-Bains, Cauteretz, and other places with his wife and children. Not long before, Arthur Clough had set out for the same parts in search of health. The following extracts from his diary are profoundly but mournfully interesting. "September 1st :—The Tennysons arrived at 6.30 yesterday. Tennyson was here with Arthur Hallam thirty-one years ago, and really finds great pleasure in the place ; they stayed here and at Cauteretz. 'Œnone,' he said, was written on the inspiration of the Pyrenees, which stood for Ida.

"September 6. Tennyson and —— have walked on to Cauteretz, and I and the family follow in a *calèche* at two.

"Cauteretz, September 7. I have been out for a walk with A. T. to a sort of island between two waterfalls, with pines on it, of which he retained a recollection from his visit of thirty-one years ago, and which, moreover, furnished a simile to 'The Princess.' He is very fond of this place, evidently."

The scene brings back the time ; two and thirty years roll away like a mist, and Arthur Hallam is with him in the valley once again ; his voice is heard in the stream, in all sounds, all silence of the deepening night.

(235) "IN THE GARDEN AT SWAINSTON." Swainston, in the Isle of Wight, was the seat of Tennyson's friend, Sir John Simeon, who is said to be the Sir Walter Vivian of "The Princess." It was in the garden at Swainston and under one of its cedar trees that "Maud" was partly written. In 1870 Sir John Simeon died at Fribourg; and Tennyson, while walking in his garden, gives him the immortality of a great poet's loving verse.

(235) "THE FLOWER." In this fable we read of Tennyson's "flower of poesy," which, according to the poet, was "little cared for;" at least, until it found many imitators. "Once in a golden hour," may be compared with "The poet in a golden clime was born." Tennyson, like Wordsworth and Milton, had lofty ideas of the poet's office, but his expression of those ideas is not always so lofty as theirs.

(236) "REQUIESCAT." Spite of the stock phrase "in its place," [1] the pathetic simplicity and sweetness of these stanzas may almost remind us of Wordsworth's "Lucy."

(236) "THE SAILOR BOY." These were the only verses published by Tennyson in 1861, the year in which he visited the valley of Cauteretz; and possibly they were written on the voyage. They appeared at Christmas in the "Victoria Regia," a volume of miscellanies edited by Emily Faithful. "The Sailor Boy" adds another to the long list of sea poems that date back to a time when our race was being rocked in its cradle, the sea; and it does honour to the daring and the pluck of the sea-ruling nation. It may further be regarded as an allegory: "Death is sure To those that stay and those that roam;" which is like Shakespeare's "Will come when it will come." Without laying further stress on this precept of the poem, we may add Longfellow's "Let us then be up and doing With a heart for any fate."

(236) "THE ISLET." From the first this poem has immediately followed "The Sailor Boy," and it is mostly allegorical: This "little Eden on earth that I know" is "a far Eden of the purple East . . . The winged storms . . . leave azure chasms of calm Over this isle . . . heavy with

---

[1] As (in Tennyson) "I will grow round him in his place."—*Fatima.* "The flower ripens in its place."—*Lotos-Eaters.*

the scent of lemon flowers . . . I have vowed Thee to be lady of the solitude . . . We shall be one . . . Within that calm circumference of bliss." To these rapturous dreamings of Shelley Tennyson seems to make reply; "Even as dreams they are unworthy; most unworthy of the high possibilities and the sacred duties of waking life."

A literal rendering would be something as follows: Dwelling apart by ourselves, seeking only our own happiness, may be likened to solitary existence on a beautiful island in the tropics; where the real work of life is suspended; where the only music is the false note of the mocking bird, and where loathsome diseases lurk in every profusion of loveliness. Like "The Voyage," this slighter poem is an occasion for vivid sketches of far-off isle and ocean.

In the original volume ("Enoch Arden") "The Islet" was followed by "The Ringlet." This poem amongst others was implied on a former page,[1] where the statement was made that certain weaknesses could be traced from the beginning to the end of Tennyson's poetical career. "The Ringlet," which was of the "Skipping Rope" character, but a better poem, was withdrawn some few years ago.

(237) "CHILD-SONGS." Both these songs were contributed in 1880 to "St. Nicholas," an American magazine for children. The rhythms of the nursery were never so melodious. But Swinburne's "In a Garden" should be compared with all other verses written for or about the very young.

(237) "THE SPITEFUL LETTER" ("Once a Week," January, 1868). In smart repartee, clever satire, easy banter—all combined with loftiness of thought and grace of manner—this poem in its present greatly improved

[1] Pages 53 and 54.

form should stand unrivalled. But Virgil could not have written such. The stanzas are addressed to no one in particular; they may be left to us as a lesson: but, after all, a better lesson is to be learnt from the next poem.

(237) "LITERARY SQUABBLES" (originally entitled "Afterthought"):[1]

> "The noblest answer unto such
> Is perfect stillness when they brawl."

"The silent stars" are the stars of "Maud" and of Lucretius that "burn and brand His nothingness into man." The epithet "stony" reminds us of the "Awful Memnonian countenances calm" of "A Fragment." "Lethe, the river of oblivion, rolls His watery labyrinth" in "Paradise Lost." These verses were written in March, 1846, as an "afterthought" to "The New Timon and the Poets," in which Tennyson a week previously had retorted upon Lord Lytton, who had attacked him in his poem "The New Timon."

(238) "THE VICTIM," accompanied by an illustration, appeared in "Good Words," January, 1868. Longfellow visited the laureate at Farringford about this time, and by a coincidence the ballad has something of Longfellow's manner, especially in the variable metre ; but possesses, nevertheless, a poetic power of its own.

(239) "WAGES" was contributed to "Macmillan's Magazine" for February, 1868, and was afterwards included in the "Holy Grail" volume. The new dress of this old scrap of philosophy is not over-poetical; among other defects the breaks in the first stanza are perplexing. The second stanza is better. We may extract the material from "In Memoriam," lxxv. (3), lxxiii. (3 and 4), xxxiv. (1), lxxv. (5). In "Parnassus" the poet is not content to be "Paid with a

---

[1] See also p. 195.

voice flying by to be lost on an endless sea ;" in spite of " A sad astrology, the boundless plan," he believes that the poet's voice will sound for ever and ever ; and that is what he asks for as the poet's "glory." It is the same with virtue ; take the charm "for ever" from her, and she crumbles into dust ; but she desires no vulgar immortality of inaction ; she demands as her meed eternal activity. Tennyson does not believe, like George Eliot, that virtue is her own reward "even here, But for one hour."[1]

(239) " THE HIGHER PANTHEISM," read previously before the Metaphysical Society, was published in the " Holy Grail " volume. This with the preceding and the two following poems forms a philosophical group.

It has already been stated [2] that the doctrine of evolution could not fail to be a potent influence with Tennyson ; and on another page [3] will be found an incidental remark to the effect that scientific thought is again making a god of nature. Before considering Tennyson's "Higher Pantheism," it will be necessary to add very briefly that many earlier religions and philosophies regarded man as one with nature ; that the Christian religion has kept them altogether apart, regarding nature as something made for man's convenience, yet often a harmful thing, to be shunned, or dominated, or despised ; and, lastly, that the intellectual ingenuity of the nineteenth century has brought them nearer together than they ever were.[4] But the first tendency of modern scientific inquiry was to leave the conception of the deity to religion whether dogmatic or emotional, while it gradually evolved man from his surroundings, and constituted him an integral

---

1 " In Memoriam," xxxv. 2.   2 See p. 26.   3 P. 33.
4 Some conjectures on p. 37 (footnote) respecting the relationship between man and his environment may seem plausible as far as man is concerned. Apart from man, what *was* his environment might be likened to the number three, if that number, after measuring three apples, sought to maintain unsymbolized its measuring potentiality ?

part of the material universe, all whose operations were found to be one with law.   Later, when science carried its spirit of inquiry into the theological field, it showed a tendency to identify its god of Law with the God of theology; and theology at the same time expressed some willingness to meet science half way—

" For if He thunder by la*w*, the thunder is yet His voice."

Here then is the " Higher Pantheism," a compromise between a strictly scientific conception of our cosmogony, and the emotional instincts and convictions of the higher philosophic and religious minds ; and Tennyson endeavours to show that the path of induction and the path of intuition converge near the forests of the infinite that bound us in.

Once more, therefore, we see Tennyson in that position of arbitrator which the leading poet of an age like ours must almost inevitably assume.   That he should not know his own mind when closely questioned on such subjects as nature and philosophy is neither surprising nor regrettable ; but that he should seek to know the unknowable and express the inexpressible is sometimes laudable, sometimes admirable, sometimes disastrous ; for here we are dealing with poetic art.   It is fairly laudable in the " Higher Pantheism," entirely admirable in " The Ancient Sage," but most disastrous in " De Profundis."

(240) " THE VOICE AND THE PEAK." [1]   This is another attempt to find a voice for the ineffable, and to apprehend the infinite.   The sentiment is often to be met with in " In Memoriam " ; as, for example, in Poem cxxiii ; we get no nearer heaven by climbing to the Peak—" Thou hast not gained a real height." [2]

Therefore when the appeal for some knowledge of the Infinite goes up from river and ocean, to the Peak that

---

[1] Cabinet edition, 1874.   [2] " The Two Voices."

stands so high above them, the poet makes the Peak reply : "The hills are shadows, and they flow From form to form, and nothing stands." But, he adds, speaking for himself, the material universe is finite, man is infinite; his thoughts wander through eternity; "Eternal process moving on, From state to state the spirit walks."[1] This view of nature is different from that of "The Higher Pantheism" which seems to confess with Pope, as also with "In Memoriam," cxxix. and cxxx. :

> " All are but parts of one stupendous whole
> Whose body nature is, and God the soul,"

a view, it may be added, which accords more exactly with many of the conclusions of modern science. Evolution has first unified science, and secondly, unified the universe. All we are certain of, says Huxley, is the fact of consciousness, thought ; to this evolution adds—we may put it in the words of Shelley—thought is the measure of the universe ; that is to say, every product of development stands in a close relation to every other product ; and, given the fact of thought in any one manifestation of the infinite making of the frame of things, then every other manifestation is a form of thought ; in the more highly organized product, thought is more highly organized ;[2] whereas some simpler consciousness of which we can form no conception may be present in the most elemental constituents of what we call matter ; " I swear I think now that everything has an immortal soul."[3] From this point of view we may better understand how it was that to Wordsworth all nature seemed alive as a form or mode of thought.

(240) "FLOWER IN THE CRANNIED WALL,"[4] has been considered on p. 38. Like some others of the philosophical pieces, it is formless, and rather unpoetical, although

---

1 "In Memoriam," lxxxii.
2 "In Memoriam," lxxxv. 6-7, and Epilogue 36.   **3** Whitman.
4 "Holy Grail" vol., 1870.

earnest and impressive. The thought occurs in many
other writers, both ancient and modern, and from one
point of view may be compared with the well-known lines
of Wordsworth :

> "To me the meanest flower that blows can give
> Thoughts that do often lie too deep for tears."

In this little poem we have at its best one of Tennyson's
later favourite phrases, the Wordsworthian "all in all."

(240) "A Dedication." This poem was printed near
the end of the "Enoch Arden" volume; and is obviously,
not explicitly, addressed to the poet's wife. So also the
dedication of "The Death of Œnone and Other Poems,"
is without a name. As these lines testify, it was a marriage
of true minds when Alfred Tennyson wedded Emily
Sellwood, and almost to be compared with the union of
Robert Browning with Elizabeth Barrett.

(241) "Experiments." This title groups together the
five poems that follow.

(241) "Boadicea." By adapting a metre of Catullus
the poet has written what are, perhaps, the most sonorous
lines in our language. He takes occasion to prophesy the
future greatness of England, especially in the passage
beginning "Thine the liberty." As in some of the verses
of "Maud" and "The May Queen," the accents, eight in
each line, become the basis of the measure, more or less
irrespective of the number of syllables.

(243) "On Translations of Homer." The substance
of a remark made in a former chapter [1] will be the best
preliminary comment on this and the following two exer-
cises in Quantity; they prove that the poet felt how difficult

---

[1] P. 80.

it was to force the classic metres into English, but prove also that if it could be done, he could do it. Further, whatever they may have that is classical will be chiefly or only their form.

These "Attempts at Classic Metres in Quantity" first appeared in the "Cornhill Magazine" for December, 1863.

(243) "MILTON." These lines are indeed worthy of their theme, though that is among the highest. The best way to appreciate them is to know "Paradise Lost" by heart. To that poem alone does the poet make any reference; and it is strange, that some critics should rank "Comus," and other minor poems of Milton, with his great Epic, to which they present no prominent feature of comparison. Although so many poets and poems may put forward a claim to the place of honour in Tennyson's favour, we may venture to mention, in this connection, that if there is one poem more than another to which the late laureate was indebted, that poem is probably "Paradise Lost." The poet singles out the two important aspects of the great Epic, "Strength and beauty met together;" he prefers the beauty, but the two

> " Kindle their image like a star
> In a sea of glassy weather;"

and if only Tennyson had possessed more of Milton's strength, he would have been a much greater poet. The *Alcaics* end in Tennyson's favourite manner, with exquisite imagery wrought into music that has a "dying fall." It may be compared with "In Memoriam," lxxxvi. (4).

(243) *Hendecasyllabics* call for little more than the remark referred to above.[1] Though these lines are more genial than usual, and merely an "experiment," they are not attractive.

[1] "On Translations of Homer."

(243) "SPECIMEN OF A TRANSLATION OF THE ILIAD IN BLANK VERSE." The following prefatory note was originally printed above this fragment : " Some, and among these one at least of our best and greatest, have endeavoured to give us the ' Iliad ' in English hexameters, and by what appears to me their failure, have gone far to prove the impossibility of the task. I have long held by our blank verse in this matter, and now after having spoken so disrespectfully here of these hexameters, I venture, or rather feel bound, to subjoin a specimen, however brief and with whatever demerits, of a blank verse translation."

On the difficult subject of translation in general a note will be given in the Chapter on " Maud."[1] Meanwhile it may be stated that opinion will differ as to the advisability or the possibility of translating Homer, the metre to be employed in any such attempt, and so forth. But the mere presence of this specimen, as well as the specimen itself, is open to some criticism. It will perhaps be sufficient to add that Tennyson's rendering of this famous passage has been greatly improved since its first appearance, that it is more successful than his " Achilles over the Trench," and that most of the notes of earlier versions have been wisely withdrawn.

(244) " THE WINDOW ; OR, THE SONG OF THE WRENS." When, in 1867, Tennyson was staying with Sir Ivor Bertie Guest at Canford Manor, Wimborne, this little cantata, or song-cycle, written for Sir—then Mr.—Arthur Sullivan's music, was printed at Sir Ivor's private press.

These songs, composed " German fashion," and twelve in number, are a fanciful and most musical story of wooing ; and in their variety, and adaptation to mood and incident, they bear some slight resemblance to the lyrics of " Maud."

1 P. 311.

ADDENDA TO CHAPTER VIII.

This chapter will close with a mention of some minor verses dating a few years later than the middle of the century, and not included in Tennyson's published works.

A poem of 1852, "Britons, guard your own," has been noticed on p. 263.

On the occasion of the marriage of the Princess Royal, January 25th, 1858, the poet added two stanzas to the National Anthem. These were printed in "The Times" of January 26th.

On March 19th, 1864, he contributed to "The Court Journal" a short "Epitaph on the Duchess of Kent." It was afterwards inscribed on Theed's statue at Frogmore.

The "Enoch Arden" volume of 1864 included "The Ringlet," which has been noticed incidentally on page 273.

"Home they brought him slain with spears," was printed in a volume of Selections in 1865. It is a good song of two stanzas, allied in subject to "Home they brought her warrior dead."

In 1868 there appeared in the March number of "Good Words" a poem entitled "1865-1866." It consisted of thirteen lines, beginning,

"I stood on a tower in the wet. . . ." [1]

As was noticed in a previous chapter,[1] the poem is a poor one, and it presents a striking example of intense emotion failing utterly to find appropriate poetical expression. Yet its leading thought, which was partly quoted on a former page,[2] possesses deep interest for all who would know the inner life of our great poet.

[1] P. 53.   [2] P. 27.

CHAPTER IX.

"IN MEMORIAM," 1850.

I.—INTRODUCTORY. Among the greater poems of Tennyson, "In Memoriam" holds a high position. It is best known and best loved; the wisest, the most spiritual, often the most beautiful. It is one of the greatest poems of the nineteenth century.

To realize its importance we have only to ask ourselves, "What would our life and thought from 1850 to 1895 have been without it?" In this respect of influence, "In Memoriam" takes rank with some of the leading productions of literary genius; it mingles with the speech of our daily life; it is sung in our hymn books, and preached with our sermons: it infiltrates the higher literature of more than forty years; it has been translated into other languages; it is referred to or quoted by a very large proportion of the best books, scientific as well as imaginative, that have been published since its appearance.[1] So much, indeed, has it been drawn upon, whether for purposes of illustration, or authority, or adornment, that a speaker or writer of good taste in the present day will scarcely venture to quote its apt, familiar, and well-loved lines.

---

[1] One instance, and of quite a recent date, would be "Problems of the Future," by S. Laing, 1893. This work, properly scientific, has many references to "In Memoriam"

As a work of literary art, therefore, it stands very high amongst us.

But hardly less important is what we may perhaps call its private influence :

> " True sorrow then is feelingly sufficed
> When with like semblance it is sympathized,"

says Shakespeare ; but it is the sympathy of a great heart that suffered as lesser hearts could never suffer, which has endeared " In Memoriam " to thousands of mourners throughout the world :

> " O wheresoever those may be
> Betwixt the slumber of the poles,
> To-day they count as kindred souls,
> They know me not, but mourn with me " (xcix.).

And the great heart of Tennyson was one of those that " mourn in hope." [1]

Further, it is popular as embodying many phases of religion and philosophy, especially such as seem best adapted to the extended and varying needs of our nine-teenth century.

Moreover, from a merely artistic point of view, we must regard, as a crowning excellence, those marvellous lyrical outbursts (Poem lxxxvi. is the very finest) that every now and then are heard above the long "monotone of pain."

To sum up, " In Memoriam " is a great work of art, the truest and the most beautiful representative of its age, and at the same time it is one of the best influences, whether external or internal, by which that age in part, and the age succeeding, have been formed.

II.—FORM AND STRUCTURE. " In Memoriam " con-sists of 131 separate poems, varying in length from twelve to 120 lines each. These poems, though not sonnets in form, are often sonnet-like in many other respects; in each we have some gem of thought set in a framework of

---

[1] " The Death of the Duke of Clarence."

beautiful verse. It will be best to call them poems, and to describe them in the poet's own words as

> " Short swallow-flights of song, that dip
> Their wings in tears, and skim away."

This moulding of passing moods into a long series of separate poems reminds us of the sonnets of Shakespeare and others ; but Tennyson reserved to himself a not un-mixed advantage, that of making his poems long or short as he pleased ; he gained freedom, but his poem lost form.[1]

At the head of these 131 poems stands a Prologue, and they are followed by an Epilogue.

Each poem is composed of stanzas formed by placing two rhyming Iambic Tetrameter lines between two others that rhyme. This form of verse, already used with effect by Lord Herbert of Cherbury, is very well adapted to the subject, which is mostly that of subdued but prolonged grief. The four lines sometimes sound like the passing bell, as in lvii. 3, 4.

Yet in the hands of such a master, the verse admits of almost infinite variation ; and it may also bring to us the joyous pealing of the Christmas bells, just as the poet heard them ring out from village churches in the undulat-ing landscape round the Lincolnshire parsonage (xxviii. 3).

Or the music of his metre may be made passionate or rapturous, and " long drawn out " by passing without a break from one stanza to another, as in the whole of poems xxii. and lxxxvi. and in the latter part of cxv.

As the rhymes occur very frequently, and the poem is a long one (it contains 2,896 lines), we must be prepared to

---

[1] Probably no other great poem is so seriously deficient in the larger composite harmony. Its generally recognized exemplar, a series of the Sonnets of Petrarch, with a few other poems, can scarcely be regarded as an exception. If we ask, " What is the structural unit of ' In Memoriam ? ' " we may get for answer, "not lines nor stanzas, but poems." To this we must reply, " That cannot be, for the poems have no common element of form, they are absolutely irregular sections ; there is no unity within their variety." See Chapter III. Appendix I. ; also pp. 310, 311.

find them sometimes inaccurate, as when the poet makes *port* rhyme with *report* (xiv.) ; sometimes also they fetter his thought and produce slight obscurity, as in this line,

> "Tho' truths in manhood darkly join." (xxxvi.)

But these blemishes are unimportant. More serious—if for a moment we regard matter as well as manner—are the occasional lapses into metrical prose, as in liii. ; or the contrasts of thought, amounting almost to contradictions, due to that other not altogether unmixed advantage, which "In Memoriam" possesses in common with "The Idylls of the King," viz., the large number of years during which the poem was in course of composition. For this long period wrought many important changes in the poet's mental and spiritual life, and we may fairly assume that poems cxxix. and cxxx. would not have been written in the same year as xlv. and xlvii. Again, in lxxv., Tennyson determines to attempt no description of his friend's greatness ; later on he devotes five poems to the subject (cix.-cxiii.). But, for all this, and much that might be added, beauty and perfection are so generally present that "In Memoriam" may be considered as a highly-finished work.

III. ITS NATURE. The "In Memoriam" is usually classed among elegies—poems of mourning. As the title "In Memoriam" implies, it may be regarded as a monument to the memory of a friend. But the poem is very much more than this. We may view it in many aspects :

> "I weep for Adonais—he is dead !
> O weep for Adonais ! "

These are the opening lines of Shelley's "Adonais" ; and in the first paragraph of Milton's "Lycidas" are the kindred words :

> "Lycidas is dead, dead ere his prime. . .
> Who would not sing for Lycidas ? "

And even in Matthew Arnold's "Thyrsis," "A Monody, to *commemorate* the author's friend," we read, near the beginning :

> " He could not wait their passing, he is dead."

> " When Sicilian shepherds lost a mate,
> Some good survivor with his flute would go. . . .
> And flute his friend, like Orpheus, from the dead."

In each of these cases we have an avowal that justifies the title " In Memoriam," and each of these lamentations was uttered, as we might say, in a breath, and for the occasion, and each lament bears the sign manual of the writer. But, as applied to Tennyson's poem, the title " In Memoriam A. H. H." might seem almost an afterthought ; no less than seventeen years elapsed between the death of Hallam and the unveiling of the memorial, and Tennyson never allowed it to bear his name.

An outpouring of grief for private consolation—

> " In words like weeds I'll wrap me o'er,
> Like coarsest clothes against the cold "—

pages from a private diary—in which we read how a strong and noble soul bore the burden of a terrible bereavement ; how love never yielded to despair, nor faith to doubt ; how a human friendship

> " Rose on stronger wings
> Unpalsied when he met with death—"

such is the first aspect of Tennyson's " In Memoriam," and however much the poem may have been built up to the music of the past,[1] it is the aspect with which we shall have to deal.

But we must not expect to find the days or weeks, or even the years of this diary marked off by dates. There is not much of external method in the composition of " In Memoriam." Certainly, commentators generally assign a definite period to the story of sorrow ; Mr. Stopford

---

[1] Especially that of Petrarch. (P. 284, footnote.)

Brooke, for example, tells us that " the poem lasts just two years and seven months." Nothing can be further from the fact. A most casual examination shows us that within the limits of 1833-1850 we can do little more than conjecture as to the date of any poem ; and two poems were added after 1850 (xxxix. in 1869, lix. in 1851). To begin with, we cannot tell whether the first Christmas mentioned is that of 1833 or 1834. Certainly it speaks of " A merry song we sung with him Last year." But "last year" might possibly be some time in 1833 prior to the death of Hallam, which took place on September 15th of that year. Again, how could the poems xxviii.-xxx., if, as Mr. Brooke says, they refer to the Christmas of 1833, be placed after poem xix., which describes the burial of Hallam, an event that did not take place until January, 1834? Nor can we willingly believe that the author of " Break, Break, Break " and " In Memoriam " would be singing any " merry song " while the dead body of his friend was not yet laid in the grave. Or take the third Christmas, which, according to Mr. Brooke, is that of the year 1835. In the poems dedicated to its memory Tennyson himself tells us,

> " Our father's dust is left alone,
> And silent under other snows " (cv.) ;

and the Tennysons left Somersby in the year 1837. The third Christmas, therefore, cannot be earlier than that year. It will be better to deal conventionally, not rigidly, with the poems of time and incident ; to allow them, like the others, to follow one another in a poetical chronology through this history of sorrow, and always to remember that, with but one or two exceptions,[1] the only reliable dates are 1833-1850.

IV. THE SUBJECT OF " IN MEMORIAM." Arthur Henry Hallam, eldest son of the historian, was born in

[1] See also p. 22, footnote.

London on the 1st of February, 1811. In 1828, when
nearly eighteen, he entered Trinity College, Cambridge.
Here he formed a close friendship with Tennyson, to
whose sister Emily he was afterwards betrothed. As
young Hallam was himself a poet, and a remarkable man
in many other respects, Tennyson's affection for his friend
soon deepened into an intense devotion.   "Certainly,"
says a recent writer, "this friendship is beautiful to look
upon ; its comparative rareness only makes it the more
refreshing.   This was no mere dining at the same club,
no mere smoking of cigars together, no mere joining in
the same jollity.   Here was a real union of heart and
mind, mutual esteem, unselfish sympathy."

This friendship lasted until 1833.   On September 15th
of that year Arthur Hallam died suddenly while abroad :

> " In Vienna's fatal walls
> God's finger touch'd him, and he slept."

Tennyson was stunned by the blow ; but he found consola-
tion in writing this poem, which tells us the story of his
great sorrow during the years that followed his friend's
death.   At first he mourns wellnigh as one that has no
hope, for a web seems woven across his sky.   Most touch-
ing is the picture of the bereaved poet as he approaches
the deserted house on a dreary autumn morning (vii.) ;
and if any calm comes to his spirit, it is the calmness
almost of despair (xi.).   But Hallam died abroad, and his
remains were being conveyed by sea to Dover, and during
this interval of four months the poet had time and strength
to right himself a little.   He can bestow a blessing on the
ship that is bringing to him one who was more than a
brother : and when the sacred dust is at last laid to rest
in Clevedon Church, the sternest hour of separation has
been so long delayed that the mourner's life does not die
within him :

> " That dies not, but endures with pain,
> And slowly forms the firmer mind."

Yet in a most perfect lyric of the simpler style (xix.) he enshrines both the sad scene and his own anguish, that sometimes ebbs a little, but oftener fills his heart too full for tears. How often the mourner's heart was too full for utterance we may gather from another beautiful lyric, "Break, break, break," which was probably written about this time.[1] From this point until the 56th poem is reached the poet passes through many phases of sorrow. We see him weeping by the grave (xxi.), or we hear him murmuring of the happy past (xxii.-xxv.), and now and then he glances sadly at love's future (xxvi.). The first Christmas comes, bringing not joy, but renewed sorrow :

> " With trembling fingers did we weave
> The holly round the Christmas hearth."

Both love and grief have sacred times and seasons— halting-places where the pilgrim finds in memory new food for joy or suffering. So is it in "In Memoriam" : Christmas, the New Year, the springtide, his friend's birthday, the anniversary of his death—all these are held solemn to the past (cv.), and they mark the stages by which the poet passes from despair to a nobler grief, which is really love that looks onward, from a sorrow for one lost friend to a joy which reveals not that friend only, but all humanity, living, for ever, in love, with God.

But we must return to that part of "In Memoriam" where the poet is still the sport of moods that are change- ful, and mostly despondent. Tremblingly he seeks for "answer, or redress" in nature, in science, in the philoso- phies (xlix.), but they can neither solve for him the mystery of pain nor show him the passage from death unto life. " Behold, we know not anything "—such is the sad burden of their reply.

Finally, with an exceeding bitter cry, he calls to his spirit friend to help him in his despair :

[1] See also pp. 192 and 193.

> " O life as futile, then, as frail !
> O for thy voice to soothe and bless !
> What hope of answer, or redress ? "

And there seems to come an answer of blended re-
signation and hope,

> " Behind the veil, behind the veil." (lvi.)

It is possible that " In Memoriam " originally ended
here.

The next poem opens with the word " Peace," and
though the victory is still far off, the poet now does sturdy
battle with despair, so that when we again meet with the
word " peace " (lxxxvi.), it is no longer a cry for strength
and courage in the fight ; it is rather the thankful out-
breathing of a warrior who pauses for a moment in a
conflict nearly won.

And through the poems that follow, loving despair is
altogether changed to loving hope ; naturally, therefore,
we find in the latter portion of " In Memoriam," the
brightest, most beautiful, and most spiritual poetry. To
treat of this at all adequately is impossible in this brief
review, especially as space must be reserved for an ex-
planation of the very important introductory stanzas.
We may only point to the many striking and effective
contrasts produced by later poems when placed by the
side of earlier poems dealing with the same subject.
Of these one of the most beautiful is that presented by the
second picture of the " Deserted House " (cxix.). Or take
the descriptions of Spring time. In poem xxxviii. spring
was forlorn as any winter :

> " No joy the blowing season gives,
> The herald melodies of spring."

In lxxxiii. it is invoked with eager but tremulous love :

> " Dip down upon the northern shore,
> O sweet new year delaying long."

But in cxv. spring and love and hope are blended in a

music that can be likened only to the rapturous melodies of the lark it sings of, and with the last long streak of snow fades also the last remembrance of long and dreary loss. Regret now blossoms as a springtide flower of love.

In the same way we should contrast and compare the three Christmas poems, or sets of poems (xxviii.-xxx. ; lxxviii ; civ., cv.); the eternal gloom of the yew-tree in ii. with the doubtful gleam of solace that lives in the yew-tree of xxxix. ; and there are many others, in most of which the natural world is laid under contribution to heighten the contrast. One such example is the anniversary of Hallam's death (lxxii.) ; there the poet turns to the disastrous day as to something that had done him and his one friend bitter wrong. How different is the calm control of xcix., in which individual sorrow is purer, truer, lovelier, because it does not forget the sorrows of our common humanity : and how exactly in each case is nature made to reflect the poet's mood. But the triumph of love over both despair and time, and the expansion of that love till it embraces all mankind, is best proclaimed by the clash of the bells as they ring in the New Year (cvi.) :

> " Ring out the grief that saps the mind . . .
> Ring in redress to all mankind."

From these poems of place and time which conduct us almost to the end of " In Memoriam," we learn how the poet gradually turned the discipline of sorrow to best and fullest account :

> " 'Tis held that sorrow makes us wise." (cviii. and cxiii.)

Sorrow made Tennyson a true poet ;[1] it may help us to live true lives. Sorrow purifies us, even as silver is tried in the fire. We have seen how it widens our sym-

---

[1] Poets, says Shelley, are

> " Cradled into poetry by wrong
> They learn in suffering what they teach in song."

pathies ; so also does it enlarge our range of vision ; and even as the dead we love (lvi.) :

> "Watch, like God, the rolling hours
> With larger, other eyes than ours,
> To make allowance for us all,"

so the living poet whose affliction had wrought for him a larger hope, and with hope an ampler love, could at last add to these precious fruits of sorrow a faith half lost in sight :

> " Far off thou art, but ever nigh ;
> I have thee still, and I rejoice ;
> I prosper, circled with thy voice ;
> I shall not lose thee tho' I die."

Surely it is not a little that we, a world of mourners, should be taught how to grieve ; that a great and noble man should have laid bare to us his spiritual life through years of much tribulation ; should have allowed us to watch the conflict waged within his soul between the powers of doubt and darkness and weakness and selfishness on the one side, and on the other, faith, light, strength, and love ; that he should have gained the victory —our victory no less than his ; for who can read "In Memoriam" without being wiser, and happier, and better ?

This, surely, is not a little. But what should be our gratitude to the great poet who has set all this before our eyes in a form of surpassing beauty, which stands moreover as the monument of a love so perfect that as long as that monument remains with us—and it will remain with us always—love itself can never die.

A few words concerning the Epilogue, the first of the 131 poems, and their Prologue, will close this section of the Chapter.

THE EPILOGUE was suggested by, and describes, the marriage of Tennyson's younger sister, Cecilia, with Edmund Law Lushington in the year 1842. This may be the date of the verses themselves ; but they speak of the " In Memoriam" as "echoes out of weaker times"— "idle brawling rhymes" made long before—a statement which need not be accepted literally.

In Shelley's lament for Keats occur these words of deepest pathos :

> " Alas, that all we loved of him should be,
> But for our grief, as if it had not been,
> And grief itself be mortal ! "

In " In Memoriam" (lxxviii.) we catch their echo—

> " O last regret, regret can die ! "

but Tennyson adds these two other lines,

> " No, mixt with all this mystic frame
> Her deep relations are the same ; "

and in the Epilogue he writes,

> " Regret is dead, but love is more "—

so much more that it can now admit and satisfy with undisturbed serenity [1] the claims of personal love, love of the family, love of mankind, and love of God.[2]

POEM I. reads like a short preface anticipating criticism. Some men might censure " In Memoriam" as being merely "Private sorrow's barren song" (xxi.), if the poet did not remind them how near akin are love and grief, and that if a man could not grieve, neither could he love.

THE PROLOGUE, dated 1849, is in some respects the most important of Tennyson's writings. From one point of view it is an *Apologia pro vita sua ;* but while essentially self-revealing, it is also a sublime poem. Again, it is another preface, and like the former one, apologetic ; but deep devotion, confession of Faith, profound thought on the mystery of Being, prophetic and stern warning, prayerful self-surrender, and a most solemn music of utterance, place it on the highest level of imaginative literature.

It is addressed to "immortal Love," and may therefore

---

[1] Stanza 4. [2] Stanzas 32-36.

be further regarded as preface and dedication in one.
Although like an overture it suggests the subject matter
of the whole work, yet its leading thought is the need of
reverence in an age that prides itself far too much upon

> "The petty cobwebs we have spun" (cxxiv.) ;

it asks forgiveness for that erring age, for its poet, for his
grief, for his " In Memoriam " ; and the wisest man in all
the world concludes his great work with a supplication of
touching humility,

> " In thy wisdom make me wise."

V.—The following commentary [1] endeavours to indicate
more clearly the course of thought that runs through the
eleven introductory stanzas.

As already suggested, they are a general Preface,
which includes Invocation, Apology, Confession of Faith,
Prayer, and also, to some extent, Dedication—a Preface,
written, as we may suppose, some twelve years after the
poem itself was completed. And just as Poem I.[2] is an
apology to the general public for a seeming indulgence in
this long poetical expression of grief, so these stanzas
contain a reverent apology to the God who, if He found
it good to take away, had first found it good to give.
Somewhat similar is the thought contained in this other
beautiful stanza by Tennyson :

> "God gives us love ; something to love
> He lends us ; but when love is grown
> To ripeness, that on which it throve
> Falls off, and love is left alone."

It is, then, as an Apology, that these stanzas have
most interest for us, and they are addressed to that Im-
mortal Love, to whom, by his search after a lost mortal
love, the poet was gradually led. With Faith as his guide
during this long journey, he passed safely by pitfalls of
reason, and stumbling-blocks of seeming facts, till he
reached the inmost regions of the spiritual life, held com-

---

[1] From " New Studies in Tennyson."   [2] See former page.

munion with his spirit friend (Poem xcv.), and with him bowed before the throne of Divine Love, "the Lord and King" (Poem cxxvi.).

We will now comment on the text in detail.

STRONG :—As opposed to our weakness, discovered by the poet's investigations ; and strong because the same investigations convinced the poet that love, the highest human aspiration, emotion, and virtue ; love begotten of God and incarnate in Christ, and thus linking the human with the divine ; and love, the essence of the Deity, was the one thing powerful in life, powerful over death, powerful for eternity.

SON OF GOD, IMMORTAL :—These epithets were anticipated in the former note ; the poem began with an individual love, and with death, and rose to the height of the great Universal Love and Immortality ; and that universal love which the poet reached through the personal could only thus be comprehended by his human mind—as begotten of the Author of all (whose most precious attribute is love), and as made divine-human in the Son ; destined again in any of its threefold characters[1] to last for ever.

But, "Il doit moins se prouver qu'il ne doit se sentir," or, in Latin, "Crede ut intelligas" (Poem cxxiv.), that is, "We feel God ; do not find him out" (by any human methods). It was not subtle analysis, but promptings of "the likest God within the soul,"[2] that revealed God to the searcher. This—and it occurs in the very first stanza —is the main argument of the poem, that belief in foundation truths rests not upon reason nor philosophy, nay, nor on the creeds themselves ; but upon convictions, high emotions, Divine instincts. Once more, the "broken light" of a human love guided the poet to that love which is the light and the life of the universe.

---

[1] Especially the first and second ; see also former note, and Poem xlvii.
[2] "The divinity that stirs within us." (Cp. Poem lv. 1.)

STANZA II.—Love, then, or the God who is Love, is the Author of all things. Stupendous and blessed thought! Ah, but then that same Being must be the Author of Death, and He seems almost to scorn us dead.

STANZA III.—But is there nothing beyond death? There must be, for the Maker is Love.

STANZA IV.—Ah, yet again ; for the love of the God-head is too high for us! But has it not been written, "Through Him, therefore, we have access unto the Father"? In such mysterious wise, then, the Divine love may reach our humanity and the *individual* man. Another mystery, "the abysmal deeps of personality" (Cp. Poem xlv.), the marvel of free will, of the responsible "Ego." No marvel; a "broken light"[1] again ; this scheme of individuals in a vast universe, and in the presence of its vaster Maker is both grand and simple ; we are created by being allowed to create ourselves.[2] This is the law within the law. ("The Two Voices.")

STANZA V.—Can a part contain the whole? Who, then, may hope to "read the riddle of the painful earth," or pluck out the heart of the mystery of his single being? Systems of thought and systems of religion, useful enough in their time and place, can never fully reveal or explain the Author of all, although through these sometimes may shine upon us uncertain rays of the one great Light for which all thirst.[3]

STANZA VI.—Therefore, yet once again, and even in this nineteenth century, we have nothing to rest on but Faith ; for what we call knowledge is derived entirely

---

[1] See especially "The Higher Pantheism." The figure, not unknown in other poets, occurs repeatedly in Tennyson.

[2]   "To work out our own salvation with fear and trembling."
                                 English Liturgy.

[3]   "Which thro' the web of being blindly wove,
    Burns bright or dim, as each are mirrors of
    The light for which all thirst."
                        Shelley, "Adonais."

from the material world, by the operation of the intellect. It could never explain the unknown. Science, no doubt, has its uses ; it may give us wider views of the material universe, and so help us, *if we learn aright*, to "look through nature up to nature's God" ; even this instrument Knowledge is one of His gifts who giveth all.

STANZA VII.—But what of the abuses of Science, especially if we may judge from the spirit of the times ?[1] I wish it all prosperity, but I trust it may still be tempered with reverence ; and may we never lose sight of the time when childlike ignorance gave us childlike faith ; and may the moral, the emotional, and the intellectual faculties still in the same well-balanced mind make unto earth and heaven "one grand sweet song"—nay, grander, as the new and gifted ages lend each their strong new harmonies.

STANZA VIII.—But alas ! in this nineteenth century are we not irreverent and foolish, and made yet more foolish and irreverent by the arrogant knowledge we vainly deem wisdom?

STANZA IX.—And am not I of all men most foolish? (See paraphrase.)[2]

STANZA X.—And my grief—alas, that too was folly.

[1] "What is she, cut from love and faith," etc. (Poem cxiv.). One of the most important of the lessons taught by this great teacher. It is the one that occurs most frequently, and is insisted upon most sternly. To our thinking the warning, the faith, the hope of Poem cxx. is of more vital interest to the world than all the achievements of modern science. Too often "Science is like the sun, which reveals the face of earth, but seals and shuts up the face of Heaven ;" and if through Science human beings are to revert to greater apes, "what matters science unto men ?" (Poem cxx. See p. 27.)

[2] "Forgive all the so-called sinful actions ; forgive all the so-called meritorious actions of my past life. *Sinful* and *meritorious* are terms that have no meaning except for the imperfect being that employs them—man. Therefore I asked thee to forgive my merit as well.* Man is worthy or unworthy only in respect to his relations with man ; though he should do all for Thee yet wouldst Thou account him an unprofitable servant."

> * "The best of what we do and are,
> Just God, forgive !"
>   WORDSWORTH.

STANZA XI.—And to pour forth that rebellious grief in this long faultful poem was folly most of all.

VI. ANALYSIS OF THE POEM. Many attempts have been made to follow the course of the poet's thought from the beginning to the end of "In Memoriam"; also to discover some natural divisions in the poem ; but none of these attempts is at all trustworthy. We cannot do better than accept the poet's own indication of parts into which the poem may be divided ; but the borders of these will not always be clearly defined. The following is the grouping supplied by the poet to Mr. Knowles, who has given it publication in "The Nineteenth Century"; and we venture to add suggestions respecting the subject of each group.

Group.	Poems.	Subject.
I.	1-8	Regrets before burial.
II.	9-20 (19?)	Interval, and burial.
III.	20-27	Regrets after burial.
IV.	28-49	Christmas, and deep musings to follow.
V.	50-58	In the depths.
VI.	59-71	A new resolve; happier recollections.
VII.	72-98	A year from birthday to birthday.
VIII.	99-103	The second birthday. Leaving Lincolnshire.
IX.	104-131	Another Christmas. A. H. H. A new year. Another spring. Concluding reflections.

CHAPTER X.

"MAUD," 1855.

I. SUBJECT OF THE POEM. The explanatory title, "A Monodrama" added in later editions, is foreshadowed in the following extract from a letter of Tennyson to Dr. Mann : "No one with this essay before him can in future pretend to misunderstand my *dramatic* poem, 'Maud'; your commentary is as true as it is full." In this letter, and by the subsequent addition "A Mono-drama," Tennyson means to tell us that his method was strictly dramatic

> "By making speak, myself kept out of view,
> The very man."
>
> BROWNING, *Sordello.*

In 1856, the year following the appearance of " Maud," Dr. R. J. Mann had published a pamphlet entitled " Maud Vindicated," in which with vigour and with insight he sought to show that " Maud " was purely objective.

The relation that should exist between the main artistic or objective purpose or element of a work of art, and the other, the usually subordinate yet sometimes eventually supreme subjective element or purpose, has been fully considered in Chapter V. It was there pointed out that this subjective, or moral, or didactic element appeared to be in excess in the two " Locksley Halls," and in some of the longer poems near to them in date ; that it slightly disfigured the characters exhibited, and gave them a tendency to caricature. At the same time we found an obvious reason, if not a necessity for that excess, in contemporary events, in the appearance of the same elements in many of the minor contemporary poems, in the poet's idiosyncrasies, and in his mode of expressing himself.

Among the poems surrounding the first "Locksley Hall," "Maud" was specially mentioned as being marred by a deliberate intrusion of personal and contemporary material. We seemed to hear the angry prophet or the noisy patriot far too much, and the sweet singer too little.

Certainly the four times repeated "curse" of "Locksley Hall," when we meet with it twice invoked in "Maud," is put into the mouth of a madman ; [1] but when the hero is sane he uses language almost as violent, as in the indignant assertion "We have made them a curse" ; or where he cynically exclaims "I will bury myself in myself, and the Devil may pipe to his own."

Such characters as those of the two "Locksley Halls" and "Maud" (other poems might be included) all serve as a *persona*, a convenient mask, by means of which the poet may disguise himself while he "foams and speaks riddles" ; characters so uproariously reprehensible that when they have interlarded the poet's soberer speech with their own insobriety he may bully them for it at his will, and shield himself from all blame. How much the better then, for him, if they show symptoms of madness ; their ravings will effectually drown his loudest vituperations.

Therefore in "Locksley Hall Sixty Years After," the querulous leading personage is careful to call himself a dreamer and a dotard : "Am I mad?" asks the lover in "Locksley Hall," though casually ; but he adds, "I know

[1] Part II., v. 6.

my words are wild." "What ; am I raging ?" cries the other lover in " Maud ; " " No matter if I go mad " ; and he goes mad soon after.

"It should be called 'Maud, or the Madness.' It is slightly akin to 'Hamlet.'" This remark of Tennyson to Mr. Knowles will be of much service to us in our endeavour to ascertain whether Dr. R. J. Mann discovered the whole truth about " Maud."

It has already been mentioned incidentally[1] that Hamlet is not a consistent character. To begin with, he is more thoughtful and less obviously mad in the later play ; and in this, as the drama proceeds, he grows in years, in disposition, in doubtfulness between sanity and insanity ; "I know my words are wild," so he, too, might say ; for with words he "unpacks his heart" ; his words, and not his actions, are governed most by Shakespeare's soul. How long and how numerous are his soliloquies ; what a personal interest he takes in the stage ; what faith he has lost in woman ; how he ponders over the problems of evil and good, of life and death. How sad he is, and with what mysterious sadness—" Thou would'st not think how ill all's here about my heart." As Shakespeare worked at his character, he drew nearer to him and nearer, gave him more of his own eight-and-thirty years, a maturer mind, a deeper reflectiveness ; he is sad most of all with Shakespeare's sadness ; and, lest he should reflect the artist too closely, Shakespeare drives him to and fro on the verge of madness.

It is in this sense, as we venture to think, that "'Maud' is slightly akin to 'Hamlet.'"

It may also be noticed that Ophelia, in contrast to Hamlet, goes mad in the ordinary way ; she has played her part by mainly contributing to the catastrophe ; Shakespeare has no further thought for her ; and she

[1] Chapter V.

leaves the stage singing a requiem for the father whom
her lover has slain. Maud, too, is unheroic enough to
make good tragedy possible ; and she vanishes from the
scene with "a cry for a brother's blood" shed by her
lover. But Tennyson's Hamlet was to die only the tem-
porary death of raving madness ; therefore Maud must
come on the stage once more, and direct the final issues ;
but how feebly ! She is dwarfed, even to insignificance,
by the personage of War. Shakespeare might have done
something like this when he was writing "King John" ;
but he never would have made his "Maud" such a traitor
to its title.

This brings us back to Dr. Mann's argument, which
seems to admit of ready refutation. "Not a murmur," he
tells us, "leaves the lips of the poet. These loud outcries
for war fitly proceed from a character sensitive, morbid,
hysterical, mad." The outcries therefore will cease when
the character has become cured of its many diseases. Is
it so ? On the contrary, in Part III., which presents
the hero redeemed and sane, denunciation of peace and
clamour for war is as loud and as unreasonable as ever.[1]

Next, as was shown in Chapter V., the lover in "Maud"
is not the only character in Tennyson's poems of the same
period who "rails at the ill :" and when we find that the
same angry protests against the time's abuse are made
not only by several fictitious characters, but also by the
poet when he speaks unequivocally for himself[2] we cannot
escape the conclusion that the character was made to suit
the occasion at least as much as the occasion happened
to suit the character. In the same chapter "marriage-

---

[1] Even in the "conscience-clause" at the end (last six lines of the poem,)
there is no thought of her who made his life "a perfumed altar-flame ;" her
for whom he "would die." He is satisfied merely because, as he thinks,
the nation has shown some spirit ; merely because he has "awaked" to the
fight, to enthusiasm for his native land, to a liking for his fellow-men that
was born on the field of battle. For these he will live his life and die his
death   [2] See next page.

hindering mammon" was mentioned as the social evil most persistently attacked by Tennyson's poetry at this time, and the appropriate passage in "Maud" was quoted from Part I. X. (2), "Bought? what is it he cannot buy?" To which we are now tempted to add, "Of course, the 'waxen-faced' millionaire intended to purchase Maud; and 'Blithe would her brother's acceptance be.'" But division 3 of the same section will furnish a typical example of the thrusting in of contemporary material. The poet is almost personal in pointing his scorn at

> "This broad-brimm'd hawker of holy things,
> Whose ear is cramm'd with his cotton. . . ."

and in the mad scene the Quaker is again censured for his love of peace.[1] If we now turn to "The Third of February, 1852," we hear Tennyson speaking absolutely for himself—

> "Tho' niggard throats of Manchester may bawl—
> We are not cotton-spinners all."

Surely an opinion publicly announced in one poem as by Tennyson himself, is no less his own for being twice included in almost the same words, though "monodramatically," in another poem of almost the same date. With one other such example this section will conclude. In "Maud," Part I., iv. (4), the monodramatic character is made to exclaim

> "For nature is one with rapine, a harm no preacher can heal;
> The Mayfly is torn by the swallow, . . ."

This is almost word for word with Tennyson's avowed utterance, as of conviction, in "In Memoriam," lvi. (4), the date being probably only a short time earlier:

[1] "There are great questions on which leaders and parties may go wrong. I did not go with the Liberal party in 1854 when they plunged into the war with Russia. I was then attacked and blamed more than I am now . . . but who now condemns me for the course I then took?"—Letter from John Bright to a correspondent, Feb. 13th, 1888.

> " Tho' Nature, red in tooth and claw
> With ravine, shriek'd against his creed."

II. THE STANZAS IN " THE TRIBUTE." The nameless stanzas contributed by Tennyson to " The Tribute " of 1837, form the very slight foundation on which " Maud " was eventually built up. This upbuilding of " Maud " came about at the suggestion of Sir John Simeon, who remarked of the poem in " The Tribute " that it seemed as if something were wanting to explain the story. But an attempt will be made in this section to show that the earlier verses were spoilt in the process of new building ; that in " Maud " they have lost their interest and become a little confusing.

The stanzas as they originally appeared formed a poem of strange and pathetic beauty. A portion of them, with certain alterations, now constitute the fourth section of the second part of " Maud " ; and nothing perhaps will show more clearly the cross purposes and crooked qualities of some parts of the longer poem than a comparison of the stanzas in " The Tribute " with those of Part II., section iv. in " Maud."

We will take the stanzas of " The Tribute " first. Here a lover has lost her whom he loved, and by whom he was beloved ; she was his " bride to be ; " he had " woo'd her for his wife ; " and suddenly death removed her from his side. The poem opens as in " Maud," Part II., section iv.; the first few stanzas are almost the same in both. Apparently the lover in " The Tribute " is a wanderer in a foreign country, for the third line of stanza 2 reads :

> " Of the land that gave me birth."

After the fifth stanza the two poems often differ ; the references to the duel scene are absent from " The Tribute." There the story in detail is as follows :—(1-2) The lover desires that the dead should still be near him, at his side ; (3) but instead of the dead love as he knew her, or as he believes her to be in "the regions of her rest," he is haunted by the vulgar ghost, her earthly shadow, " not thou, but like to thee." And on that account the more he yearns for the visitation of her real presence ; yearns to know the nature of her being, and its home.

But the earthly shadow, the mere mechanic apparition, alone is present to him :—(4) " It leads me forth at evening . . . . in a cold white robe." (5-6) His dreamings in the night-time die away in terror when it comes "without knowledge, without pity" to stand persistent by his bed. (8) The dreary morning dawns only to be made yet more dreary by the " dreary phantom." (9) It pursues him as day advances even through " the hubbub of the market." (10) Then more than ever, amid the throng of men, he seeks for solace in the happy past ; (11) and when daylight is at its broadest, and the din of life is loudest, and the shadow flits nearest about him, he would fain creep into some dark cavern and weep out his soul to his love. Thus, as in the two " Marianas" and other poems, description has followed the daily round of sadness. (12) Then he angrily adjures the Shadow to be gone ; " Get thee hence, nor come again ;" and sets about explaining the weird apparition in terms of science :

> " 'Tis the blot upon the brain
> That *will* show itself without."

At this point we must bring in two passages from " In Memoriam" that explain what precedes, and illustrate Tennyson's theory of the dead who die not:

> " If any vision should reveal
> Thy likeness, I might count it vain
> As but the canker of the brain. . . ." (xcii.)

> " No visual shade of some one lost,
> But he, the Spirit himself, may come
> Where all the nerve of sense is numb
> Spirit to Spirit, Ghost to Ghost." (xciii.)

The remaining six stanzas of the poem in " The Tribute" are merely an application of the doctrine involved in the above quotations to a particular experience.

Stanza (13) is as printed in "Maud" (12), of course omitting the line, "Or to say 'Forgive the wrong.'"

> (Stanza 14) "But she tarries in her place,
> And I paint the beauteous face
> Of the maiden that I lost,
> In my *inner eyes* again,
> Lest my heart be overborne
> By the thing I hold in scorn,
> By a dull *mechanic ghost*
> And a *juggle of the brain*."

Some of the words in italics are repeated in "Maud;" the "blot upon the brain" of these two poems is the "*canker of the brain*" quoted above from "In Memoriam." The "*inner eyes*" are explained in stanzas 15 and 16:

> (15) "I can shadow forth my bride
> As I knew her, fair and kind,
> As I woo'd her for my wife;
> She is lovely by my side
> In the silence of my life—
> 'Tis a *phantom of the mind*,"

which phantom we are told in (16) is fair and good, and guards his life from ill,

> "Tho' its ghastly sister glide
> And be moved around me still
> With the moving of the blood
> That is moved not of the will."

The last two lines convey a further explanation of stanza 8 in the "Maud" version, "the blot upon the brain That *will* (*sic*) show itself without."

That the "drearier phantom" is a product of physical derangement as opposed to the spiritual presence within his spirit, is set forth in the next stanza (17):

> "Let it pass, the dreary brow,
> Let the dismal face go by.
> Will it lead me to the grave?
> Then I lose it: it will fly:
> Can it overlast the nerves
> Can it overlive the eye?"

This is the ghostly disease of " Maud," Part II., section
ii. 5. In Part III. vi. 1, Maud " seem'd to divide in a
dream from a band of the blest," saying, " I tarry for
thee." Of this we have the germ in the last stanza (18) of
of the poem in " The Tribute " :

> " But the other, like a star,
> Thro' the channel windeth far
>   Till it fade and fail and die,
> To its Archetype that waits
> Clad in light by golden gates—
> Clad in light the spirit waits
>   To embrace me in the sky. "

And now we understand what otherwise is scarcely in-
telligible, the third division of Part III. vi. in " Maud."
The " *morbid eye* " finds a meaning in the line, " Can it
overlive the eye ? " and one symptom of the " old hysterical
mock-disease " is the " disease " of II. ii. 5 ; and the
" dreary phantom " is the " hard mechanic ghost " of that
passage, and the " shadow " of II. iv. 3.

Of the poem in " The Tribute " it is hard to speak tem-
perately ; the plaintive strange sweet music that it mur-
murs to itself murmurs ever in the ears of him who has once
heard it. But the stanzas in " Maud " are very different ; the
shadow, the mechanic ghost, appears before Maud is dead,
II. i. 2, II. ii. 5 ; and is explained as a " juggle born of the
brain ; " when she has died, the same shadow, as it seems,
" the blot upon the brain " appears again, stripped of half
its ghostly mystery. Maud comes from " a stiller world of
the dead " (Cymbeline) and stands by the madman in his
madness ; she comes again—it was but a dream (III. vi. 2) ;
and ultimately the " dreary phantom " flies to the scene
of war—leaves him at peace because he is going to war.
These various appearances are a little confusing. The
subject cannot be fully dealt with in this chapter ; but a
careful examination of the stanzas of II. iv. will show
further that they do not form a consistent poem when re-
garded by themselves, and much less when taken in their

connection with the rest of the Monodrama ; at several points they fail to be in keeping with the former drift of the story. It will also appear that this inconsistency is due partly to the war motive forced into the poem, and partly to the eccentricities of the leading character. When we think of the other lover in " The Tribute," we may be inclined to marvel that Maud could ever have loved the madman of the longer poem.

III. THE MADNESS. (1) In the plot of "Maud" lurk several improbabilities—incidents of doubtful dramatic propriety. From these we will single out for brief examination the celebrated mad scene (Part II. v.)

"The Princess," like "Maud," is, properly speaking, a monologue ; and when in Canto VI. of "The Princess" the next character begins his long soliloquy, he is some-what puzzled how to relate events he has not seen ; incidents that occurred while he was unconscious, or his ravings while he was delirious in fever. He attempts to overcome the difficulty, as will be understood from the following doubtful lines :

> " Seeing, I saw not, hearing not, I heard :
> Tho' if I saw not, yet they told me all
> So often that I speak as having seen."

We might grant this possible in the case of a prince, even to the extent of recording the mutterings of a mind wandering in disease. But Maud's lover is a friendless man, a fugitive among men ; he has been the inmate of a madhouse "so long" (Part III. i.), it may be years. No one would be likely to tell him what he said during that time. Ophelia either speaks her madness to the audience, or some other character repeats what he has heard her say. This holds good of all other examples of insanity in literature that we can remember.

(2) In "The Two Voices" there is an allusion to madness which seems at variance with Tennyson's treatment of the subject in this section :

> " And men, whose reason long was blind,
> From cells of madness unconfined
> Oft lose whole years of darker mind."

In the same poem we are told that men who have recovered from a trance often forget what then passed through their minds until they fall into a trance again. And in "In Memoriam," lxxi., trance and madness are said to be akin. It is not usual, we believe, for men who have been mad to recall the ravings of their insanity. It would, therefore, seem improbable that this insane person should remember what occurred during his period of confinement in Bedlam.

(3) Doubtless there are various forms of madness, most of which include unconscious cerebration and wild speech. But this mad scene is surely too rational, too consecutive to represent the incoherent ravings of a friendless lunatic long confined in a mad cell. There is too much method in his madness, whether as regards the matter or its arrangement. This any reader of the poem will be able to discover. The maniac recalls the past in an exact sequence of events and censorious reflections, varied only by a curious new topic—the " churchmen " who " fain would kill their church."

(4) When brought to bear on the mental aberration and jangled utterance of madness, criticism is reduced to conjecture. The lover in this section fancies, madman-like, (1) that he is dead, (2) that he is not mad ; he has also a confused recollection of the past. This, according to Tennyson, in " In Memoriam," lxxi. and iv., is sometimes the peculiarity of dreams ; but, as we may judge from this stanza and the references to " The Two Voices," it is an exceptional occurrence. Further, the madman fancies he has been thrust into a " shallow grave," " only a yard beneath the street." There is no end to the din above him : yet he can hear the dead men chatter ; he is in a " world " of the dead ; the dead go ever around

him ; Maud, who has come from another stiller world, stands by him silent ; then he returns to the yard-deep grave that he seems to have converted into a " world." All this, however, is conjecture.

(5) But the conjecture may be admitted to have some purpose in it ; because " The whole of the stanzas where he is mad in Bedlam, from ' Dead, long dead,' to ' Deeper, ever so little deeper,' were written in twenty minutes, and some mad doctor wrote to me that nothing since Shakespeare has been so good for madness as this." This remark made by Tennyson when reading his " Maud " to some friends, should be received, we think, with reverential regret.

(6) With this regret in our minds, we now glance at the form of the section. It is more irregular than usual. The subject of excess in irregularity has been noticed in Chapter III. p. 75. A few words may be added here.

This series of lyrical structures in " Maud " may be compared to a succession of emotional waves breaking on a beach that gives them utterance and uncertain rest. From this point of view they are admirably adapted to an impulsive character who reveals his history by a series of moody outbursts. But, after all, waves are more or less regular and similar, and the sometimes symmetrical, sometimes formless lyrics of " Maud " do not as a whole produce quite the unity of impression left on the mind by the unsymmetrical symmetry of such an architectural experiment as the interior of Roslin Chapel. We can understand that they " take the shape " each of some new emotional phase ; but until emotional phases are capable of rigid classification, they may not become substitutes for the definite structural units of poetry. It is delightful to hear the lines of Shakespeare as they pass from rhythmless metre to metrical rhythm (pp. 104-5) ; but the next stage is disintegration. We may be amused to see the " Parts of Speech " melt down in the crucible of philology ; we should not be amused to see English blank verse—the finest art form ever moulded by man—reduced to the amorphous pulp of Macpherson's " Fingal." And this is true of the larger structural units and structures of verse ; the time has not yet come when emotional form may be transfigured into formless emotion ; we cannot watch the operation of the law that governs such a change as that, for it is not visible to mortal eye ; absolute beauty must dwell a little longer in the heavens. And now, returning to our subject, the first two lines of this fifth lyric of Part II. in " Maud" may be said to suggest the fitful utterance of a maniac ; but they are not poetry. Neither are they prose ; for they rhyme with a line in the context. The last division again (11) is neither verse nor prose.

Ophelia turns her passion to prettiness sometimes in prose, sometimes in verse ; but there is no halting between the two.

IV. THE MUSIC OF MAUD. The present writer once read a French version of " Maud." It yielded him many a merry laugh, but, with that, much concern for the unhappy translator. Translate " Maud " into French ! you might as well try to send a nightingale's song to France in a bottle securely corked. (Alas, we are near doing that now.) Some poetry, Byron's for example, can be reproduced just a little in another language :

> " You may break, you may shatter the vase if you will,
> But the scent of the roses will cling round it still."

But those parts of " Maud " whose word-music of emotion thrills you till the dull touch of intellect is felt no longer— attempt to translate these—

> " You seize the flower—the bloom is shed ! "

Of this fine intangible poetry, which is so abundant in " Maud," some account has been given on p. 78 ; and it will be referred to again in the commentary appended below.

It has been said that Tennyson could not bear to hear his songs sung ; that is excellent. Some of us will never forget hearing Sims Reeves sing " Come into the garden, Maud." We admired Sims Reeves immensely, but we hoped never to hear him sing that song again. It may be recited till one's breath is caught away ; but it ought not to be sung. These remarks apply also to such pieces as " Sweet and low," "Ask me no more," " Tears, idle tears." Poetry [1] does sometimes transcend music ; and then music must keep away from it. Though slightly irregular in form, yet in regard to their number and the delicate intellectual accompaniment of their melody, the stanzas " Come into the garden, Maud," are the most perfect specimens of their kind. But they have no kind ; and if music spoils them, what shall talking do ?

This leads us to a final criticism on " Maud ; " it can hardly be fairer than the one inscribed in his volume of " Maud " by the writer of these comments many years ago : " Tennyson's worst poem but finest poetry."

V. A COMMENTARY ON " MAUD." [2]

PART I.

SECTION I.—The hero tells his tale of death and villainy ; "and are we not all villains ? And no wonder ; ' For the jingling of the guinea helps the hurt that Honour feels.' Better war, loud war, if in peace we murder each

---

[1] Poetry in which faultless form is vitalized by faultless spirit ; so vitalized, indeed, that form and spirit "touch, mingle, are transfigured," as far as may be in poetic art. Such poetry has a charm not inferior to the charm of music, in which the transfiguration is complete ; nay, rather, superior, because expressed in that word-symbolism by whose aid the sound-symbolism of music was developed, and to which, consciously or unconsciously, the eloquence of music must for many generations longer be related.

[2] From " New Studies in Tennyson."

other for gold. In such a sordid age I may well be misanthropos, and hate mankind. I am ready to hate Maud."

SECTION II.—Maud comes on the scene, and her influence begins to operate at once, for he falls to criticising her.

SECTION III.—The new influence in Sleep (as in the "In Memoriam"). With one touch of sadness in her beauty she rebukes him for hostile and prejudiced criticism.

SECTION IV.—Her influence falters for awhile. Springtime and Maud are powerless as yet to redeem such an one, though both flash like a light on his darkness. Moreover, a slight misunderstanding (stanza 3), while it heightens dramatic effect, makes the misanthrope a cynic also ; and in such a mood he will almost mock at his deliverer (stanza 10).

SECTION V.—*Her Voice.* With wonderful felicity the poet presents her SINGING—singing a song that will move even him ; a song of the one virtue he recognizes— patriotism.

Note the fine art whereby the section begins and ends with "A voice." By that voice—only thus far—he allows her influence ; and he fights against her influence still.

SECTION VI.—*Her Smile.* By way of contrast, nature frowns after a night brightened by her recollected smile. For he still plays with his doubts ; and these give him an occasion (8) to introduce autobiographical grounds for his melancholy. But that smile—he cannot forget it ; and he just realizes how different his life *might* be. So this section begins and ends with a smile. (Note the rise and decline of verse and thought in 3.)

SECTION VII.—The new emotion in his mind calls up an incident of the past, which establishes the hero's right to make advances. Note the same device in " The Princess."

SECTION VIII.—The next meeting, which borrows **a** certain charm from surroundings.

SECTION IX.—A new character—the rival wooer. Contrast metre of this with former section ; for it indicates a reaction. Notice also the background of nature in harmony with the foreground of incident.

SECTION X.—Jealousy—indispensable element in a story of love—quickens the hero's passion and our interest. Once more he turns round on his time to upbraid it. Yet he takes a lesson from Maud (4) ; begins to change love of self for love of her : " O for a man, a statesman great enough and good enough for me—for Maud " (5) ; and again, self-correction (6), otherwise he would have been extravagant.

SECTION XI.—

> " A trembling apprehension always waits
> Our highest joys."
>
> SHIRLEY.

This section hints at an arrangement for the next.

SECTION XII.—*The Woodland Meeting.* The rooks miss Maud, and caw their consternation ; the shriller [1] songsters of the wood answer with many a sympathetic trill ; the rooks again grow hoarsely anxious, for is not the young lord-lover waiting at the Hall ? But Maud's spaniel shows his teeth to the rival, who has come a little too late.

SECTION XIII.—The course of true love never did run smooth. A first check—her brother. (The miserly father shuns the honest light of day.) As to Maud's mother, she is a reflection of the mother in " The Princess," and of the poet's own mother. A couplet (4) of self-castigation, again, as at end of Section X.

SECTION XIV.—He surveys the situation, and prepares us for the meeting of XVI. and XVII. (1) Early morning in Maud's garden ; (2) her bower. (3) He has not lost

---

[1] The low vowel in M*au*d suggests the note of the rooks ; the high vowel in here, the note of the songsters

the tendency to analyse emotions ; (compare with " In Memoriam.") (4) He has looked unconcerned on death hitherto ; but now he shudders at sleep, the mere semblance of death ;—now, for he thinks much of Maud, and begins to think that no man may even die unto himself.

SECTION XV.—If then Maud has become so dear to him, surely he must make himself worthier—if heavenly grace permit. Here, at least, is a life-duty. Any man can die for a woman, but few are the men who will live for one. Further, " Love annihilates self, even while exalting it, and crowns life in a twofold ecstasy of renunciation and attainment " ; or thus :

> " He doth not love himself aright
> Who doth not love another more."

SECTION XVI.—In the absence of the brother they meet—but first, one other doubt ; (2) and yet one fear ; (3) " Let not the sight of her beauty bereave me of the power to speak my love."

SECTION XVII.—*The " Wilt thou?" and " The happy 'Yes.'"*—Here in word-music, quivering with expectant rapture or tremulous with ecstasy beyond the reach of thought, the poet thrills us into sacred sympathy with the most exquisite emotion of human life.

SECTION XVIII.—Exquisite word-music again ; its keynote is " calming itself." For it tells of tranquil possession of perfect happiness. Contrast rhythm with that of former section. XVII. is as a mountain streamlet hurrying joyously impatient to reach the valley of its desire ; XVIII. as a full-flowing river—" Full to the banks—close on the promised good."

In Division 3 of this section the nameless hero takes the natural world into his confidence, and, like the lover in the " Talking Oak " unburdens his heart to a tree ; and in (4) he talks calmly to the stars that govern our conditions with an iron tyranny ; " Astronomy and Geology, terrible Muses."—*Parnassus.* " What is it all but a

trouble of ants in the gleam of a million million of suns?"
—*Vastness.* But this "iron hollow of doubtful heaven"
can "numb him not or torture not again";

> " For love possess'd the atmosphere,
> And fill'd the breast with purer breath . . .
> (Div. 6.) With farther lookings on."
>   *Miller's Daughter.*

And not only Life, but Death also, is transformed by
Love; and Nature in the light of love displays new beauty.

(Division 7.) But fair as may be the everlasting reign
of love beyond the grave,

> (" And if God will
> I shall but love thee better after death."
>   E. B. BROWNING.)

let true life and its true love come first (" In Memoriam,"
lxxxv.); and in this best way shall the life and love that
follows death be truer.[1] Note the emphatic *thou* of the
seventh line; for to the *new counsellor*, Maud, he lovingly
confides his first doubt.

(Division 8.) "What charm in words, a charm no
words could give!" and I must not mar this enchanted
and enchanting music with more than just one comment;
we notice at the end of the division that the culmination
of ecstasy gives the cue for tragedy to enter.

SECTION XIX.—Two short lines serve to indicate the
tragic turning—forecast the catastrophe. Compare the
stage direction "Enter a servant," "Julius Cæsar,"
III. i. 121; the effect is much the same in each case. In
2 and 3 we have another apology for the morbid condition
of the hero when he first appeared on the stage; in 4 and 5

---

[1] The meaning of the last two lines in Division 7 is as follows : The silken
cord of love is strengthened by the inweaving of Death's *dark* strand (a
" strand " is one of the smaller cords—sometimes of a different colour—that
when twisted with others form the larger cord). The thought appears to be
twofold : 1st "The approach of death should make us dearer to each other;"
2nd, "But death is immortality, and immortality alone can make love per-
fect." See "In Memoriam," xxxiv. ; and "Locksley Hall Sixty Years After,"
couplet 36.

renewed justification of his relationship to Maud ; in 6, the *villain* of the play ; in 7, woman's kinder, perhaps juster, estimate of man ; and Maud, the reconciler, relates an incident that adds deadly pathos to the duel. ("A cry for a brother's blood"; see Part II. i. 1). In 8 and 9 we witness a mental struggle that ends in a kind result of love, and is moreover introductory to 10. The mercurial moods of the lover are nowhere better described than in this latter division.

Section XX.—Much as in "In Memoriam," the trouble is sometimes *transferred*. It is Maud's turn to be melancholy ; and no wonder (compare with incident in "Aylmer's Field") ; the brother has been roughly urging on the suit of the lord rival. The plainness of her dresses ! Plain to the rival, of course ; but to the lover, perfection. She must wear another dress to-morrow, and entertain, with whatever grace, the villain or the fop. But he too shall see his Maud in "gloss of satin and glimmer of pearls ;" and she will be gracious to him.

Section XXI.—How this is to be accomplished.

Section XXII.—First compare this matchless lyric with the lines in "The Princess," "Now sleeps the crimson petal" (VII. 161). Stanzas 1 and 2 sketch *le lieu de la scène ;* 3, the night before the dawn to him who waited ; 4 and 5, communings with her two flowers ; 6 and 7, the bulbul and the rose in Gulistan, and the sensations and recollections that follow ; 8, in the other serenade the flowers all sleep ; here the lilies and roses watch with the watcher ; 9, as in "Becket," [1] so here ; the lily and the rose are chief among flowers, and are fittest emblems of fairest womanhood ; but Maud is "lily and rose in one." [2] The

---

[1] "If Rosamund is
The world's rose, as her name imports her, she
Was the world's lily."

[2] "They made her lily and rose in one."
            Ancient Sage.

sun is just rising, but to her flowers "Maud" shall be a brighter sun. 10, a sunlit dewdrop shaken from the passion flower of XIV. (1), tells that she is coming : "In a moment we shall meet."[1]   After the fitting and prophetic climax of 11,[2] the curtain falls.   It rises again on

PART II.,

in which, after the duel, we discover (1) some return of the old malady, followed (2) by broodings in exile ; (3), tells us that Maud has died of a broken heart ; (4), is some portion of the beautiful lyric round which by accretion the whole poem shaped itself ; (5), the delirium of madness, which has some resemblance to the fever scene in "The Princess," Canto VII.

PART III.

"So then to love is good, to lose is good,
    If but the loser bow to penance given ;
Thou wilt have purged the grossness of my blood,
    Thou wilt have taught me look for thee in Heaven."

And now the two main motives, love, and the yet stronger patriotism, are blended into one redeeming life purpose.

---

[1] Part II. iv. (6).

[2]   "Shake hands, my friend, across the brink
        Of that deep grave to which I go.
            . . . . I cannot sink
        So far, far down, but I shall know
        Thy voice, and hearken from below."

From "My life is full of weary days."   Also Cf. "New Year's Eve :"

            "I shall hear you when you pass
        With your feet above my head. . . ."

CHAPTER XI.

"IDYLLS OF THE KING."

I. INTRODUCTORY. It is possible that no reliable estimate of this poem can be formed in our day. Most probably the task will be left to some future Addison, and to the host of critics who will criticise his criticisms, generation after generation. The question, "What sort of poems are the 'Idylls'?" is profoundly interesting, but very far-reaching; indeed, the whole subject is so vast, and beset with such extraordinary difficulties, that within the compass of this Handbook suggestions must be offered rather than conclusions.

At first sight nothing can seem easier than to create the minor work of art by the side of the major one—to write, that is, a useful and impressive account whether of the poem as a whole, or of the separate Idylls, or of the characters. But this paper may possibly serve a better purpose if, like the chapter on "The Princess," it seeks rather to show with the utmost brevity that any such treatment of the subject is liable to be not only imperfect but also misleading.

For example: critics are almost unanimous in regarding a uniform magnificence of style as the chief merit of Tennyson's poem, and the greater number claim also for the Idylls an epic unity of design and construction. But in a passage from "New Studies in Tennyson," which is appended to this chapter, the present writer has already attempted to show that in point of style and construction generally the poem is by no means uniform.

Some of the opinions expressed in this Appendix received remarkable corroboration when Mr. Knowles published his "Aspects of Tennyson (II.)" in the "Nineteenth Century" for January, 1893. For example, the poet is represented as making the following statements: "It is necessary to respect the limits. . . . I soon found that if *I* meant to make any mark at all it must be by shortness, for all the men before me had been so diffuse, and all the big things had been done. . . . A small vessel on fine lines is likely to float further than a great raft." Of the "In Memoriam" he said: "The general way of its being written was so queer that if there were a blank space I would put in a poem." Of "Maud": "It should be called 'Maud; or, the Madness.' It is slightly akin to 'Hamlet.'" Also of the "Idylls of the King" he remarked: "When I was twenty-four I meant to write a whole great poem on it, and began to do it in the 'Morte d'Arthur.' I said I should do it in twenty years, but the Reviews stopped me."

Without abusing the poet's confidence we may fairly repeat that although Tennyson, like Milton at an age almost as early, determined to write "a whole great poem," he was nevertheless of the opinion that if he meant to make any mark at all it must be by shortness; and further, that he allowed "the Reviews" to stop him. And this hesitation to attempt a very great work of artistic oneness leads us to conjecture that the greater works which the poet did attempt might possibly fail to some extent in unity of design, unity of composition, and unity of effect.

As a fact, we have seen something of this in the chapters on "The Princess," "In Memoriam," and

"Maud." We noticed, for example, that the long period during which "In Memoriam" was in course of composition exposed the poet to some risk of impairing his unity of impression.[1] This risk became much more serious in the writing of a work so difficult and so vast as the "Idylls"; and, as noticed in the Appendix, other influences tended to interrupt and protract its composition.

II. A CHRONOLOGICAL VIEW OF THE POEM. The plausibility of such a conjecture will appear more plainly as we approach our next subject, the history of the composition of the "Idylls." This history is briefly summarized in the following chronological table:

1833. In this year, as we may say, the poet[2] contemplates writing his "whole great poem." The "Lady of Shalott," in the 1833 volume, is the first fragment of Arthurian romance turned into poetry by Tennyson. The "Palace of Art" in the same volume introduces "That deep-wounded child of Pendragon,"[3] and speaks of *Alfred* as "the flower of Kings." This is the "Flos regum" of Joseph of Exeter, and it is significant that Tennyson at this period gives that well-known title to Alfred.

1837. Landor tells us that a MS. poem by Tennyson on the death of Arthur was read to him, and he speaks of the work as being "more Homeric than any poem of our time."

1842. The poem Landor has mentioned appears in the volume of 1842, having a Prologue entitled "The

---

[1] It is interesting to note that many a commentator has found "In Memoriam" capable of rigid analysis, but that each has analysed it differently; and Tennyson himself differently last of all.

[2] Now 24 years of age.

[3] In later editions: "Mythic Uther's deeply-wounded son."

Epic," and followed by an Epilogue without any title. In the Table of Contents "The Epic" and "Morte d'Arthur" appear as independent poems, otherwise we might have regarded the Epilogue as included in "The Epic." The same volume contained the two splendid Arthurian Lyrics, "Sir Galahad" and "Sir Launcelot and Queen Guinevere." This last is styled "A Fragment."

1857. "Enid and Nimuë: The True and the False." (Privately printed.)[1]

1858. "The Detection of Guinevere and the Last Interview with Arthur" (Clough, "Remains," vol. i., p. 235; or p. 287 in one vol. ed.).

1859. "The True and the False. Four Idylls of the King." Also "Idylls of the King (Enid, Vivien, Elaine, Guinevere)."

1862. New Edition of the "Idylls," with dedication to the memory of the Prince Consort.

1869 (dated 1870). The "Holy Grail" volume, containing "The Coming of Arthur," "The Holy Grail," "Pelleas and Ettarre," and "The Passing of Arthur."

1871. "The Last Tournament" (in "The Contemporary Review" for December).

1872. "Gareth and Lynette." (1873.) "To the Queen" appended to the Idylls. In an edition of this year many passages were added—*e.g.*, lines 9-28 to the "Passing of Arthur," and the marriage song to "The Coming of Arthur."

1874. A new passage of 150 lines introduced into "Merlin and Vivien" (following the fifth line).

1885. "Balin and Balan" in the "Tiresias" volume.

1888. "Geraint and Enid" is divided into "The Marriage of Geraint" and "Geraint and Enid."

---

[1] Nimuë in the South Kensington Museum is marked "Revise."

This table, which might possibly be made yet more complete, is of the first importance in any attempt to survey the "Idylls of the King." With its aid we have now to discover how the poet wrought at his poem, and what were his own opinions concerning it. It is always well to inquire of the poet first.

Setting aside the lyrics, which have been dealt with elsewhere, we notice that Tennyson begins by turning into blank verse a portion of the twenty-first book of Sir Thomas Malory's "Le Morte Darthur." Possibly he had written more, but for publication he chooses the most interesting passage in Malory, and the one that gives a name to the whole volume; and he mostly adopts Malory's purely romantic treatment of the subject.

If we now turn to "The Epic," we discover much that is interesting and important. It is not advisable to take the poet literally when he says that the Epic, his "King Arthur," consisted of some twelve books, all of which were burnt except "Morte d'Arthur," which constituted the eleventh. If we are asked, as sometimes happens, "What then would have been the subject of the twelfth book?" we may answer, "Paradise Regained." [1] The tradition "that he shall come again" is common to many heroes of legend and romance. [2] Malory's tradition continues, "and he shal wynne the holy crosse." But Malory himself adds, "rather I wyl say here in thys world he changed his lyf." With the life of Christ before him, Tennyson might have chosen the first of these fables; but it is doubtful whether the Nineteenth Century would have made any such twelfth book possible. The mystical

---

[1] "Thou hast said much here of 'Paradise Lost, but what hast thou to say of Paradise found ?" Ellwood to Milton.

[2] Among the many other heroes of history or romance who were to come again are Charlemagne and Holger Danske, one of his twelve peers; Barbarossa, Roderick, Desmond, Sebastian of Brazil, the Incas of "Westward Ho !", Hiawatha.

number of twelve books, however, have been written, or made, for in 1888 the "Enid" of 1859 was divided into "The Marriage of Geraint" and "Geraint and Enid."

At this earlier stage of 1842 the author blames his work for being "Homeric"; "a truth," he thought, would look "freshest in the fashion of the day." He distrusts only the resemblance, not the Homeric qualities, the simplicity, directness, dignity, truth of sentiment, fidelity to legend, delight in the mere story, dramatic description, and so forth; and from the Classics, especially the Greek epics, and such materials as the Bible, the Book of Common Prayer, Malory, "Paradise Lost," and the "Hyperion" of Keats have bequeathed to him he constructs a blank verse that may bear some comparison with the "strong-wing'd music of Homer."

At present, therefore, his doctrine is essentially epical, and of the highest order of epic, although in the epilogue to "Morte d'Arthur" he admits "some modern touches here and there." Also, in a dream, he somewhat significantly sees Arthur "like a modern gentleman Of stateliest port"; and there is the slightest possible suggestion, not as yet of allegory, but merely of a moral purpose, in the lines, "Come again, and thrice as fair. . . . With all good things, and war shall be no more."

We can never be sure how long before the date of its appearance any particular Idyll or part of it was written; but, on the hypothesis that each poem was finished only a short time before publication, we next speak of the volume of 1857. This, however, as mentioned in the Table, was not published. A few copies only were printed for private circulation. The title-page is as follows: "Enid and Nimuë: The True and the False, by Alfred Tennyson, Poet Laureate, London. Moxon: 1857."

This volume contains two of the Idylls, "Enid" and "Vivien," in an earlier form.

In the year 1859 a proof was printed with half-title, "The True and the False. Four Idylls of the King;" and, for full title, "The True and the False. Four Idylls of the King, by Alfred Tennyson, P.L., D.C.L. London: Edward Moxon & Co., Dover Street. 1859."

These title-pages are given in full because something useful to our purpose may be learnt from them. In this second volume we find the two former stories, "Enid" and "Nimuë" (considerably altered), together with two new ones, "Elaine" and "Guinevere." In the table of contents "Nimuë" is cancelled; and "Vivien" is the name already adopted in the body of the book. Both volumes contain corrections of great interest to the student of Tennyson.

To turn now to the title-pages. In the distinction "The True and the False," we have the first reliable indication of moral purpose; but, again, not as yet of any allegorical intention. That some importance may be attached to this title seems clear from the fact that in the 1859 copy it twice takes precedence over "Idylls of the King." Herein we recognize also the principle of antithesis or contrast, the helpful setting off of character against character, most common to beginners in dramatic art. This important element will receive fuller notice below. Further, it appears that the title, "Idylls of the King," was selected not earlier than 1857 nor later than 1859. One would think that the poet, in defiance of the "Reviews" that "stopped him," now cautiously ventured to link these stories to the fortunes of "Flos regum"; and this idyllic treatment of the great epic theme was probably suggested by Theocritus.

But there is another point. Proof copies of the "Enoch Arden" volume of 1864 were styled "Idylls of the Hearth." "Idylls of the King," and "Idylls of the Hearth," are therefore near enough in date to imply that in the former of the two we may discover Tennyson's unwillingness to regard his four pictures of women with their tinge of parable as books of an epic ; that he almost preferred to class them with the " Idylls " of the " Enoch Arden " volume.

When, later, in 1859, these four stories appeared as " Idylls of the King," they were drawn yet nearer to the central myth by the motto " Flos regum Arthurus."

We now come to the year 1870, in which four more " Idylls " were published [1]—" The Coming of Arthur," " The Holy Grail," " Pelleas and Ettarre," and " The Passing of Arthur." In this volume also the poet supplies us with hints respecting his design. Important and significant changes are made in the titles, for " Enid," " Vivien," and " Elaine " become respectively " Geraint and Enid," " Merlin and Vivien," and " Lancelot and Elaine " ; and these later titles are less suggestive of studies of women, and more clearly connected with the Arthurian legends. The " Idylls " are now spoken of as " the whole series " ; there is the " Round Table " [2] of six idylls, or poems (both these terms are used, but not at present the term *books*), and it is preceded by " The Coming of Arthur," and followed by " The Passing of Arthur." Concerning the latter poem we are informed in a note : " This last, the earliest written of the poems, is here connected with the rest in accordance with an early project of the author's."

Does this include the whole of " The Passing of

[1] " The Holy Grail and other Poems." *Flos Regum Arthurus* is retained on the title-page.

[2] A curious title, and probably an afterthought. According to the poet as quoted below, King Arthur means the soul, and the Round Table the passions and capacities of a man. If so, this is no longer the Round Table (printed in small capitals in early editions) of " Morte d'Arthur," which was " an image of the mighty world " ; it is rather the Round Table of " Balin and Balan " :

> " This old sun-worship, boy, will rise again,
> And beat the cross to earth, and break the King
> And all his table."

This subject is referred to again in Section V.

Arthur"? probably not. And here we may notice some subsequent additions to this idyll ; such are the " weird rhyme," " From the great deep to the great deep he goes," which is repeated from " The Coming of Arthur " ; also lines 9 to 28, which appear to be suggested by " The Last Tournament." Already therefore we may venture to regard "The Last Tournament " (1871) as an afterthought, arising probably out of the passage in "Guinevere ;" "Then came the sin of Tristram and Isolt ;" but also thrust into the story in order to give weird and incomprehensible colour to the consequences of the crime of Guinevere ; and we may also remind ourselves with due reservation of Tennyson's remark to Mr. Knowles concerning " In Memoriam" : " The general way of its being written was so queer that if there were a blank space I would put in a poem."

The year 1874 brings us to the long passage added to " Merlin and Vivien." Coleridge has described a speech of Iago's as " The motive-hunting of a motiveless malignity." That description applies in part to these 150 lines. But in providing Vivien with questionable motive, Tennyson has brushed over the tinge of parable with some gaudy paint of allegory ; she was born "Among the dead and sown upon the wind." 1885, the last year in this chronicle, gave us " Balin and Balan," which we may regard as another interpolation of motive. It was announced as " an introduction to ' Merlin and Vivien.'" It serves as an introduction both to "The Holy Grail" and to " Merlin and Vivien." It is a first attack on what may be called sensual religion, and being the latest written of the " Idylls," brings in Vivien less as a woman and more as an allegorical creation of " Sense at war with Soul." These words take us back to the year 1862, in which the poet makes avowal of some moral and allegorical method and purpose ; for in the solemn " Dedication " of that year occurs the phrase, " My own ideal Knight," (sub-

sequently altered to "my king's ideal knight"); and the
same words take us on to the year 1873,[1] when the grace-
ful lines "To the Queen," were placed after the "Idylls."
It is in these lines that we find Tennyson's most explicit
avowal of allegory; the passage is well known; it begins,
"Accept this old imperfect tale . . ." Although expres-
sions of an allegorical intention almost as precise are found
scattered about the "Idylls," it is perhaps a pity that the
poet turned commentator in this way; for critics have
fastened upon the passage and made somewhat too much
of it.   Of course we must accept it, but with due discretion
and some caution.

   Much more is to be learnt from the poet; but only a few
words may be added here.   In the lines just referred to,
Tennyson implies that he does not approve of Malleor's
conception of King Arthur.   Then he gives such a sketch
of his own times, "signs of storm," as remind us forcibly
of "Locksley Hall Sixty Years After," and seem to furnish
another reason for the introduction of "The Last Tourna-
ment," as well as for lines 9 to 28 of "The Passing of
Arthur."   The poet ends, however, as he usually does,
with a faint forecast of hope.

[1] It may here be noticed that this "Dedication to the Queen," which
speaks of the poem as complete, was followed by 150 lines added to "Vivien,"
by Balin and Balan, and by various other additions. At this time of dedication,
the poem was probably regarded as complete within the compass of its ten
books; but when in 1885 "Balin and Balan" formed an eleventh book, it
may have suggested the formation of a twelfth by the division of "Geraint
and Enid" (1888).

[2] In Chapter V. "Locksley Hall" was regarded as a summing up of sen-
timents expressed in many contemporary poems, including the first four
"Idylls of the King;" in the same way "Locksley Hall Sixty Years
After" gathers up such similar utterances as are scattered among the poems
that surround it, again including the later "Idylls of the the King;" one
example may suffice; the 1872 addition to "The Passing of Arthur"—

                    "All my realm
          Reels back into the beast"

(where "beast" may be read in two senses), corresponds to a line in "Locks-
ley Hall Sixty Years After:"

   "Have we risen from out the beast, then back into the beast again?"

Next we have to note that after 1842 the poem is never spoken of as an epic ;[1] the latest title applied being "Idylls of the King. In Twelve Books." And although called "Books," the divisions of the poem have each of them *a story-telling name*.

Lastly, we return to Mr. Knowles, with whom Lord Tennyson was accustomed to talk over the "Cycle of his 'Idylls,' to see how their treatment would come ;" and to whom he dictated a prose sketch of "Balin and Balan" which is referred to below. Mr. Knowles repeats the poet's own words : "By King Arthur I always meant the soul, and by the Round Table the passions and capacities of a man."

When Tennyson's biography comes to be written, we may learn something more of the poet's dealings with his subject. At present we are bound to collect and weigh such fragments of external evidence as the foregoing, before we proceed to the more fascinating department of internal evidence.

III. WHAT WE LEARN FROM THIS HISTORY. "Paradise Lost" was under contemplation for a very long period ; but with the exception of one passage, and a few details, the poem was written in from five to six years, and was under revision for two years longer. If, as Tennyson says in the "Holy Grail" volume, "The Passing of Arthur" was earliest written, and the project of the poem also was early, we may set down some fifty years as the period of the composition of the "Idylls of the King." According to the poet's own showing, his mode of treatment varied from "Homeric echoes" to "The True and the False," from that to the sketching an "ideal knight," and from that again to the "Shadowing" of "Sense at war with Soul."

---

[1] Excepting in the poet's conversations with his friends. Otherwise the work is styled "These Idylls" ("Dedication to the Prince Consort"); "This old imperfect tale " ("To the Queen").

Legend, early epic, parable, allegory, mediæval romance, the modern moral—all these may be traced in the development of one of the characters, King Arthur.

As regards the introductory and personal verses, he is "King Arthur" in "The Epic" of 1842 ; then he becomes "my own ideal knight"[1] in 1862 ; and he shadows sense at war with soul in the epilogue of 1873.

And more or less throughout the "Idylls" he presents these varying phases of character. Moreover, this holds true of many of the personages who move about the king.

But these inconsistencies are not confined to the characters ; they are abundantly evident in the narrative itself. The early ballads are purely romantic in treatment. "Morte d'Arthur" is romance dressed in the robes of early epic, often to be recognized by a single line—"Authority forgets a dying king." The first four idylls are written while the poet is still studying his problems of women in their relation to men ; and the later allegorical idylls reflect the period of "Locksley Hall Sixty Years After."[2] In fact, as hinted already, we have before us something of the medley of "The Princess" ; the difference is of degree rather than of kind ; and these new difficulties must be dealt with much as in Chapter VII.

Therefore from the poet himself in the first instance, and then from the briefest glance at his poems, we gather evidence adverse to any opinion that the "Idylls" form an epic of recognized type ; we also discover under several aspects a want of absolute uniformity of treatment ; and the blemish appears to be due most of all to the fact that the poem was "at first tentative, was so long in hand."[3]

---

1 By this—before the reading was changed—Tennyson meant Arthur himself. "Arthur" was first in his mind ; and only thus could he pay the high compliment to The Prince Consort, who serves moveover as a model for the poet while he sketches his blameless king. The change to "my king's ideal knight" was made necessary by later additions to "The Idylls."

2 These views will be enlarged in the next section.

3 See Appendix to this Chapter, p. 360.

IV. SOME FURTHER CONSIDERATIONS. (*a*) *The Form of the Poem.* We have now to strengthen this first impression of inconsistency by examining more closely the leading features of the " Idylls of the King;" and we will begin by glancing at the style of the poem. To this division of our subject the Appendix already mentioned will again serve as a convenient introduction ; for the latter part deals with another blemish, closely allied to irregularity of structure ; a wavering treatment of subject extending over as many as fifty years must tend to impair symmetry of outward form.[1]

It is scarcely possible to over-estimate the importance attaching to form and finish in a long poem ; the unity of effect produced by the epic or dramatic genius which has been great enough and fortunate enough to preserve uniformity of design and treatment, is so far-reaching as to include the rhythm of a single line. What charms us most in a work of art is the degree in which it manifests the creative presence of the artist operating intensely throughout, so that the smallest detail glows with the heat of his imagination, and, moreover, is made *rememberable*[2] because of its exquisite relation to every other detail and to the whole. It is this which gives to " Paradise Lost " what Matthew Arnold has called its "unfailing level of style."

We are told that by way of explanation Lord Tennyson remarked to a friend that the first and last of his twelve books were intentionally made more archaic than the other ten known as the " Round Table." If this were the case, the explanation might be regarded as tending to prove that the poet had made his task an easier one ; for he must have noticed that his earliest fragment, the " Morte D'Arthur," was obviously archaic when compared

---

[1] Some further remarks under this head will be found on p. 54.
[2] See also Introduction to Chapter XIV.

with many other parts of his work, and required to be supported in some way.

But it has not been supported in the way he has indicated. Apart from the question, why should the first and last books be more archaic than the rest, we may be content with noticing first that they are not consistently archaic beyond the others ; they contain the same anachronisms, triplets, inconsistencies of style, and characters, and events ; but also, as a fact, " The Coming of Arthur " is not nearly so archaic as " The Passing of Arthur " ; and, what is more striking and more important to our purpose, " The Passing of Arthur" contains within itself passages totally different in style and sentiment from what may be called the central portion, the " Morte D'Arthur" of 1842. Compare the rhythm of the following with that of any four lines in the earlier fragment :

> "O me, be yon dark Queens in yon black boat,
> Who shriek'd and wail'd, the three whereat we gazed
> On that high day, when, clothed with living light,
> They stood before his throne in silence, friends. . . ."

In the same way both the style and the sentiment of the speech beginning " I found Him in the shining of the stars . . . ." may be contrasted with "The old order changeth, yielding place to new. . . . ."

In connection with the question of a more archaic style, we may refer to Tennyson's inquiry in " The Epic,'

> " Why bring the style of those heroic days ? "

which reminds us just a little of " what style could suit ? " in " The Princess." But the words in " The Epic " have an extended sense. The poet feared that " mere Homeric echoes " were " nothing worth " ; that it was idle to re-model models. The real point to consider is, how the re-modelling was effected. Virgil may be said to have re-modelled Homer, and with good success. The ideal past of epic or drama is seldom wholly consistent ; and in most cases it must be made enough real by a reference to contemporary humanity.

On the other hand, it is no defence of Tennyson to plead that in modernizing his characters he had Malory for precedent; for first, as in "The Princess," they are modernized only in part, and not consistently; whereas Malory makes them mediæval and romantic throughout. Also, the legends were nearer to Malory's own times—to his speech, his sentiments; for the mythical Prince Arthur and his subject Kelts need scarcely be reckoned with in this connection.

Under the head of style, we may next draw attention to Tennyson's mode of telling his story. The ordinary epic is introduced by ἄειδε, θεὰ. . . . or by "Cano," followed by "Musa, memora," or it is, "Sing, Heavenly Muse; aid my song that I may tell," etc. Again, as in "The Princess," Tennyson chooses a kind of compromise between epic and narrative; the plan, namely, of disconnected stories told by more than one story-teller. Among narrators in the "Idylls," the poet of course takes the first place, but never in the first person; he is introduced as "he that tells the tale." Otherwise we listen to Malory, Sir Percivale, or Sir Bedivere. Sometimes, again, we are left in doubt as to who the story-teller may be, or we are reminded, or again left in doubt, by a curious interpolation. To whom, for example, does the poet refer in "The Coming of Arthur"—"Thereafter—as he speaks who tells the tale"? Sometimes, on the other hand, the reference is plainer: "He that told the tale in olden times" at the end of "Gareth and Lynette" is presumably Malory, and "he, that told it later" is presumably Tennyson. But these interpolations—and there are others—are curious and confusing.

Apart from some differences of style pointed out in the Appendix to this Chapter, Tennyson was entirely fortunate in his choice and treatment of verse. This alone makes any comparison of the " Idylls " with the " Faerie Queene" misleading. The mazy murmuring of Spenser's great poem has a wondrous beauty ; but in a language like ours (as Shakespeare and Milton had the genius to discover), rhyme alone—to say nothing of stanza—is probably fatal to the dignity of a very great poem ; it is too persistently obvious as a structural expedient ; it cannot be disguised ; the bone frame of such metrical devices will stick out here and there, however much you may try to cover it with the flesh and form of rhythm ; it makes impossible the finer and larger phrasing of blank verse, the law beyond the law.

Yet in this varyingly magnificent blank verse of the "Idylls," rhyming lines are sparingly admitted ; sometimes they take the form of the "triplets of old time," whose three lines rhyme together ; otherwise only the first two rhyme, and the third line constitutes a refrain. Other variations are to be met with in other songs that diversify the poem. Such songs seem foreign to the well-recognized epic.[1] Virgil tells us the minstrel's theme, but not his song ; Milton makes his splendid hymns blank verse with the rest. Rhyme, again, would be too light ; it would impair the dignity of such a great poem as " Paradise Lost."

Lastly, a word may be said on the mystic changing year of the " Idylls." Though often a delightful device of the laureate's, and not unknown to old romance, this association of each important event with some appropriate season is a little too pronounced in Tennyson's poem. When Guinevere was married, "The sacred altar blossom'd white with may." Lancelot had gone to fetch her in April—"the maiden spring." The birds "made melody

---

1 It may almost be questioned whether songs are strictly appropriate to epic or even to narrative poetry of any kind. In drama, of course, they are assigned to a character who sings them. Otherwise they are merely repeated by the narrator

on branch and melody in mid air " when Gareth joyously set out for Camelot. And so it is throughout the story; a storm was brewing when Vivien began to practise upon Merlin ; the last Tournament was fought in the autumn,

> " And the wan day
> Went glooming down in wet and weariness."

Like Enoch Arden, Arthur returned

> " All in a death-dumb autumn-dripping gloom."

The last weird battle was fought in the death-white mists of winter ; and at the close of all

> " The new sun rose, bringing the new year."

All this—and more that might be added—gives the poem an appearance of stiffness and unreality ; and we cannot help suspecting that the seasons are forced upon the romance in order to make it a closer allegory of individual or national life :

> " Star of the morning, Hope in the sunrise, gloom of the evening, life at a close."—*Vastness.*

(*b*) *The subject matter.* From this brief consideration of the form of the poem we may now turn to as brief a survey of the subject matter.

Our study of " The Princess " in Chapter VII. lends support to the conjecture already put forward, that such a brief survey will be best obtained by tracing the development of one of the leading characters ; for every influence of the poet's creative energy bears directly or indirectly on this development. And from what was discovered in the same chapter, we may also conclude that an examination of the one character will bring into full view any improbabilities or inconsistencies that may be inherent in the work as a whole.

But first we must do justice to the poet by remembering that ideal conditions are to be assumed before ideal writing can be fairly criticised. On the other hand, we must refer to the former division of this section, and remind ourselves that ideal conditions which held good in the days of Malory may be inadmissible in our own day ; and further, that we may reject any ideal conditions that are not consistent throughout.

Again, as Ida served our purpose in " The Princess," so in this instance we will select Guinevere. This may be a departure from the usual course ; but, whatever Tennyson meant Arthur to be, Guinevere is certainly Queen of the tragedy ; she, according to the poet, governs all the tragic issues ; she is the dram of ill that corrupts all the nobler metal to its own scandal.

We might, therefore, fairly entitle this section of our chapter

" THE STORY OF QUEEN GUINEVERE."

(1) And first let us speak of the four women—Enid, Vivien, Elaine, Guinevere. By the poet's own showing, these are types of " The True and the False." Therefore the salient features—and it may be added thus early, the distorted features—in the character of each will be due to this early device of contrast.

These women may be variously contrasted ; the true wife may be set over against the false wife, and the harlot of the cities against the lily maid of Astolat.

Or, as in the copy of " The True and the False," Vivien may be confronted by Enid ; and then the Queen will be moved to uneasy pity by Elaine. As pointed out in Chapter V., these characters belong originally to the period of " Locksley Hall," and its multitude of love problems. Viewed in this light, we can understand any exaggeration involved in their contrasts ; we can understand why such a study as Vivien—a study that seems to draw upon what the poet in " The Princess " has called " strange experiences "—should claim a place in art at all. Hence, also, we may understand why Geraint is over-stupid and Arthur under-wise.

But most important it is to observe that in these first
"Idylls" we have illustrations of the ethics of "The
Princess." To take one example : the maxim, "Work no
more alone," or "each fulfils defects in each," will explain
the poet's treatment of Guinevere. Ida, as the opposite to
Guinevere, fulfils defects in the Prince ; and while Arthur
is left to work alone, the Prince and the Princess

> "Will walk this world
> Yoked in all exercise of noble end."

This reference to the intended husband of Ida leads us to
compare him with the husband of Guinevere ; and we
shall notice many resemblances. Arthur is introduced to
us in the very first "Idyll" as a man "Vext with waste
dreams." These are the "waking dreams" that vexed the
Prince in "The Princess,"[1] dreams which only a self-
sacrificing woman could kill ; and in each poem, although
it might be well doubted whether the malady was curable,
the woman has the task assigned to her in a somewhat
arbitrary fashion :

> "For saving I be joined
> To her that is the fairest under heaven,
> I seem as nothing in the mighty world,
> And cannot will my will nor work my work
> Wholly."

We might well fancy Guinevere's scornful reply :

> "Poor boy," she said ; "can he not read? no books?
> Quoit, tennis, ball ; no games? nor deals in that
> Which men delight in, martial exercise?"
>
> > *The Princess.*

But here we are admonished of those ideal conditions
which we must be prepared to accept. We do accept
them, and shall not refer to them again ; nor again, as in
the present instance, shall we expressly show that they
are inconsistent.

---

[1] Dreams, as was noticed elsewhere, that vexed the poet himself.

In this case Arthur must bear witness against himself:

> "And all this throve until I wedded thee,"

a contradiction that the poet has not evaded by the later reading,

> "And all this throve before I wedded thee."

What it was that throve may be learnt from the context, and from many another passage.[1]

(2) But Guinevere was married to so many Arthurs; how could she please them all? Some have been glanced at already; they must now be regarded more attentively. There is no Keltic chieftain among them, but there is the Arthur of mediæval romance, whom we all love—him of the old Morte D'Arthur, ideal knight, Flos Regum, every inch a king. There was also this dreamer, vext with waste dreams,

> "A moral child, without the craft to rule,"

as Vivien had called him; faultily faultless, wanting warmth and colour, as Guinevere had judged him; the

---

[1]
> "To hear high talk of noble deeds
> As in the golden days before thy sin,"

or again:
> "Until it came, a kingdom's curse, with thee."

After protesting that all was well before Guinevere came, the king argues ("Guinevere") that all will go ill now that her guilt is discovered:

> "For which of us, who might be left, could speak," etc.
> *Guinevere.*

in other words, the mischief spread by the story over a dozen years, would begin from that present.

But of course when "The Coming of Arthur" was written, the poet found it advisable to differ from Malory, and from his own previous statements, and allow Arthur to effect little or nothing before his marriage.

It is also worthy of notice, that when all the battles had been fought, and the king's opinion of his knights was most favourable, and his confidence in Guinevere still unshaken (see "The Holy Grail," *passim*), he was more than ever vexed with "visions of the night or of the day." The malady therefore, as we have already ventured to judge, was exceedingly difficult of cure, or perhaps incurable.

"impeccable prig" of Mr. Swinburne ; the Arthur of the second Locksley Hall.

But in fairness to the poet we should hear in some of these opinions an echo of the scoffing of the scribes, " He hath Beelzebub" ; and having taken into account a few slight differences, we look next on Tennyson's most prominent idea, the Christ-like Arthur :[1]

> " No man,
> But Michael trampling Satan."
> *The Last Tournament.*

Achilles, Ulysses, Æneas, Beatrice, Satan, all move at times through the golden mist ; and we also love this Arthur of Tennyson's favourite motto, " Be ye perfect." He moves in pure severity of perfect light, a great reformer, divine and human,

> " In whom high God hath breathed a secret thing,"

a man not easily to be loved by woman, not to be loved at all in this world by such a woman as Guinevere ; yet from her, as from Princess Ida, the poet extorts a confession quite foreign to her nature and her case :

> " It was my duty to have loved the highest ;
> It surely was my profit, had I known."

Much truer to the story are those other words of Guinevere:

> " But who can gaze upon the sun in heaven? "

There is yet another Arthur ; him also Tennyson de-

---

[1] Common to Tennyson's "Arthur" and to Christ, are mystic origin and destiny, and men's doubt concerning it :

> " From the great deep to the great deep he goes "

(which belongs to the "De Profundis" period ; not to that of "Morte D'Arthur"), a spotless character ("in him was no guile"), the scoffing of man, the going about doing good, ceaseless struggle with evil, reforming zeal, seeming failure, the agony ("My God, thou hast forgotten me in my death." —*The Passing of Arthur*). To these may be added the mysterious passing away, and a mysterious coming again. The precedent of Christ to a large extent modified Tennyson's conception of "Arthur."

lighted to honour ; he is the "modern gentleman Of state-
liest port" of the Epilogue to "Morte D'Arthur." And
others might be recognized, most of whom would be

> "A noble type
> Appearing ere the times were ripe."

But to speak generally of all the various aspects of this
central figure of the poem, we may venture to add that
Lord Tennyson's remark to Mr. Knowles—"By King
Arthur I always meant the soul," might perhaps, without
presumption, be altered to "By King Arthur I gradually
came to mean the soul." If the poet had not incorporated
his "Morte D'Arthur" of 1842 into "The Passing of
Arthur" of 1872, we should have had less difficulty in
understanding his statement. And as the remainder of
the last book of the twelve was adapted to the old incor-
porated fragment which, as already seen, represented
Arthur more purely as a hero of romance, it follows that
the poet's remark applies less closely to the last book of
his poem than it does to the others. For example, in the
very first book of the "Idylls" (1872), readers of Tenny-
son will easily discover for themselves that Arthur is
"more than man." And it has already been noticed that
the line in "The Coming of Arthur,"

> "From the great deep to the great deep he goes,"

was repeated in the passages added to the "Morte
D'Arthur" in 1872.

Next we will observe the manner of the wooing. If
Lancelot's failure was the misfortune of circumstance,
so yet more truly was Guinevere's. When Arthur rode
by her castle walls, "She saw him not, or mark'd not if
she saw." A rumour even ran that she took Lancelot for
the king.[1]

[1] Earlier reading, "She took him for the King." Present reading, "A
rumour runs, she took him for the king."

She sighed to find her journey with Lancelot done. As to the king, she

> "Thought him cold,
> High, self-contained, and passionless, not like him,
> Not like my Lancelot."

She did not choose Arthur ; she was chosen in spite of herself ; and the result was disaster. For a commentary we may refer once more to "The Princess," "Man to command, and woman to obey." Elaine, on the other hand, "being so very wilful," did choose Lancelot, and with little enough ground for her choice ; and yet our sympathies are with Elaine rather than with Guinevere.

(3) We now approach the main subject—Queen Guinevere as responsible for the great catastrophe ; and it shall be stated in none other words than her own :

> "The sombre close of that voluptuous day
> Which wrought the ruin of my lord the king."

But not of the king only :

> "For now the Heathen of the Northern Sea,
> Lured by the crimes and frailties of the Court,
> Begin to slay the folk and spoil the land."

"The Idylls" are usually regarded as the history of a king and a kingdom that were ruined through the fault of one woman ; and if the poem is viewed as an allegory, the story is yet the same, and must be consistent. This woman, as we understand,

> "Like another Helen fired another Troy ; "

or she was another beautiful, baneful Eve who lost us another Eden. And in the two quotations above, she has pronounced plain judgment upon herself.

Nevertheless, those who read the poem with more than ordinary attention, may perhaps discover that this, the very framework of the story, is fabricated throughout of improbabilities, contradictions, and impossibilities. What the poet meant is one thing, but his means of effecting it are quite another thing. The case against Guinevere is conducted without any show of fairness or reason ; the verdict is by no means supported by the evidence. And, briefly, the fact is, that just as in many other long poems,[1] so in this, Tennyson's ethical intention spoilt his story. The ethical intention was good ; but it was to be exhibited in a work of art ; and as the ethical intention was constantly permitted to mar the beauty and impressiveness of the work of art, both ethics and art are reduced to a lower level. This was not the case in " The Æneid," in the " Divine Comedy," nor in " Paradise Lost."

The story itself, or something like it, might have been a very good one. Viewed broadly, it tells of the ever-renewed war between good and evil :

> " Evolution ever climbing after some ideal good,
> And Reversion ever dragging Evolution in the mud."

It is the constantly recurring history of the individual, the seldomer but not less common rise, culmination, and decline of a nationality.[2] But as applied to a court, whatever that may be, and to such a court as that of the Keltic or Mediæval Prince, we scarcely know how to take the legend thus recast by Tennyson, especially as it further concerned itself with Arthur's kingdom, whatever that may have been :

> " All my realm
> Reels back into the beast."

For, first, these knights of a new as opposed to " that old knight-errantry," were bound by vows that made them almost a monastic order ; and yet, under the circumstances, their pristine utter purity is as improbable[3] as

---

[1] "The Princess," the two "Locksley Hall's," "Maud," "Aylmer's Field," "The Promise of May."

[2] Its moral appears in many a line of Tennyson: *e.g.*, as quoted above,

> "Have we risen from out the beast, then back into the beast again ? "

[3] For example, Sir Gawain and Sir Modred were of their company ; and Sir Kay was "the most ungentle knight in Arthur's Hall," and was disobedient to the king.

their subsequent wholesale corruption—a corruption, we may repeat, that is sometimes spread over the whole kingdom.

Next, we have seen that in " Morte D'Arthur" the Round Table is "the goodliest fellowship of famous knights," and an "image of the mighty world"; whereas later, and in a manner at variance with Malory's explanation or Tennyson's first conception, it symbolizes "the passions and capacities of a man."

But whatever this Court, Round Table, or Kingdom may have been, it lasted, as we guess, some twelve years,[1] and after having been gradually undermined by rumours of the love of Lancelot and Queen Guinevere, it fell with a crash when their love was detected.

This may appear plausible enough at first sight; but a closer examination of the twelve books seems to prove that scarcely a single effect in this long history of ruin can be traced to any clear or sufficient cause; rumour always strangely lives or as strangely dies; and even the "Detection of Guinevere" is on many sides unsupported by the circumstances.

To make this plain would demand an elaborate analysis of each Idyll and the comparison of a very large number of passages. On the other hand, fragments of evidence such as might be brought forward in a short commentary would be altogether inconclusive and misleading. Even the middle course of examining more closely some one or two links in the chain of evidence must be attended with grave disadvantages; but as it is the only one open to us we propose to deal with not more than the story of Vivien; and we choose this with a purpose, for the incident of Balin and the testimony of Merlin are the weightiest evidence brought into court by the prosecution.

We will even begin by making a concession to the

---

[1] The flight of time is seldom clearly marked in " The Idylls."

adversary, and attempt to date back the love of Lancelot
and Guinevere to the time when they rode together in the
boyhood of the year on their way to Camelot.   It was a
long ride ; Lancelot had left among the flowers in April
and he returned among the flowers in May.   Day after
day they rode, rapt in sweet talk ; and although it suits
the poet in this connection to assure us that as yet no sin
was dreamed, nevertheless in other passages where he is
less guarded this ride is looked back to as to the beginning
of love :

> " Prince, we have ridden before among the flowers."

> "As once of old—among the flowers—they rode."

They rode, and during that long ride together they
tasted surely of the magic cup.   For our thoughts wander
to that other twain of kindred beautiful romance who
journeyed on the same errand, and were bound by the
same hopeless love.

It is noon in some delicious dale ; the silk pavilions of
King Arthur are raised for brief repast ; the wine-cup is
placed upon the board ; they pledge each other, Lancelot
and Guinevere.   And now, as they ride forth once more,
our ears in fancy listen to the words that tremble from his
lips, and catch the faltering syllables of her reply :

> " Holy Mother, by thy Child-God save me
>   From this fever of a bliss not mine !—
> Lady, 'twas a charmed cup we tasted—
>   Lady, there is poison in that wine ! "

> *   *   *   *

> " Nay, sir knight, what answer should I yield thee?
>   (Jesu—Mary—shield me from my shame !)
> Lancelot—nay—I perish with my passion,
>   Feel—ah God—like thee—the wizard flame."

> *   *   *   *

Our glance must also be turned for a moment upon the
second poem, " Gareth and Lynette."   From two or three
passages we gather that some years have past, and now
Sir Kay warns Lancelot :

"That thine own fineness, Lancelot, some fine day
Undo thee not."

Certainly, as we have just inferred, the love of Lancelot and Guinevere dates from that memorable ride ; but what did Sir Kay know about it ? The court is spoken of as absolutely pure. Gareth found nothing but purity there.

In "The Marriage of Geraint," which we may presume is a yet later event,[1] "A rumour rose about the Queen . . ." and in "Geraint and Enid," Geraint at first does not rest so well contented as "Before the Queen's fair name was breathed upon" ; yet a little later "He rested well content that all was well." The spiteful whisper died. And, what is very significant, he *crowned a happy life* of at least several years, and more probably of many years' fighting in battle for the blameless King. What is to be said about the rumour after that lapse of time?

We now come to "Balin and Balan," and in this poem Balin, like Gareth before him and Pelleas after him, is permitted to move about the court ; and, like them, he hears nothing whatever of any rumour. But he is permitted to see (what apparently no one else had seen, and what he discovered to no one else but his brother) the eye of Lancelot dwell upon the Queen and her hue change beneath the earnest gaze. He seems to be doubtful as to any construction that might be placed upon the interview ; but, blaming his troublesome temper, and mad for strange adventure, he dash'd away. And although he never heard so much as a whisper at Arthur's court, he is told at the court of Pellam:

"This fair wife-worship cloaks a secret shame."

Yet again Balin dismisses his doubts, and turns fiercely upon his anger:

"O me, that such a name as Guinevere's
Which our high Lancelot hath so lifted up

---

[1] Other passages suggest a considerable interval.

And been thereby uplifted, should thro' me,
My violence, and my villainy, come to shame."

These words he addressed to Vivien, and she had much
more to tell him ; but, as "she lied with ease," her slander
would not have been mentioned here but for the fact that
it brought to Balin's mind "that dark bower at Camelot,"
and revived his doubts. Yet he told Vivien nothing about
them. As to the rest of the story, the brothers die believing
the Queen innocent. But two points are to be noted ; one,
that Balin's doubts were revived not by substantial rumour
but by sheer falsehood, and the other that the poet ranks
the remarks of Vivien as evidence. How clearly he in-
tended this may be understood from the prose version,[1]
for after the death of the brothers, Vivien "sped stealthily
away to King Mark, and after to Arthur's court, and there
she told how she had overheard from Knights of Arthur's
Table scandal beyond all disproof about Sir Lancelot and
Queen Guinevere. And thus in truth the 'Dolorous
Stroke'[2] was struck which first shook to its base the
stately order of the Table Round."

From this Idyll therefore it appears that, in spite of the
conclusions of the prose version and of whatever corrup-
tion or whatever rumour prevailed at Arthur's court,
Vivien knew nothing about them ; nor does she know
anything at the opening of the second paragraph of the
next Idyll, "Merlin and Vivien."

But strange as are all these proceedings of Vivien, and
the dramatic use the poet expects to make of them, her
actions and their relation to the tragedy are in "Merlin
and Vivien" stranger still. This was to be expected, for,
as explained above, the poem when first written had a
purpose more moral than dramatic.

Again the rumour comes from without, as in the case of
the Red Knight. Mark hears a minstrel sing of certain

1 "Aspects of Tennyson," "Nineteenth Century," January, 1893.
2 Title of the prose version of "Balin and Balan."

mediæval, Platonic, supersensual notions prevailing at Arthur's court:

> "To worship woman as true wife beyond
> All hopes of gaining."

After a conversation with Mark that is abhorrent, Vivien sets out for Camelot on her mission of absolute mischief; and we must be careful to notice that the scene of her exploits is not to be a corrupt or even a corruptible court, but one in which men are "passionate for an utter purity." Nor is it to the knights alone that she imputes her own evil nature: "This Arthur pure ! . . . . There is no being pure." At present, therefore, it is not the guilt of Guinevere that makes Vivien possible. This is a very important point. All the evidence adduced up to the present proves that the court is pure, and it is this utter purity that attracts Vivien.

She arrives at a time of golden rest. The heathen lie at Arthur's feet. (Spite of Guinevere, therefore, thus much of the King's purpose has been fulfilled.) After long pry-ing, and without making any warrantable discovery, she sows one ill hint from ear to ear and leaves death in the living waters. But the court was decent; the knights heard and let her be ; therefore she hated the knights and set herself to practise upon Merlin.

"Set up the charge," says Merlin, "to stand or fall."

In reply to her charge Merlin makes some doubtful admissions, but in the older edition adds:

> " Sir Lancelot went ambassador at first
> To fetch her, and she took him for the king ;
> She fixt her fancy on him ; let him be."

Later he is convinced that there is no truth in her accusations generally, for—

> "She cloaks the scar of some repulse with lies ;
> I well believe she tempted them and fail'd. . . ."[1]

---

[1] A few words remain to be added respecting the evidence supplied by Merlin. He is the first to give any support to the rumour—or rather to the

Hence we understand that the poet's purpose has been less to expose Guinevere than to paint Vivien.

Now Merlin had dreamt[1] that the King's high purpose was "broken by the worm"—by Vivien, that is, and not by Guinevere. Guinevere loves in secret, but her love is falsely true ; and the passage added in 1874 only shifts yet more of the blame on Vivien, and by no means discloses any demoralization in the court. On the contrary, it is Vivien who calls upon us to follow her through the fiery flood, and not Guinevere.

(4) And now we have to notice the fact that other causes besides the sin of Guinevere are assigned to this ruin of king and kingdom. Indeed, if we refer to "Morte d'Arthur," Guinevere had nothing whatever to do with it. There—and it is much the same in Malory—the cause of downfall is rebellion ; that, and nothing else. "I perish by this people which I made!" is Arthur's angry

rumour of a rumour ; and that support, as we have just seen, is almost wholly withdrawn. Moreover, he dies soon after. Apart from this, how was it, again, that Balin had heard nothing ; that Pelleas afterwards heard nothing, although he had been—according to Percival's showing—"One of our free-spoken Table"? How was it that the rumour which reached Mark was not of scandal, but of mediæval woman-worship? How is it that in the next "Idyll"—in which however the contradictions are much more numerous— Lancelot and Guinevere are set before the world in a new relation:

> "Our knights, at feast,
> Have pledged us in this union, while the king
> Would listen smiling."

Nor can Merlin's estimate of the "Round Table" be altogether trustworthy :

> "My friends of old,
> All brave, and many generous, and some chaste."

Modred had received no meed of bravery ; and purity among the knights has appeared in every previous reliable line of the poem.

[1] In this dream is Tennyson's own "moral" of the poem ; it should be compared with "Locksley Hall Sixty Years After," to which it is near in date.

exclamation to Sir Bedivere; and this making of a people is fully explained in "The Coming of Arthur." The true old times are only just dead ; the sequel of to-day, that and that alone, unsolders the goodly fellowship of knights. This is still the impression left on the mind even when we have read the additions in "The Passing of Arthur," including those that were made in 1872 ; for, by a possible oversight, the poet allows Sir Bedivere to listen to the new causes of disaster—a traitorous wife and friend, a realm that reels back into the beast, and the rest—but nevertheless retains all the original passage, and makes both King Arthur and Sir Bedivere act and speak throughout the remainder of the poem as though Guinevere and Lancelot had never been heard of.

But not only Guinevere and Lancelot, for the Holy Grail has to be reckoned with as another cause of the widespread ruin. To begin with, it had long ago destroyed nine-tenths of that goodly fellowship of knights which, according to Sir Bedivere, were nevertheless unsoldered by "the sequel of to-day." No doubt Tennyson had more than one reason for writing the Holy Grail into his series of poems. It was in the book of Malory, it was most famous among legends, it enabled the poet to paint on a larger canvas the St. Agnes and Sir Galahad of former years,[1] and would serve as another opportunity for condemning religious enthusiasts.[2] Perhaps it would relieve Guinevere of some of this enormous burden of working confusion in the Table Round, or at least serve both to bring into stronger relief the effect of her crime,

---

[1] For St. Simeon a place was found in "Balin and Balan," as King Pellam.

[2] Against extravagance of any kind in religion, he raised his voice to the last, as in the somewhat inartistic line of "The Northern Cobbler"—"An Muggins 'e preäch'd o' Hell-fire an' the loov o' God fur men." Even "Rizpah" is in some danger of being spoilt by the two stanzas beginning "Election, Election and Reprobation."

and be at the same time a secondary cause of con-
fusion.[1]

But here again we are in doubt; for, first, the Holy
Grail is never mentioned together with Guinevere as an
influence for evil or a cause of disaster. And in the Idyll
devoted to this fascinating legend we read that the Holy
Cup left the world because of the sin of the world; that it
might be expected to return only when the world had
become pure; that when the Holy Thing did come again,
then arose a hope that all the world might be healed; that
the King pronounced it "A sign to maim this Order which
I made," and that as the knights rode away on their quest
the Queen shrieked aloud:

"This madness has come on us for our sins."

Therefore the Holy Grail legend as employed by Tenny-
son presents strange contrasts; nor can the opinion of
Guinevere be accepted by anyone who reads the poem
attentively; nor was the Holy Quest a last effort of
religion, amid general demoralization; apart from other
abundant evidence, the king says expressly that his knights
are all men "With strength and will to right the wrong'd,"
and he rejoices in his Table Round; and a better religion
had prevailed from the first—the "Cross and Table."
Nor, as we have mentioned, is the quest of the Grail any-
where cited as a consequence or an auxiliary of the sin
of Guinevere; for instance, although its results are so
disastrous, no word of it is heard in Arthur's parting speech
to Guinevere, nor in "The Passing of Arthur." But, once
introduced, Tennyson was obliged to make the search for
the Grail an evil, not a good; the story could not have
been worked in otherwise.

(5) This subject must be left not more than touched
upon as we turn to the remaining consideration that arises

---

[1] In "Malory," Arthur is troubled only because he knows how many good
knights must be lost in the quest.

out of this long history of crime. Speaking broadly, was it probable that such widespread and various evil should be due to rumour so vague and so contradictory,[1] but more, was it possible that for twelve years at least the king should have dwelt in the midst of this rumour, a witness of all its supposed effects, and yet have no suspicion of it whatever? That Malory put this question to himself appears from his remark, " For, as the French book saith, the king had a deeming"; and that Tennyson was not unaware of the difficulty is seen in the following readings :[2] in "Enid and Nimuë" the important line runs thus :

> " And troubled in his heart about the Queen."

This, in "The True and the False : Four Idylls of the King," is corrected to, "Vext at a rumour rife about the Queen,"—and this line kept its place till 1874. As to the reading adopted in that year,

> " Vext at a rumour issued from herself,
> Of some corruption crept among his knights,"

we need only say that conjecture as to what it means— taking all circumstances into consideration—is entirely baffled ; but it may be noticed that the rumour, as in so many other instances, proceeds from the malignant lips of a stranger.

We can easily understand why the poet should delay the discovery—at least on Arthur's part :

> " Man—is he man at all, who knows and winks? "

---

[1] We may as well remark here upon the startling fact that no proof was forthcoming till all the mischief had been done ; we may further remark that the rumour remains rumour to the very last, proceeds mostly from a foreign source, and never becomes "The world's loud whisper breaking into storm ;" for in spite of the "open shame" spoken of by the Lord of Astolat and Sir Pelleas, it appears so late as in "Guinevere" as a "smouldering scandal " that only *may*

> " Break and blaze
> Before the people, and our lord the king."

[2] These existed before "Balin and Balan" was added in the expectation of making the matter clearer.

was Vivien's old insinuation ; and Tennyson is determined to combat Malory's looser doctrine, and to insist on the principle set forth with undue emphasis in " Guinevere," in the passage beginning :

> " I hold that man the worst of public foes. . . . "

In all this he is more concerned with the interests of modern society than with those of his poem.

But why should Guinevere bear so much of the blame ? How much may be gathered from many passages ; but the utter severity of the poet is best discovered by the word he prints in italics in the following :

> " That *she* is woman, whose disloyal life
> Hath wrought confusion in the Table Round."

In a story older still, the woman who had sinned sought pity, if not pardon, in her plea, " The serpent beguiled me, and I did eat."   And in Malory, at the close of the volume, we read as follows :—" When Sir Lancelot was brought to her, then she said to all the ladies, ' Through this man and me hath all this war been wrought.' "[1]   In other respects Malory is more impartial than Tennyson, for the queen dismisses Lancelot against his will.

Tennyson's is the old doctrine that allows man license, and woman none.   This may be seen by a comparison of his assurance to Lancelot,

> " Never yet
> Could all of true and noble in knight and man
> Twine round one sin,"

with all that long strange speech[2] that the King spoke to the Queen, who grovelled at his feet :

> " Yet must I leave thee, woman, to thy shame. . . ."

---

[1] This admission on the part of Guinevere would be misleading if we did not remember that in Malory the Queen's offence is treason rather than unfaithfulness.

[2] *Inter alia*, the King, who first of all had contemplated giving his Queen over to " the flaming death," often employs language that belongs to the loftiest ideal of modern civilisation.

Lancelot is left with a future before him.[1]   There is no hope for Guinevere in this world.[2]

"The woman is so hard upon the woman." So Tennyson had written in "The Princess." But here it is the man—the poet—who is so hard upon the woman. And if space permitted it might be shown more clearly that as a consequence he has destroyed almost all the probabilities of his story. Once more, the intense ethical purpose that we first associated with the "Locksley Hall" period, and that showed itself most plainly in the first four "Idylls," was forced into the poem to the very last, and continued to spoil its art.

Following the course taken in the chapter on "The Princess," we have thus been led to notice some apparent defects in the construction of "The Idylls of the King." It is held by most critics that the ten stories with their prologue and epilogue possess a certain unity which makes the whole poem truly epic in its grandeur and completeness ; some find this unifying element in the gradually developed story of one great sin and its spreading taint ; others in the moral purpose that pervades the poem ; and others again in the seeming fact that every episode, incident, and personage is bound up with the fortunes of King Arthur.

But it is certainly doubtful whether Tennyson has succeeded in making his twelve "Idylls" veritable members of an organic whole, so that the cycle of them may bear the immortal name of Epic. The mode of composition of the "Idylls," the frequent and long interruptions, the poet's habit of construction as seen in other poems, his doctrine concerning long poems, a distrust of his own ability to produce the highest work of sustained effort ; his first thought of writing "a whole great poem," the

---

[1] "Therefore, Sir Lancelot, go to thy realm, and there take thee a wife, and live with her in joy and bliss. . . ."—*Malory.*

[2] "Mine will ever be a name of scorn."—*Guinevere.*

name *epic* that he then associated with it, the adverse criticism, combined with his own conviction, that forced him to be contented with semi-isolated stories ; the other fact that ultimately he set himself to modify the construction and arrangement of his stories so that they might become parts of a unifying main plot ; that he added to the number of them until it reached the mystic twelve ; and again the fact that he still called his stories by their names, nor ever gave to his work a more ambitious title than " Idylls "—all this has been touched upon. And to this we may now add, as on our own part, that during a very long period of development the poet's treatment of his subject grew less romantic and more moral or more allegorical, until the intrusion of ethical design destroyed the symmetry of his creation ; that, as a further consequence, the story sometimes wants swiftness and coherence, and the characters a dramatic reality ; that some of the episodes appear too loosely attached to the body of the organism to be called its members, and that others, if members, seem to be redundant. But at this point we find ourselves compelled to resort to historical and comparative methods : or, rather, we are led back to our starting-point—the future Addison and his successors.

To those, however, who urge that Tennyson's " Idylls " have all the epic grandeur, we counter-urge that epic completeness must be recognized before epic grandeur can be admitted.

And now, as in the Chapter on "The Princess," whatever may be the value of this inquiry into the unity of the poem as related to the breadth of its conception, there is yet to be added a reference to the truth, the beauty, the magnificence of the parts. Such a poem as Guinevere might almost be regarded as an epic in miniature; "The Holy Grail" has all the dim rich splendour of a gothic cathedral. But the space at our disposal for praising the " Idylls of the King " is very limited, and yet it need not be larger ; for we have merely to question whether, when Shakespeare and Milton have been placed apart, there can be found in our English literature a more considerable poetical achievement than the Arthurian poems of Tennyson.

APPENDIX TO CHAPTER XI.

From " New Studies in Tennyson."

I venture to think that many critics of the Poet Laureate have allowed zeal for his well-earned honour to blunt their sense of the honour due to other great masters of song. If, therefore, I seem harsh, or even unjust, in some of my remarks, I must ask you to say of me, " It was not that he loved Tennyson less, but that he loved Shakespeare and Milton more."

Indeed, my lecture may very well begin with a caution. For in some recent reviews that I have brought with me, I find Lord Tennyson constantly bracketed with Shakespeare : and as to Milton, he *is* included in a list of eight other poets who have gained the favour of one of these reviewers, but with this exception, no mention is made of him.

Now I wish strongly to protest against this careless use of Shakespeare's name, and this equally careless omission of Milton's ; and, remember, I speak of a prevailing tendency. In spite of our modern aversion to comparative criticism, I shall be bold enough to assert that we English possess two poets of the very first class, and only two— Shakespeare and Milton ; and if we graduate the scale evenly, we shall probably find no poet at all to place in the second class, although there are several who may take rank in a third. But this, you will say, is going too far.

I do not think so. However, Chaucer, Spenser, Lord Tennyson and the rest shall form a second class, if you will; and further, if you will, Lord Tennyson shall rank first in that second class. I shall be content, provided I check this tendency of our time to forget Milton, and to degrade Shakespeare. Degrade is exactly the word. Would you believe such appalling ignorance as this exhibited by a recent critic of considerable repute : " Shakespeare," he said, "and Sheridan, our two great dramatists." [1]

By a similar fad of modern criticism, another critic of higher repute prefers " Comus " to " Paradise Lost," and the " Faerie Queene " to either. I am sure you will not wish me to make any further comment on such strange notions.

And why, it will be asked, are Shakespeare and Milton the two, and the only two, very great poets in our English literature ? To answer that question fully would be impossible here. For although I intend to examine Tennyson's claim to poetic greatness under the three heads of Epic, Dramatic, and Lyric poetry—and in this order—I shall nevertheless say little or nothing that is not suggested to me in the pages of these reviews as I turn them over. I will, however, briefly explain, that word, image, foot, line, stanza, song, epic, drama, and the rest are some of them structural elements in forms of poetical expression, and some of them forms of poetical expression in themselves —the epic and the drama [2] being generally regarded as the greatest of these forms. Now I will call your attention to one quality of the best work produced by the two artists, Shakespeare and Milton ; it is on the largest, the grandest scale. In certain works of art, magnitude contributes most of all to the sum total of pleasing impressions ; conversely, to create on this great scale is

---

[1] Apart from other differences, the difference of *form* is beyond calculation. See Chapter XIV.

[2] The question whether under ordinary circumstances drama is a fit subject for poetic treatment was reserved for a second lecture.

often the highest effort and the highest achievement of genius.

But the grandeur of the whole lends grandeur to each part. This incidental remark is not exactly a step in the direction of my argument, yet I am glad that the words have been uttered, for they give me an opportunity of telling you something that came under my notice a few years ago—a phenomenon that does bear directly on my argument. Well, it was this : some years ago literary experts and others were invited to send to one of our leading magazines their favourite passages of poetry. To the editor's hand there came extracts from almost any English poet—if I may trust my memory—except Shakespeare and Milton. I seem to remember also that the modern poets were most in favour, and that if Shakespeare was represented two or three times, scarcely any contributor cared to take a few lines from Milton. I cannot understand this. I should have thought there was really no choice in the matter. Two pieces, as I think, were sent up by each authority. What could one possibly be supposed to do in such a case other than select from Shakespeare—it might be the storm scene in "Lear," the dialogue between Othello and Iago, or that between Brutus and Cassius ; and from Milton, the Morning Hymn of Adam and Eve, the description of Eden, Satan's address to the Sun, and so forth. Now, if we choose the marvellous storm-scene in "Lear," or the Morning Hymn —for which no epithet is found in earthly language—we do this, as I have suggested already, not only because the part is excellent in itself, but also, and much more, because *it borrows wondrous strength and beauty from every other part, and from the magnificent total of scheme and scope.* Stupendous was the genius that created "King Lear" and "Paradise Lost." There were giants on the earth in those days.

That Tennyson knew what was required of a very great

poet, is evident from the outset. He began his Epic in good time ; the first fragment, " Morte d'Arthur," being published in 1842, and it had been in course of composition probably from a much earlier date ; and although his dramas came very late, they were written with determination, and soon multiplied.

But if the young poet had made up his mind to attempt the highest poetic achievement by writing epic and drama, it seems equally clear that from the first he distrusted his capability of doing either. To use his own words, he had " a mint of reasons "[1] for this. Later on he styled the first four books of his epic " Idylls,"[2] a title implying, amongst other things, that these four stories (now known as the third and fourth, the fifth, the sixth, and the eleventh) were more or less disconnected. This lack of epic completeness I shall refer to again.

As to Tennyson's dramatic works, they were at first monologues, monodramas, and the like experiments ; or were such as " The Princess,"—" Medleys," full of the poet's apologies.

The same hesitation to attempt a very great work of artistic oneness may be traced in many other poems ; for example, in the isolated sections of the " In Memoriam," where again apologies are numerous, and where we discover the significant utterance,

> " Nor dare she trust a larger lay. . . ."

After doing full justice to the context, we cannot help reading the line as one amongst many of like import, whether in this work or in others. Even " Maud," the most successful of his earlier dramatic efforts, was con-

---

[1] See "The Epic."

[2] Spelt " Idyls" in earlier volumes. The spelling "Idyll," which is closer to the original Greek, once helped to distinguish the heroic descriptive poem from such pastorals as those of Theocritus. But the distinction has ceased to be maintained by such a means, and the later spelling of the term is now adopted without discrimination.

structed in a tentative, desultory manner, and the various editions of the poem prove that the author was for some time uncertain as to the real character of what he had created.

Now, comparatively speaking, nothing is easier than to write a poem on a small scale (hence the lyric has always ranked lowest), or a poem that may end anywhere and anyhow, or that never ends at all ; poems—(but again, perhaps, I ought to crave your indulgence if in my respect for our two great masters I cast a careless eye on lesser artists ; indeed, I am about to make a terrible onslaught on all such)—poems like the " Canterbury Tales " (never finished),

> " Artistry's haunting curse, the incomplete "

(though I do not wish to apply this quotation too closely); poems such as the "Faerie Queene" (again, never finished), "The Essay on Man" (always a puzzle to its author), "The Excursion" (part of a poem never finished), "Don Juan" (which, if it "begins with a beginning," can hardly be said to end with an ending : "Nothing so difficult as a beginning In poesy, unless, perhaps, the end,") "Childe Harold's Pilgrimage" (a unique example of vacillating composition), "Endymion" (a series of "Rich windows that exclude the light"), "The Revolt of Islam" ("And passages that lead to nothing"), the "In Memoriam" to which critics alone have given shape—

> " If shape it might be called, that shape had none " ;

poems that were, so to speak, "allowed to write themselves," being more or less prolix, diffuse, pieces of patchwork, wanting proportion, lacking the well-known essentials of beginning, middle, and end, the end seen from the beginning, adjustment of parts to the magnificent whole, composite harmony ; and of course they lack also vastness, *they lack stupendous, concentrated, sustained, and successful effort*, and with that they lack grandeur.

It is the custom of critics to argue that Tennyson's choice of what was easiest merely implied a meritorious love of the simple ; it was a characteristic simplicity, they tell us, that preferred the uncomplicated monologue to the complex drama, the short idyll to the long epic. Their argument is easily disposed of. Had Shakespeare written nothing but monologues and Milton nothing but idylls, the later poet might have surpassed them both. As things are, Shakespeare and Milton are great, and he in comparison is less great.

Even if Tennyson's " King Arthur " satisfied some of the requirements of a great epic poem, the fact that it was at first tentative, was so long in hand, tells terribly against it. Making due allowance for change of theme, we seem to discover as much difference in point of style between the superb " Morte d'Arthur " and " Pelleas and Ettarre " as between " Paradise Lost " and " Paradise Regained " ; and of course books I. to XII. of " Paradise Lost " exhibit the same " unfailing level of style " ; the whole sublime poem being, in fact, wrought out by the blind poet in about six years.

Again, the change in style is all for the worse. " Morte d'Arthur " was written while Tennyson still believed, and rightly, that Scott, Byron, and even Shelley had exhausted the charm of somewhat lawless vigour, and that the perfect form of Keats was to be the new and successful manner in poetry. In later years he seems to have placed less confidence in that belief.

It is a change, indeed, that we witness in most poets whose period of authorship is long—notably in Shakespeare and Milton. Compare, for instance, " Julius Cæsar " with " The Tempest," or " Paradise Lost " with " Samson Agonistes." It comes of many years, the desire and need of change, weariness of struggle between impetuous thought and prescribed art form ; it is a change that *sometimes* verges on license, not freedom ; it interrupts, for example, with extra syllables, the stately movement of the blank verse :

> " And so went back, and seeing them yet in sleep,
> Said, ' Ye that so dishallow the holy sleep.' " . . .

These two consecutive lines from " Pelleas and Ettarre " would have been impossible in the " Morte d'Arthur." Or if we except them as forming a kind of couplet, and as having a rhythm peculiar to themselves, I will choose the following two from the immediate context—

> " Fingering at his sword-handle until he stood . . .
> And the sword of the tourney across her throat. . . ."

Many others you can find for yourselves in the same two short paragraphs ; so many, that, as before, making allowance for a lighter theme, we may yet reasonably regard the blank verse of the later poem as something quite different from that of the " Morte d'Arthur," and as marking a tendency towards undue license.

The same phenomenon is seen when we compare " Locksley Hall " with " Locksley Hall Sixty Years After " ; and, more generally, in the many lighter measures of the Laureate's later poems.

The defence set up by reviewers, that we must consider the " Idylls " as a modern Faerie Queene, serves finally to establish my conclusion, that if the chief test of a poet's greatness be greatness, the production, we will say, of at least one very great and perfect work, then Tennyson fails to rank as a poet of the very first order ; we may not concede to him superlative grandeur, unfaltering strength, nor, as in Shakespeare's case, the freshness also of unconscious genius.

CHAPTER XII.

"BALLADS, AND OTHER POEMS."[1]

THIS volume of 184 pages took the public by surprise in 1880, and the surprise was a delightful one. Everybody welcomed the appearance of a collection of poems— ballads, lyrics, idylls, and monologues like those of earlier years which brought his first fame to the poet. And the new poems showed no signs of weakness ; on the contrary, though less lavishly adorned they had more dramatic power. This might have been expected, for most of them were written at a time when Tennyson was hard at work on his drama. It may be added that the Ballads, as would be inferred from the title, are a special feature of the volume.

(499) "To ALFRED TENNYSON, MY GRANDSON." "Glorious poet" reminds us of Longfellow, who called children "living poems," in much the same spirit as Byron's when he apostrophised the stars as the "poetry of heaven." As in others of Tennyson's verses for children, the lines all rhyme together.

(499). "THE FIRST QUARREL" is the first among

1 "The Lover's Tale" (476), together with "The Golden Supper" (493), has been noticed in Chapter II.

many poems in this new series that deal with difficult problems arising out of the relations between man and woman. Formerly the poet pondered over disappointed love, due mostly to "marriage-hindering mammon"; but now he approaches subjects more delicate, more distressful, and more profound. Nor does he make known to us his own opinions so clearly as of old; and this partly because his method is more strictly dramatic. Or if we can draw his moral with any confidence, we find it to be at variance with the lesson taught by some other poem that treats of a kindred subject, as when we compare "The First Quarrel" with "The Wreck." "I felt I had been to blame" is Nell's conviction, and Tennyson's too, as we may presume. It would not often be the conviction of the modern novelist. And in "The Wreck" the woman who has been false to a bad husband loses both lover and child.

Apart from any ethical purpose underlying these poems, they are dramatically effective, and true to the life; but not every aspect of life is true to art.

In these later volumes Tennyson often employs a galloping line of six accents with a variable number of syllables clustering around each; and in most cases a strong pause marks the middle of the line. Also, the number of lines in each stanza is seldom fixed. In this poem they range from two to eighteen. This tendency towards freedom of movement as the poet nears the end of his career, has been noticed in the preceding Chapter.

(501) "RIZPAH." The date 17—, prefixed to this poem, refers the groundwork of the incident to the eighteenth century, when bodies of criminals were hanged in chains until they became skeletons. The name of the mother, as was noticed under "Claribel," is chosen by the poet for its literary associations, which in this case are suggestive of his subject. "Rizpah . . . from the beginning of har-

vest until water dropped upon them out of heaven, . . . suffered neither the birds of the air to rest on them by day, nor the beasts of the field by night. . . . And they gathered the bones of them that were hanged." (2nd Samuel xxi. 10—13.) So, too, as in "The Grandmother," the name of the son is Willie. The description of a mother's devotion to her offspring in Robert Buchanan's 'Book of Orm" (1870), may also be mentioned in connection with "Rizpah."

The voice in the wind in the first stanza reminds us of Gawain's "Hollow, hollow, hollow, all delight"; and the "Follow, follow," or the "wind wailing for ever" in "The Princess"; the "motherless bleat," in "The Children's Hospital"; the "music on the wind" in "The May Queen"; the "wind of memory murmuring the past" in "In Memoriam."

In this poem Tennyson makes ample amends for the very feeble expression of a mother's love, as we read it in "The Princess." Nothing, perhaps, could be weaker than Lady Psyche's lamentation, "Ah me, my babe, my blossom." . . . But here the strongest and the most sacred of instincts, made yet stronger and more sacred by a situation of terrible pathos, is wrought into words and sung into immortal song as it never had been before.

(504) "The Northern Cobbler" is based upon Mr. Robert Crompton's ballad in the Irish dialect, "Facing the Inimy" (1875). There we read how a cobbler

> "Hammered and stitched and hammered away,
>   Whilst, labelled 'Potheen,'
>   A bottle was seen
> On his small window-shelf." . . .

> "That's the Inimy! Micky Muldoon would say . . .
> And I noticed the spirit from day to day
>   It never grew less, no, never!"

Though not so striking as a character sketch, this

poem rivals in many other respects the two "Northern Farmers."

(507) "THE REVENGE." For the incidents of this splendid ballad, Tennyson has relied mainly upon Sir Walter Raleigh's report of the engagement, which was published in the same year, 1591. Sir Richard Grenville is a well-known figure in Charles Kingsley's "Westward Ho!" At the time of the Armada he was commissioned by Elizabeth to protect Cornwall and Devon; and in 1591 was sent out with a small squadron to intercept a Spanish treasure fleet. The rest of his story is told in the poem.

In movement, the ballad of "The Revenge" closely resembles "The Battle of the Baltic," by Campbell; and it has one or two recollections of Macaulay's "Armada." Campbell's ballad, however, is almost symmetrical, but Tennyson allows himself so much license of construction, that in spite of some rhythmic sequences, the poem leaves on the mind no distinct impression of form; and thus he gives a more than Elizabethan freedom to his work. Otherwise, in simplicity, force, swiftness, spirit—in all that appertains to the daring of the old English sea-dogs, the ballad is magnificent.

"The Revenge" was first printed in "The Nineteenth Century" for March, 1878. Some few years previously Gerald Massey had published a ballad of nineteen stanzas on the same subject.

(509) "THE SISTERS." This idyllic monologue recalls some of the beauty and truth of "The Gardener's Daughter," and other poems of the volume of 1842. Such passages as "The aërial poplar wave, an amber spire"[1]; "Down to the snowlike sparkle of a cloth On fern and foxglove . . . passing jest"; "Born of the fool

---

[1] "Nec gemere aëria cessabit turtur ab ulmo"; with this should be compared "The moan of doves in immemorial elms."

this Age that doubts of all"—these, and a hundred others are excellent. But the story is painful and improbable; and the words, "the love I bore them both," which are the pivot of the poem, seem to ring false; and they almost spoil the splendid paragraph, "Now in this passage," etc. The very objective view of nature in "We left her happy . . . . to our joy," is characteristic of Tennyson, though he spells the great mother's name with a capital. Twice he repeats the Platonic doctrine already often hinted at, as in "The Passing of Arthur," in the paragraph near the beginning, "I found Him in the shining of the stars"; for we hear that "a man's ideal Is high in Heaven, and lodged with Plato's God"; and that "this gross hard-seeming world Is our misshaping vision of the Powers Behind the world." Here and there other poets lend their aid; Wordsworth's ("Vaudracour and Julia"):

> "All Paradise
> Could by the simple opening of a door
> Let itself in upon him,"

may compare with "I stood upon the stairs of Paradise," etc. In Wordsworth, also, is found the phrase "diviner air" of the first song in this poem, and in the fifth stanza of the "Welcome to Alexandrovna." Also Wordsworth's "intellectual all-in-all," is like "his own imperial all-in-all." "Home-return" is in Shakespeare. Many other resemblances will occur to the reader; these are mentioned as reminding him that the imitative tendency is strong in Tennyson to the last; so also is the tendency to repeat himself, though, considering the poet's advanced age, that is not more marked than in his earlier years. One example from many in this poem will be sufficient; the second line of Evelyn's song, "Thro' the heat, the drowth, the dust, the glare," recalls the line of Edwin Morris, "For in the dust and drowth of London life"; and the song itself is a beautiful variation upon the melody of "In Memoriam," lxxxvi.

(514) "THE VILLAGE WIFE: OR, THE ENTAIL."[1]
There is dry humour but perhaps too much word-play
in this story told by "A hignorant village wife" of the ruin of
the "owd Squire" who "niver knawed nowt but boöks."

(517) "IN THE CHILDREN'S HOSPITAL." This pathetic
story, said to be a true one, of the little child putting out
her arms on the counterpane, in order that Christ might
know the sufferer who needed his love, appeared in De-
cember, 1872, in a London local magazine called "St.
Cyprian's Banner." It was entitled "Alice's Christmas
Day," and was related by a Sister of Mercy.

Tennyson takes occasion to rebuke somewhat harshly
the very rare roughness of the hospital surgeon. He in-
sists upon the need of kind words as "a medicine in
themselves," of kindly looks as "a light of healing." "He
handled him gently enough ; but his voice and his face
were not kind." But as a general fact, no men discharge
their terrible duties with greater patience and tenderness.
Also he repeats in almost stronger terms than of old his
indignation expressed in "The Princess" against "Those
monstrous males that carve the living hound And cram
him with the fragments of the grave." More graciously,
but with no less earnestness, he dwells on the power of
personal religion : " How could I serve in the wards if the
hope of the world were a lie ?" adding, as for himself,
" Lord, how long ?" and answering, " It will come by-and-
by." Beautifully he pleads for the presence of all things
fair and fragrant, flowers that "freshen and sweeten the
wards like the waft of an angel's wing ;" or the picture—
" Little children should come to me." To " the fool this
Age that doubts of all" the last words here quoted from
its poet may be as a stumbling block and a rock of offence.
" Say that his day is done ! Ah, why should we care what

they say?" But the question, What is the debt of the humanities to religion, and of religion to theology, will belong to a consideration of "The Promise of May."

(518) "DEDICATORY POEM TO THE PRINCESS ALICE." In December, 1878, "the fatal kiss Born of true life and love" had touched the lips of the Queen's second daughter, the Princess Alice; and to her sacred memory, in lines equally sacred, the Poet Laureate dedicated the poem that follows. The two poems were published together in "The Nineteenth Century" for April, 1879.

(519) "THE DEFENCE OF LUCKNOW." In this ballad the six-accent line we have met with so often among these later poems gives place here and there to one of seven accents, and with good effect, as in the first and last lines of the first stanza. The last line of the stanza, though the language is somewhat strained, serves as a long-drawn triumphant refrain. We miss the simplicity and with that the graphic strength of "The Revenge;" and though "The Defence of Lucknow" is rapid to breathlessness, yet it seems overweighted with detail, and fails a little at the close. But we may be deeply thankful for such another immortal song well mated with an immortal deed.

(521) "SIR JOHN OLDCASTLE, LORD COBHAM." This monologue gives a better dramatic account of itself than the one in the first "Locksley Hall," although the first two lines are obvious as a device, and the friend's coming is referred to very often in the course of the long soliloquy.

In the earlier volumes these studies of character were mostly mythical or of an older world : now the poet more than rivals the modern historian; and in this poem he reminds us that he has become a student of history to such purpose as was never attained before. "Harold" had appeared four years earlier; and some four years later he gave to the world that historical masterwork, "Becket." In his vivid, sympathetic, and favourable sketch of Oldcastle, Tennyson was assisted by the "Ecclesiastical Biography" of Dr. Christopher Wordsworth. According to Dr. Stubbs, the creed of the Lollard leader was "sounder than the principles which guided either his moral or political conduct."

(525) "COLUMBUS." This is another sympathetic portrait from history, but not a perfect one, nor is it always good poetry. Columbus in prison is visited by a friend from the Court, to whom he has much to tell concerning his experience of life. Columbus at this time was about fifty-five years old, and he speaks, not with the garrulity of age, but with the long bitterness of disappointment and injustice ; nevertheless his words are often effusive, and the poem is not very successful. Nor is the workmanship throughout so fine as usual. As in some of Tennyson's other monologues, a dramatic element is introduced by implied remarks of the listener. The materials of this monologue are derived mostly from the Diary of Columbus ; but it also has many poetical resemblances to a poem by Mr. Joseph Ellis, entitled, "Columbus at Seville." This poem was published by Pickering in 1869 and 1876 in a volume entitled "Cæsar in Egypt, Costanza, and other Poems." Although the work of Mr. Ellis is also based on the Diary of Columbus, the parallel passages leave room for an opinion that the Laureate made use of it. In this connection the "Vox Clamantis" of Mr. Eric Mackay, published by Stewart, may be read with some caution.

(529) "THE VOYAGE OF MAELDUNE." Dr. Joyce's "Old Celtic Romances," published in 1879, were probably the groundwork of this poem. They are a translation of the old Irish legend mentioned by the poet. He adapts it at will to his own purpose—a second series of poetical

magic-lantern slides,[1] with a moral[2] inscribed on the last. Apart from the moral he seems to embody in his poem just a little of the popular notion that the Irishman must be fighting.

Where imagery is abundant in Tennyson's poetry, we may expect to find resemblances to Shelley ; and there are many in this poem. The following passage will serve as an example. In the description of the "undersea isle" in v., "the water is clearer than air ;" in Shelley it is "the wave's intenser day;" both poets behold "palaces" and "towers" in the garden of the deep ; when the sur face of the water was troubled "the Paradise trembled away" in the one poet ; in the other, the sea-blooms and the oozy woods "tremble and despoil themselves."

The same galloping six accents bear us swiftly through these rare and beautiful scenes of fancy.

(532 and 533) "DE PROFUNDIS." It is strange that the poet who wrote "Tears, idle tears" as his way of uttering St. Paul's "groanings which cannot be uttered,"[3] should also be the author of "De Profundis ;" for while the poetic quality of the earlier lyric is beyond all praise, it is doubtful whether many of the lines now before us are poetry at all. Certainly "The Human Cry" is not ; and we will glance at that first. The poet surely has been groping about among the ashes of his youth :

> " I feel there is something ; but how and what ?
> I know there is somewhat, but what and why ?
> I cannot tell if that somewhat be I. . . .
> Why deep is not high, and high is not deep. . . .
> Why two and two make four ; why round is not square. . . ."
> *From " The ' How' and the ' Why,'" in the volume of* 1830.

Not " The Human Cry " alone, but the whole poem, is an overstrained attempt to utter the unutterable :

---

[1] See p. 87.   [2] "Vengeance is mine."   [3] P. 252, footnote.

> "Of this divisible-indivisible world
> Among the numerable-innumerable. . . ."

these and the following five lines pass beyond the bounds of art. Perhaps the best comment on such poetry is a quotation that will throw it into relief by resemblance or contrast, or both in one :

> "Searching an infinite Where,
> Probing a bottomless When,
> Dreamfully wandering,
> Ceaselessly pondering,
> What is the Wherefore of men :
> Bartering life for a There,
> Selling his soul for a Then. . . ."

and the rest of this little poem ("The Philosopher and the Philanthropist," written by J.K.S. when a boy at Eton) would serve for the purpose.

The germ of "De Profundis" will be found in two lines of "In Memoriam,"

> "A soul shall draw from out the vast,
> And strike his being into bounds."
> *(Epilogue, 34.)*

Already in "The Two Voices" and "In Memoriam" the genesis of the soul has been a matter of speculation, as also its future destiny. The views embodied in this poem are figured forth in "Crossing the Bar" :

> "When that which drew from out the boundless deep
> Turns again home,"

which is Shelley's "That Power. . . . Which hath withdrawn his being to its own." Or, in the "Idylls of the King :"

> "From the great deep to the great deep he goes."

Again, in "The Higher Pantheism," "This weight of body and limb Are they not sign and symbol of thy division from Him?" or, in "The Ancient Sage,"

> "But that one ripple on the boundless deep
> Feels that the deep is boundless, and itself
> For ever changing form, but evermore
> One with the boundless motion of the deep.'

But there is more than this in " De Profundis." Having in section I. conducted the human soul from the shore of the great deep, through a personal existence in this world to the shore of the great deep again, the poet in a second Greeting proceeds to ponder over the great deep itself, and over those " abysmal deeps of personality," already referred to in "In Memoriam," xlv. The spirit, a broken light from that one light, " drew to this shore " to learn by this fleshly sign, " that this is I " (" In Memoriam," xlv). It " wailed being born," as in the Greek of Plotinus ;[1] it will have to choose between the darker and the sunnier side of doubt ; and at last, after passing through many states of being, return to Him who wrought "this main-miracle, that thou art thou." This part of the argument is important, for it presents one of the poet's views of immortality. The poem closes with " The Human Cry," which, however earnest, is too grotesque for comment ; and those who would be convinced of this, need only compare it with the opening stanzas of " In Memoriam."

In this brief survey no mention could be made of the many metaphysical points common also to " The Ancient Sage."

(533) "PREFATORY SONNET TO THE NINETEENTH CENTURY" (March, 1877). Tennyson's varying attitude towards doubt has received occasional consideration in previous Chapters.[2] To the passages already quoted from " In Memoriam" we will now add—" He fought his doubts" ; " Defects of doubt, and taints of blood "; " doubt and death, Ill brethren" ; " You tell me doubt is devil-born —I know not." Recently, in " The Sisters," we noticed the line " Born of the fool this Age that doubts of all"; we have in this sonnet " Sunless gulfs of doubt "; in " Despair," " Doubt is the lord of this dunghill "; lastly, in " The

---

[1] "Ennead." V. I. i
[2] Pages 18, 81, 118.

Ancient Sage," there are two sides to doubt, a sunnier and
a darker side ; and in this we arrive at the usual Tenny-
sonian compromise. And we cannot too often call to our
minds the importance of this judicial attitude of the poet
towards the shifting thought of fifty years, of which this
sonnet is a striking epitome ; and we do him honour for
venturing on those sunless seas of doubt ; and for planting
the flag of poetry upon many a newly discovered land.
While other great literary artists of our time—Browning
and Ruskin, for instance—lowered the value of their
teaching by basing it in greater part and to the very last,
on the older systems of thought, Tennyson stood amongst
us scattering from one lavish hand choice dried fruits of
the past, and with the other gathering for us the ripest of
many tempting clusters of the present.

The month in which this sonnet appeared is given in a
very picturesque phrase—"This roaring moon of daffodil
and crocus."

(533) "To the Rev. W. H. Brookfield." In 1875
this sonnet was prefixed to Lord Lyttleton's "Memoir of
William Henry Brookfield," one of Tennyson's old college
friends. There is a touching reference to Arthur Hallam,
"The lost light of those dawn-golden times"; it speaks
of a love

> "Abiding with me till I sail
> To seek thee on the mystic deeps."

σκιᾶς ὄναρ ἄνθρωπος (dream of a shadow—such is man,) is from
Pindar, eighth Pythian, 136. The sentiment is often
reversed, as in Shelley's "Shadow of some golden dream,"
or in "The Princess," "I myself, the shadow of a dream."

(533) "Montenegro," (534) "To Victor Hugo."
These two sonnets were contributed to the "Nineteenth
Century," the first in March, and the second in June, 1877.
They are a valuable addition to the long list of poems in
which Tennyson gives honour to gallantry or genius.

It is just worthy of notice that the one sonnet applauds the "smallest among peoples" for maintaining their nationality, while the other would bring in the day when all men will make one people.

(534) "BATTLE OF BRUNANBURH." In the "Anglo-Saxon Chronicle," poetry takes the place of prose for the years 937, 942, 973, and 975. The first of these entries, a stirring ode on the Battle of Brunanburh, forms the groundwork of Tennyson's poem. With fine effect the poet adheres closely to the form of his original. But not to the form alone; for the prose rendering of Hallam Tennyson, "the raven with horny beak," becomes in his father's poem, "the horny-*nibb'd* raven"; and thus, with the aid of verse, the Laureate could retain the graphic *nebban* of the "Chronicle." It is a pleasure to have in modern English such a reproduction of the form and the spirit of this fine old song.

(536) "ACHILLES OVER THE TRENCH," contributed to "The Nineteenth Century" for August, 1877. (See p. 280.)

(537) "TO PRINCESS FREDERICA." On April 24th, 1880, the Princess Frederica of Hanover was married to the Baron von Pawel Rammingen. Her father, who was afflicted with blindness, had been King of Hanover from 1851 till 1866.

(537) "SIR J. FRANKLIN." Sir John Franklin was born at Spilsby, near Somersby, and was uncle of the poet's wife. These lines to his memory were written in 1877.

(537) "TO DANTE." These are among the best of Tennyson's shorter memorial verses. They owe much to the graceful art of the figure at the close.

CHAPTER XIII.

"TIRESIAS, AND OTHER POEMS."

IN 1885 Tennyson published "Tiresias and Other Poems," a volume of 204 pages as vigorous as its predecessor of 1880. And in the next year, 1886, " Locksley Hall Sixty Years After" appeared with two other poems and "The Promise of May," forming a volume of 201 pages. " The Cup" had been produced at the Lyceum in 1881, "The Promise of May " at the Globe Theatre in 1882 ; in 1884 "The Falcon" and " Becket" were published ; and in 1889 "Demeter, and Other Poems" followed " Locksley Hall Sixty Years After." Such a record of ten years' labour by a poet of more than threescore and ten is without a parallel ; and by a strange coincidence, the productiveness of Robert Browning during the same ten years and at nearly the same period of life would rank next in power and quantity.

It is to Robert Browning that the " Tiresias " volume is dedicated in the following terms : " To my good friend Robert Browning, whose genius and geniality will best appreciate what may be best and make most allowance for what may be worst, this volume is affectionately dedicated."

An inscription in simpler language appears on the

opening page of "Locksley Hall Sixty Years After":
"To my wife I dedicate this Dramatic Monologue and the Poems which follow."

In the one-volume edition the group headed "Tiresias, and Other Poems," really includes the contents of both the volumes we have been describing, excepting that "Balin and Balan" is omitted from the "Tiresias" volume, and "The Promise of May" from "Locksley Hall Sixty Years After." The other two poems in the latter volume, "The Fleet," and "Opening of the Indian and Colonial Exhibition by the Queen," are placed near the end of the group.

(560) "Locksley Hall Sixty Years After."

As "Locksley Hall" was the most important among the poems of Tennyson's early volumes, so "Locksley Hall Sixty Years After" takes a high position, perhaps the highest, among the shorter poems of the later period ; it may therefore be considered first. With this exception, the group will be reviewed in order as printed.

I. Introductory.—It was noticed in the chapter on "Locksley Hall" that, adopting approximate dates, the hero of that poem would be about the same age as the poet—say 30 years. When some fifty years had passed, Tennyson published his "Locksley Hall Sixty Years After ;" by that time he was three years short of eighty, and eighty is the age assigned to the hero on this his second appearance. This, then, is the first point to notice ; the poet may be supposed in each case to be about as old as his hero. As to the "Sixty Years After," they are put roughly. Supposing the first "Locksley Hall" to have been written a few years before 1842, and this poem not long before 1886, a period of something less than fifty years lies between. But the sixty years are conventional ; nor need they apply rigidly to the poems, but generally to the subject matter. Yet, knowing as we do our poet's carefulness in regard to dating as far back as possible, we may leave the question open.

This poem was probably rough-cast, if not finished, some time before 1886 ; certainly, two of its couplets were first of all inserted in the " Locksley Hall " of 1842, viz. : 7 and 8 of the new poem between 19 and 20 of the former one. It is further interesting to notice that " The Two Voices Sixty Years After," in other words, " The Ancient Sage," was published in the " Tiresias " volume of the year before (1885) ; and we remember that " Locksley Hall " and " The Two Voices " appeared together in 1842.

A third parallel between the first and the second " Locksley Hall," will be found in their environment. This has already been suggested on p. 159. The poems there referred to as being near to the second " Locksley Hall " in subject and in date would be such as some of the later " Idylls of the King," together with passages recently added to the earlier ones ; also " Despair " (1881) ; " The Promise of May " (1882) ; the " Epilogue to The Charge of the Heavy Brigade (1882) ; " Freedom " (1884) ; " Vastness " (1885) ; and the two other occasional pieces published in the " Locksley Hall " volume of 1885 ; also, and most important, and of later date, many of the poems in the " Tiresias " volume of 1886, and the " Demeter " volume of 1889. Such are the songs, some grave, some serious, some almost despondent, notes from which may all be heard in the stormy music of " Locksley Hall Sixty Years After."

II. ITS PERSONAL CHARACTER.—Possibly enough was said in the chapter on the companion poem to establish the poet's relationship to the speaker of this later monologue. And in the notes on the " Supposed Confessions of a Second-rate Sensitive Mind," which is the first in this series of self-examining and self-revealing soliloquies, some explanation was given of the way in which Tennyson appears to have availed himself of this mode of utterance.

And the series is a long one ; in poems beginning with
the " Supposed Confessions " of 1830, and ending with
"Akbar's Dream," of 1889, the Laureate occasionally
revealed his view of contemporary life—but at the same
time concealed something—by dressing himself up, more
or less exactly, as one of his leading characters.

III. HOW THE POEM DEALS WITH PROBLEMS OF
EVIL.—We have again to notice that the poet generally
makes out as good a case as possible against himself. He
does full justice to the darker side of doubt before turning
towards us the narrowest crescent of the sunnier side. He
dwells long on the subject of evil before a hint of redeem-
ing good is offered. Though not quite so valiant, perhaps,
yet, like Browning, he is " ever a fighter," and he seems
inclined, if we may take a hint from his " Northern
Cobbler," to make the most of his enemy. But, as we
have remarked elsewhere, Tennyson is too cautious to be
sanguine ; he is disposed to take life seriously rather than
confidently ; Browning will believe where Tennyson can
only trust.

Light is struck from hardest stone ; and the blacker the
darkness, the brighter is that light. In part, at least,
this is Tennyson's way; and he is not alone in this.
When the curtain falls on the last scene of " King Lear,"
our hearts are full—not of the tragedy, but of the loveliness
of goodness that the tragedy made possible. The world,
we whisper, that owns Cordelia, must be owned by God.
In " The Two Voices " " the arguments," to repeat Tenny-
son's opinion of " In Memoriam," " are about as good on
one side as the other ; " but the poem concludes with
something more powerful than argument ; it is a picture :

> " These three made unity so sweet. . . .
> I blest them "—

even as we bless Cordelia.

The hostile forces in " The Princess " falter on both
sides before the presence of a little child ; the problems

of " In Memoriam " find their fittest solution in the mere
fact of a marriage ; the holy love between the man and
woman in " Despair " proved that for them despair was
in reality impossible : the two men and two women found
faithful in " Locksley Hall Sixty Years After " [1] proclaim
to us that the protest was pitched too high ; that the aged
" dotard " might safely have lowered the note of his
pessimism—though certainly that would have spoilt some
of the sounding couplets ; and we further wonder why,
with four such examples of goodness within his experience,
he had not thought of reforming himself—and, next to
that, of reforming others. Nor will the hero of " Locksley
Hall a Thousand Years After " be a consistent pessimist
if he has lived to respect one man or one woman—
including himself.

IV. COMPARED WITH "LOCKSLEY HALL."—(a) *As
Monologues*: "Locksley Hall" was a soliloquy ; "Locksley
Hall Sixty Years After" has the advantage of being
rather more dramatic, for the one speaker addresses
another person whose remarks he repeats in a frag-
mentary and ejaculatory manner ; for example the fifth
and sixth couplets expanded might read " *Grandson* :—
' My curse on the old dotard ; as though he had any love
to give her ; but she jilted me for him just because he had
lots of money.' *Grandfather* :—' Why should you curse
him ? pity him, rather ; he has put a halter round his
neck ; and as to dotard, an old man might easily be
gulled by such a woman, but surely you ought to have
had more sense. However, I suppose you loved her well
enough, and you might have made her happy—but no,
impossible ; and we shall see whether the fortune she has
married is going to bring her any happiness.' " This
semi-dramatic device is employed by Tennyson in many
other poems, such as : "The Northern Cobbler," "Northern

---

[1] Couplets 24, 25, 29, 32, 120, 134.

Farmer," "Despair," "Happy," "Rizpah," "The First Quarrel," "The Village Wife," "Columbus," "Romney's Remorse," "Charity." He must have felt the awkwardness of some of the situations in "Locksley Hall"; as noticed already, the idea of a soldier waiting until his "merry comrades" call him, is not exactly a good one. "Sir John Oldcastle" is an improvement in this respect; the speaker in that poem is waiting for a friend who had appointed to meet him. On the other hand, a fuller form of drama, as in "Walking to the Mail," involved yet greater difficulties; therefore Tennyson often preferred the middle course, which was more graphic than a mere soliloquy or a story told to no one, and yet avoided the troublesome dramatic elements of characters and incident.

(b) *Their Subject.* As to the subject of these poems, everything has gone wrong, first in the ardent eyes of youth and early manhood, next in the dimmer eyes of fourscore years.[1] Ultimately, as explained in Chapter V., these views of the world, with more or less of exactness, represent respectively those of Tennyson when he is at the age of about thirty and eighty.

To realize the two characters of the one individual and to discriminate between them is not such an easy task as might be imagined. The hero of the earlier poem suddenly sees everything with a "jaundiced eye;" the world is the same world, but he has been unfortunate in a love affair, and forthwith that world is to him—he uses the words of Hamlet—"out of joint." The Prince told Princess Ida that if she withheld her love she "might shock him even to death Or baser courses, children of despair." This lover crossed in love does not seek refuge in death from broken heart, nor in suicide, nor riotous living; his disease takes a form more agreeable to the poet's purpose. After some years he recovers confidence,

---

1 "Aged eyes may take," etc., is the "moral" of the poem.

partially, if not entirely, and begins again to look forward.[1] In the later poem the same character appears at the age of eighty; once more the time is out of joint; but why? If we admit that his conduct in the first poem was to some extent habitual, and not determined by one sudden and overwhelming cause; and if we further admit that his disappointment expressed itself strangely and extravagantly; or if, not content with this, we have recourse to the later poem for a somewhat enlarged portrait of the ardent young lover,

"Gone the fires of youth, the follies, furies, curses, passionate tears. . . .

Fires that shook me once, but now to silent ashes fall'n away,"

then how can we understand the aged hero when he confesses himself "heated,"[2] or again, when he tells us that the curses of his youth are gone, and yet a little later on in the poem,[3] and when almost breathless with cursing, protests that he must curse his fill, being old. Other difficulties attend any careful study of these two characters; but it will be best to admit conventionally that the young man of "Locksley Hall" would be intolerant in old age, and more than other old men accustomed to abuse the present and to look back with fondness to the past; only we have to repeat that this motive for the poem is in reality cancelled by the lines quoted above. Yet more, in couplets 24 and 26, we are told that Edith healed him of his disease, and that with her for forty years his life "in golden sequence ran."

From this glance at the characters, we may turn for a moment to the leading topics of the two poems. Some of these were indicated in Chapter V.; others are best studied in connection with the contemporary poems assigned to them severally in that and the present Chapter. For example, the germ in "Locksley Hall," "Knowledge

---

[1] Couplets 87 and 94.   [2] Couplet 76.   [3] Couplets 76 and 77.

comes, but wisdom lingers," was found fully developed in
" In Memoriam " ; immortality and many kindred sub-
jects in " Locksley Hall Sixty Years After," are amply
and wisely discussed in the " Ancient Sage." Others,
such as Science, Art, Evolution, Social Evils, War, The
Future, have already been touched upon in these pages ;
for it is scarcely possible to review the writings of Tenny-
son without frequent reference to those storehouses of his
favourite themes, the two " Locksley Halls." It remains
to be noticed that some of the topics included in " Locksley
Hall Sixty Years After" seem to have been worked into
the couplets several years earlier than the date of publica-
tion, 1886.

(*c*) *Their Style.* Under this head a strange phenomenon
presents itself, which, however, is fully explained in the
Appendix to Chapter XI. In point of style the two poems
are exactly reversed; the angry and impetuous utterance
of "youthful jealousy"[1] is restrained by an almost un-
varied evenness of rhythm, whereas the reflections of the
"old white-headed dreamer"[2] rush along in lines as
tumultuous as a torrent. There are passages in the earlier
poem where the even flow of the river of verse is broken
by boulders[3] or quickened to a rapid ;[4] and in the torrent
stream of the later poem are placid coves[5] where the
moon and "Venus near her" smile reflected in unutterable
beauty; but the main characteristics of the two works
are strikingly different, and are exactly the opposite to
what we should have expected. To descend to particulars :
half a trochaic line in " Locksley Hall " is now and then
changed to iambic ; but except for an extra syllable or
two this is almost the only important variation admitted ;
whereas in the later poem the trochaic measure is diver-

---

[1] " Locksley Hall," couplet 120.
[2] " Locksley Hall Sixty Years After," couplet 19.
[3] Couplets 48, 49.   [4] Couplets 91, 92.
[5] Couplets 16-18, 85, 89-96, 105, 106, 129, 130, 137-140.

sified by numberless devices ; only one can be mentioned here, which especially makes the metre more turbulent, viz., the introduction of many extra syllables ; unless we point to the rhyme " Zolaism " which borders on the double. The length of the poems deserves attention ; the 141 couplets of " Locksley Hall Sixty Years After " as against 97 of " Locksley Hall " may suggest the garrulity of age ; and the breaks indicated by asterisks may mark some wavering in the course of thought, due to the same cause. Otherwise they are not easily accounted for.

A somewhat similar phenomenon appears when the blemishes of the two poems are considered ; the faults of the first poem are due to excess of weakness, and of the second to excess of strength. In " Locksley Hall " there is much that might almost be called effusive, thin, effeminate ; and not seldom we seem aware that the poetry is careful patchwork and not careless passion. On the contrary " Locksley Hall Sixty Years After " is often Byronic in its fullness and force. In every way it is a much more powerful poem than its predecessor.

But lastly, we apply ourselves to the pleasant duty of pointing out some of the literary merits of these wonderful poems ; and perhaps it may not be impertinent to praise even " Locksley Hall " as now we view it by the side of its companion of more recent years. We notice first the absolute fitness of its charm—the charm of youth; its enchantment over us is " the fulness of the spring ;" we hear the copses ringing ; our being becomes renewed by all objects of new life and loveliness ; and the distance of the future melts away into the hues of hope.

In the maturer poem there is nothing so buoyant, and fresh, and young; yet it holds us enchanted with a spell as strong. " Locksley Hall " sent a joyous thrill through our blood ; but there are passages in " Locksley Hall Sixty Years After " that make the heart ache with their beauty.

(538) TIRESIAS. "Tiresias" is less modern in treatment than Tennyson's other classical poems, and on that account partly it is less interesting ; also, the workmanship is below the level of "Ulysses," "Tithonus," "Lucretius ;" yet it contains noble passages, with a modern touch here and there. In the lines "To E. Fitzgerald" (537) it is referred to as "dating many a year ago."

"Tiresias" is suggested by the "Phœnissæ" of Euripides and the "Septem contra Thebas" of Æschylus. The Theban "prophet old" addresses himself to Menœceus, gives him one of the varying accounts of his blindness, and prophesies that if Menœceus will slay himself, Thebes will be victorious over the Argives. The best thing in the poem is the description of Pallas "climbing from the bath ;" the nine closing lines, also magnificent, are adapted from Pindar.

The prefatory lines "To E. Fitzgerald" are a poetical *tour de force ;* they run on without a break to the close. "Your Omar" which "drew Full-handed plaudits from the best," is Fitzgerald's "Translation of the Rubaiyat of Omar Khayyam," 1858.

"Tiresias," which the poet's son Hallam found "In some forgotten book of mine," was sent to Fitzgerald in 1883, but too late to receive a criticism that might "require A less diffuse and opulent end." In the pathetic "Epilogue," which, though shorter, yet being sadder, has one or two breaks, we meet with another of Tennyson's many —almost angry—demands for man's immortality—

"If night, what barren toil to be !"

(541) "THE WRECK." This is one of the many problems of marriage pondered over by Tennyson. An emotional girl who loves her Shelley, has been "given" to a man of the world—a man in stature, a dwarf in intellect, who loves his Tables of Trade and Finance ; he is heartless; chills her efforts to please him, and greets their

firstborn with the exclamation, "Pity it isn't a boy." She leaves her husband and her baby girl ; spends "ten long days of summer and sin" with a man who is a dwarf in stature but a giant in intellect ; then a storm brings to her the cry of her child ; the man falls dead at her feet. She is saved from the wreck to learn that her little one had "gone" after "'Ten long sweet summer days' of fever, and want of care !"

The moral is obvious. Marriage is an institution so useful as to be deemed necessary; but no law is so just as not to be unjust to an individual here and there ; and we cannot sacrifice the law for the sake of the individual. Had Milton's plea for divorce been successful, society would have perished.

(544) " DESPAIR." The leading thought of this poem is expressed in the following line of Division V. : "We had past from a cheerless night to the glare of a drearier day." In these words the poet compares the effect produced on average human life by the "fatalist creed" on the one hand, and by "the Age" (with its capital letter) on the other. The "cramping creeds," we are told, had maddened the people, and must vanish, together with the hell they had invented ; and, as we are also told, the "new dark ages" with their "know-nothing books" had "crazed" their victim. . . . . "O yes" . . . . This important fact has sometimes been overlooked ; the poet denounces, with equal sternness, both the creed that maddens and the Age that crazes.

And what are we to learn from this ? Is there any hope ? We seem to learn at least one lesson ; it is not new to these pages—"There's nothing we can call our own but love." Love runs its course through the poem like a streamlet through a dark valley, revealing itself to us in silver glimpses here and there, till it passes from our sight towards the sea—the sea to which these two gave up their love. "Fear? Am I not with you?" . . . "And she laid her hand in my own" . . . "And we turned to each other" . . . "Dear love" . . . "She is gone! can I stay?" . . . "Never a kiss so sad." . . . There we may pause ; what a mistake they made, this loving pair ; what unequivocal logic is love's : "Never a kiss so sad"! surely, surely, the kiss should have been their happiest, sealing the bliss of the past—pledge of the peace to be theirs at once—and for ever ! "There's nothing we can call our own but love." They just forgot that, and the kiss was sad.

With Lear and Cordelia it was exactly the opposite : when both had "incurred the worst," the words of the old king to Cordelia were such as these,

> " Come, let's away to prison :
> We two alone will sing like birds i' the cage. . . .
>   And we'll wear out
> In a wall'd prison, packs and sects of great ones
> That ebb and flow by the moon. . . ."

Why? merely because Lear had come to learn what the husband and wife in "Despair" manifested, yet failed to realize,

> "There's nothing we can call our own but love."

Nor did the author of "Despair" realize this very obvious moral of his poem, for in the prefatory note already referred to[1] he assures us that the pair were "utterly miserable."

If we now ask, what does Tennyson wish us to understand from this poem, we first answer, "Despair" is followed immediately by "The Ancient Sage" ; they may be regarded as separate portions of an improved "Two Voices ;" and it is to "The Ancient Sage" that we must appeal for the poet's explanation of this tragedy. But before passing on to this long commentary on "Despair,"

[1] See p. 119.

we may apply to the latter poem a statement by Tennyson already referred to : "All the arguments are about as good on one side as the other, and thus throw man back more on the primitive impulses and feelings." Now these two sides, according to the poet, have two distinct names ; one in this poem "the darker side" of doubt ; the other in the next poem, "the sunnier side of doubt." "Thrown back on the primitive impulses and feelings," we seldom fail to recognize these two sides, and we naturally choose the sunnier,[1] "the larger hope"; bred up by "their know-nothing books," we may even then exclaim "Ah ! yet—I have had some glimmer, at times, Of a God behind all, the great God, for aught that I know"; but we shall naturally "lean to the darker side." This is the second moral to be drawn from "Despair." Yet a third aspect of the poem also forms a fitting introduction to "The Ancient Sage." The poet, as we have seen, equally condemns the "know-all chapel," and "the know-nothing books," the dogmatic assertion of the "creed,"[2] and the dogmatic negation of the agnostic.[3]

(547) "THE ANCIENT SAGE." An alternative title for this poem, as suggested in a former chapter, was "The Two Voices Sixty Years After"; but, prompted by the last sentence in our review of "Despair," and mindful also of "The Higher Pantheism," we will now propose to style it "The Higher Agnosticism." From this point of view we shall be enabled to deal briefly with a poem that might otherwise make an excessive demand upon our space.

So long as agnosticism contents itself with a rejection of the "know-all" doctrine ("Despair," xvi), it is comparatively harmless ; but when in its turn it grows positive, and draws up its creeds—"I do not believe more than I can see" ; "The mind is limited to a knowledge of phe-

---

[1] Few find in the fact of choice a necessity for *pessimism.*
[2] Division iv.
[3] Division xvi.

nomena " ; " I never believe in anything unless I have an absolutely scientific ground for believing in it "—when it formulates such creeds as these, it deserves the poet's stern rebuke in " Despair." Take the last of them ; it admits of ready refutation ; no absolutely scientific ground has yet been discovered for believing in anything ; all physical questions are speedily lost in metaphysical issues. " The most unreasonable of men," said a great thinker, " are those who will have a reason for everything." This lower agnosticism is of more recent date ; but the higher agnosticism has been professed by great souls from Socrates downwards. In " The Ancient Sage " it is admirably expressed in the following words :

> " For nothing worthy proving can be proven,
> Nor yet disproven : wherefore be thou wise,
> Cleave ever to the sunnier side of doubt."

This doctrine points to a middle course ; it does not limit human knowledge to phenomena ; it respects " the primitive impulses and feelings " ; those intuitions that lie deeper than knowledge and transcend phenomena ; by which, when experience fails, we believe in " that which is " [1] with greater assurance than experience itself could warrant.

Further than this we cannot go ; and at least the fact that the lower negations themselves rest on mere assumption, leaves us a heart to learn the other great lesson of the poem,

> " Let be thy wail, and help thy fellow men."

This corresponds exactly to the first moral we drew from " Despair "—

> " There's nothing we can call our own but love ; '

and this, again, was the conclusion of " The Two Voices." [2]

From the higher position whence this bird's-eye view of

---

[1] " In Memoriam," xcv. (10), and cxxiv.

[2] See p. 147.

" The Ancient Sage " was obtained, we must now descend to a more particular but brief examination of its doctrines. We have in this poem a summary of the Poet's opinions on the many mysteries of our being ; and the Sage may stand, in the first instance, for Tennyson himself. He comes forth from his ancient city accompanied by a young man, " Worn from wasteful living," whose notions of life are contained in the text, " Let us eat and drink, for to-morrow we die."

Some of these notions the young man has written down in verse ; he has the scroll with him ; and as they proceed on their way, the Ancient Sage reads his young friend's rhyming lines, but pauses at intervals to add blank verse comments of his own.

The first few lines of the lyric imply that only the world as we see it is ours ; there is nothing beneath or beyond appearances. " The likest god," the Sage answers, " is within you." Then, quoting the modern philosopher who first defined the limits of knowledge, he adds :

" When thou sendest thy free soul thro' heaven,

*　　　　*　　　　*　　　　*

Thou seest the Nameless of the hundred names."

" But the Nameless never came among us ; he cannot be proved."

" Nothing, O my son, can be proved, and nothing disproved ; therefore art thou free to believe ; by faith alone canst thou embrace the Power who brings good out of evil."

" What Power ?　An intelligence like our own ? or blind chance ? "

" His work is not yet finished ; we are parts, and cannot see the whole."

" There is no power but Time ; and Time destroys all."

" Our thin minds break into Thens and Whens an eternal Now."

"One common end o'ertakes life's idle dreaming—
Dust, darkness, tears."

"The doors of night may be the gates of Light."

"We are but as a ripple on the boundless deep."

"My son, that ripple is boundless, because the deep is boundless. In spirit I have seemed to traverse an eternal past ; in a trance I am flashed at times through an eternal future."

"But why is this life so evil and so sad ?"

"Good and evil, like Time, are relative terms that lose their meaning in the eternal act of creation ; they will lose their meaning to us even here, if we do our best."

As was stated in the remarks on "The Two Voices," we do not expect to find a system of philosophy in a short poem ; nor can any attempt be made in a book like the present to test the soundness of the poet's doctrines. It will be enough to notice that they are mostly "new-old," and are gathered from many writers. Some of the speculations of this poem and "The Two Voices," date back to the days of Plato ; the teaching of "The Ancient Sage" is referred by Tennyson to "A thousand summers ere the time of Christ." But probably some two hundred years before Plato is all the poet meant. In that age, a contemporary of "Eastern Confutzee"[1] lived another Chinese philosopher, Lau-Tsze, whose works, translated by John Chambers, seem to have furnished Tennyson with material for such passages as the one beginning, "The Abysm of all Abysms," which again suggests the 106th couplet of "Locksley Hall Sixty Years After." It may further be noticed that the many writers from Lau-Tsze to Wordsworth, who suggest theories to the later poet, also supply him now and then with his phraseology.

Lastly, much of "The Ancient Sage" is found in

---

[1] Mentioned in 1st edition of "The Palace of Art."

Tennyson's earlier work ; the relativity of time in the passage, " The days and hours . . . serve thy will," is expressed as fully and clearly in " The Princess." [1] " The Passion of the Past " has already been referred to ; [2] as also the description of trance, [3] " And more, my son . . ."—read best of all in " In Memoriam " xcv. ; and not unknown to other writers, Wordsworth, Plotinus, Sir Thomas Browne, John Addington Symonds. The theory of polarity, " No night no day ! " " No ill no good ! " presents itself frequently in Tennyson from first to last.

Turning now from the thought of the poem to its form, we must admire one of the finest metrical contrasts in literature ; and we immediately recollect " The Brook." Here the rhyming tetrameters and trimeters suggest the careless levity of unbelief, and where they break for a moment the calm faith of the blank verse, they remind us of those mountain torrents that foam into the Tay until the mighty river widens to the ocean, and they are heard no more.

(552) "THE FLIGHT." This is in some respects a companion poem to the " The Wreck." The problem there left to be solved by suffering in obedience to law is here anticipated, and calls for no solution. The bride of " The Flight " does not stay to be "given." [4] On the early morning of the day fixed for her marriage with a man she loathes, she flies with her sister to seek some distant shore where haply she may meet with her beloved Edwin. It is much weaker work than " The Wreck " ; the story drags ; its May Queen stanza (more particularly of the " Conclusion ") suits it somewhat ill, having all the old drawbacks with but little of the old charm.

---

[1] III. 306-313.　　　　　　　[2] Chapter VII., Appendix.
[3] Pp. 62, 63, 103, etc.　　　　[4] " The Wreck," II. 1.

(555) "To-morrow." See pp. 268 and 269; and especially the note on the Irish dialect, p. 268.

(557) "The Spinster's Sweet-arts." Although the present writer is more familiar with the dialects of the north of England than with the Irish brogue of the former poem, he has placed them on the same literary footing. Still, no commentator can omit to recognize in "The Spinster's Sweet-arts" a study both clever and amusing.

(568) "Prologue to General Hamley." In 1873 General Hamley, a friend of the poet, had contributed to Blackwood a very clever parody of Tennyson in his "Sir Tray; an Arthurian Legend." These prefatory lines open with an excellent bit of painting from nature.

(568) "The Charge of the Heavy Brigade at Balaclava" ("Macmillan's Magazine," 1881), is another "song that nerves a nation's heart;" and though, like the other, not free from flaws, is a fine companion poem to the "Charge of the Light Brigade." "Like drops of blood in a dark-gray sea" is a daring simile.

(569) "Epilogue." "Irene" (Greek for "peace") may stand for those—and there would be many of them—who expressed to the poet their entire disapproval of war. The sentiment of the poem has been noticed elsewhere, especially the theory of the source of evil —"Perchance from some abuse of Will In worlds before the man."

(570) "To Virgil." Though written at request for the nineteenth centenary of Virgil's death, this is a beautiful poem, and hardly less inspired than the lines to Catullus. Truly a great poet can criticise a great poet. "Thou majestic in thy sadness at the doubtful doom of human kind": all who have loved Virgil will marvel at and love that line; it is exactly what they must have felt,

and felt a yearning to express. Nor would they be greatly inclined to dispute the epithet "stateliest" as applied to the metre of the poet.

(571) "THE DEAD PROPHET, 182—." Does 182— imply a poem of early years? It seems too vigorous for any date before 1830, though the thought occurs early enough. Stanza IX. has something in common with "The Poet"; V. and VI. are graphic. But the poem is unworthy of Tennyson. It might be advisable to protest with dignity once or twice against hostile or vicious criticism; but there were probably times when indifference on the part of the Laureate would have been more effective than any protest. On this occasion he may almost seem to be addressing the critics who had recently condemned his "Promise of May."

(573) "EARLY SPRING." What a transition! An angel of light stands singing where but a moment before a demon of darkness lay howling. It may be a fancy, but more than once we seem to trace a purpose in the sequence of poems. Further criticism of "Early Spring" is not needed; we could not praise the poem more highly; to praise it less would be unjust.[1]

(573) "PREFATORY POEM TO MY BROTHER'S SONNETS." This was the latest record of a brother's love, which is so familiar to all who read "In Memoriam," lxxxix. and cii. Charles Tennyson-Turner died at Cheltenham, April 25th, 1879. In 1835 he assumed the name of his uncle, the Rev. S. Turner, vicar of Grasby, to whose living he succeeded. He was well known as a writer of sonnets, in one of which he tells us "The seal of Truth is Beauty."

(574) "FRATER AVE ATQUE VALE" ("The Nineteenth

---

[1] "Early Spring" was published in "The Youth's Companion," 1884.

Century," March, 1883). Sirmio, now Sirmione, is a peninsula ("all but island") on the shores of Lake Benacus (now Garda). This was a favourite spot with the poet Catullus, as he tells us in his poems. The words " Frater Ave atque Vale" are found at the end of the pathetic lament of Catullus for his brother. Nothing but the tender regret of a great poet could have made lovely poetry of nine lines all rhyming together.

(574) " HELEN'S TOWER." Privately printed by Lord Dufferin. The pamphlet containing "Helen's Tower" bears an engraving of the tower on the title page ; within are two poems, both unsigned. The first is, " To my dear son, on his 21st birthday, with a Silver Lamp," and it is from the pen of Lady Dufferin ; the second is Tennyson's. On the last page are the words, " On Wednesday, October 23rd, 1861, Helen's Tower was finished."

" Browning's ' Sonnet to my Mother,' following the title-page, he sent me as a dedication to Helen's Tower, for which Tennyson also composed a poetical inscription. This tower I built on a hill at Clandeboye, overlooking a lovely view of the sea, in order to contain the verses which my mother wrote to me the day that I came of age." (From a Memoir by her son, the Marquis of Dufferin and Ava, prefixed to a volume of Poems by Helen, Lady Dufferin. John Murray, 1894).

(574 and 575) " EPITAPHS." Tennyson's poetical work is so extensive and so various, that it must sometimes fail to maintain its author's average reputation. His epitaphs are not very successful. They are mostly epigrammatic in form, and may have been suggested by some of the epigrams of Simonides. The familiar phrase " Light of Light" is employed as finely as the kindred phrase of Keats, " Light in light" ("In Memoriam," xci. 4 ; " Happy," x.)

(575) "To the Duke of Argyll." "Ever-changing circumstance" has already been referred to on pages 37 and 95. In these eleven lines of blank verse we may also notice Tennyson's deference to "never-changing Law."

(575) "Hands all round." (See also p. 263). This song was sung at St. James's Hall by Mr. Santley in March, 1882, to music by Mrs. Tennyson. It is very spirited, being one of the best of the patriotic songs. In 1881, at the suggestion of Sir F. Young, the "Examiner" copy of 1852 was altered so as to include the Colonies. In many lines we are reminded of Tennyson's love of compromise :

> "That man's the best Cosmopolite
> Who loves his native country best."

(575) "Freedom," ("Macmillan's Magazine," December, 1884). The goal of ethical progress is personal and social freedom. Something like this may be discovered in Tennyson's excellent poem.

(576) "H.R.H. Princess Beatrice." These lines were printed in "The Times," July 23rd, 1885. On that day H.R.H. Princess Beatrice was married to Prince Henry of Battenberg, who, however, continued to live with the Queen.

The blank verse of this poem is scarcely so good as usual ; and but for the three lines at the close, some of the imagery might border on the fanciful.

(577) "The Fleet." Printed in "The Times," April 23rd, 1885, under the heading "The Fleet. (On its Reported Insufficiency)." These stanzas may have been suggested by the Debate on the Navy Estimates, April 20th. They are a fitting introduction to the poem that follows. The poet gives expression to an opinion that

passes ever and again over the minds of Englishmen like
" a great third wave "—" The fleet of England is her all-
in-all."

(577) "OPENING OF THE INDIAN AND COLONIAL
EXHIBITION." Though not so good as the former Ex-
hibition Ode, this was very appropriate to the new occa-
sion. In the third stanza it contains a graphic description
of the founding of the United States. The Colonial Exhi-
bition was opened May 4th, 1886.

This poem was written at the request of the Prince of
Wales ; and the impressive companion lines in the
Epilogue to the "Idylls of the King" are said to have
been suggested by Lady Franklin. These two poems form
a striking additional proof of the intense interest taken by
the poet in our " ever-broadening England."

(578) "POETS AND THEIR BIBLIOGRAPHIES." Again
we have " laudator temporis acti." This unthankful theme
has been glanced at more than once in these pages.
Nor is the sonnet a very good one : the line

"You see your Art still shrined in human shelves"

is one of the worst Tennyson ever published.

It will be observed that the poets selected are Latin.
And here it will be interesting to notice that partly owing
to circumstances, and partly to inclination, Tennyson has
cast a flower of poetry at the feet of three Latin poets, and
not one Greek. For his " Lucretius," though unavowed,
is a splendid tribute to that poet. Certainly Homer occu-
pies an honoured place in " The Princess" and " The
Palace of Art" and the " Epilogue to the Charge of the
Heavy Brigade." But with this exception, no Greek poet
is specially mentioned by Tennyson.[1] Like himself, the

---

[1] The poem " To Virgil" contains an incidental reference to Hesiod—
"he that sang the Works and Days."

Latin poets were mostly imitative and artistic, and he may have felt that he was more akin to them.

Horace, whom he resembles in manner only, and that occasionally, he here styles "popular;" that is the best he could say of a poet possessing—or owning to—little feeling, and a low order of imagination. Catullus wears "a wreath of sweeter bay"; love with Horace was fashion, with Catullus, passion.

(578) "TO W. C. MACREADY." In February, 1851, at a farewell banquet to the famous actor, W. C. Macready, this sonnet was read to the guests by John Forster. It had been written for the occasion by Tennyson, and was printed in "The Household Narrative of Current Events," and other periodicals. "Full-handed thunders" is a variation of "full-handed plaudits" in the lines "To E. Fitzgerald." The poet's opinions of modern drama are interesting; the lines "Nor flicker down to brainless pantomime, And those gilt gauds men-children swarm to see," are a picturesque description of a modern perverted taste. The tribute to Shakespeare recalls a phrase in "The Palace of Art,"—" Shakespeare bland and mild."

CHAPTER XIV.

THE DRAMAS.

I. Introductory. We are constantly told that dramatic
literature is intended primarily for stage representation.
But this statement will be subject to modification accord-
ing to the varying conditions imposed by the progress of
time. When a play by Shakespeare can be bought for a
penny, and a novel for threepence, the dramatist may
perhaps be pardoned if he gives a second thought to the
readers.

This, however, is certain; the playwright should in
every instance adapt his work to the actor; he should at
least write under the impression that his play will be re-
presented as actual life upon the boards of a theatre; he
cannot lose by preparing it for this final and supreme
test of dramatic worth. Doubtless his capacity for creat-
ing an infinite variety of dramatic activities directed
towards an issue clear to himself from the first, and always
complete at the last, and his faculty of giving them expres-
sion in language that will appeal with equal power to
boxes and gallery, will be tried to the uttermost; but un-
less he submits on every occasion to this sternest and
loftiest artistic training, he will not succeed.

When, therefore, we read in Tennyson's own words
that his "Becket" was "not intended in its present form

to meet the exigencies of our modern theatre," we read also its doom.[1]

Some measure of success may attend the piece when arranged for the stage by Sir. H. Irving, and interpreted by himself and a powerful company, aided by all the modern scenic accessories ; and the words of the author shall not be accepted too literally ; we will regard them rather as his habitual "prelude of disparagement;" and further, we may admit that in writing " Becket " he kept the theatre more carefully in view than before. But in order to understand the significance that still underlies his admission, we have only to refer to the one fortunate artist who produced drama at once popular, of the highest poetic merit, and of lofty purport. When Shakespeare wrote a play, he sat, as it were, on the stage, with his audience before him. He knew the tread of the stage ; he heard his every sentence declaimed ; saw every movement, every gesture interpreted by the actor even as he was writing ; he watched the faces of the gallants above or around him, and of the groundlings below. Such a statement as Tennyson's would have been absolutely impossible with Shakespeare ; we seem to hear him exclaim with astonishment, " If I did not write every word of this for the stage, what did I write it for ? Certainly not to be read ; who is going to read it ?—when, where, how, why ? "

Another useful hint is supplied by " The Promise of May." The author did not see why[2] "the great moral and social questions of the time ought not to be touched upon in a modern play." There was no reason why they should not ; but all that could be heard of " The Promise of May " before it appeared was to one and the same effect—it would deal with Agnosticism. Therefore it is

---

[1] Cf. also the note at end of Act II. in " The Foresters," where the poet in the stage copy transfers his Fairy Scene to the end of Act III. " for the sake of modern dramatic effect."

[2] Letter to Mr. Hall Caine.

presumable that a dominating purpose, moral and not artistic, was present with Tennyson when he wrote. Such a writer would scarcely keep his moral sufficiently under control. Again we refer to Shakespeare. His first business was to write a good and a successful play ; if some one had worked at the subject before, so much the better ; his re-cast would be all the more popular. Every one knew something about Julius Cæsar and Brutus ; they had already been dramatized, and were excellent material in every way. He liked the characters certainly ; but he must let them evolve themselves as the drama might determine, and not that they might please himself. He would set them in motion towards a catastrophe, and they would proceed of themselves, so to speak. Everything else, notions of imperial authority, of republican independence, the fickleness of the mob, would be incidental to the main purpose, a good and paying play.

This mention of Julius Cæsar leads up to a third short note. In Shakespeare's day history, even English history, was story. Tennyson might have done better with more romantic materials—and he did try them later, but his efforts are best regarded as experiments. Like Shakespeare, he wisely adopted history for dramatic practice ; but Shakespeare's best plays are not historical—not English history. Tennyson began too late. Age overtook him before he could get through his dramatic apprenticeship.

It is often argued that because Tennyson and Browning wrote many monodramas, they either had not the faculty of writing drama, or they destroyed it. This is partly true ; yet Shakespeare at the outset wrote his monodramas —plays with one, or at the most, two characters, like "Richard II.," "King John," "Richard III.," "A Midsummer Night's Dream," and others. He also began with some less dramatic work, "Venus and Adonis," and "Lucrece" ; and in a tentative way pieced out dramas that we know little about. But he was fortunate enough to get to work on complex drama very early in his career, and to write more of it than any other man.

In close connection with this habit of drawing one character with one environment, as opposed to the creation of characters through the medium of the infinite relations of life, we may note the tendency towards a subjective treatment manifested by most modern dramatists. Byron wrote autobiographies rather than dramas; and in many plays of Browning, Swinburne, and Tennyson the spirit of the author peers at times through the mask of his characters, or flits among them like an unquiet ghost. This disadvantage, however, is not always present, nor always disastrous when it is present; and again, it is least of all present in Shakespeare.

The classic verse drama, and dramas in prose, were removed from consideration when we spoke of Shakespeare as the one literary dramatist of the world; and on his single authority we assume that drama is a fit subject for poetic treatment. We recollect no other instance of very good poetic drama suitable for realistic stage representation at long intervals of time. But a most important consideration now follows; after all, Shakespeare lives in literature, not on the stage; his influence is perpetuated and transmitted through literature, not through the theatre. Some plays of Shakespeare are not acted at all; and for every time a play is acted it is read perhaps a million times. The present writer knew his Shakespeare almost by heart before he went for the first time in his life to see one of the great poet's plays performed at a theatre. The play was "Hamlet"; Irving and Ellen Terry were among the caste. "Well," said a friend, when it was over, "and what did you think of it?" "Two things," was the reply; "first, if good poetic drama can be acted, Shakespeare can; next, Shakespeare cannot be acted. I was never so disappointed in my life." This

took place more than twenty years ago, and the speaker
on that occasion has not found it necessary to change his
opinion.[1]

Drama, therefore, of this highest type, has a literary as
well as a spectacular aspect.

We are now in a position to ask, have the dramas of
Tennyson qualities that insure success in the theatre or
the library or both? Before answering the question we
shall do well to repeat that only one man has written plays
which have achieved an unqualified reputation both on
the stage and in the region of the higher literary art ; and
we have next to repeat that even Shakespeare is more
read than acted in the present day.

Without attempting to discuss the question of decline
in our modern drama, we may briefly notice some of the
changes that have overtaken dramatic art since the days
of Shakespeare. In his hands it had reached a perfection
that is lost to it probably for ever. Into the lifeless pro-
duct of the unities he had infused a new life by adjusting
novel complexities to a nobler symmetry. His other
achievement was to educate up to this highest level of art
a nation that had lent him much of its own creative
energy. All poetry is feigning ; it is foolishness to those
who have not learnt that the most real life may be sought
in the regions of the ideal ; and this loftiest form of the
poetic art, the Shakespearian drama, is the most difficult
to live up to.

Passing over the closing of theatres by the Puritans,
and the license of reaction that followed the Restoration,
we come to cheap printing. The drama could now be
read at home, if read at all. But cheap printing made a
market for the novel, which is little better than drama

---

[1] This may be an extreme case, but it finds a partial explanation in the
remark on p. 312, "and then music must keep away from it" ; also, in the
words of Keats, "Heard melodies are sweet, but those unheard Are
sweeter."

stripped of all the permanent adornments of art, and without any of its concentrated strength. Just as the poetic drama (and here the unities did good service) was the crowning achievement of literary form, so the novel exhibits the most striking example of an ever-recurring tendency to break loose from the fortifying and beautifying restraints of form. The unities had prescribed for the play a reasonable beginning, middle, and end ; they had assigned to it those other due limits that alone enable the human mind to comprehend the entirety of an artist's creation, to embrace all its beauty while the heart beats once, to form of it a perfect and a perpetual image in the mind. From this we turn to the novel ; one aspect alone will detain us ; why should it be included within one volume or three volumes? why should it not extend to thirty volumes? You cannot make every word of this peculiar product of imaginative literature a part of your life—and in a work of real literary art every word is vital, and every word can be remembered by reason of its exquisite adaptation to every other word and to the whole. Chiefly on this account was poetry called into being. One play of Shakespeare is vastly more precious than the entire mass of prose fiction. Briefly, a novel is as a stone flung into the stagnant pool of some human existence ; the surface stirs lazily for a moment, then returns to its dead level of stagnation ; and there is another stone at the bottom for an idle weed to cling to.

Thus the British public are no longer compelled to make their way to a playhouse where they will receive education in such high art as Shakespeare had provided ; they can carry their theatre about in their pockets—a theatre whose tendency is far less elevating. Hence their taste degenerates ; instead of being ennobled by a trilogy, they are too often debased by a novel. And now, when they go to the theatre, they go to stare at sensuous if not sensual scenery, to admire the costume of an actress or to giggle at a farce.   If the only modern art is bill-sticking, the only modern drama is the ballet—or "those gilt-gauds men-children swarm to see" (p. 397).

Of course, there is a large section of the public who can appreciate a good play, and make fit audience for a good poetic dramatist ; but of the average playgoer the above is most frequently true.   Blank verse of itself is a bar to success ; the verse that takes the popular ear is the jingle of the "brainless pantomime" (p. 397).   Truth must now be dressed up in tawdrier garments ; light or farcical drama expressed in prose holds its own against anything in Shakespeare.   This, again, may seem an ill-considered assertion ; but we have merely to ask whether Shakespeare's blank verse ever had such a run as "Our Boys."   No ; the difference is enormous and altogether convincing.

Many other causes combine to make high class plays comparatively unprofitable in our time ; but they cannot be specified here : enough may have been advanced to show that the poet-dramatist will at least find it difficult to fill the pockets of the proprietors of our modern English theatre. We may add the noteworthy fact that Tennyson has generally secured a better audience in the United States and the Colonies.   Also, what has been said of the acted poetic drama of to-day will be partly true of this drama in its literary aspects ; it cannot compete with the novel.

At the close of these preliminary considerations we now make the inquiry :   What are the characteristics of Tennyson's dramatic work?   The question will be partly answered in the following short notices of the several plays.   Meanwhile, a few general remarks may conclude this introductory section.

Long before the poet had written a single play, much less had attempted to put one on the boards of a theatre, most critics seemed to have made up their minds that Tennyson could not, or should not, write dramas.   In this respect he suffered injustice both from reviewers and from the public. On the other hand, was it worth his while to attempt this poetic drama? Possibly not. At least, we cannot admit the defence set up by some writers, that if Tennyson lacks power to produce technically perfect poetic drama, he lacks it with Homer and Dante, against whom it is never urged that they did not write in dramatic forms. This is surely absurd ; first, these poets satisfy our test of greatness ; apart from drama, each produced a perfect work on the grandest scale ; second, they did not attempt drama, and, therefore, we bring no charge of dramatic weakness against them. On the other hand, had Milton persisted in his second intention, and thrown " Paradise Lost " into dramatic form ("Samson Agonistes" does not concern us), and failed to satisfy dramatic requirements, he would have paid the penalty of being placed one or two classes lower ; but his superb poetic instinct preserved him from that fate.

Tennyson certainly began too late. He had scarcely freed himself from Shakespeare when death overtook him. He has left us plays which are often very good reading, but he had not quite learnt to write with his eye on the stage, to allow his characters to create themselves, to make the dramatic end, and that alone, justify and energize even the minutest dramatic development. His knowledge of plays was in excess of his experience as playwright, and that is one reason why he did not better adapt his genius to the conditions of his own day. It is impossible to regard his dramatic work as " The very age and body of the time." Our age may not be favourable to great creative poetry, whether dramatic or epic ; yet, had he begun earlier, all this might have been different. But he chose—as he remarked to Mr. Knowles—to respect the limitations. Therefore he began with the simplest forms of poetry, passing gradually on to the more complex. Probably he was right, especially in such a doubtful epoch. Had he set his life on the cast of the drama he might have failed altogether before the hazard of the die. On the other hand, his life, though long and fortunate, was only long enough to make him eminent as a lyric and a narrative poet, and praiseworthy as a dramatic poet.

THE HISTORICAL PLAYS: "QUEEN MARY," "HAROLD," "BECKET."

Towards the close of "Harold," "Becket," and "Queen Mary" respectively, the following passages occur:

> "*William.* Make them again one people—Norman, English."
>
> "*John of Salisbury.* Thou hast waged God's war against the King."
>
> "*Bagenhall.* God save the Crown! the Papacy is no more."

In other words, the three plays illustrate three critical periods in our national history, and thus form a kind of trilogy. The first of these periods made England a nation, well governed, and a member of civilized Europe; the second did much to save England from the tyranny that in France enslaved the people until 1789; and the third was important in preventing England from becoming a Catholic appendage of Catholic Spain.

Tennyson never worked without a conscience and an aim, and we may be sure that one of his purposes in writing these historical dramas was to exhibit in an idealized form three important stages of our national development.

But a great epoch is always the environment of great persons; hence the poet would be able to embody the spirit of each event in some leading character who should also give a name to his drama. In respect to the first and the second of these an interesting reference may be found in "The Foresters": "I love him as a damsel of his day might have loved Harold the Saxon. . . . Your great man fights not for himself, but for the people of England. . . . And how often in old histories have the great men striven against the stream, and how often in the long sweep of years to come must the great man strive against it again to save his country and the liberties of his people?"

Such a man also was Tennyson's Robin Hood. As to the third of these plays, Mary's death is Elizabeth's opportunity :

> "*Cecil.*   Never English monarch dying left England so little."
> "*Elizabeth.*   But with Cecil's aid,
> And others, if our person be secured,
> We will make England great."

"QUEEN MARY" (579).

"Queen Mary" was published in 1875. The following year, April 18th, it was played in an abridged form at the Lyceum, with Miss Bateman as Queen Mary and Sir H. Irving as Philip. In spite of clever acting and gorgeous scenery the piece enjoyed only a short run. Tennyson's first attempt to dramatize English history was also his least successful. The play is long, heavy, and dull. It lacks the most important element of all, a single and powerful tragic force—force that moves swiftly to the issue and carries all with it. Instead of this, two elements of suspense confuse whatever interest they severally possess ; the first centres in Mary's anxiety to gain Philip for a husband, the second in her anxious hope for the birth of a child. Also, many of the characters have an interest that is too special and apart from the major motives of the drama.

Indeed, we may say that some of the characters are drawn too well ; but not Philip and Mary, who are excellent. Philip cold, sensual, selfish, on whose dead heart the one word "policy" would be found written ; and Mary—no historian could ever do the unhappy queen such fair justice. But here we must be on our guard against a common error. A critic has been known to call "Becket" Tennyson's greatest work because it was such excellent history. That might become the very reason why "Becket" should be his worst work, for good history may make bad drama. Apart from this question, the portrait of Mary is admirable indeed. Many others of the characters are finely sketched, but, as observed above, they often resemble separate studies rather than human beings hurrying through the life of drama.

The dialogue is sometimes tedious, and delays the action. The style and diction are severely bare and stiff. Seldom does the poet adorn his work with the old imaginative beauty. The passage, "There runs a shallow brook . . . ." spoken by Lady Clarence in the fifth scene of Act V., reminds us of the idyllic charm which Tennyson has laid aside in order to adopt a somewhat formal and self-conscious dramatic manner. We shall find much more poetry in "Harold" and "Becket."

"HAROLD" (652)

appeared in 1876 (dated 1877). This play has never been put upon the stage, but the very considerable advance it manifests in every department of dramatic business is one ground for the statement hazarded on a former page that Tennyson began writing his dramas too late in life. Action, plot, dialogue,—singleness, continuity, and fulfilment of interest—all these are better in "Harold" than in "Queen Mary." The style is freer and wealthier; and although not flawless in respect of composition, especially as regards stage representation, the work is very readable both as play and poem. The most effective passage to the reader—and it would be the same on the stage—is the description of the fight at Senlac, where the chanting of the monks is borne to us ever and again as the din of battle rises and falls.

In one respect Harold and William bear a resemblance to Brutus and Octavius; the better man is no match for the more cunning. Harold betrays at once his weakness and his strength in the lines, "How should the King of England waste the fields Of England, his own people?" In the same spirit Brutus spared Mark Antony. Edith is a noble character, and in her sudden transformation from

girl to woman reminds us of some of Shakespeare's
heroines. Aldwyth's weakness is a foil to Edith's strength,
and it seems better to die with her who meets death
triumphantly, "Thy wife am I for ever and evermore,"
than with the miserable schemer who lives only to wail
"My punishment is greater than I can bear." As Portia
is Brutus over again in the form of a woman, so Edith
may be regarded as the counterpart of Harold, and then
Aldwyth is the shadow of William. And as it was with
the two women so may it be said of the two men—as
Tennyson himself has said it—better to fall with the
Saxon than to reign with the Norman.

"BECKET" (693).

Though next in order in the Table of Contents,
"Becket" was not published till 1884, before which date
"The Promise of May," "The Falcon," and "The Cup"
had been acted. But it naturally follows the other two
historical plays.

Again the poet gives evidence of rapid progress in
dramatic art, and his "Becket," whether read as printed,
or seen on the stage as adapted by Sir H. Irving, may
perhaps be considered as successful as any drama of the
kind out of Shakespeare. The character of Becket is by
far the best thing in the play. Next to this in interest,
and bound up with it, is the long struggle between Becket
and the King, from the game of chess in the first scene to
the magnificent climax in the cathedral at the close. But
the poet was also fortunate in his creation of Rosamund de
Clifford. By his treatment of her story he has secured an
effect which may be described as a bright idyllic vein
running through the dark mass of tragic ore. From
whatever point of view we regard the play, whether as to
character, plot, dialogue, or dramatic movement generally,
we must pronounce it a powerful work ; and again, con-
sidering the advanced age of the author and his limited

experience in this the most difficult form of art, we remain convinced not only that he possessed dramatic genius, but also that a difference of ten years might have made him —if it be at all possible in our day—a great dramatist.

"THE CUP" (750).

In 1881 this play was produced by Sir H. Irving at the Lyceum, and with much success—a success that seems at first sight out of proportion to the merit of the piece. But it gained greatly by being short, concise, and not too thoughtful for a modern taste. The story, which occurs in Plutarch's "De Mulierum Virtutibus," is as follows : Camma, wife of Sinnatus, Tetrarch of Galatia, is beloved by Synorix, an ex-Tetrarch. He murders Sinnatus, who a short time previously had saved his life. Camma flies to the Temple of Artemis.

In the second act, she is priestess of the temple. But Synorix still pleads for her hand. Recognizing an opportunity of revenge, she consents to marry him—but in the temple. According to the custom of the country, the two must first "drink together from one cup." Camma has poisoned the wine ; and Synorix, who had been false to Galatia as well as a murderer, "Poor worm, crawls down his own black hole ;" and Camma goes "on her last voyage" to meet Sinnatus.

"THE FALCON" (767).

"The Falcon" was produced at St. James's Theatre, December 18th, 1879. Mrs. Kendal represented The Lady Giovanna. This comedietta of one scene is quite a failure on the boards ; and when reading it we have sensations of the kind that used to be aroused by "The Skipping Rope," and are reminded that Tennyson's smile is too grim for this sort of work. But the material is equally unsuited to its purpose ; it is altogether too thin and bizarre to be amusing or even interesting. As a story in Boccaccio's "Decameron," or as a "Tale of a Wayside Inn,"[1] it may serve well enough ; but no amount of ingenuity could make good English Comedy out of elements so foreign, so fanciful, and so insufficient as Tennyson's "Falcon."

Count Federigo degli Alberighi loves the wealthy widow The Lady Giovanna. He had loved her before her marriage, and now he spends all his money in the purchase of a diamond necklace that may win her favour. The Count has a falcon that he loves almost as much as he loves the lady. It happens that her son, who is so ill that the mother speaks of him as "my dying boy," has such a longing for the Count's falcon that nothing but the possession of it may save his life. The Lady Giovanna goes to the house of the penniless Count to beg the bird of him, and she invites herself to breakfast. The Count's larder is empty. He hesitates between his love for his falcon and his love for Giovanna. He chooses the latter, and the poor bird is killed to supply the table. While the meal is being prepared, the Count reminds Giovanna of their early love. But the mother is most in her heart ; and she asks the falcon for her sick boy. Then she learns that the Count has killed it for her sake, and she yields him her love.

This sketch alone will reveal some of the many weaknesses inherent in the drama. The Count's love for his bird is a very doubtful motive to an English audience ; and the stronger motive that impelled the mother to approach the Count, to beg of him what he loved so well, to turn from him when he withheld it, wastes itself in a futility that is fatal to the other dramatic issues.

"THE PROMISE OF MAY" (778).

This play was produced at the Globe Theatre, Novem-

---

[1] The Student's Tale—"The Falcon of Sir Federigo."—LONGFELLOW.

ber 11th, 1882, under the direction of Mrs. Bernard-Beere. It was a complete failure. On the night of November 14th of the same year, as the piece was nearing the close of the first act, the Marquis of Queensberry sprang to his feet exclaiming " I beg to protest . . . . " ; but adding, " I will wait till the end of the act," he returned to his seat. When the curtain had fallen he again stood up, and, confessing himself an agnostic, declared that Tennyson's Edgar was an "abominable caricature" into whose mouth the poet had put sentiments that did not exist among freethinkers.

The passages in the play to which the speaker referred are the long soliloquy of Edgar, beginning " Jealous of me with Eva !" and some of the speeches which subsequently in the same act he addresses to Eva. Had the marquis understood Tennyson's method of dealing with such subjects (see p. 378), and his habit of expressing himself through the lips of a character purposely exaggerated— both of which he might have learnt from the two "Locksley Halls" and " Maud"; or had Tennyson, on the other hand, been content with the monodramatic pulpit from which he had so often thundered unanswerable, the painful scene at the Globe might have been avoided. What Tennyson seizes upon in such cases, is the *tendency;* the agnostic of to-day can afford to be moral ; he must be moral ; morality is in the air he breathes ; it flows in his veins ; he shakes it everywhere by the hand ; but, sternest truth of all, he is heir to the glorious humanities fought for and won by century after century of Christian life. He cannot spend this inheritance in a day ; but, living henceforth without an ideal, he or his children after him will squander the priceless bequest. We cannot— even in the nineteenth century—live by bread alone :

> "A soul with no religion—
> My mother used to say that such a one
> Was without rudder, anchor, compass—might be

> Blown every way with every gust, and wreck
> On any rock."
>
> *Promise of May*, Act III.

" See thou fail not," were Tennyson's words of apprehension and warning so long before as 1850 ("In Memoriam," xxxiii.) ; and this drama of "The Promise of May" is a latter-day sermon on the old text.

While we are regarding the play in its ethical aspect, we may remember the significance of mere titles in Tennyson, and briefly consider the words " The Promise of May." The tragic note is struck early, and their first and obvious interpretation will be found at the beginning as well as the end of the drama—" O joy for the promise of May . . . . O grief for the promise of May." The salt wind of agnosticism will wither away the beauty from nature and from human life ; a kite will stoop down and still the cooing of the dove. Or again, near the end, we learn that five years of shame and suffering have broken the heart of one so lovely in the promise of her May. It is woman therefore, the mainstay of society, who will have most to fear from such a disruption of society as the poet dreams of. From first to last Tennyson refuses to believe that woman can ever be identified with man : from first to last he assigns to her a position in which, if we may judge from this play, she can retain one at least of her old prerogatives ; for though in future years man may not any longer permit her to be a blessing to him, he will not withhold from her the privilege of suffering for him.

But, as already hinted, the stage is no safe place for preaching a sermon. "The Promise of May" suffered both internally and externally from a pronounced ethical intention. The poet probably fondled his moral purpose to the detriment of his dramatic duties ; and a section of the public came prepared to express disapproval. Others of the audience soon felt called upon to condemn what they regarded as a repulsive character placed in situations of doubtful propriety.

Yet the failure of the play should be traced, not to character nor morality nor incident, but to general weakness of composition. Still, it would be a pity if a work containing so much of the wealth and the beauty of genius should be lost sight of, or remembered only as a literary curiosity. And it is by no means impossible that "The Promise of May" will be read and admired when every ethical novel of our time has long been forgotten.

"THE FORESTERS" (857).

This romantic pastoral drama was produced at Daly's Theatre, New York, on the 19th of March, 1892. A few weeks later it was published by Messrs. Macmillan. It met with good fortune on the American stage; and we have before noticed, among the varying conditions of dramatic success, that Tennyson's plays have sometimes been appreciated by the younger England when they have failed to satisfy the mother country.

This latest of Tennyson's dramas is even more Shakespearean than the historical plays; yet it is not so suitably nor so consistently Shakespearean as they are. But first, one does not see why it need be Shakespearean at all. The mere fact that it copies the manner of one man in a bygone age makes it much less interesting to us.

Next, we can hardly fail to detect an unpleasant element of burlesque or pantomime which may imply that the poet was determined in this instance to write down to the modern stage, if he had not the strength to lift it to his level. The Fairy Scene, fortunately, is not like anything in Shakespeare. Once more we are reminded of "The Skipping Rope"; for this scene is sheer pantomime; it has nothing in common with the delicate grace of the elves in "A Midsummer Night's Dream." Something

like it in manner, but less obtrusive, is the dialogue
between Robin and Marian at the opening of Act IV.—

> " *Marian.* The sweet light of a mother's eye,
> That beam of dawn upon the opening flower. . . ."

If Shakespeare were writing the scene, he might put
such language into the mouth of Robin, but not of Marian
—of lovesick Orlando, but not of smart Rosalind. Further
on we read :

> " *Marian.* And out upon all simple batchelors !
> Ah well ! thou seest the land has come between us,
> And my sick father here has come between us,
> And this rich Sheriff too has come between us ;
> So is it not all over now between us ? "

And again a few lines further on :

> " *Marian.* What wilt thou do with the bond then ?
> *Robin.* Wait and see.
> What wilt thou do with the Sheriff ?
> *Marian.* Wait and see."

These two passages are below the standard of " As You
Like It " ; to find parallels we should have to refer to
" Love's Labour's Lost." And in such passages, again,
we fear lest the poet may seem to " flicker down to brain-
'ess pantomime," or at the least to low comedy.

From this consideration of the dialogue, we should
naturally proceed to the characters ; Marian, for example,
according to the scene, or the part of the scene, is liable
to change, not her mood, but her personality ; in fact, as
the play goes forward, she catches the manners of some
half-dozen of the heroines of Shakespeare.

But these trifling violations of dramatic propriety vanish
altogether from our mind as we think of the great poet, of
his advanced age, his sylvan theme, his charming play.
If any plea were needed, he has one formulated in words
spoken by his Robin Hood :—" Being out of the law, how
should we break the law ? if we broke into it again we

should break the law, and then we were no longer out-laws."

Before taking leave of Tennyson's dramas, a word should be said about the songs. Two of these in " The Foresters" had appeared before ; the song in Act II., "There is no land like England," is adapted from the " National Song " of the 1830 volume ; and the " New Review " for March, 1891, first published the musical but mournful "To Sleep ! " in Act I., Scene 3. The songs in the dramas generally are excellent in themselves and appropriate to the context.

CHAPTER XV.

"DEMETER AND OTHER POEMS."

"DEMETER and Other Poems" was published on December 13th, 1889, and it is said that 20,000 copies were sold within a week. Tennyson was now eighty years of age; and although in this and the other late volumes we may miss youthful fancy and ardour, we discover maturity of imagination fine as ever and a strengthening sobriety of thought. Nor does the art form suffer except from an occasional laxity. We may add that at this stage a new question of date will sometimes arise; we shall now have to inquire, how recent is this poem? is it the production of the poet of fourscore years, or was it found on "sallow scraps of manuscript"?

(804) "TO THE MARQUIS OF DUFFERIN AND AVA." Tennyson's younger son, Lionel, was attacked by fever in India, and died on his journey home, 20th April, 1886. He had received great kindness from Lord Dufferin, to whom he became much attached. In the rhythm o this tender poem a very notable line occurs—"Fell—and flashed into the Red Sea." No such variation of the metrical structure occurs in all the stanzas of "In Memoriam"; nearest would come the line, "On the bald

street breaks the blank day" (ix.). The "Might have
been" is from " In Memoriam," lxxv. 4.

(805) "ON THE JUBILEE OF QUEEN VICTORIA." These
lines are another experiment in metrical contrast, but not
a very successful one. They were first published in
"Macmillan's Magazine," for April, 1887, under the title
of "Carmen Seculare." The characteristic sections ix.
and xi. further illustrate some remarks which will be
found on many former pages, such as 25-28, 266, 378.

(806) "DEMETER AND PERSEPHONE (IN ENNA)." The
lines to Professor Jebb contain a very apt figure, that of
the wheat which after thousands of years of burial in
Egypt bore sweet grain in England. But the story of
Ceres and Proserpine, long buried in its Sicilian haunt,[1]
has blossomed on our colder island into an alien flower.
It is useless to ask which is the more beautiful, the old
classic legend or the modern adaptation of it in Tenny-
son's "Demeter and Persephone"; both are beautiful,
and we can possess them both.

Tennyson's poem is the occasion of yet another and a
magnificent song to the honour and glory of motherhood ;
and the Earth-mother becomes a type of all the mothers
of humanity. Among the many modern touches given to
the classic theme, the most notable is Demeter's "Gods
indeed . . . ," and her interpretation of the dark saying
of the Fates, "There is a Fate beyond us"; the classic
ground is abandoned abruptly when we read of younger
kindlier gods who will "send the noon into the night and
break The sunless halls of Hades into Heaven."

To his title, "Demeter and Persephone," the poet adds
the words " in Enna," because he gives us only one episode
of the story ; but into that one episode he contrives to

1 Belike the tale, wept over otherwhere
  Of those old days is clean forgotten there."
                                    The Earthly Paradise.

introduce almost the whole legend. The episode will be best explained by the following abstract from Ovid's "Metamorphoses," at the end of which it will be added.

Persephone, daughter of Demeter and Zeus, is carried off by Dis whilst she is gathering flowers in the fields near Enna in Sicily. Dis descends with her to Hades, where she becomes his queen. Meanwhile, the mother seeks her daughter through all lands—"The world was too little for her in this search." When at last she learns her daughter's fate, she appeals to Zeus, who, after some demur, arranges that Persephone shall live half the year with her husband, and half with her mother. In Tennyson's poem the mother pours out her heart to her child then first reclaimed.

Much of the material of "Demeter and Persephone" is classical in origin, yet enough remains of Tennyson's own, whether of thought or form, to fill us with wonder and admiration. Close examination of the poem will further reveal old familiar phrases and sentiments of which the following are a few examples : "climate-changing bird," "can no more," "from state to state," "thro' clouded memories" ; "the wail of midnight winds," that "shrilled their answer." The "shrilly whinnyings" may be compared with the "whinny shrills" of "The Princess" ; there also is a form of "thridded."

In style the poem comes nearest to "Tithonus" ; only the verse is more bountiful and joyous and made almost articulate with the yearning love of a mother for her child. Of all the classical pieces this is the most tenderly English.

(809) "Owd Roä." (See p. 269, footnote.) With touches of humour here and there, a farmer tells his son how Old Rover saved the lad's life ten years before.

(812) "Vastness" was published in "Macmillan's

Magazine," March, 1885.   Much may be learnt from the
title of this poem, and much from the " Epilogue to the
Charge of the Heavy Brigade " :

" The vast sun-cluster's gather'd blaze . . . Amaze our
brief humanities—no! . . . . the man remains."   No con-
viction is so constantly forced upon Tennyson as this : if
we end in being our own corpse-coffins, then life is no
better than " a trouble of ants in the gleam of a million
million of suns."   But in this vastness lives our hope ;
" we that are not all, As parts can see but part " ; on the
scale of infinity all is well; "the dead are not dead, but
alive."

For other expressions of this belief see " In Memoriam,"
xxxiv., xxxv. ; " Locksley Hall Sixty Years After," 30-36 ;
and there are yet more, especially of this later period.
Here again we have the history of the poet's many dis-
illusions, followed by an impetuous assertion of hope, and
in this respect as in some others, the poem closely
resembles " Locksley Hall Sixty Years After."   For one
example of the first, we may mention stanza 7, which
deals with commerce ; and as to the second, in spite of the
vagueness of the close, the poem is powerful and impres-
sive, and with the main argument we may compare Keble,

> " For dreary were this earth, if earth were all,
> Tho' brighten'd oft by dear Affection's kiss."

(813) "THE RING."   Here a story, improbable, and in
some other respects like the story of " The Sisters," serves
chiefly as a frame for much picturesque philosophy.   It
would seem that as the great poet drew towards his earthly
end, his thoughts wandered oftener and farther beyond
the confines of earth ; and in his autumn he frequently
dwells on the eternal miracle of spring.

At the outset of this existence—as stated in " De Pro-
fundis,"—we wail being born ; but in " The Ring," the
dead have " gone up so far " that they too are losing their

moments of earth as we forget our pain of birth and our lament for antenatal life. This theory of " Æonian Evolution" is set forth towards the end of the poem; but it occurs in another passage near the beginning :—" No sudden heaven, nor sudden hell; My Miriam breaks her latest earthly link With me to-day."

Thus then the dead may linger lovingly about us for awhile. But in " In Memoriam," xli.-xlvii., li., lxxxv., xciii., cxxix., cxxx., the poet inclines to the belief that the bond which binds the dead to the living is never broken. And in " The Sisters " we find no hint of final separation ; the man who loved them both has reached " the quiet of declining life," and yet they glide about him still.

As in " Rizpah " and other poems, the wind becomes a medium of communication between " the Ghost in Man " and " the Ghost that once was Man,"—" one silent voice Came on the wind " : and similarly in four or five other passages. Beautiful is the line, " And utter knowledge is but utter love"; which condenses the fuller thought of " In Memoriam," li., and lxxxv. 6, 7, 20-23, and of " Epilogue," 36 and 37. Also we notice that, as once before, the poet speaks of a light in the eyes of the dead that comes from the other life.

Tennyson never wholly rids himself of the older notion, "God made the woman for the use of man " ; this is another instance in which " The Ring " resembles " The Sisters." The attitude of the man is entirely condescending ; not so much in this poem as in many others ; though here " No voice for either spoke within my heart " ; and either is looked upon as a bride to be won by a ring ; and both, of course, are in love with a man whose intimacy is at least an unknown quantity. Also, at the end, "the larger woman-world " is—as it was in " The Princess " and " In Memoriam "—the world " Of wives and mothers." It is the same in " Becket "—" So rare the household honey-making bee, Man's help."

The poem contains much beauty of language and description, some of it old, some new :—"A thousand squares of corn and meadow" ; " Made every moment of her after life A virgin victim to her memory" ; " Making with a kindly pinch Each poor pale cheek a momentary rose" ; " The tiny fist Had grasped a daisy from your mother's grave " ; the figure following, " I gazed into the mirror" ; and the passage beginning, " My people too were scared with eerie sounds " ; all these are of Tennyson's best. The expression " all-in-all " again occurs ; it has done duty very often indeed ; " that All-in-all " ("Akbar's Dream "). We recognize also " Æonian," " I loved and love," " statue-like,' and the rest. But more important to our purpose at this stage of our inquiry is the verse structure ; absolutely bad lines are always rare in Tennyson ; the most daring experiments occur in " The Princess " ; yet it may be doubted whether there is a really reprehensible line in that poem. Here we may find one occasionally :—" And all ablaze too plunging in the lake" ; " At times, too, shrilling in her angrier moods."

(821) " FORLORN." As so often in Tennyson, and less often in Shelley, the metre and the thought are as bride and bridegroom. In this ballad it might seem that the mere metrical arrangement could by itself tell the tale of feverous shame and shuddering despair. As to the tale itself, it is another of this series of stern lessons bearing on the relation between the sexes ; though we may doubt whether the poet has not weakened rather than strengthened his poem by adding disease to crime—" You that lie with wasted lungs."

(822) " HAPPY—THE LEPER'S BRIDE." In this ballad on the other hand disease purifies love ; " Happy " follows " Forlorn," and not without purpose ; the principle they illustrate is the same ; the sacredness of love, the sanctity

of marriage; but the first poem, if not the second also, borders on the repulsive. Again, in "Happy," Tennyson separates the "human ghost" from the "poor rib-grated dungeon of the body"; and as in "In Memoriam," poems cxxii. and lxxxv., "moving each to music" they "shall flash thro' one another." But Tennyson has told us that "The living soul" of this 85th poem is not Hallam's, but the "general soul." The cheerful metre of "Happy" is an old one made delightfully new.

(825) "To Ulysses." As in the address to E. Fitzgerald, so in this to W. G. Palgrave, the lines run on without a break; and it is curious to note the novel music of the "In Memoriam" stanza. The poem contains light, clear sketches of nature; and in poetical guise gives its own date—"The century's three strong eights."

(826) "To Mary Boyle." There is something of Horace in this little ode, but much more that Horace could not have written. It is graceful, thoughtful, pathetic; but it is less hopeful than Tennyson's wont. Addressed to a woman, the stanzas are delicate and the tone is feminine. It was just the opposite with the verses "To E. Fitzgerald" and "To Ulysses." The half a hundred years and the rick-fire days, of which the poet makes a figure in the fourth Canto of "The Princess," take us back to Somersby, which the Tennysons did not leave till 1837.

(827) "The Progress of Spring." This poem, "Found yesterday—forgotten mine own rhyme By mine old self," and dating about 1836, is apparently not quite finished; but it would be difficult to find a more delightful or more spiritual study of the gradual yearly return of life and beauty to the English landscape.

(829) "MERLIN AND THE GLEAM." This poem reads like an expansion of two lines in "Freedom":

> "O follower of the Vision, still
> In motion to the distant gleam,"

to which may be added "The Voyage," when "one fair Vision ever fled. . . . And still we followed where she led."

As we approach the end of the volume, the poems become more personal and more sacred. In this, though the metre is almost archaic, we have a beautiful and touching description of the life of the great artist, who in seeking the ideal probably achieved more real good for the modern higher life than any other man of his time. First the gleam flickered above the springs of fancy, then for ten years, repelled by the croak of critics, it retreated, but the poet followed still, and it glanced on lyric and monologue and idyll, it illumined the legend of Arthur the King, threw a divine light on the lament for Arthur Hallam, mingled a ray of immortality with the melodies that sang through the world in later years ; and now, having led the poet to the land's last limit, it stood hovering "on the border Of boundless Ocean, And all but in Heaven."

In section 9, those whose journey lies before them are bidden to follow the Gleam. For these the quest of ideal truth and beauty should be easier now that the great magician has trodden all their road, leaving footprints into which they may press their steps. To make these footprints clearer is the main purpose of this "Handbook to Tennyson."

The poet had already chosen Merlin as a *nom de plume* when he contributed "Britons guard your own" and other poems to "The Examiner," in 1852.

It is not easy to piece out the allegory of "Merlin and the Gleam." The poet traverses life from the "morning hills" down by cataract and wilderness over the level to the ocean shore. Those he leaves behind are young mariners charged to launch their vessel upon the ocean which is about to withdraw his being to its own (p. 371).

(831) "ROMNEY'S REMORSE." This is yet another story founded on the relationship of marriage. An artist who had deserted his wife in order that he might be free to follow art, comes back to her at last, and dies blest by her loving care. " To you my days have been a life-long lie Grafted on half a truth," the half-truth being Sir Joshua's remark that "marriage spoilt an artist." This half-truth looks a whole falsehood in the searching light of such another poem as " The Wreck," or in such a sentence as the following from this poem, " The world would lose, if such a wife as you Should vanish unrecorded"; or again, where the artist says of his desertion, " One truth will damn me with the mindless mob." Here Tennyson takes up once more his unthankful theme of adverse criticism in life or after death. The mindless mob, first of all, are exposed to his contempt as often as Shakespeare's ; but with Shakespeare there was a difference. Next, he would again anticipate the " myriad lies that blacken round The corpse of every man that gains a name." How strange it is, and how sad withal, that the great poet who could write a line like this, "What is true at last shall tell," should by his querulous apprehensions call down upon himself some of the condemnation which he dreaded.

The last scene in the history of this half-truth is laid in another world than ours—" Why left you wife and child? for my sake? According to my word? . . . ."

There are good things in the poem—the lovely picture of mother and child, " I dream'd last night. . . ." We meet with the staghorn moss, the white heather, the placid lake, the falling water, the murmuring bee, and all the breath and beauty of the mountain side.

"What artist ever yet Could make pure light live on the canvas?" "the chasm between Work and Ideal," are deeply interesting as expressions relating to art. By the side of the first we place Browning's "And so *they are better painted*"; the second is a truism of every true artist.

(834) "PARNASSUS." The purport of the quotations from Horace is as follows :

> "My work is finished. Yea, this book of song
> Is Flaccus' stately monument, more strong,
> More lasting than the proud memorial brass,
> Than brazen-moulded bust. It doth surpass
> The height of regal pyramid ; no shower
> Shall this corrode, nor have the north winds power
> On this, to shake it, nor the all-conquering years,
> Nay, nor the yearless æons."

Horace suggests the theme, but not its unexpected development.

The poets on the summit of "Parnassus" have been beautiful crowned forms ; may he be one with them, rolling his music till it mingles with the music of the spheres. But! there stand also—in modern times—two shapes, not beautiful, but huge, ever huger, dwarfing the muses, deadening their song.

For the voice of Geology is that of an "ever-breaking shore That tumbled in the Godless deep," and more fearful still is the funeral chant of Astronomy :

> "Stars and systems through dead space are drifting,
> To shine no more."

In "Literary Squabbles" we hear both of these terrible Muses rolling their doom. "Parnassus" has nothing to do with the inroads made by science into the regions of emotion and imagination ; it is merely the counter reflection to "Quod non . . . . possit diruere . . . ." etc., a counter reflection that might also be set down in Latin :

> "Nec me animi fallit, quam res nova miraque menti
> Accidat, exitium cœli terræque futurum."

"The sight confuses," says Tennyson.

> "Et quam difficile id mihi sit pervincere dictis,"

adds Lucretius.

There is a third reflection. This also we shall find both in Tennyson and Lucretius :

> " In a boundless universe
> Is boundless better, boundless worse "—
>> *Two Voices.*

> "Sic igitur mundi naturam totius ætas
> Mutat, et ex alio terram status excipit alter,
> Quod potuit, nequeat ; possit, quod non tulit ante."
>> *De Rerum Natura.*

In Section III. of "Parnassus" Tennyson reaches beyond his predecessor on the poetic throne :

> " If thou, indeed, derive thy light from Heaven,
> Then to the measure of that heaven-born light,
> Shine, Poet ! in thy place, and be content."
>> WORDSWORTH.

(834) "BY AN EVOLUTIONIST." As bodily existence was given to us in order that we might learn the " me " and the " not me " (" In Memoriam," xlv.), so also was it given to us that we might " move upwards " by " working out the beast " ; which reminds us of Milton's " Till body up to spirit work."

This, then, is the Ascent of Man from one point of view. Also we were told in " In Memoriam" that only thus might the ascent be made. The doctrine is fully stated in the fifty-third section of that poem.

But the first stanza of " By an Evolutionist " implies that " we are raised a spiritual body." We are raised then by death, as well as by a life that works out the beast.

One thought remains. These are the reflections of age ; it is the aged man who "hears the yelp of the beast"; " in the Past " he " sank with the body at times." The doctrine therefore of " In Memoriam," liii. must not be preached as a truth to the young that eddy round and round. Still, let us hope that there are exceptional cases in which the beast is worked out earlier—in middle age, youth, childhood.

The poem is a little uncouth in form and in thought.

(835) " Far-Far-Away." (See Appendix to Chap. VII).

(835) " Politics." (See p. 21.)

(835) " Beautiful City." " The red fool-fury of the Seine " has all along been eyed with suspicion by our poet. These lines may date near to 1889, for we have met with "raving Paris" so recently as " Locksley Hall Sixty Years After." In that poem also may be found a couplet of kindred thought, "And Reversion ever dragging Evolution in the mud."

(836) " The Roses on the Terrace." These lines were probably addressed to a sister of Mary Boyle. (See p. 423.)

(836) " The Play," may have been suggested by Quarles :

> " My soul, sit thou a patient looker-on,
> Judge not the play before the play is done.
> Its plot has many changes : ev'ry day
> Speaks a new scene : the last act crowns the play."

" Gloom'd " in the first line is one of Tennyson's earlier words. As a participle it is awkward. Of these four lines the first and third are very poor.

(836) " On One who Affected an Effeminate Manner." (836) " To One who Ran Down the English." Like " The Play," these two pieces that follow it are " poor indeed."

(836) "THE SNOWDROP." Spelt by age, this trifle has claim to our respect.

(836) "THE THROSTLE." (" The New Review," October, 1889.)—But this is something very different. Its only rival, as far as we can recollect, is Mr. Swinburne's "Itylus." Also it may be compared with Tennyson's earlier effort, "The Owl"; and with "The Swallow Song" in "The Princess."

(836) "THE OAK"—This is another inspiration, of which the briefest criticism will also be the best. The thing described and the describing verse have grown incorporate into one monumental Being.

(837) "IN MEMORIAM—W. G. WARD." The subject of these memorial lines was William George Ward, the theologian, who died in 1882. He was the author of "Ideal of a Christian Church, etc.," a work whose ultramontanism was described by Dr. Pusey as being " very strong."

CHAPTER XVI.

"THE DEATH OF ŒNONE, AKBAR'S DREAM, AND OTHER POEMS."[1]

LORD TENNYSON died on the 6th of October, 1892, and this last volume was published a few weeks later. A mournful sacredness invests its pages, and criticism should speak softly. The book opens with a beautiful and tender dedication to his wife—"JUNE BRACKEN AND HEATHER."

(838) "TO THE MASTER OF BALLIOL."—These lines to the late Professor Jowett contain an allusion to the "downward thunder of the brook," which in the first "Œnone" fell "In cataract after cataract to the sea."

(838) "THE DEATH OF ŒNONE."—As we left the lonely mountain nymph of the earlier poem, the noise of

---

[1] Omitted poems of Tennyson's later years are some introductory verses to "Rosa Rosarum," by E. V. B. (the Hon. Mrs. Boyle), (1884) ; a stanza contributed to a small pamphlet printed for the benefit of the Chelsea Hospital for Women (March, 1884) ; a stanza in the volume of his poems that was presented to the Princess Louise of Schleswig-Holstein by representatives of the nurses of England ; lines on the christening of the infant daughter of the Duchess of Fife ; lines to the memory of J. R. Lowell ; and a prefatory stanza of four lines to "Pearl" (edited by Mr. Israel Gollancz).

battle was ringing in our ears. Now the ten years' war of Troy is over ; but in her cave Œnone sits still desolate ; the wandering ivy and vine that hung in rich festoons are dead cords dripping with the wintry mist. Through these her sad eyes look down the long glen, or rest on the naked bower where once she saw her Paris judge of gods. On a sudden he comes again, no longer beauteous as a god, but livid, moaning, pierced by a poisoned dart. Only Œnone may heal his wound—" Go back to thine adulteress and die."

He groaned, turned, passed downward through the mist, fell headlong dead. The mountain shepherds came ; they built for their old playmate a funeral pyre. In her dream she heard a wailing, " Come to me, Œnone ! " Led by the silent cry and the low gleam of death, she paced the torrent path, to the broader vale, came to the pile, cast herself upon it, and past in fire with him.

It would be idle to speak of this poem as betraying little or no falling off in power or beauty. As a fact it presents signs of decaying strength in every aspect, and should certainly be among the latest compositions of the poet. The story can scarcely bear a classic name ; its one classical element is the unforgiving daughter of the river-god ; and, of course, there is some local colouring, such as mountain shepherds and the funeral pyre. The descriptive passages are less striking, and less perfect. But they possess nearly all the old charm ; they are well adapted to the wintry theme, and they are sparse accordingly ; yet " Which drowsed in gloom, self-darken'd from the west " ; " She waked a bird of prey that screamed and past," are examples which to those who recall the poet's earlier imagery must seem a little at fault. The verse shows more signs of weakness ; it has not entirely lost the old movement and melody, but at times it falters. The very first line runs into the second after the manner of certain verses in " The Princess," rather than that of the classical

poems. In "The Princess," moreover, nearly every personage who comes on the stage makes his or her strongly accented bow from the forefront of the line, and pauses :—
"The Princess, liker to the inhabitant . . . ." "Melissa, with her hand upon the lock . . . " ; and although the posture is not unknown in the earlier classical poems and the "Idylls of the King," yet Paris three times occupies that prominent position in the later "Œnone." This may be of design ; but turning to peculiarities not of design, we may point out the following among many lines that drag : "Amazed, and ever seeming stared upon . . . ." "One raised the Prince, one sleek'd the squalid hair" ; "Which drowsed in gloom, self-darken'd from the west" ; "His face deform'd by lurid blotch and blain" ; "Fell headlong dead ; and of the shepherds one . . . ." This last line, which is the most striking example, will also discover—as do many of the others—the extent to which the master's hand has lost its cunning in the arrangement of vowel sounds. But the subject cannot be pursued further.

And now, on the other hand, we have one more of those many beautiful and often sad stories arising out of married love or the loss of it, which the poet has delighted to tell in his latter years. We might see in "The Death of Œnone" the counterpart of "Romney's Remorse" ; add to that poem the word "Adulterer," and the tragedy enacted on the mountain slope by Ilion becomes possible even in the nineteenth century.

But lastly, in deep reverence to goddess and nymph and demigod, and to the great poet who has so often newly-created both these and their divine abodes, we may thankfully read "The Death of Œnone" as a "Grecian tale re-told."[1]

(840) "St. Telemachus." There are fewer signs of

---

[1] Re-told also—or part of it—by Landor and William Morris

declining power in this poem ; the extra syllables in the blank verse—" That Rome no more should wallow in this old lust "—might scarcely determine a recent date. It may nearly belong to the most perfect period of Tennyson's authorship. Some of the descriptive passages are very fine—the call of God that drove Telemachus to Rome ; the unchristian splendour of the Christian city ; the pagan crowd ; the Colosseum where 80,000 Christians watched man murder man ; his deed that woke the world. The dramatic situation is a noble one ; the saint who had so long been lazying out his life in self-suppression, makes swift atonement by one deed of self-sacrifice.

(842) " Akbar's Dream." This fine poem breathes of that tolerance and love and peace which possesses great and good souls when nearing their earthly goal. Akbar, like Tennyson himself, seeks

> " To spread the Divine Faith
> Like calming oil on all their stormy creeds."

The figure here employed is but one in a poem peculiarly rich in metaphor—" The wild horse, anger, plunged to fling me, and failed " ; " To hunt the tiger of oppression out " ; " Those cobras ever setting up their hoods " ; are a few among many. Very interesting is the prophecy after the event—" From out the sunset poured . . . . My mission be accomplished " ; and a graceful poetic tribute to our Indian Empire. The Hymn to the Sun at the close is in Tennyson's happiest manner.

(847) " The Bandit's Death " has much but not all of the old dramatic power and picturesqueness. A woman lives with a bandit who killed her husband. She bears him a son—a link between them. Some time after this, when they are hiding from soldiers, the bandit strangles the child, lest its crying should betray them ; he

curses himself for the deed, yet sleeps. Then the mother kills the bandit with the dagger that has slain her husband. The peculiarity of "The Bandit's Death" is that of a double motive. It would seem as though in this last poem Tennyson strove to blend the instincts of wifehood and motherhood into one stronger passion. But our divided interest militates against his purpose ; although we may understand that whereas the wife merely endured a murderer, the mother struck him dead.

(848) "THE CHURCH-WARDEN AND THE CURATE." Of all the poems in dialect this is perhaps the most humorous. It is founded on a tale told in the Memoirs of Julian Young. (See p. 269, footnote.)

(850) "CHARITY." This is the last of the many poems —mostly dramatic monologues—that are founded on the relation of the sexes. A woman who has been ruined is dressing a grave with flowers. She is approached by another beast of prey in the form of a man—the friend of him who had ruined her. She reads him a stern lesson and then tells the story of the grave·—" 'Will you move a little that way ? your shadow falls on the grave.' He married the heiress of half a shire ; I sent him a wail and a curse and his money. He was killed in the train ; and his wife was widowed on her bridal day. But she found my letter upon him ; she came and nursed me when my dead child was born. At last I learnt who the Christ-like creature was ; together we prayed for him. She became a hospital nurse, and died of a fever caught in the wards. She had left me money. God sees not her like anywhere in this pitiless world. 'Get you gone ; I am dressing her grave with flowers.'"

The poem is better than "The Bandit's Death ;" and the subject befits the pen of one that writes amid the closing scenes of life. It is the story of George Eliot's

"Romola," and it carries with it the same moral—"Man, can you even guess at the love of a soul for a soul?"

(851) "KAPIOLANI" is less advanced in doctrine than "Akbar's Dream"; Akbar desired to worship beneath "a dome of nobler span" than pagod, mosque, or church; Kapiolani would worship in church rather than pagod; would abjure the Spirit of Evil, and call on the power adored by the Christian.

(852) "THE DAWN." This is an expansion of two lines added to the first edition of the "Ode sung at the opening of the International Exhibition":

> "Is the time so far away?
> Far—how far no tongue can say."

In "The Princess" the thought is more hopefully expressed:

> "This fine old world of ours is but a child
> Yet in the go-cart. Patience! Give it time
> To learn its limbs: there is a hand that guides."

But now, looking back upon a long life, the poet will naturally mourn over the slow Ascent of Man.

(852) "THE MAKING OF MAN." And here, after looking at that darker side of doubt, and in the mood of reaction so habitual to him, the poet fixes his prophetic eye where even the fainter red of the dawn is fading away in the light of a rising sun.

(853) "THE DREAMER." This is a cast into a deeper future. "The Making of Man" concerned itself with this earth that we sometimes care to cherish and to deem worthy of the Maker; "where the races flower and fade . . . till the peoples all are one." But while earth follows the Sun, the Sun himself is racing from heaven to heaven;

and in the eternal making of the frame of things, less is to be lost than won ; the Reign of the Meek may begin upon earth, but their reign shall know no end ; merged in the music of the spheres, the fitful moan of earth shall become an everlasting harmony.

(853) "MECHANOPHILUS." A deeply interesting elaboration of the following couplet of " Locksley Hall :

"Men, my brothers, men the workers, ever reaping something new ;
That which they have done but earnest of the things that they shall do."

The poem is an unqualified pæan to practical science and the industries. In later life the poet would have added language like Ruskin's in the preface to " Sesame and Lilies," new edition ; or like Carlyle's at the time of the first exhibition ; or like his own in " Locksley Hall Sixty Years After"—"Art and grace are less and less.'' As in the seventh stanza, both form and substance are occasionally imperfect.

(854) "RIFLEMEN FORM." In " The Times" for May 9th, 1859, these patriotic verses, now slightly altered, were entitled " The War," and were followed by the signature " T." Owing to the hostile attitude of France, the War Office, in May, 1859, sanctioned the establishment of Volunteers, and before the end of the year nearly 200,000 were enrolled in our citizen army.

(854) "THE TOURNEY." A spirited ballad of the times when men fought themselves into a lady's favour.

(854) "THE WANDERER." A simple lay of hospitality and the grateful guest.

(855) "POETS AND CRITICS." These last words to the critics are less ungracious ; had none others appeared

before them, they would have been more worthy of a place in the volume. We may be ill-advised, but we venture to think that in these pages also "perfect stillness" would be best. The critic was never so kindly, so sagacious, nor so much of an artist as in the days of Matthew Arnold and his successors. As to the "But seldom comes the poet here," it takes the tone of Horace:

> " Mediocribus esse poetis
> Non homines, non di non concessere columnæ."

We hear it also in "The Poet," "The Poet's Mind," and "Poets, those rare souls," in "The Princess." Longfellow, somewhere, has a beautiful thought for the poet who is second or third, or yet more humbly placed in the world's esteem ; and this chance reference to Longfellow brings to our mind his well-known lines, so unassuming and so winning:

> "If any thought of mine, or sung or told,
> Has ever given delight or consolation,
> Ye have repaid me back a thousandfold."

Longfellow may not be a great poet in the eyes of the world ; but, strange to say, there are times when we would not wish him greater.

(855) "A VOICE SPAKE OUT OF THE SKIES." This is a variation of the doctrine so often insisted upon by Tennyson, and set forth in its finest form in "Locksley Hall Sixty Years After":

> "Take the charm 'for ever' from them, and they crumble into dust."

(855) "DOUBT AND PRAYER." (855) "FAITH." (855) "THE SILENT VOICES." (856) "GOD AND THE UNI-VERSE." In these four sacred poems the poet already holds communion with an unseen world ; but at times he turns lovingly towards us whom he is leaving, and his words have a power that can never pass away.

(856) "The Death of the Duke of Clarence and Avondale" ("Nineteenth Century," February, 1892). Eight months before his own death, Tennyson discharged this last sad duty as Laureate ; and the lines are strikingly appropriate as the final message from a great poet to a sorrowing people.

(894) "Crossing the Bar."

> *Beloved Guide, unchanging Friend,*
> *No sadness of farewell from me,*
> *No murmur at death's mystery,*
> *For thou art with me till the end.*
>
> Oct. 6th, 1892.

CHRONOLOGICAL TABLE.

1807 Frederick Tennyson b.

1808 Charles Tennyson b.

1809 Alfred Tennyson b. (Aug. 6).

1811 Arthur Hallam b.

1816 Tennyson entered Louth Grammar School.

1820 Tennyson left Louth Grammar School at Christmas.

1826-7 *Poems by Two Brothers.*

1828 Tennyson enters Trinity College, Cambridge (Oct. 28). Friendship with Hallam begins. *The Lover's Tale.*

1829 *Timbuctoo.*

1830 *Poems, chiefly Lyrical* (Published by E. Wilson). Tennyson and Hallam visited the Pyrenees together.

1831 Tennyson contributed *Anacreontics, No More,* and *A Fragment* to "The Gem." Also a Sonnet *Check every outflash, every ruder sally* to "The Englishman's Magazine" for August. Tennyson's father died, and the poet left Cambridge.

1832 Contributed a Sonnet *Me my own fate to lasting sorrow doometh* to "Friendship's Offering;" also a Sonnet *There are three things which fill my heart with sighs* to "The Yorkshire Literary Annual."

1832-3 *Poems,* by Alfred Tennyson (Published by Moxon).

1833 *The Lover's Tale* printed and suppressed. Reprinted

Check every outflash . . . . in " Friendship's Offering." A. Hallam died at Vienna, Sept. 15.

1834 Hallam buried at Clevedon, Jan. 6th.

1837 Contributed *O that 'twere possible* to " The Tribute," and *St. Agnes* to " The Keepsake." The Tennysons leave Somersby.

1838 Tennyson in London joins the Anonymous Club, which includes Carlyle, Sterling, Thackeray, Forster, Lushington, Macready, Landor.

1842 *Poems*, by Alfred Tennyson, in Two Volumes. Cecilia Tennyson married Edmund Law Lushington (Oct. 10th).

1845 Tennyson receives a pension of £200.

1846 Contributed to " Punch " *The New Timon and the Poets* (Feb. 28) ; also *Afterthought*, to the same periodical (March 7).

1847 *The Princess ; A Medley.*

1849 Lines in "The Examiner" for March, *To ——, You might have won the Poet's Name.*

1850 *In Memoriam.* Contributed *Here often, when a child, I lay reclin'd*, to " The Manchester Athenæum Album." Married Emily Sellwood at Shiplake Church, Oxfordshire, June 13. Resides at Twickenham. Appointed to succeed Wordsworth as Poet Laureate (Nov.).

1851 Contributed *What time I wasted Youthful Hours*, and *Come not when I am Dead*, to "The Keepsake." Sonnet *To W. C. Macready.* Dedication *To the Queen* in seventh ed. of Poems. Presented to the Queen as Poet Laureate (Mar. 6).

1852 *Ode on the Death of the Duke of Wellington.* The following poems were contributed to " The Examiner" :—*Britons guard your own* (Jan. 31), *Hands all Round*, and *The Third of February* (Feb. 7). Hallam Tennyson b.

1853 Removes to Farringford, Freshwater.

1854 *The Charge of the Light Brigade.* Lionel Tennyson b.

1855 *Maud and Other Poems.* Oxford confers on Tennyson the degree of D.C.L. (May).

1857 *Enid and Nimuë : The True and the False.*

1858 Tennyson added two stanzas to the National Anthem. They were printed in " The Times," Jan. 29.

1859 *The True and the False. Four Idylls of the King. Idylls of the King. The Grandmother's Apology* contributed to " Once a Week " (July 16). *The War*, signed T., printed in " The Times," May 9. Visited Portugal with F. T. Palgrave.

1860 *Sea-Dreams ; an Idyll* contributed to " Macmillan's Magazine " for Jan. *Tithonus* to "Cornhill " (Feb.).

1861 *The Sailor Boy*, contributed to "Victoria Regia." Revisited the Pyrenees. Wrote *Helen's Tower.*

1862 New edition of " Idylls of the King," with *Dedication* to the Prince Consort. Wrote *Ode : May the First*, 1862, printed in "Fraser's Magazine," June.

1863 *A Welcome*, published March 7, on the arrival of the Princess Alexandra. Contributed *Attempts at Classic Metres in Quantity* to "Cornhill," Dec.

1864 *Enoch Arden, etc. Epitaph on the late Duchess of Kent* (published in " The Court Journal," Mar. 19).

1865 " A selection from the works of Alfred Tennyson," contained six new poems : *The Captain* (said to be founded on fact), *On a Mourner, Home they brought him slain with spears*, and *Three Sonnets to a Coquette.* A Baronetcy offered to Tennyson and refused by him. Tennyson's mother died, aged 84, at Hampstead, Feb. 21. She was buried at Highgate.

1867 *The Window; or, the Song of the Wrens* (published 1870), and *The Victim*, both printed privately. Tennyson purchased the Aldworth estate, Sussex.

1868 Contributed *The Victim* to " Good Words " (Jan.).
On a Spiteful Letter to " Once a Week " (Jan.).
Wages to " Macmillan's Magazine " (Feb.). " 1865-
1866 " to " Good Words " (March). *Lucretius*
to " Macmillan's Magazine " (May). Longfellow
visited Tennyson.

1869 Elected an Hon. Fellow of Trin. Coll. Camb.

1869-70 *The Holy Grail and Other Poems.*

1871 *The Last Tournament,* contributed to " The Con-
temporary Review " (Dec.).

1872 *Gareth and Lynette, etc. To the Queen* (1873).

1874 *A Welcome to Marie Alexandrovna, Duchess of
Edinburgh.* Cabinet edition of Works, containing
important additions.

1875 *Queen Mary : A Drama.* Sonnet *To the Rev. W.
H. Brookfield.* Author's edition of Works, con-
taining some important changes.

1876-7 *Harold : A Drama. Prefatory Sonnet to the
Nineteenth Century* (March). *Montenegro,* to the
same. *To Victor Hugo,* to the same (June).
Achilles over the Trench, to the same (August).
Lines on *Sir John Franklin.*

1878 *The Revenge : A Ballad of the Fleet,* contributed to
" The Nineteenth Century " (Mar.). Tennyson in
Ireland.

1879 *The Lover's Tale* published. *The Falcon* produced
at St. James's Theatre (Dec.). *Midnight, June
30, 1879. Dedicatory Poem to the Princess Alice*
and *The Defence of Lucknow* to " The Nineteenth
Century " (April).

1880 *Ballads and Other Poems.* Contributed two Child-
Songs to " St. Nicholas." Cabinet edition, 12
vols., completed.

1881 *The Cup* produced at the Lyceum. *Despair* to " The
Nineteenth Century " (Nov.). Becomes Vice-
President of the Welsh National Eisteddfod.

1882 *The Charge of the Heavy Brigade*, to "Macmillan's
Magazine" (March). *To Virgil*, "The Nine-
teenth Century" (Nov.). *The Promise of May*,
produced at the Globe. Santley sings *Hands all
Round*. Tennyson's *Letter to Mr. Dawson*.

1883 *Frater, Ave atque Vale*, to "The Nineteenth Cen-
tury" (March). Sea trip with Mr. Gladstone.
Rents a house in Lower Belgrave Street, London.

1884 *The Cup* and *The Falcon* published. *Becket. Free-
dom*, to "Macmillan's Magazine" (Dec.). New
edition of Works in 7 vols. and 1 vol. Tennyson
raised to the Peerage as Baron of Aldworth and
Freshwater. Becomes President of the Incor-
porated Society of Authors. The Hon. Hallam
Tennyson married Miss A. G. F. Boyle.

1885 *Tiresias and Other Poems. The Fleet*, to "The
Times" (Apr. 23rd). *To H.R.H. Princess Beatrice*,
to "The Times" (July 23). *Vastness*, to "Mac-
millan's Magazine" (Nov.).

1886 *Locksley Hall Sixty Years After, etc. Indian and
Colonial Exhibition Ode*. Lionel Tennyson died
at Sea, April 20.

1887 *Carmen Seculare* (The Jubilee Ode), to "Mac-
millan's Magazine" (Apr.).

1888 New edition of Works in 8 vols. In this, *Geraint
and Enid* is divided into *The Marriage of Geraint*,
and *Geraint and Enid*. It reprints several poems
formerly suppressed.

1889 *Demeter and Other Poems* (Dec. 13). (20,000 copies
sold within a week). *The Throstle* (previously
printed in the New York "World") was con-
tributed to "The New Review" (Oct.). In the
new 1 vol. edition of 807 pages, first appears the
title : *Idylls of the King, in Twelve Books*.

1891 Song *To Sleep*, to "The New Review" (Mar.).

1892 *The Death of the Duke of Clarence and Avondale*,

to " The Nineteenth Century " (Feb.). *The Foresters.*

Lord Tennyson died at Aldworth, October 6th, aged 83. He was buried in Westminster Abbey, on the 12th of October.

The Death of Œnone, Akbar's Dream, and Other Poems (October 28).

1893 *Becket : A Tragedy.* "Globe" 8vo. edition in 10 vols. completed.

1894 *Tennyson's Works complete in 1 vol.* Crown 8vo., pp. 898.

NOTE.—To the above may be added the minor poems mentioned at the foot of page 430.

INDEX.

Titles of poems not contained in the One Volume Edition referred to in the Preface are printed in italics.

Numbers that stand first are a special reference.